Where Roads Will Never Reach

Where Roads Will Never Reach

*Wilderness and Its
Visionaries in the
Northern Rockies*

Frederick H. Swanson

The University of Utah Press
Salt Lake City

The Defiance House Man colophon is a registered trademark
of the University of Utah Press. It is based upon a four-foot-tall,
Ancient Puebloan pictograph (late PIII) near Glen Canyon, Utah.

19 18 17 16 15   1 2 3 4 5

LIBRARY OF CONGRESS CATALOGING-IN-PUBLICATION DATA

Swanson, Frederick H. (Frederick Harold), 1952-
  Where roads will never reach : wilderness and its visionaries in the
Northern Rockies / Frederick H. Swanson.
    pages cm
  Includes bibliographical references and index.
    ISBN 978-1-60781-403-0 (cloth : alkaline paper)
    ISBN 978-1-60781-404-7 (paperback : alkaline paper)
    ISBN 978-1-60781-405-4 (e-book)
  1. Rocky Mountains--Description and travel. 2. Rocky
Mountains--Environmental conditions. 3. National parks and
reserves--Rocky Mountains. 4. Wilderness areas--Rocky Mountains.
5. Nature conservation--Rocky Mountains. I. Title.
  F721.S93 2015
  333.78'2097865--dc23
                                                    2014038397

Printed and bound by Sheridan Books, Inc., Ann Arbor, Michigan.

In memory of Kenneth Bohlig

Contents

Maps

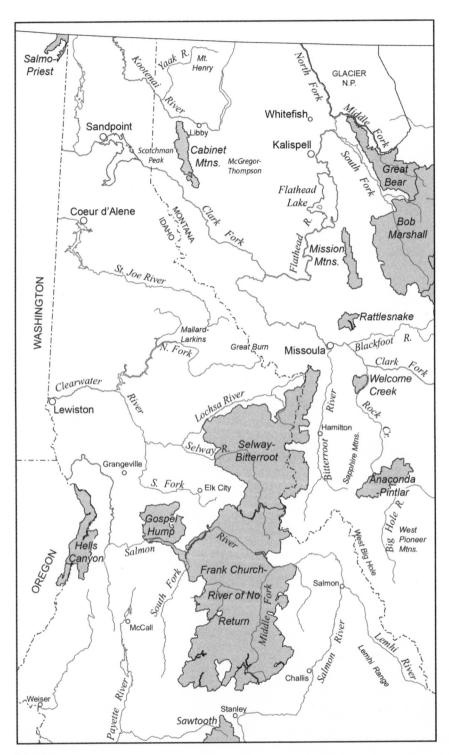

MAP A

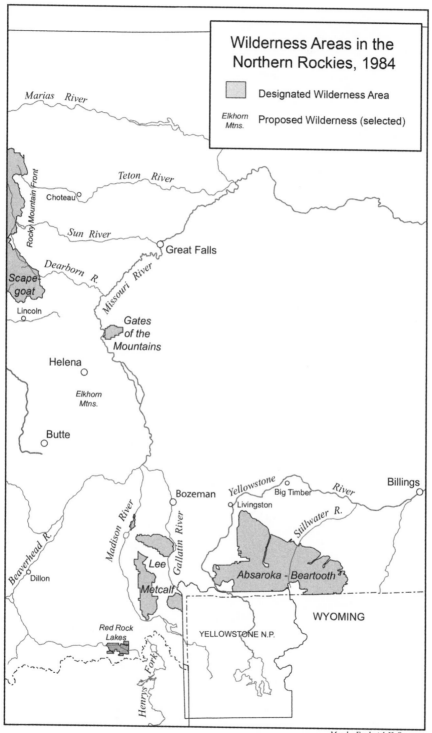

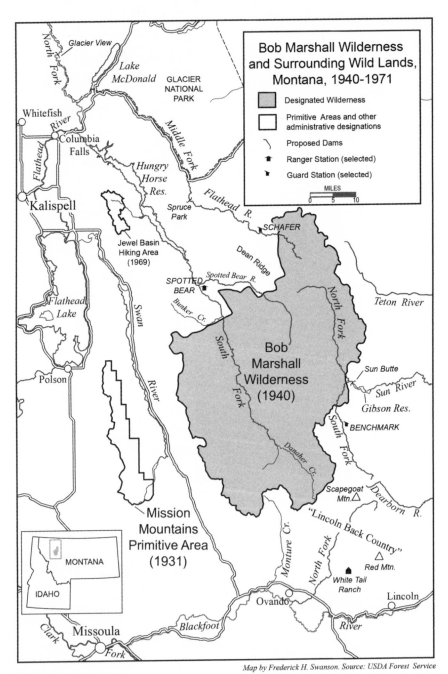

Bob Marshall Wilderness
and Surrounding Wild Lands,
Montana, 1940-1971

Designated Wilderness

Primitive Areas and other
administrative designations

Proposed Dams

Ranger Station (selected)

Guard Station (selected)

MILES
0   5   10

Glacier View

North Fork

Lake
McDonald

GLACIER
NATIONAL
PARK

Whitefish

Flathead River

Columbia
Falls

Middle Fork

Hungry
Horse
Res.

Flathead R.

SCHAFER

Kalispell

Spruce
Park

Dean Ridge

North Fork

Teton River

Jewel Basin
Hiking Area
(1969)

SPOTTED
BEAR

Spotted Bear R.

Bunker Cr.

South Fork

Bob
Marshall
Wilderness
(1940)

Sun Butte

Flathead
Lake

Swan River

Sun River

Gibson Res.

Polson

South Fork

BENCHMARK

Danaher Cr.

Scapegoat
Mtn. △

Dearborn R.

Mission
Mountains
Primitive Area
(1931)

Monture Cr.

North Fork

"Lincoln Back Country"

△

Red Mtn.

MONTANA

IDAHO

White Tail
Ranch

Lincoln

Ovando

Missoula

Blackfoot

River

Clark

Fork

Map by Frederick H. Swanson. Source: USDA Forest Service

MAP B

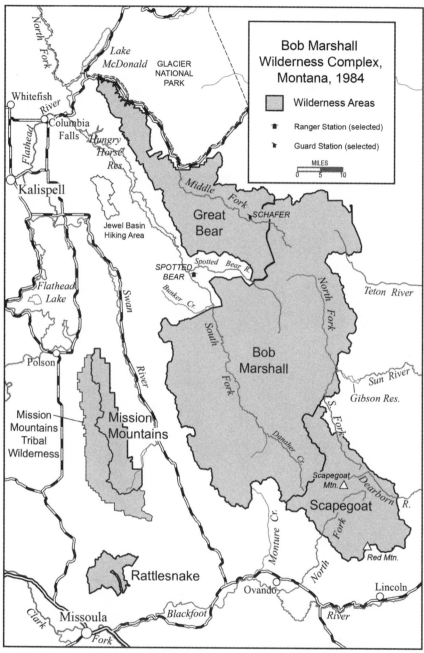

Bob Marshall
Wilderness Complex,
Montana, 1984

Wilderness Areas

Ranger Station (selected)

Guard Station (selected)

MILES
0   5   10

North Fork

Lake
McDonald

GLACIER
NATIONAL
PARK

Whitefish

River

Columbia
Falls

Flathead

Hungry
Horse
Res.

Kalispell

Jewel Basin
Hiking Area

Middle

Fork

Great
Bear

SCHAFER

SPOTTED
BEAR

Spotted Bear R.

Flathead
Lake

Swan

Bunker
Cr.

South

Fork

North

Fork

Teton River

Bob
Marshall

Polson

River

Mission
Mountains
Tribal
Wilderness

Mission
Mountains

Sun River

Gibson Res.

S. Fork

Danaher Cr.

Scapegoat
Mtn. △

Dearborn R.

Scapegoat

North

Fork

Red Mtn.

Rattlesnake

Monture Cr.

Ovando

Lincoln

Clark

Missoula

Blackfoot

River

Fork

MAP C

Map by Frederick H. Swanson. Sources: USDA
Forest Service and Montana NRIS

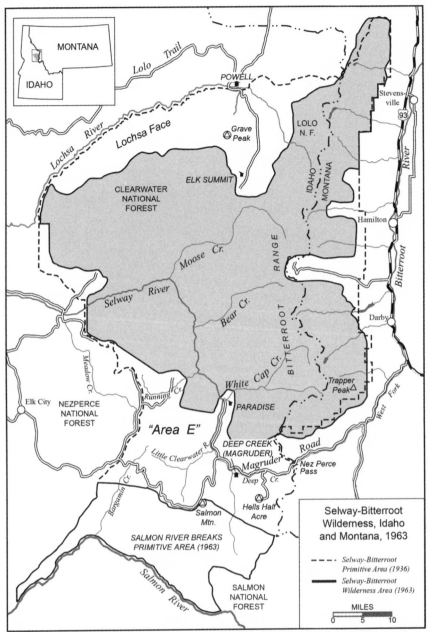

MONTANA

IDAHO

Lolo Trail

Lochsa River

POWELL

Stevens-
ville

93

Lochsa Face

Grave
Peak

LOLO
N. F.

Lochsa River

ELK SUMMIT

CLEARWATER
NATIONAL
FOREST

IDAHO

MONTANA

Hamilton

RANGE

Moose Cr.

Selway River

Bear Cr.

BITTERROOT

Darby

Bitterroot

Meadow Cr.

White Cap Cr.

Trapper
Peak

Elk City

NEZPERCE
NATIONAL
FOREST

Running Cr.

PARADISE

"Area E"

West Fork

Little Clearwater R.

DEEP CREEK
(MAGRUDER)

Magruder Road

Nez Perce
Pass

Borgamin Cr.

Deep Cr.

Salmon
Mtn.

Hells Half
Acre

SALMON RIVER BREAKS
PRIMITIVE AREA (1963)

Salmon River

SALMON
NATIONAL
FOREST

Selway-Bitterroot
Wilderness, Idaho
and Montana, 1963

- - - - Selway-Bitterroot
Primitive Area (1936)

———— Selway-Bitterroot
Wilderness Area (1963)

MILES

0   5   10

Map by Frederick H. Swanson. Source: USDA Forest Service

Map D

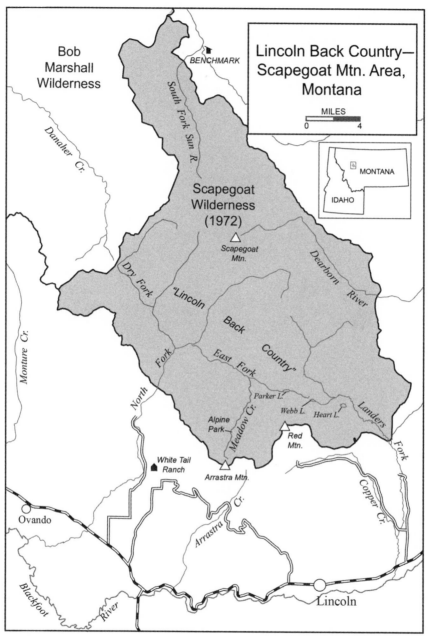

Bob
Marshall
Wilderness

BENCHMARK

South Fork Sun R.

Danaher Cr.

Scapegoat
Wilderness
(1972)

Scapegoat
Mtn.

Dearborn River

Dry Fork

"Lincoln

Back

Country"

East Fork

Monture Cr.

North Fork

Parker L.

Webb L.   Heart L.

Landers Fork

Alpine
Park

Meadow Cr.

Red
Mtn.

White Tail
Ranch

Arrastra Mtn.

Copper Cr.

Ovando

Arrastra   Cr.

Blackfoot   River

Lincoln

**Lincoln Back Country—
Scapegoat Mtn. Area,
Montana**

MILES
0   4

MONTANA

IDAHO

Map E

*Map by Frederick H. Swanson. Sources:
USDA Forest Service and Montana NRIS*

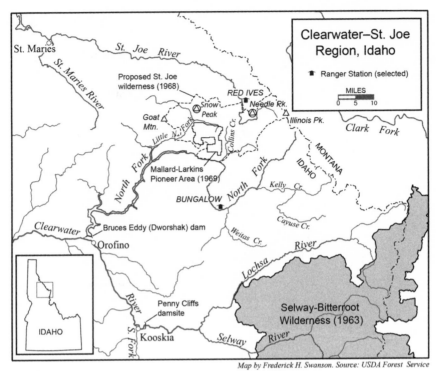

Clearwater–St. Joe
Region, Idaho

Ranger Station (selected)

MILES
0   5   10

St. Maries

St. Joe River

St. Maries River

Proposed St. Joe
wilderness (1968)

RED IVES
Needle Rk.

Snow
Peak

Goat
Mtn.

Collins Cr.

Illinois Pk.

Clark Fork

Little N. Fork

North Fork

North Fork

MONTANA

IDAHO

Kelly Cr.

Mallard-Larkins
Pioneer Area (1969)

BUNGALOW

Cayuse Cr.

Clearwater

Bruces Eddy (Dworshak) dam

Weitas Cr.

River

Orofino

Lochsa

IDAHO

Penny Cliffs
damsite

Selway-Bitterroot
Wilderness (1963)

S. Fork

River

Kooskia

Selway River

Map by Frederick H. Swanson. Source: USDA Forest Service

MAP F

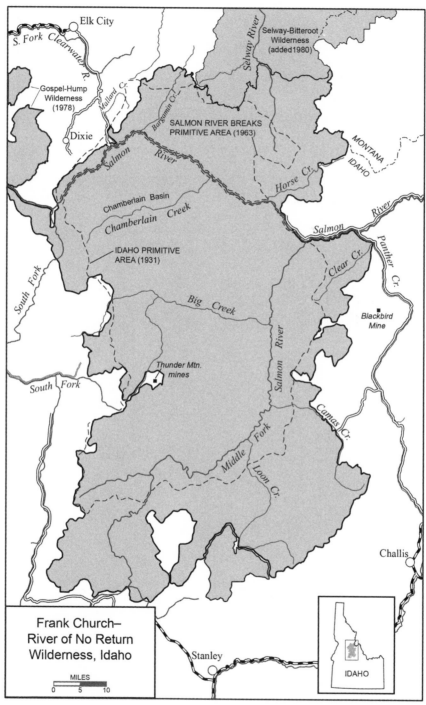

Elk City

S. Fork Clearwater R.

Selway River

Selway-Bitterroot
Wilderness
(added 1980)

Gospel-Hump
Wilderness
(1978)

Mallard Cr.

Bargamin Cr.

SALMON RIVER BREAKS
PRIMITIVE AREA (1963)

Dixie

MONTANA
IDAHO

Salmon   River

Horse Cr.

Salmon   River

Chamberlain Basin

Chamberlain   Creek

Clear Cr.

Panther Cr.

IDAHO PRIMITIVE
AREA (1931)

South Fork

Big   Creek

Blackbird
Mine

Salmon River

South Fork

Thunder Mtn.
mines

Middle   Fork

Camas Cr.

Loon Cr.

Challis

Frank Church–
River of No Return
Wilderness, Idaho

MILES
0   5   10

Stanley

IDAHO

MAP G

Map by Frederick H. Swanson. Source: USDA Forest Service

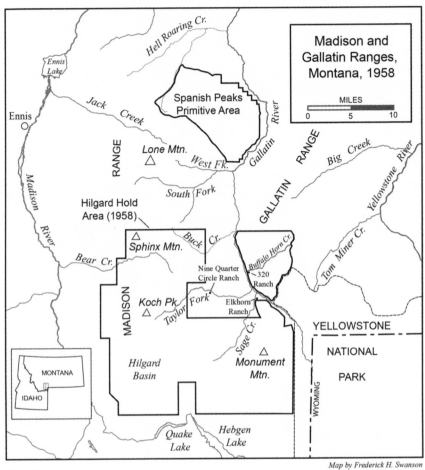

Hell Roaring Cr.

Ennis
Lake

Ennis

Jack Creek

Madison River

RANGE

Lone Mtn.

West Fk.

South Fork

Gallatin River

Spanish Peaks
Primitive Area

GALLATIN

GALLATIN RANGE

Big Creek

Yellowstone River

Hilgard Hold
Area (1958)

Sphinx Mtn.

Buck Cr.

Bear Cr.

MADISON

Koch Pk.

Taylor Fork

Nine Quarter
Circle Ranch

Elkhorn
Ranch

Buffalo Horn Cr.

320
Ranch

Tom Miner Cr.

YELLOWSTONE

NATIONAL

PARK

Sage Cr.

Monument
Mtn.

Hilgard
Basin

MONTANA

IDAHO

Quake
Lake

Hebgen
Lake

WYOMING

Madison and
Gallatin Ranges,
Montana, 1958

MILES

0   5   10

Map by Frederick H. Swanson
Source: USDA Forest Service

MAP H

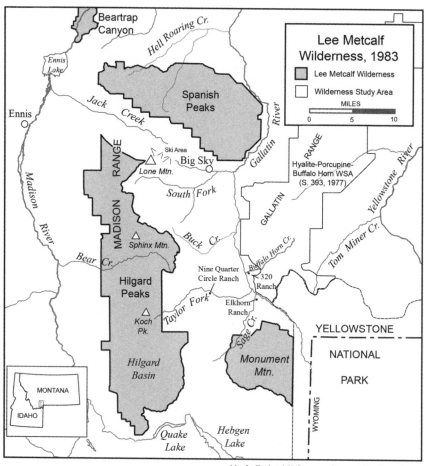

Beartrap
Canyon

Hell Roaring Cr.

Ennis
Lake

Jack Creek

Ennis

Spanish
Peaks

Gallatin River

Lee Metcalf
Wilderness, 1983

Lee Metcalf Wilderness

Wilderness Study Area

MILES

0   5   10

Ski Area
Lone Mtn. △⚡ Big Sky

MADISON RANGE

South Fork

GALLATIN RANGE

Hyalite-Porcupine-
Buffalo Horn WSA
(S. 393, 1977)

Yellowstone River

Madison River

Buck Cr.

Sphinx Mtn. △

Bear Cr.

Hilgard
Peaks

Buffalo Horn Cr.

Tom Miner Cr.

Nine Quarter
Circle Ranch

320
Ranch

△
Koch
Pk.

Taylor Fork

Elkhorn
Ranch

Sage Cr.

YELLOWSTONE

Hilgard
Basin

Monument
Mtn.

NATIONAL

PARK

MONTANA

IDAHO

WYOMING

Quake
Lake

Hebgen
Lake

MAP I

Map by Frederick H. Swanson. Source: USDA Forest Service

Introduction

For those who enjoyed hunting America's greatest big game, fishing for wild trout, or simply wandering on foot or horseback through the high open, Idaho and Montana were the places to live in the years following World War II. The mountains that bled fire in the summers of 1910, 1929, and 1934 were slowly recovering under the watchful care of Forest Service rangers. Tremendous elk herds fattened on new browse growing in the fires' wake. Streams full of trout beckoned to anglers. An active outfitting industry catered to travelers who wished to explore the nation's largest wilderness and primitive areas. From the Clearwater, Selway, and Salmon Rivers to the high Absaroka Range and Beartooth Plateau, the Northern Rockies offered a chance to immerse oneself in a world that had disappeared from much of America.

The Forest Service's zeal in guarding these and other forest and mountain landscapes throughout the West brought it a nation's accolades and earned its officers a degree of autonomy unprecedented for a federal agency. But as the staff of its Northern Region, who oversaw seventeen national forests in northern Idaho and western Montana, moved from fighting fires, building trails, and monitoring sheep allotments to laying out roads and timber sales—part of a comprehensive effort to bring these forests under intensive management—they found that some outdoor lovers were lining up in determined opposition.

1

Beginning in the mid-1950s, well before environmental issues reached national prominence, a few dozen hunters, anglers, and outfitters in these states began to question the Forest Service's policy of devoting nearly all of the region's timber stands to producing wood fiber for a growing nation. They were the vanguard of a much larger movement that attracted wide public support in these states and helped transform the nation's wilderness policy.

To the timber planners and road engineers based at the Northern Region's headquarters in Missoula, Montana, the forest stands under their care were an untapped resource of pine, spruce, and fir. Eager to assist in America's postwar transformation into the world's wealthiest nation and greatest consumer of resources, they sought to apply the principles of sustained-yield timber harvesting to as much forestland as possible, as rapidly as their budgets allowed. The high-standard gravel roads needed for this program would open up many of the region's remote drainage basins to recreational use, a public benefit that the regional staff assumed would be greeted favorably. None of these individuals anticipated the storm that followed once their plans surfaced in towns such as Kalispell, Lewiston, Helena, and Bozeman. Certain sportsmen and women living in those towns and nearby rural areas assumed that the forests that provided limitless backcountry adventures would always be there to enjoy. Their reaction caught federal resource managers (and the state's political leaders) by surprise and signaled a turnabout in how federal lands in these states would be managed.

This book tells how a relative handful of citizens living amid the forests of the Northern Rockies halted the federal resource bureaucracy's plans to develop large expanses of roadless land within their figurative backyards. These outdoors people and their allies in the national wilderness preservation movement not only interrupted major timber harvesting projects within some of the nation's most emblematic wildlands, they helped achieve something we do not often see in America: the establishment of a durable public policy with widespread popular support, despite the opposition of a respected federal agency and its powerful client industries. The story of how these wilderness lands came to be recognized and preserved has antecedents in the battles over federal river-basin development in the 1940s, when wilderness and wildlife advocates found common cause with the Forest Service, and it reaches back even earlier, to the agency's attempts during the 1920s and 1930s to pacify wilderness enthusiasts by designating millions of acres of primitive areas in the national forests of the West. This story parallels wilderness controversies in other parts of the West, but in the Northern Rockies the importance that activists placed on wildlife habitat distinguished their efforts and anticipated the flowering of the biodiversity protection movement during the 1980s.

Recreationists made use of nearly all of the thirty-nine million acres of national forest lands in Idaho and Montana, but the ultimate outdoor experiences—the kind that drew enthusiasts from all over the country—were found in the far backcountry, up in the headwaters of the Selway, Clearwater, Salmon, Flathead, and Missouri Rivers. Here one could find traces of the old American idea that beyond the roads' end lay a land untarnished by the graspings of our materialist culture, a land in which a man or woman might find a welcome refreshment of the soul. In small numbers at first, but with steadily growing ranks through the 1960s as the federal timber program gained speed, these outdoors people raised alarms about the loss of wild landscapes they had long enjoyed. Initially they objected to the giant dams that the Corps of Engineers and Bureau of Reclamation proposed to throw across the Flathead, Sun, and Clearwater Rivers; then, when the Forest Service took up the call for full timber development in the Northern Rockies, they used their new-found political voices to oppose this program as well. They objected not just to clear-cutting the forest, which was unsightly enough, but especially to the construction of high-standard logging roads in backcountry areas. These roads were essential to the forest development program, but they removed a quality of the landscape that these men and women prized above all else: its sense of remoteness.

This was a difficult idea to express, and it was especially difficult to compare to the board feet of sawtimber that had flowed out of these mountains in record quantities during the postwar decades. So the wilderness activists of that era put it in more concrete terms: principally elk, trout, and grizzly bears. They feared that their forests might no longer offer a chance to track a wily bull elk across a mountain clearing on a crisp October day, unhindered by a dozen other motor-equipped sportsmen. Or to thrill to the flash of a native cutthroat trout in a stream unsullied by sediment from logging roads. Or simply to stand on top of a windswept limestone escarpment and look across miles of undeveloped country, knowing there were grizzly bears wandering among those slopes and mountain goats clambering on far-off crags. Their desire to maintain a certain way of life—one that was closely intertwined with the land and its native creatures— motivated their efforts to maintain wild forests and mountain areas as more or less self-sustaining and self-willed landscapes, free from the massive interference of the modern forest management paradigm.

The postwar wilderness preservation movement emerged as a national force following the battle over Echo Park Dam in Dinosaur National Monument during the mid-1950s, yet Montana and Idaho citizens were working even earlier to halt massive river development projects in their own states. By 1954, having stalled dams that would have inundated parts of Glacier National Park, the Bob Marshall Wilderness, and the Selway-Bitterroot Primitive Area, and having forged a strategic alliance with the leaders of the nation's principal conservation groups, they took on timber sales and road projects that threatened to disrupt their use of unprotected wildlands surrounding the latter two preserves. More than three decades of bitter confrontation with the Forest Service followed in which they succeeded in gaining congressional designation of millions of acres of new wilderness areas in both states. In doing so they forced the Forest Service to substantially revamp its timber management plans, with lasting consequences for the region's timber industry.

These activists operated without a blueprint for how they might achieve large-scale landscape protection. This was a loosely coordinated, geographically atomized, and thoroughly ad hoc set of campaigns, which until 1964 had only the most rudimentary legal and policy framework on which to stand. Its leaders were typically active in local wildlife clubs; few of them had ever stood before a committee of Congress. Exemplifying the tradition of the dedicated amateur, which historian Stephen Fox traces to John Muir, they came from all corners of society and all levels of economic status.[1] Some were recent transplants to the region while others came from pioneer roots. What they shared was a love for the backcountry and its wildlife. By emphasizing the need to protect forest habitats for game species such as elk and to maintain unpolluted streams for wild trout and salmon, wilderness advocates tapped into popular feelings in the Northern Rockies states, undermining claims that wilderness designations would close off hunting and fishing.

These campaigns originated by and large with local residents. They sought help from national conservation organizations but were not directed by them. In most cases they advertised their cause with nothing more sophisticated than a single-page brochure. All this counteracted the image of wilderness proponents as elitist outsiders with little understanding of local needs and lifestyles. Eventually the wilderness movement would embrace modern techniques of public persuasion and increasingly draw on support from the East and West Coasts, but it is noteworthy that some of the movement's greatest successes were achieved with the simplest of methods. This occurred, I believe, because activists in Idaho and Montana presented a heartfelt and compelling message: *save the land because wild creatures depend on it.* And because we, in turn, need close contact with those creatures and their habitats. This message echoed in meeting halls, newspaper columns, and public hearings, leading legislators such as Montana's

Lee Metcalf and Idaho's Frank Church to craft new wilderness legislation in spite of its costs to the region's timber industry.

The nature of the preservation battle changed radically in the early 1970s in response to the Forest Service's Roadless Area Review and Evaluation (RARE) program, which forced activists to examine hundreds of potential new wilderness areas and learn a new vocabulary of technical and economic analysis.[2] Employing this language (and new laws such as the National Environmental Policy Act) helped give the wilderness movement a solid factual grounding, but I argue that it also led to its losing hold of this elemental message—and suffering a crisis of purpose as a result. The growing awareness during the 1980s of protecting the biosphere in all its diversity added a further dimension to the activists' work, but this, too, threatened to alienate hunters and others who had historically been a key part of the American wilderness movement.

In his book *Driven Wild: How the Fight against Automobiles Launched the Modern Wilderness Movement*, historian Paul Sutter has shown how the founders of the Wilderness Society were motivated primarily by opposition to high-standard tourist roads invading wild mountain regions. Ecological concerns initially played much less of a role, Sutter believes, even though the society's founders "understood quite well what wilderness did and did not preserve ecologically."[3] In the Northern Rockies, grassroots activists shared this antipathy to wilderness-busting roads, but they infused their work from the start with concern for the welfare of wild creatures. They saw how elk, grizzly bears, and other creatures retreated at the advance of logging roads, and they featured these animals strongly in their campaigns. In doing so they helped bridge the recreational arguments of the prewar generation and the biocentric approach to conservation that came to the fore in the late 1980s.

It was two biologists, in fact, who steered the Wilderness Society toward greater engagement with wildlife issues in the postwar era. Olaus Murie, who was Howard Zahniser's right-hand man and director of the Wilderness Society from 1945 to his death in 1963, was a tireless exponent of wildlife's needs as well as of the psychological benefits that humans gain from close association with wild creatures. Stewart Brandborg, who replaced Zahniser as the society's executive director in 1964, also understood how wilderness designations directly benefited many species of wildlife. Both Murie and Brandborg had strong ties to the Northern Rockies and spent much of their time cultivating its grass roots. In *The Promise of Wilderness*, James Turner's masterful overview of the modern American wilderness movement, Murie and Brandborg gain long overdue credit, as do the local and statewide groups they worked with such as the

Montana Wilderness Association (MWA).[4] Yet many activists in these states were promoting wilderness designations at least a decade before the MWA was formed. This was not unique to the Northern Rockies, and historians are beginning to fill in the important role citizens played in public lands politics during the postwar decades in the Pacific Northwest and other regions.[5]

The early successes of wilderness activists in the Northern Rockies contravene the popular impression of the 1950s as a time of apathetic, let-George-do-it political doldrums in America. In an era when resource professionals were accorded great respect and deference, these activists confounded the engineers in the federal dam-building bureaus and challenged the Forest Service's assumed expertise in forestland management. They forced the latter agency to substantially broaden its vision beyond supplying timber and to accept (albeit slowly and grudgingly) that wilderness meant more than rugged mountain peaks and scenic alpine basins.

This book examines wilderness controversies in Idaho and Montana from 1954 through 1983, and summarizes action on a host of unsuccessful bills since then. (In December 2014 Montana's "wilderness drought" ended when Congress approved a 67,000-acre addition to the Bob Marshall and Scapegoat Wilderness Areas along the Rocky Mountain Front.) Few of these battles have been chronicled in any depth, although the struggles over the Idaho Primitive Area and Montana's Scapegoat Wilderness have been reviewed in more general works.[6] I include these areas here, but also a half dozen that are less well known, such as the upper Clearwater River of Idaho, where a sawmill engineer named Morton Brigham carried on a personal grudge match with the Forest Service for nearly four decades; and the upper Selway River, where Doris Milner, a Montana housewife with an uncanny sense for influencing policy makers, led a successful campaign to halt a major logging program. Other, more recent campaigns include the relatively tiny Scotchman Peak area straddling the Idaho-Montana border; the Great Burn area to its south; the scenic but terribly conflicted Madison Range and West Big Hole areas in southwestern Montana; and the upper reaches of the Flathead River, including its wild Middle Fork. As a setting for these conflicts I discuss the establishment of the Northern Region's primitive areas during the 1930s and the subsequent controversy over proposed dams that would have impinged on several of them. In a work of this length I regret that I must pass over a number of important wilderness battlegrounds, ranging from the Selkirk Mountains of northern Idaho to the island mountain ranges of central Montana, each of which has its unique value and its passionate advocates.

I also sidestep a current intellectual battlefield: the question of how extensively the Northern Rockies were influenced by aboriginal fire and hunting, and the related question of whether wilderness areas remain "natural" in any meaningful sense. Our species' millennia-long occupation of the plains and river valleys has significantly altered and redistributed the region's mammalian fauna. The human use (and control) of wildfire has influenced forest composition throughout the West, although the timing, extent, and degree of those changes as compared to those resulting from natural wildfire are disputed.[7] Regardless of these influences, the struggles over wilderness designations in the Northern Rockies had more to do with how present-day humans would use this landscape than with any vision of a pristine, unoccupied wilderness. The activists portrayed in this book worried less about the purity of their wilderness than whether they could hold back the machines of Progress. They were not seeking a mythic, idealized Nature that existed apart from humans; rather, they sought an intimate engagement with the creatures, forces, and qualities we most often associate with nature, particularly the free-roaming populations of wildlife found in unroaded settings.

Humans were visitors to wilderness lands, it was true, but the way in which they visited them mattered. The hunters, anglers, and outfitters working in the Northern Rockies agreed with Olaus Murie that modern humans had much to gain from a quiet, careful, observant approach to the natural world. Roads had no place in such landscapes, they insisted. Still, as Kevin Marsh observed of similar battles in the Pacific Northwest, these political debates focused not on the wilderness *idea* so much as on wilderness *places*.[8] If these places happened to have been occupied or traversed at times by aboriginal peoples, this only added to their interest. Experienced wilderness travelers knew that forests burned and that humans sometimes burned them. They made use of old cabins, corrals, and spring boxes the settlers left behind, transitory signs of human impermanence in an enormous landscape. What these men and women could not abide was graded and engineered logging roads and the endless, noisy human activity and landscape manipulation the roads brought.

Finally, as these words show, I admit to bias: my heart is, and always has been, with the preservationists. Our national forests must continue to provide timber, minerals, livestock forage, and motorized recreation, and I have tried to present the arguments for those uses. But read the words of those who sought something different in these woods and mountains and ask yourself: Is what they saw real? And if it is merely a symbol, can that still inspire us and enrich our lives?

Prologue
The Headwaters of the Gallatin River, September 1958

For five days the riders trailed through the expansive meadows and lake basins of southwestern Montana's Madison Range, making camp as the late-summer sun dropped beneath a jagged wall of metamorphosed peaks. This subalpine landscape stood a world apart from the tourist-mobbed geyser basins in nearby Yellowstone National Park—a circumstance that appealed to the horsemen and horsewomen leading this outing, who owned or operated four of the major guest ranches in the upper Gallatin River drainage. Their clients on this trip were a select group of current and former government men who were used to backcountry travel. Three wore the green uniform of the U.S. Forest Service and were officially in charge of this delightful wild country. Another worked for the Montana Fish and Game Department, and the sole out-of-state visitor, Dr. Olaus Murie of the Wilderness Society, had been a prominent field researcher with the federal Biological Survey.

The ride gave these enthusiasts the chance to savor encompassing views over the forests of pine, spruce, and fir that blanketed the Gallatin's headwaters. Breezes rippled the surface of mountain tarns, Clark's jays gave raucous calls from whitebark pines, and the fading blooms of asters and cottongrass spelled the end to another season in the timberline country. When the party reassembled following their outing within the dining hall of Howard and Bonnie

Kelsey's Nine Quarter Circle Ranch in the Taylor Fork drainage, their conversation turned to the fate of this relatively unknown mountain expanse. For more than a decade these outfitters had been pressing the Forest Service to classify a quarter million acres in the Madison and Gallatin mountain ranges as a wilderness area, and now, in this first week of September 1958, it was time to bring the issue to a head.

The outfitters had invited Olaus Murie to Montana in order to bring a national perspective to their discussions and perhaps add some of the political clout that they lacked. The renowned biologist, now sixty-nine years old, served as the Wilderness Society's president and chief spokesman in the West. He and his wife, Mardy, lived in a rustic log cabin close by the Snake River in Wyoming's Jackson Hole, where he had spent years studying Rocky Mountain elk in the surrounding mountains.[1] Murie had conducted similar research in Montana's Bob Marshall Wilderness in the 1930s, as well as major field studies of wolves and caribou in Alaska. He was as comfortable living in primitive environments as any of these trail riders, yet as they gathered next to the lodge's river-rock fireplace, Murie noted wryly that "after a five-day idyllic experience such as we have just had, we always have to have a meeting: we have to discuss the mundane and realistic matters; this is necessary."[2]

Murie's job took him to many such meetings—perhaps a few too many for an outdoorsman who reveled in the far solitudes. A soft-spoken, reticent man who seemed more comfortable in intimate gatherings with friends or sketching and painting wildlife in his studio, he nonetheless spent weeks traveling to meetings such as this, offering encouragement to sportsmen and women, outfitters, fellow game biologists, agency men, and anyone else willing to raise a voice for the dwindling wild country that he and Mardy had come to love. "There can be great inspiration from a trip into wild country," he told his listeners at the Kelseys' lodge. In recent years he had observed a welcome tendency for Americans to "take a little higher view of things. More and more people are really interested in what is happening to their environment." The Gallatin outfitters were feeling impatient with the slow process of protecting this area, but Murie told them that time was on their side—if they could stave off the various development schemes that kept popping up for forested lands such as these.

Murie was used to western prerogatives and knew that it was up to these Montanans to chart a plan for protecting the Madison and Gallatin Ranges. He listened as Vic Benson, owner of the Covered Wagon Ranch at the mouth of Taylor Fork and president of the national Dude Ranchers' Association, spoke of the intangible qualities of the land they had ridden through. "This area has a great sweep and expanse, a sense of freedom," Benson told the attendees. Four years ago he had traveled to the North American Wildlife Conference in Chicago to speak with Murie and other conservation leaders about setting up a sizable wilderness area in these mountains. It would begin at Yellowstone Park's northwestern edge and extend north along the twin mountain ranges flanking the Gallatin River, one arm reaching to Hyalite Peak south of Bozeman and the other to the Spanish Peaks west of the river. Many Montana organizations were sympathetic to the idea, Benson added, even the state's Farm Bureau. But Forest Service officials had requested that they "not push along too fast and asked that we be considerate and quiet," he said. "So we did not come out and seek further national support."

These were only the latest of many such discussions that dated to the early 1940s, when Grace and Ernest Miller, owners of the Elkhorn Ranch on nearby Sage Creek, had approached the Forest Service about setting aside some of the land they used for their pack trips so that it would not fall to the logger's saw. There appeared to be little urgency at the time, but a Bozeman-area lumber firm was now cutting timber from private lands in the Gallatin drainage, and Forest Service officials from the regional office in Missoula were talking of dramatically expanding harvests from national forest lands as well.

Grace Miller, who had joined this day's discussion, was particularly exercised about motorcycle riders from Bozeman and Billings who frequented the trails her outfit had traditionally used. The machines were causing erosion and scaring her wranglers' horses, she said. She still hoped to see a wilderness area established in at least part of these mountains, and her fellow outfitters and landowners in the upper Gallatin agreed. They included Jim Goodrich of the 320 Ranch at the mouth of Buffalo Horn Creek, which was the largest dude ranch operation in the canyon, and Marc Patten, who with his wife Doris raised quarter horses at their ranch opposite Black Butte at the edge of Yellowstone Park. Patten spoke for all of them when he said, "I gather that the Forest Service would like to have this matter lie low for a while, but the people won't be satisfied until they get a definite promise of a holding action." He turned to the three agency men present. "Is this possible?" he asked. "We can't work without your cooperation, and yet the people are perturbed."

George Duvendack, the supervisor of the Gallatin National Forest, had accompanied the outfitters on their ride and appeared more open than his predecessors to the idea of land preservation. "I assure you we are sympathetic," he told the participants. "If we were not so constituted we would not be in the Forest Service." He said he had watched the forests fall around his grandfather's

Ohio farm, and he shared with many of his colleagues a "deep concern with maintaining wild places." The Forest Service had already set aside thirteen million acres nationwide as wilderness areas, but he believed more were needed. He told the dude ranchers that "probably this region would be an ideal place to take trees out of timber production."

Duvendack had put his finger on the main issue. The Forest Service was established in 1905 as a resource production agency, only later taking on the slippery mission of providing recreation to a public that craved all manner of outdoor diversions.[3] Building roads and campgrounds was one way to meet this need, and for the most part such uses were compatible with timbering. But these outfitters and their allies in Montana's conservation movement were talking about something more difficult. Duvendack's colleagues at the meeting— Frank Bailey of the neighboring Beaverhead National Forest and Ed Barry from the Forest Service's regional office in Missoula—wanted the sportsmen to moderate their demands. Their boss, regional forester Charles Tebbe, had just approved a bold new program of expanded timber cutting and road building to tap the underutilized potential of western Montana's national forests. Its title, *Full Use and Development of Montana's Timber Resources*, was telling. Much of the outfitters' quarter-million-acre proposal was slated for eventual logging, and Barry counseled the attendees to "be a lot more realistic about the area you can get and then stick to that."

Barry alluded to a further complication: his agency was negotiating with the Northern Pacific Railway to exchange its intermingled lands in the Madison and Gallatin drainages, which formed a checkerboard of alternate square-mile sections in major portions of both mountain ranges. This was a tedious and tricky process that would not benefit from a new controversy over wilderness. The railroad, in fact, had sent two of its top men to this meeting: Dwight Edgell came from its Saint Paul headquarters, while S. G. Merryman of its Portland, Oregon, office managed the railroad's vast timber and land holdings, granted to the company in 1864 to finance construction of a transcontinental rail link. Edgell told the group that his company would need to exchange the land it owned within the proposed wilderness before there could be any such designation. "We are putting all our lands under management, and we expect to be in the timber business a long time," he told the group.

Merryman assured them that in the meantime, "there is nothing happening here that should disturb you. I don't feel there is any real rush and I don't see any way we could get around to do this job in the very next few years. The area I am thinking of here is not going to be damaged for wilderness purposes in these intervening years." He was referring to the higher-elevation lands through which the outfitters had led this party; farther down the Gallatin lay better stands of timber, also in checkerboard ownership, which if consolidated would form an ideal timber tract. None of the three—Merryman, Edgell, or Barry—stated the obvious prospect: that by sorting out these confused ownerships, both the Forest Service and the railroad could expedite their plans to harvest timber.

In this fashion the principal users of the upper Gallatin drainage laid out their overlapping and often conflicting interests. Some were based on simple economics: the railroad wanted to develop its timberlands, while the outfitters needed mountain scenery unspoiled by roads, clear-cuts, or buzzing motorbikes if they were to attract well-paying clients. Each favored clear guidelines that would segregate incompatible uses—what historian Kevin Marsh has termed "drawing lines in the forest" to rationalize management.[4] Timbering could take place on the middle and lower slopes while recreation would reign in the high country. Hikers and motorcyclists would benefit from designating separate trails on which each could travel in peace. These conflicts, according to Forest Service officers such as Ed Barry, could be dealt with through careful application of the multiple-use doctrine, which held that many forest uses—even timbering and recreation—could be made compatible through foresight and planning. This was a kind of land-use zoning, an attempt to regulate the use of a natural resource commons in which traditional activities such as hunting and trail riding conflicted with industrial demands and new forms of motorized recreation.[5]

There was one issue, however, that worked at cross-purposes to the lines-on-a-map approach, as Howard Kelsey reminded the guests gathered at his lodge. "No wilderness is real wilderness without big game," he noted, and his fellow outfitters were inclined to agree. They derived much of their income during Montana's hunting season, which was one of the longest and most productive in the nation. Bob Cooney, a biologist who worked for the Montana Fish and Game Department, amplified this point. Montana's wild country was shrinking, he said, and along with it the quality of its hunting and fishing. "When you get to hunting elk from roads, it loses its charm," Cooney suggested. Some people, he added, simply wanted to see or photograph wild animals, including the state's most emblematic creature. "The only way to have grizzly bears," he said, "is to have a considerable amount of wild country." This was a use of the forest commons that depended on it simply being left alone—an approach the officers of the Forest Service had great difficulty accepting.

Kenneth Baldwin, an avid hunter and hiker from Bozeman and president of the Gallatin Sportsmen's Association, had not participated in the recent trail ride, but having explored these mountains for years he knew that they contained values beyond recreation (as usually conceived) or even quality hunting. Wilderness was an important benchmark for scientific research, he told the group, observing that eastern Montana's prairie provided a wealth of animal habitats and must not be neglected. Drawing lines was a start, and at the end of the meeting he would recommend specific boundaries for the upper Gallatin area, but there were more complex ecological and societal issues to consider than merely providing a hunting playground for eastern dudes or trails for local hikers.

The Forest Service's leadership seems to have missed this fundamental issue entirely—the role that wild creatures played in an increasingly humanized landscape. Elk, bear, pronghorn, mountain sheep, and anadromous trout knew nothing of lines and boundaries. Their world was mapped by age-old migratory routes, wintering grounds, and summer feeding ranges. No single land designation could take these patterns into account, although biologists such as Cooney and Murie believed that wilderness designations, if widely and generously applied, were the best available proxy. From the late 1940s onward they pressed the Forest Service and other federal agencies to pay attention to wildlife's needs before turning public lands over to massive development programs such as hydropower reservoirs, highways, and logging roads.

The discussions over the country north of Yellowstone National Park represented both facets of this emerging conflict. High up among the picturesque lakes of Hilgard Basin—the centerpiece of the Madison Range—lay some of the finest recreational country imaginable. This was what Forest Service officers thought of when they envisioned a system of wilderness areas on their domain. To the east and south of the Hilgard peaks, however, was a more subdued landscape featuring huge meadows in which elk feasted on the rich greenery and, sometimes, became feasts for grizzlies. Decent timber stands lined many of the approach valleys to this high country, making wilderness designation problematic to the foresters, yet wildlife enthusiasts and outfitters alike understood their importance as seasonal cover and winter range. They would continue to press for a wider application of the wilderness concept in order to protect the area's abundant, free-ranging wildlife. On this depended a way of life they had enjoyed for decades.

The horsemen and women of Gallatin Canyon and their friends in the outdoors and wildlife community knew they needed a connection to a Washington power base, for they faced an intimidating federal bureaucracy and, in the

Northern Pacific, one of the country's most powerful corporations. Their September meeting was one of many held in Montana and Idaho during the 1950s that cemented a working coalition with the Wilderness Society and its allies— one that would help set in motion a tremendous expansion of the nation's designated wilderness system. At that time the states of Montana and Idaho contained eleven Forest Service–administered wilderness, wild, and primitive areas comprising some 4.8 million acres. Most were interim designations, however, and elsewhere in the West the agency was opening its primitive areas to new road construction and logging. This boded ill for the Madison and Gallatin Ranges, which enjoyed no formal protection under agency regulations.[6]

The men and women gathered at the Kelseys' lodge concluded their meeting by helping Ken Baldwin draw boundary lines for a 220,000-acre protected area within the upper Gallatin River drainage. Ed Barry passed the map on to Charles Tebbe, who agreed to not conduct any development activities within what became known as the Hilgard Hold Area. A quarter century would pass, however, before Congress would decide whether to ratify this attempt at land-use zoning. By then, thanks to the pioneering work of Cooney, Murie, and others, the importance of wilderness areas to wildlife would be better understood, and the new science of conservation biology would introduce terms like *corridors* and *connectivity* to the debate.[7] A new generation of advocates would draw more lines on maps, outlining a 500,000-acre protected landscape in the Madison and Gallatin Ranges that they felt was needed to protect elk herds, free-roaming grizzlies, wolves, and many other creatures. At issue was the question of how humans could make room for the interplay of wild animals and the natural forces that had guided their evolution for eons.

The leaders of the wilderness movement in the Northern Rockies never constrained their efforts, as some histories imply, to preserving popular hiking trails and treeless mountain basins. They enjoyed their recreation, to be sure, but for most of them wildlife was key to their enjoyment, and not necessarily the huntable or catchable variety. The growing scientific understanding of the importance of varied and undisturbed habitats led them to broaden their campaigns beyond the scenic high country. In these mountains the work of conservation biology would begin, decades before the term was coined. The discussion that Olaus Murie was hearing in that remote lodge in the autumn of 1958 stemmed from an emerging grassroots movement—one that might transform how humans coexisted with their fellow inhabitants of the Northern Rockies. This was an ambition much grander, and fraught with deeper policy implications, than creating recreational preserves for hikers and horse riders.

The Forest Service men listening to the discussion at the Kelseys' lodge must have wondered what lay in store for their carefully designed management plans. Ed Barry had in mind an equally grand vision for the mountain ranges of the Northern Rockies—one that involved graded forest highways coursing through the high timber, bringing mountain lakes and subalpine basins within easy reach of the motoring public as well as opening timber stands for the region's burgeoning timber industry. He and his colleagues wanted to apply the principles of modern American forestry to the upper Gallatin, replacing a lightly used forest landscape with something much more productive of resources. Their nervousness at this meeting attested to a developing conflict they knew was coming and did not know how to resolve.

1

The Blueprint for Our Folly
The Upper Flathead, 1947–1959

A decade before the Gallatin Canyon outfitters met with Northern Region officials to plot the future of the Madison Range, their counterparts in northwestern Montana were trying to hold back reclamation and flood-control projects from inundating portions of Glacier National Park and the Bob Marshall Wilderness. Dams, not logging, prompted the first stirrings of a wilderness movement in the Northern Rockies. With the National Park Service and the Forest Service as their allies, sportsmen in the Flathead Valley honed their techniques of arousing public concern and built a close relationship with national conservation leaders such as the Wilderness Society's Olaus Murie and Howard Zahniser. Soon the sportsmen would turn these same techniques against the Forest Service after it began to emulate the federal reclamation agencies with its own comprehensive resource development program.

During the early 1900s the leaders of various federal agencies—among them the Geological Survey, Army Corps of Engineers, Bureau of Reclamation, and Forest Service—brought the principles of scientific resource management to bear on the public domain in the western states.[1] The first three concerned themselves with harnessing rivers and providing irrigation, while the Forest Service was charged with bringing order to the vast yet poorly administered system of forest reserves created in the late nineteenth century. Established in 1905 as an arm of the utilitarian-minded Department of Agriculture, this agency stood ready to follow its chief, Gifford Pinchot, into battle. Its enemies were fire, rapacious private enterprise, and public apathy; its ultimate goal the orderly regulation of the western forests through applied silviculture.

Within District 1 of the Forest Service (later the Northern Region), demand for public timber rose steadily following the great fires of 1910, but the Great Depression forced the agency to revert to a mostly custodial posture of fire control, trail building, and land surveys, waiting for the day when private industry in northern Idaho and western Montana would finish cutting its lands and come calling. Such was not the case for the Corps of Engineers and Bureau of Reclamation, which responded to the Depression with monumental water storage projects such as Fort Peck Dam in eastern Montana and Bonneville and Grand Coulee on the Columbia River. Following World War II, these traditional rivals for congressional appropriations agreed on a joint plan for harnessing the Columbia's headwater streams. It called for an astonishing number of impoundments on the Snake, Clearwater, Clark Fork, and Flathead Rivers, as well as in the upper Missouri River basin. Even tributary streams such as Montana's Bull River, Blackfoot River, and Rock Creek were slated for impoundment in an ambitious effort to reduce flood hazards, provide irrigation water, and (at favorable sites) generate power.[2]

During the New Deal the federal reclamation agencies cemented their relationships with major construction firms and the northwestern states' congressional delegations—an "iron triangle" that looked to new challenges in harnessing the nation's rivers. In 1944 Montana senator James Murray and western district representative Mike Mansfield pushed a bill through Congress to authorize the Hungry Horse project on the South Fork of the Flathead River, one of two principal drainages flowing out of the northwestern side of the Bob Marshall Wilderness. Murray and Mansfield touted this project as an alternative to raising Kerr Dam below Flathead Lake, which would have inundated several towns and spoiled one of Montana's most popular recreation destinations.[3] Three years later, contractors for the Bureau of Reclamation began clearing land for the 564-foot-high Hungry Horse Dam and its 34-mile-long reservoir, which flooded the South Fork's timbered and largely undeveloped valley nearly to the Spotted Bear Ranger Station. After its completion in 1953, the dam's turbines supplied electric power to the reduction pots at the Anaconda Company's new aluminum smelter at Columbia Falls. If dams, reservoirs, and smelters overrode such niceties as air quality, trout habitat, and hiking trails, there were higher values to consider. In brochures, filmstrips, and annual reports, these federal agencies extolled the strong hand of humanity against the destructive forces of nature.

Northern Idaho lagged somewhat in postwar resource development, but the mines and smelters in the Wallace-Kellogg corridor remained busy and the Potlatch Corporation was building a new pulp mill at Lewiston. Plans were under way to dam the Snake River in and below Hells Canyon to generate power and open the river to barge traffic. Idaho senator Henry Dworshak wanted to build one or more high dams on the Clearwater River, a cool and inviting forest stream that flowed westward out of the Bitterroot Range. Chamber of commerce boosters from Walla Walla to Kooskia hoped to connect the towns along the Clearwater with Missoula via the planned Lewis-Clark Highway, thus modernizing the ancient trade route the Nez Perce had forged over Lolo Pass. The route was named for the explorers Meriwether Lewis and William Clark, whose starving journey through this snowy wilderness in 1805 bore little resemblance to the comfort of modern-day motorists who, beginning in 1962, cruised the smooth asphalt curves alongside the Lochsa River.

For a handful of hunters, anglers, and hikers living in towns from Lewiston to Kalispell, this great industrial expansion foretold the end of the nearly limitless wanderings they had enjoyed in one of America's least developed regions. Well into the 1940s they lacked a strong voice; Ken Baldwin and others had formed the Montana Wildlife Federation in 1936 to represent the dozens of rod-and-gun clubs across the state, but these stuck mostly to issues of game limits and hunting seasons. Before long, though, as outdoors people headed for the woods and encountered the very industrialization they had hoped to leave behind, some would raise pointed questions about the effects of hydropower, flood control, and highway projects on stream habitats and wintering areas for big game. Uncertain at first whether they could block popular public-works projects, they began to mount ad hoc campaigns to protect what they regarded as a hunting and fishing commons—an essential part of their way of life in this still-undeveloped part of the country.[4]

The question came to the fore in 1947 when the Army Corps of Engineers unveiled a proposal for another great dam in the Flathead River drainage. This one, called Glacier View, was to span the North Fork of the Flathead River below Dutch Creek, northwest of Lake McDonald, and flood the North Fork's broad valley nearly to the outlet of Kintla Lake. The North Fork was quintessential Montana—an arrow-straight glacial trench that lay between the hulking peaks of Glacier and the only slightly less imposing Whitefish Range. Its few hundred residents clustered around the remote hamlet of Polebridge, many of them thankful for the miles of potholed gravel road that separated them from the centers of civilization at Columbia Falls, Whitefish, and Kalispell. Few of them were pleased over their impending relocation, and they and their allies among Montana's sportsmen saw great value in maintaining the winter range lining the bottomlands along the North Fork.

The three-million-acre-foot reservoir created by Glacier View Dam would provide flood control, water storage, and lake-based recreation along Glacier National Park's western edge. It would also slip water into the park itself, which dismayed officials of the National Park Service. Its director, Newton Drury, was aware of a Bureau of Reclamation proposal to flood Utah's Dinosaur National Monument at Echo Park and Split Mountain on the Green River, as well as a planned water diversion within Colorado's Rocky Mountain National Park. The inundation of Glacier, even if limited to its westernmost portion, was likewise anathema. At a preliminary hearing on the proposal held in Kalispell in April 1947, Glacier superintendent John Emmert issued a statement faulting the Corps of Engineers for proposing to "seriously impair the primitive character of this highly prized North Fork section of the park by the creation of a fluctuating artificial body of water. . . . The submerged area both within and outside the park would encompass practically all of the present winter range of moose, elk, and white-tailed deer in the northwestern portion of the park."[5]

The Corps of Engineers held another public hearing in Kalispell in May 1948, following a winter in which heavy rainfall and rapid snowmelt caused severe flooding throughout the Columbia River system. The floods added a sense of urgency to headwaters storage projects such as Glacier View, but despite local support for the dam among business and community boosters, some local sportsmen objected to the loss of a valuable stream and its associated bottomland habitat. Park Service director Newton Drury reiterated his agency's opposition,[6] and Olaus Murie traveled to Kalispell to testify on behalf of the Wilderness Society. Testimony at the 1948 hearing ran forty to nine against the project, according to Murie, including opposition from the Montana Dude Ranch Association, the Whitefish Chamber of Commerce, and the Glacier Park Hotel Company. Forty residents of the North Fork wrote letters protesting the project. The clash amounted to a rehearsal for the epic confrontation that was brewing over Dinosaur.[7] Unlike in Utah, the Glacier View project drew significant local opposition to flooding this isolated and highly scenic river valley.

At the second Kalispell hearing, Olaus Murie sat next to a Montana farmer who he presumed would be speaking in favor of the dam. After Murie delivered his testimony and returned to his seat, the man reached for his hand, saying "Good!

I am a member of your society!"[8] He was Winton Weydemeyer, the president of the Montana State Grange, who lived in the tiny community of Fortine in north-western Montana. He then stood up and gave what Murie called "the most fundamental testimony of the hearing," telling the Corps of Engineers that although part of his farmland was underwater, he was against this dam.

> The proposal to dam the North Fork of the Flathead [Weydemeyer said] is in perfect harmony with the national water policy we have been following, of treating results rather than causes. Throwing dams across our streams is in too many cases only an emergency measure, instituted to overcome in part the results of abuse of our watershed. Here is the pattern we follow, the blueprint for our folly; we cut down the forests which form Nature's water reservoirs faster than they grow; we allow burned watershed areas to lie idle and eroding; we overgraze the grasslands upon which the rain falls; as a result, there occurs rapid run-off of water from rain and melting snow, with accompanying soil erosion and silting of our streams and reservoirs. When floods occur, do we hasten to protect the lands from whence the water flows? No, instead we pour more concrete or dirt across the silt-laden streams.[9]

An agriculturist trained at Montana State College in Bozeman, Weydemeyer viewed conservation through a different lens than the Corps of Engineers or even the sportsmen seeking to protect big-game winter ranges. To him, floods were an indication of poor land use, and it is no coincidence that he had been corresponding since 1925 with Aldo Leopold, the best-known exponent of such a perspective. Just as Ken Baldwin had urged the Gallatin Canyon outfitters to consider the value of different ecosystems to science, Weydemeyer recognized the interrelatedness of human land uses. These were fitful attempts to grasp at larger understandings, but it is significant that such questions were being raised in Montana in 1948, a year before the publication of Leopold's *A Sand County Almanac*, which thrust the question of land health before a larger audience.

With conservationists united in opposition to Glacier View, and conservatives nationwide branding federal river basin development as "creeping socialism," the dam faced uncertain prospects in Congress. In 1949 Newton Drury was able to persuade Interior Secretary Julius Krug to broker an agreement with the secretary of the army to eliminate the dam from the Corps of Engineers' Columbia Basin projects.[10] A smaller dam downstream from Flathead

Lake near the town of Paradise was also shelved pending further study; this project was a favorite of public-power advocates who hoped it would lead to the construction of another Anaconda smelter in the economically depressed lower Flathead Valley. Conservationists in Montana cheered the dams' cancellation, but their celebration (as in many other campaigns stretching back to Yosemite's Hetch Hetchy Valley) was short lived. Mike Mansfield, an advocate of cheap hydropower for public utilities, introduced legislation in 1949 to revive Glacier View, telling his constituents that it would be "of inestimable value to the people of Montana" and would "completely eliminate" flood damage on the upper Flathead. He asked Krug to reconsider, since the reservoir would disturb only 1 percent of Glacier National Park—"all of it in a little used valley on the westerly fringe, and completely outside the rugged, glacier-covered areas for which the park is famous."[11]

Krug was not persuaded that any portion of Glacier was expendable and stated in reply to Mansfield that "the losses in wildlife resources, in forested wilderness, in scenic beauty, and in recreational value to our whole Nation, in my opinion, are far greater than pictured by the dam's proponents." His opposition effectively closed prospects for the dam and helped set a precedent for the subsequent battle in Dinosaur National Monument.[12] Mansfield, who was elected to the Senate in 1952, turned his attention to a new proposal to divert water from the Middle Fork of the Flathead at Spruce Park, which would boost the generating capacity of Hungry Horse Reservoir.[13]

Lee Metcalf, a liberal Democrat who served on the Montana Supreme Court, was elected that year to fill Mansfield's western district House seat. He initially joined his colleague in supporting Glacier View, believing it would not cause "appreciable harm" to the park.[14] A strong supporter of consumer-owned electric utilities and co-ops, Metcalf viewed inexpensive federal hydropower as a means of undercutting the politically powerful Montana Power Company, a private utility that was historically allied with the Anaconda Copper Company. The public-power issue was less prominent at Dinosaur, where Metcalf worked closely with the Wilderness Society and other conservation groups to halt the Echo Park project. Led by David Brower of the Sierra Club, Howard Zahniser of the Wilderness Society, and Fred Packard of the National Parks Association, they won a stipulation in the 1956 Colorado River Storage Project Act that no dam or reservoir built under the act would inundate any national park or monument. The provision applied only to the upper Colorado, but it set a clear precedent for the rest of the national park system. Zahniser informed readers of the Kalispell *Daily Inter Lake* that they "might as well conclude now" that Glacier

View would not be authorized. "Why not instead cherish Glacier National Park for what it is—one of the greatest tourist attractions that Kalispell and other communities in the region could ever hope for, and prized in its natural state by Americans from all over the nation and by visitors from all over the world?"[15]

After witnessing the combined power of the nation's conservationists in the Echo Park battle, Metcalf retreated to a more ambivalent position on Glacier View. In 1955 he told Mel Ruder, the influential publisher of the *Hungry Horse News* and a dam supporter, that he might introduce authorizing legislation "at some more opportune time in the future."[16] Glacier View did not disappear from the drafting boards of the Corps of Engineers, however, and local businesses continued to tout the dam as a means of attracting high-paying construction and smelter jobs. Ruder acknowledged that recreation and wildlife were important but noted that "we are also well aware of the snow water potential for hydro-electric power. The question remains just where on the Flathead River can this area have a second dam? We don't know of a better way to create lasting jobs for men."[17]

Ruder framed the question as a choice between jobs and amenities such as recreation and wildlife, as if the answer were self-evident. But for Dallas Eklund, an avid angler from Kalispell, the perennial threat to the Flathead's free-flowing waters and its surrounding park and wilderness lands represented a "big steal" of the public's wildlife. In a letter to the *Daily Inter Lake* he termed Glacier National Park a "game reservoir" that permitted the take of more than two hundred elk from the adjacent national forest lands along the North Fork. "One has only to look at what is happening on the South Fork above Hungry Horse Dam, where twenty-three thousand acres of winter range and habitat for big game herds was flooded," he wrote. The dam also removed one-third of the available spawning habitat for Flathead Lake's migratory trout.[18] To Eklund, the park was more than a tourist attraction; it provided seamless habitat that complemented the forestlands of the North Fork.

Wildlife was the predominant concern for Montana sportsmen at Glacier View, whereas the nation's principal conservation groups framed the issue as a battle for the integrity of the national park system. Mel Ruder's utilitarian approach had wide appeal in Montana and Idaho, however, and advocates for each side faced off again and again over new river development proposals. Choosing the highest and best uses of wild forest landscapes like those of the North Fork exposed deep contradictions in the conservation movement. Was it better to construct a large dam and reservoir to control floods and provide cheap hydropower, or should the government keep the headwater forests and winter range intact? Standing trees and elk habitat had their uses, too, and in the Northern Rockies they constituted a significant economic resource. These questions did not revolve solely around Glacier's touristic value. Sportsmen and wildlife advocates pointed to the need for a full complement of natural habitats spanning the park and forest boundary in order to maintain valuable game populations.

The question of utility depended on who was drawing up the balance sheet. Mel Ruder saw in the Flathead River's rampaging floods little more than potential energy flowing to the Pacific. The engineers and managers working for the dam-building bureaus also thought of themselves as conservationists who were preventing the waste of a natural resource. Through their efforts rivers were being harnessed, croplands were growing wheat and corn, and towns and cities were being protected from flooding. But Dallas Eklund, Winton Weydemeyer, Olaus Murie, and their friends were searching for a new ethic that might soften the hard edges of utilitarianism and the technoindustrial questing of the postwar era. Unwilling to leave river basin development to the government's reclamation experts, they were laying the groundwork for later campaigns involving the Forest Service and its timber management policies. Despite the high regard in which technical experts were held in America, these activists insisted on broader measures of the public good. Some part of the natural world must be allowed to work out its own ends, they claimed. If Americans would exercise some restraint, their descendants might enjoy seeing a wild cutthroat trout rise to the fly in the Flathead's clear August waters.

2

Selway Wilderness
The Forest Service and the Primitive Areas, 1926–1940

Well before conflicts over reclamation dams brought preservation issues before a wider public, a few individuals within the Forest Service were trying to advance wilderness as a legitimate land designation—at least where significant timber resources were not involved. Their interest centered on some of the largest roadless tracts in the West, including Idaho's Bitterroot Range, the source of the Lochsa and Selway Rivers. Frank Jefferson, the supervisor of the Selway National Forest during the 1920s, called these mountains "one of the most beautiful portions of Idaho" and predicted that they would "eventually be discovered as such by the wilderness loving fraternity." Within the Selway drainage, he wrote, "three semi-civilized Forest Rangers, a few Forest Guards and a strand of number nine wire constitute the extent of its contamination by civilization."[1] Officially, however, the agency considered the Selway drainage to be a "low value area," where rugged terrain, poor road access, and a lack of merchantable timber limited management options. The agency's hesitant embrace of wilderness in these mountains set the stage for conflicts that would not be resolved for another half century.

To Bob Marshall, the most influential advocate among the Forest Service's nascent pro-wilderness faction, the Bitterroot Range encompassed "the greatest forest wilderness still left in this country." In the winter of 1926, while based in Missoula as part of the agency's research staff, Marshall set out on an overnight snowshoe trip west from Lolo Hot Springs, following a recent extension of the Forest Service truck trail that led over Lolo Pass and onward into the Lochsa drainage. Halting at the pass, he observed the snowbound track leading down toward the Powell Ranger Station, which was still one of the most isolated administrative posts in the nation. When completed westward, the road would "cut this great wilderness in two," Marshall realized. "I am certainly glad I had the chance of standing at its edge in mid-winter, before this wilderness is ruined forever by a highway."[2]

In Marshall's view, a true wilderness needed to be big enough to contain a full day's hike in one direction—which for him could be thirty, forty, or even fifty miles of rugged mountain country. On a 1927 exploration of the northern Bitterroots, Marshall was enthralled by "needlelike peaks rising unscalably into the sky, spacious plateaus suddenly dropping into gloomy gorges, wooded basins meeting on irregular fronts with snag-strewn burns, deep blue ponds and bright parks alleviating the harshness of granite, goats moving with poise and dignity among the ledges impending over air."[3]

Notwithstanding the primeval allure of the Selway and Lochsa backcountry, Frank Jefferson and his fellow forest supervisors oversaw the construction of several hundred miles of primitive roads into the headwaters of these streams during the 1930s as part of regional forester Evan Kelley's overriding commitment to fire control. The "truck trails," as they were called, gave employment to Depression-era work crews as well as access for the agency's smokechasers. Hunting parties and auto tourists, too, followed the trails' jouncing courses to reach heretofore inaccessible lakes and streams. The Lolo Trail, an evolving braid of routes on which generations of Nez Perce Indians had traveled to the buffalo prairies of Montana, gave way (as Bob Marshall feared) to the rattle of truck engines as Kelley's crews bladed a rough-and-tumble roadway from Musselshell Meadow east of Weippe, Idaho, to the Powell Ranger Station on the Lochsa River.[4] Another truck trail led from Powell south past the meadows at Elk Summit, where it descended into the upper drainage of Moose Creek in the Selway River drainage.

Farther south, Civilian Conservation Corps youths helped complete a vehicle route from Darby, Montana, to Elk City, Idaho. This route, a narrow dirt track through the deeply canyoned topography of the upper Selway River, was named after Lloyd Magruder, a gold rush–era packer who was murdered in the area. Few officials in the agency questioned whether these roads should be built or how far they should extend. One that did was Elers Koch, who had overseen the Selway country from 1906 to 1908 as supervisor of the Bitterroot National

Forest. Writing in the February 1935 issue of the *Journal of Forestry*, he lamented the loss of wilderness values that accompanied the Northern Region's truck trail program. "The Lolo Trail is no more," he wrote. "The bulldozer blade has ripped out the hoof tracks of Chief Joseph's ponies. . . . It is gone, and in its place there is only the print of the automobile tire in the dust."[5]

Koch's impassioned comments added another log to the fire in a decade-old debate within forestry circles about the role that wilderness lands might play in American life. The Forest Service tended to look at such preserves as one aspect of recreational planning, a tradition that began in 1924 with the designation of New Mexico's Gila Wilderness Reserve. Aldo Leopold, a former district ranger and a pioneering ecologist, urged district forester Frank Pooler to set up the 695,000-acre area as a prime example of a wild region "big enough to absorb the average man's two weeks' vacation without getting him tangled up in his own back track."[6] Leopold believed that there were deeper rewards to such a trip than could be gained from camping or fishing alongside a road. "Driving a pack train across or along a graded highway is distinctly not a pack trip," he advised. "It is merely exercise, with about the same flavor as lifting dumbbells." Pooler approved tentative boundaries for the Gila reserve under the umbrella of recreation management, without specific direction or authority from Washington.[7]

Similar initiatives came from district foresters in Idaho, Montana, and Wyoming, who in the mid-1920s outlined five large roadless tracts that were to be segregated from resource uses. These took in the spectacular Grand Teton massif, an area to the east of the Tetons around Two Ocean Pass, the Absaroka Range east of Yellowstone National Park, the Middle Fork of the Salmon River, and the headwaters of the Blackfoot River. These reserves, according to James Gilligan, who studied the origins of the agency's primitive and wilderness area program for his 1953 doctoral dissertation, "were selected as areas temporarily restricted from road and summer home development rather than to represent a positive new policy of use."[8] Without any firm directive to limit uses, such areas were at best the germ seed for wilderness preservation. In 1926 chief forester William Greeley, responding to the increasingly public stance Aldo Leopold and Bob Marshall were taking in promoting wilderness set-asides, detailed Leon F. Kneipp, who headed the agency's recreation and lands branch, to make a broadbrush inventory of undeveloped lands on the national forests. Kneipp identified seventy-four roadless areas of at least 360 square miles (230,400 acres), nearly all in the western national forests, which aggregated to fifty-five million acres.[9] Using this inventory as a starting point, Greeley asked his district foresters in the West to review their development plans to ensure that they did not "contemplate a needless invasion of areas adapted to wilderness forms of use." He did not propose any uniform standards or any formal designation for such areas, however.[10]

Unsatisfied with his agency's fitful attempts at protecting wild lands, Marshall produced his own inventory as a starting point for further designations. In 1927 he outlined every remaining roadless area of a million acres or more on the national forests—many of which he had traversed himself. The largest of these lay in central Idaho in the Salmon and Selway drainages, an enormous landscape of beargrass-covered ridges and deep river canyons that he estimated took in 11,982 sections of forestland, or some 7.6 million acres. The upper Flathead River drainage, by Marshall's estimate, contained a 2,360,000-acre roadless area, while a conjoined "Beartooth-Absaroka" area came in at just under a million acres.[11] Marshall did not publicize his list, but it formed the basis for his incessant prodding of the federal bureaucracy to protect large wild areas.

Additional impetus came from the National Conference on Outdoor Recreation, an informal organization of more than one hundred heads of federal, state, and private agencies chartered by President Coolidge. The group included L. F. Kneipp and Franklin Reed, a district forester in charge of the agency's eastern national forests. At the group's first meeting in May 1924, Kneipp was "amazed" to find "almost unanimous sentiment" against building roads into undeveloped areas of the national forests.[12] At its second meeting in 1928, the group (at Reed's and Kneipp's urging) asked the Forest Service to set aside five large roadless areas in the Northern Rockies: 485,000 acres in the Whitefish Range, 600,000 acres in the upper Flathead River drainage, a half million acres on the Beartooth Plateau, a million acres in the Selway drainage, and the largest of all, a 1,250,000-acre expanse surrounding the Middle Fork of the Salmon River.[13] District forester Fred Morrell, however, favored setting aside only the Beartooth Plateau, since the forest resources of the Absaroka Range and the Flathead and Selway drainages might one day prove useful. He told Reed that their use by "a relatively small portion of the recreation seeking public makes me question the wisdom of keeping them shut up forever."[14]

Morrell was expressing a common Forest Service belief that the utility of the national forests derived mostly from their stocks of sawtimber. In a personal note to Reed, he professed impatience with recreationists who wanted vast areas set aside as wilderness preserves. A road up the South Fork of the Flathead River "would not change the aspect of the three quarters of a million acres of land that it would tap. The chap who longs for the wilderness could lose the road by traveling 100 yards in any direction." He likened Marshall, Leopold, and their followers to an "aristocracy of recreationists" who were mainly interested in getting away from their fellow humans.[15] Such areas were unlikely to be developed for many years, he added, and thus did not merit special protection.

The first Service-wide codification of the wilderness concept came in 1929 when L. F. Kneipp drafted Regulation L-20, which specified that undeveloped forest and mountain areas could be designated to maintain "primitive conditions of environment, transportation, habitation, and subsistence, with a view to conserving the value of such areas for purposes of public education, inspiration, and recreation."[16] Chief forester Robert Stuart, who replaced William Greeley in 1928, hoped that a system of primitive areas would satisfy the increasingly vocal wilderness enthusiasts within and outside his agency. He informed his district foresters that "this much can be given them without an unwise subordination of our protective and administrative obligations." He underscored that such areas would be subject to somewhat loose control, with "no hard and fast rules, principles, or standards" to govern their use and development. The ideal of absolute land preservation, he said, "probably is beyond the ability of any administrative agency."[17]

Stuart's comments reflected the deep ambivalence among many Forest Service officers toward the idea of placing large blocks of land off limits to development. While many agency staffers enjoyed hunting and fishing in the Northern Rockies' backcountry, and certain old-timers such as Elers Koch still valued woodcraft and primitive travel skills, most assumed that modern methods of fire control, timber salvage, and silviculture would soon supplant the old ways. American industry would eventually catch up with these remote areas, and once their stands of timber had grown a little more and new access roads were built, the farthest reaches of the Selway or the Flathead would prove profitable to log. To foresters such as Fred Morrell and Frank Jefferson, the primitive areas were a temporary expedient—a political accommodation to a small group of vocal citizens whose demands they scarcely understood.

Evan Kelley, who was known as "Major" for his service in France during World War I, replaced Morrell in 1929 and brought a somewhat more favorable attitude toward wildland withdrawals. In 1931 he approved Montana's first primitive areas under Regulation L-20, covering 584,000 acres in the South Fork of the Flathead River and 67,000 acres west of the Swan River in the Mission Range. The latter's spectacularly carved peaks and deep glacial lakes gave the range an Alpine aura and attracted numerous fishing and camping parties. Both primitive areas were sparsely forested and extensively burned, so they presented little controversy. Their designation also helped the Forest Service guard against the depredations of a sister agency, the National Park Service, which was on the lookout for scenic landscapes to add to its domain. There were active proposals to create new national parks or monuments in some of Montana's most impressive mountain ranges, including the Beartooth Plateau and the Cabinet Mountains. A slate of primitive areas might head off these proposals and round out the Forest Service's recreational program, which up to now had consisted mostly of building a few roadside campgrounds and issuing leases for summer cabins along prime lakeshores.[18]

District 4 (later the Intermountain Region, headquartered in Ogden, Utah) established an even larger reservation within central Idaho, encompassing just over a million acres in the remote breaks and uplands centering on the Middle Fork of the Salmon River. This proposal arose out of a pack trip that district forester Richard Rutledge made in 1927 with Idaho governor H. C. Baldridge and several prominent Idaho businessmen. Impressed with the fine hunting and fishing in the area, Baldridge, a Republican, convened a committee consisting of various ranching, mining, and business executives to consider protected status for the Middle Fork drainage. Rutledge provided tentative boundaries for a new primitive area and assured the men that existing mining uses could continue and private lands would be respected. With these assurances, Baldridge's committee gave its assent, and in February 1931 chief forester Stuart approved the 1,087,744-acre Idaho Primitive Area, the largest thus far in the national forest system. Even so, Stuart felt it necessary to add that should a demand for timber or mineral resources arise, his agency "would feel free to modify the plan of management."[19]

In 1935 Bob Marshall chided his mentor, chief forester Ferdinand Silcox, for what he termed "an almost total disregard for any form of outdoor recreational planning which seems to have occurred in many of your regions." He noted that Park Service director Arno Cammerer was "turning yearning eyes toward every pretty spot in the National Forests."[20] Marshall was likely thinking of the Selway River drainage, which remained open to road construction under Evan Kelley's truck trail program. That year Marshall contributed an article on the Selway to the inaugural issue of *Living Wilderness*, the magazine of the Wilderness Society, an organization he had helped found that year. In it he urged that the area be "set aside as a great wilderness and that all the Forest Service truck trail programs within it be abandoned."[21] Major Kelley defended his truck trails as "absolutely necessary" for fire protection. "Why should we pay so much attention to Bob Marshall's advocacies?" he complained. "He is only one man of many thousands who have opinions in regard to the uses which should be made of the National Forests."[22] But the young forester had tapped into an undercurrent of longing for the primeval that Elers Koch and a handful of cooperators in the agency could understand. By November Silcox had given his general approval for a new primitive area in the Selway, and in June 1936 Kelley reached agreement with Koch, Marshall, and his local forest supervisors on its boundaries. The proposed order went back to the chief's office, where on July 3, 1936, Silcox signed a directive establishing the 1,875,000-acre Selway-Bitterroot Primitive Area, the largest in the country, which stretched for sixty rugged miles from the Lochsa to the Salmon.[23]

Whatever his reservations, Kelley went on to praise the primitive area program at a recreation conference held in Hailey, Idaho, later that summer. "Many men, and women too, deep down, crave the natural amusements and soul gratifications which issue only from living now and then far removed from life's nerve-wracking whirl," he said. "They yearn for solitude—to live in and listen to the wilderness."[24] Still, he insisted on completing the roads planned within the Selway-Bitterroot Primitive Area, including one that was being blasted through the talus slides of Lost Horse Canyon to give fire crews quick access to the upper Moose Creek drainage.[25] Three primitive airstrips already existed in the Selway and were used by hunters and Forest Service crews; these would remain open and new ones could be built as needed for fire control. While the primitive area gave recognition to the Selway as a wild landscape, its designation erected no solid barriers against development. That would not come until advocates built a wider base of support for the wilderness concept.

In 1936 Bob Marshall released the results of his latest inventory of roadless areas, again conducted without official sanction. Writing in *Living Wilderness*, he and cartographer Althea Dobbins identified forty-eight forest tracts of 300,000 acres or larger, most of which were located in the western national forests. Among the largest was a 2,800,000-acre tract in the Salmon River canyons, which owing to road construction was now a fraction of the huge area Marshall had identified in 1927. Fifth on their list was a two-million-acre area in the South Fork of the Flathead River, which was far larger than the Forest Service's designated primitive area.[26] Partly at Marshall's urging, and with support from Meyer Wolff, Major Kelley's chief of recreation and lands, two more primitive areas were set aside adjacent to the South Fork: the 240,000-acre Sun River area in 1934 and the 125,900-acre Pentagon area in 1936. Together these formed the headwaters of some of Montana's most beautiful rivers: the Flathead, Teton, Sun, Dearborn, and Blackfoot. A 31,000-acre strip in the upper Spotted Bear drainage was initially omitted from these primitive areas because of interest in road and water power development, but it was added to the Pentagon area in 1939, joining it to the Sun River. Then, following Marshall's untimely death in late 1939, Evan Kelley recommended that all three areas be joined into a single 950,000-acre wilderness area, to be named for the nation's most persistent wilderness advocate. Secretary of Agriculture Henry Wallace issued the order designating the Bob Marshall Wilderness on August 14, 1940, establishing what many would regard as America's premier example of forestland preservation.[27]

Interest was also growing in Montana's other mountain landscapes as potential recreational preserves. Marshall and Dobbins outlined a 300,000-acre roadless area in the Mission Range in their 1936 report, far larger than the 67,000-acre primitive area set aside in 1931, although chief Silcox expanded it to 75,500 acres in 1939. (The western part of the Missions lay on the Flathead Indian Reservation, whose leaders adopted an innovative tribal wilderness in 1979.) The Spanish Peaks west of Bozeman contained little timber and presented conflicts only from summertime livestock grazing and the inholdings of the Northern Pacific Railway. With support from Northern Region staff, including Meyer Wolff, Robert Stuart designated a 50,000-acre primitive area in the Spanish Peaks in April 1932. Southeast of Livingston, the northernmost reach of the Absaroka Range (64,000 acres) and the lofty Beartooth Plateau west of Red Lodge (230,000 acres) were designated in 1932, although the two areas were separated by a historic wagon track that led up the Boulder River to Cooke City at the northeastern margin of Yellowstone. In the Cabinet Mountains of northwestern Montana, densely vegetated slopes guarded a narrow string of seldom-climbed peaks, which Ferdinand Silcox, Stuart's replacement, set aside in 1935 as a 90,000-acre primitive area.

Sportsmen and civic groups in the Butte-Anaconda area expressed support for reserving the massive 10,000-foot peaks of the Anaconda Range, which overlooked lovely subalpine lakes stocked with trout. Bob Marshall had urged their classification under Regulation L-20, leading Meyer Wolff to observe that "the more of these we dedicate, the better satisfied are the Bob Marshalls."[28] No difference in management would result either way, he added, and in 1937 Evan Kelley gave his blessing to the 145,000-acre Anaconda-Pintlar Primitive Area, protecting about half of the lands that Marshall and Dobbins believed were still undeveloped.[29]

As yet there were few resource conflicts within the new primitive areas, although that would change as the Northern Region broadened the scope of its timber program. Although these areas were initially set aside to fill a vacuum in recreational needs, there was little discussion of their value for wildlife or as ecological benchmarks in an increasingly developed forest landscape. Nor did the Forest Service amend its fire control policies in the primitive areas, despite a sharp remonstration from Elers Koch on the excessive expense (and ultimate futility) of trying to control huge blazes in these so-called low-value landscapes.[30] He was reacting to the enormous control efforts made during the great fires of 1929 and 1934, which raged out of control in the upper Selway. These fires allowed extensive brush fields to spring up along the Lochsa and upper Selway Rivers, offering excellent browse for a growing elk herd. Few hunters could afford to hire a guide to pack deep into the wilderness, and with little winter range available to support the elk, the Forest Service feared massive die-offs. The state of Idaho managed a game preserve on the south side of the Lochsa that predated the primitive area, so its cooperation was crucial. In 1937 it opened the preserve to hunting on a lottery basis; some hunters took advantage of the primitive area's airstrips to gain access to its interior.[31]

Some fish and game officials proposed a simpler solution to the Selway's elk problem: more roads to bring in more hunters. In 1940 L. F. "Duff" Jefferson, supervisor of the Clearwater National Forest (and Frank Jefferson's brother), raised the possibility of drawing back the protected boundary as part of a new wilderness area to be classified under the recently adopted "U" regulations, which Bob Marshall had written and chief forester Silcox approved in 1939. Bitterroot National Forest supervisor G. M. Brandborg also requested a review, pointing out that the Magruder Road nearly bisected the primitive area and had orphaned several hundred thousand acres of otherwise wild land south of the road.[32] From Missoula, Meyer Wolff counseled a wait-and-see attitude toward the Selway, fearing that any move to shrink the protected area (even under the more restrictive U-1 regulation) would engender much controversy. Major Kelley advised chief Silcox that the Selway possessed little more than a "monotony of color, character of topography, burned-over land, hot canyons, poor soil and lack of grass and lakes."[33] Most Forest Service staffers seemed to see little of interest in the area beyond its large acreage of unused (and probably unusable) country. The reclassification effort was dropped for the time being, and no attempt was made to reclassify the region's other primitive areas for two decades.

The U regulations were one of Bob Marshall's last gifts to the wilderness movement, coming only two months before his death in November 1939. They rescinded the L-20 regulation and with it some of the loopholes that permitted roads and other developments to be built in the primitive areas. Regulation U-1 permitted the secretary of agriculture to establish areas of more than one hundred thousand acres as wilderness areas, in which no roads, motorized transportation, commercial timber cutting, or major recreation developments such as summer homes or resorts would be allowed. Regulation U-2 provided for "wild areas" of between five thousand and one hundred thousand acres, which were to be managed in the same way as their larger sisters. Regulation U-3 established a category for recreation areas in which more developed facilities would be allowed.[34] Each primitive area would eventually be reviewed and its boundaries adjusted as needed before being reclassified as a wilderness or wild area, but there was no timetable in which to accomplish this. Meanwhile they would be administered under the stricter U regulations, which may have prompted supervisors Jefferson and Brandborg to call for a boundary review in the Selway-Bitterroot.

What the U regulations did not include was a clear statement of goals for the new system of wilderness areas. Were they to be the leftovers or "worthless lands" that contained little usable timber?[35] Or would the agency take positive steps to identify candidate areas for preservation and show the public the benefits of its program, ranging from primitive recreation to watershed and wildlife needs? Unless forest supervisors and regional office staff identified and protected suitable areas before they were committed to other uses, little might come of Marshall and Silcox's visionary initiative.

Meyer Wolff and Evan Kelley could reasonably claim that in designating the Northern Region's seven primitive areas and the Bob Marshall Wilderness, their agency had taken a major step toward integrating wildland values into its multiple-use program. In reclassifying the Selway-Bitterroot under U-1, the Forest Service again had the opportunity to display great vision in upholding a magnificent wilderness resource, but here, too, it would waver between the conflicting aims of land preservation, administrative convenience, and potential resource production. During the 1940s and early 1950s agency leaders remained uncertain of the role that wilderness areas could play in their overall program of national forest management, and they lacked a coherent process for dealing with the conflicts that kept coming up when their development plans ran afoul of some sporting or preservationist group that wanted the area left alone.

For that matter, public advocacy groups such as the Wilderness Society also operated without a well-defined program for preserving areas of wilderness. Outside of Bob Marshall, no officer of the Wilderness Society or the Sierra Club had taken a strong interest in the Selway-Bitterroot or the other primitive areas in the Northern Region, and with Marshall gone they lacked anyone with a comprehensive, on-the-ground understanding of the diverse wildland areas on the western national forests. No longer could they call on an agency insider such as Marshall, Elers Koch, or Meyer Wolff to cajole reluctant bureaucrats into action. The preservation movement needed to set forth its goals, determine what values and resources were found in such areas, and, equally important, devise a working definition of what constituted a wilderness. Only then could its leaders determine how much wilderness was left in the nation and how to go about protecting it.

3

The "Bob" Besieged
The Sun River, 1947–1953

By labeling the Glacier View Dam as a precedent-setting threat to the integrity of the national park system, preservation groups drew on Americans' strong interest in maintaining these natural treasures. Scenic park lands were not to be trifled with, even for the hallowed purposes of flood control and hydropower generation. Montana's wildlife advocates faced a far harder task in calling attention to the habitat needs of elk, moose, mountain goats, and grizzly bears on national forest lands south of Glacier. Most Americans knew little about the huge wilderness expanse named for Bob Marshall in 1940, and even less of the undesignated wildlands that surrounded this area. The threats to this greater ecosystem led wildlife advocates to call for extending the wilderness umbrella over the entire area, in direct conflict with the Forest Service's timbering plans. At first, though, preservationists found useful allies within the agency in opposing the impoundment of the Sun River at the eastern edge of America's largest wilderness area. Even more than at Glacier View, this conservation emergency would galvanize Montana's outfitters and wildlife enthusiasts, with important ramifications for efforts to protect this biologically important region.

The "Bob," as it was known in Montana, anchored the Forest Service's system of protected reserves and helped establish the agency's reputation as a guardian of inspiring mountain scenery. Meyer Wolff, chief of the Northern Region's recreation and lands division, described it as a "vast wild region" in which "the smoke of a thousand camp fires might never merge." Writing in the Wilderness Society's journal in 1941, one year after the area was established, he noted that the area was "not just a wilderness left over after progressive encroachment of unrestricted development had ceased."[1] But the "Bob" was exactly that, if you considered the work that several generations of trappers, homesteaders, loggers, and railroad builders had carried out around the margins of the area before the Forest Service took control. Even the remote Danaher Valley, a favorite destination for horse packers, displayed the remains of settled homesteads. Nor were the nation's resource developers quite done with this wilderness, as conservationists like Wolff soon learned. The Army Corps of Engineers' rival in casting concrete—the Interior Department's Bureau of Reclamation—had its eyes on the east side of the mountains where the Sun River emerged from the wilderness.

In 1929 the bureau completed Gibson Dam on the main stem of the Sun River, six miles below the confluence of the river's North and South Forks. Its reservoir supplied irrigation water to wheat farms in the prairies east of the mountains, but the bureau wanted to augment this storage by building a second dam upstream from Gibson Reservoir. Two sites were investigated: Upper Sun Butte would be situated on the North Fork of the Sun River a mile above its confluence with the South Fork, while the Wilson Dam, later known as Lower Sun Butte, would be situated directly at the confluence and would extend its reservoir up both forks, reaching up to eleven miles back into the Bob Marshall Wilderness. This would necessitate the removal of up to fifty-five thousand acres from the wilderness, according to the Forest Service. Bob Cooney of the Montana Fish and Game Department tipped off the Wilderness Society's Howard Zahniser to the proposal in February 1947. The reservoir, he wrote, "would not only flood some of the finest and most critical winter elk range on the Sun River drainage, but would be almost completely included within the Bob Marshall Wilderness Area. I may be an alarmist in this matter, but certainly think that we should get busy in stirring up the proper sentiment for blocking plans for this reservoir development now when they are in their infancy."[2]

Zahniser made inquiries with the U.S. Fish and Wildlife Service and discovered that the project was already authorized under the Flood Control Act of 1944. Olaus Murie, who had met Bob Cooney while studying elk herds in the Bob Marshall Wilderness during the 1930s, learned that the Forest Service had made specific allowance for the project when it set up the Sun River Primitive Area in 1934. Despite this, Murie assured Cooney that the question was "far from hopeless." He noted that Zahniser had recently succeeded in obtaining a public hearing on a proposed Bureau of Reclamation dam on Lake Solitude in

Wyoming's Cloud Peak Primitive Area. All three men understood, though, that a lengthy struggle lay ahead over these and other reclamation projects. Even the federal Office of Indian Affairs was getting into the act, Cooney learned, by proposing to divert irrigation water from the Mission Mountains Primitive Area to the west side of the range via tunnels leading from Gray Wolf, High Park, Turquoise, and Glacier Lakes.[3]

Kenneth Reid, the executive director of the Izaak Walton League of America, shared Zahniser's opinion of dams and reservoirs on free-flowing rivers, telling him that such projects were "particularly poisonous and obnoxious. They ignore all natural values on fine clear streams and ignore entirely the fact that the area has been officially set aside as a wilderness area."[4] He believed that if Reclamation would back off on just 20 percent of its projects, the bureau could avoid most of the public's objections. Zahniser, meanwhile, asked Clarence Cottam, the acting director of the Fish and Wildlife Service, whether his agency would issue an adverse opinion on the Wilson project, but he demurred. The Bureau of Reclamation had considerable clout in Congress and Zahniser, like Reid, was left to look for some means of compromise—perhaps by locating the dam farther downstream. He suggested to Joe White, an outfitter who worked out of Choteau, a small town on the plains east of the Bob Marshall, that "with proper concern for wilderness values on the part of reclamation officials the irrigation needs can be satisfactorily met without jeopardizing wilderness preservation."[5]

Many Montanans who lived along the Sun River feared its flood potential, however, and voiced their support for the Wilson Dam at a Corps of Engineers hearing held in Great Falls in June 1948. (While the dam was a Reclamation project, evaluating flood risks and control projects fell to the Army Engineers.) Meyer Wolff presented a statement signed by regional forester P. D. "Pete" Hanson claiming that the dam "would cause grave sacrifices and losses of other national forest resources and values. It would invade a designated wilderness area, one of the scarce remaining tracts of this character in the United States, which are of great future social value to the people of the Nation."[6]

During the late 1940s the leaders of the national conservation organizations counted the Forest Service as an ally on many fronts, ranging from dams in wilderness areas to their running battle with stockmen's groups that were agitating for preferential treatment in their grazing permits. The writer Bernard DeVoto brought both issues to national attention with his articles in *Harper's Magazine*,[7] but Murie, Zahniser, and Cooney still needed local citizens who were willing to speak out against the prevailing reclamation mindset. In 1947 and 1948—a time when federal dam-building agencies still enjoyed almost unlimited power in

Washington and in the Northern Rockies—such citizens were hard to find, and they were often afraid to risk their jobs in a political climate that looked upon challenges to authority as potentially subversive.

Anticipating a tough struggle against these multifarious incursions into wild habitats, Bob Cooney told Olaus Murie in 1947 that "we need an organization here on the ground that would be definitely responsible for looking after the local threats to the Wilderness Areas. I have in mind the possibility of developing a Montana Wilderness Society as a unit of the National Society if possible." Murie brushed aside the suggestion, advising Cooney that the society's role was to "organize the idealism and worthy impulses" of local conservationists and "channel them into a force that can be effective in the conservation of wilderness values. We will get nowhere if each state or region, or local community, began building up its own local rules in such a matter."[8] The society's leaders preferred to work with small ad hoc groups in each state instead of dealing with a statewide organization that would mimic its own role. Murie suggested that Cooney form such a group to fight the Wilson Dam. Cooney's idea of an umbrella organization would lie fallow until 1958, when wildlife activist Ken Baldwin gathered various wilderness supporters to form the Montana Wilderness Association.

It was not just the prospect of flooding the Bob Marshall that pained Cooney; his department had been working for years to build up the Sun River elk herd, now one of the nation's largest at around three thousand animals. Each spring the herd left its windblown winter range in the foothills east of the Rockies and dispersed throughout the "Bob." Elk were more than an amenity in Montana; along with the grizzly bear they were a powerful symbol of the state's forests, mountains, and open spaces. Elk put meat on the table for many Montanans, attracted well-heeled easterners who hired guides at good wages, and presented a thrilling sight when silhouetted on a ridge or massed in a mountain meadow. Having them close at hand reminded rural residents of why they chose to put up with the state's harsh winters and omnipresent poverty.

In 1913 the Montana state legislature, responding to sportsmen's concerns about livestock competing with elk for forage in the upper Sun River drainage, decreed a game preserve in nearly two hundred thousand acres of the Lewis and Clark National Forest east of the Continental Divide. Livestock grazing and hunting were prohibited, creating a kind of "mini-Yellowstone" (as one writer described it) for elk and Rocky Mountain bighorn sheep. As in the national park, the preserve provided mostly summer range and spring calving grounds. Winter range—the crucial element in elk and bighorn survival—lay outside the preserve on privately owned ranch lands downstream along the Sun. As the burgeoning elk herd depleted forage and spilled out of the preserve, ranchers complained about hundreds of animals living off their haystacks. Ugly episodes of starvation and disease followed. The Fish and Game Department was anxious to maintain the herds at an optimum size, and in 1947 it got a break when two ranchers put up $10,000 to option some prime land for what would become the Sun River Game Range, a state-managed winter range in which regulated hunting was allowed.[9]

The Sun River elk herd moved up in the spring from its winter range to calve in extensive meadows at Pretty Prairie and North Fork Flats, both of which lay within the proposed Wilson Reservoir. As the high country opened up, the elk migrated farther into the Bob Marshall, many continuing over the Continental Divide into the drainage of the Middle Fork of the Flathead River. About 275 bighorn sheep also used this range—a substantial portion of the 1,200 believed to live in Montana.[10] The proposed reservoir would pinch off these ancestral travel corridors, according to the federal Fish and Wildlife Service, leading migrating elk into "firing lines" at the edges of the preserve. The result could be a gruesome slaughter like the one that took place at the northern edge of Yellowstone in the 1920s.[11] Adding to concerns over big game, a dam at either the upper or lower Sun Butte site would interrupt fish spawning migrations out of Gibson Reservoir.

To wildlife interests, the Wilson–Sun Butte project looked like a sure loser. Bob Cooney took Murie's advice and helped local ranchers and sportsmen set up the Sun River Game Conservation Committee to combat the Reclamation juggernaut. The group sponsored a series of springtime trail rides through the reservoir site to publicize the issue and educate government officials. A 1951 ride involving officials from the Montana Fish and Game Department, U.S. Fish and Wildlife Service, Forest Service, and Bureau of Reclamation turned into a kind of referendum on the project. Lou Siniff, the group's secretary, noted that "along the trip many head of elk were seen on the flats and along the slopes. As it was calving time, the party rode to within a few feet of four calves trying to conceal themselves in the grass. On the return trip the reclamation department officials pointed out the approximate flood mark of the proposed dam across the North Fork of Sun River at Sheep Reef. Sheep Reef is located slightly more than a mile above Allan Ranch and is appropriately named, as mountain sheep were sighted on both the inbound and outbound trips of the party."[12]

At a meeting held that evening, Harold Aldrich, director of the bureau's Upper Missouri Division, defended the dam as a multipurpose project that would provide needed power, flood control, and irrigation. He said his engineers had spent considerable time searching for alternative sites, including the option of raising Gibson Dam, which he said would impound only another thirty to forty thousand acre-feet. Downstream flooding remained a disputed issue in the dam negotiations. Siniff noted afterward that on the day of their ride, the two branches of the Sun were at a normal level and had been so for a week, while the main stem was out of its banks lower down near Augusta. The flooding, he maintained, came from a much wider drainage area than the Bob Marshall Wilderness.

In the spring of 1952 regional forester P. D. Hanson reiterated his agency's opposition to the dam in a letter to Oscar Chapman, President Truman's secretary of the interior. Chapman agreed to intervene and ordered the Bureau of Reclamation to suspend its studies on the project.[13] Once again it was a temporary victory. That October an alarmed Bob Cooney informed Olaus Murie that a recent bureau report stated that dam studies would be continued at both the upper and lower Sun Butte sites. Joe Penfold, the Denver-based western field representative of the Izaak Walton League, made inquiries of Interior Department officials and was told that Chapman's order meant only that no on-the-ground investigations would be conducted within the Bob Marshall Wilderness. Outside the wilderness—that is, at the dam site itself and in the rest of the drainage basin—Reclamation's studies would continue. It was a self-serving interpretation, and Penfold told an outdoor columnist for the *Billings Gazette* that "while Chapman has not rescinded his order to Reclamation to keep the hell out of the Bob Marshall Wilderness Area, it would appear that Reclamation can go right ahead to complete its report and perhaps set in motion the procedures which result in obtaining authorization. I don't like it one little bit."[14] Both here and at Echo Park, conservationists were learning that government bureaus were not easily deterred from their intended goals.

Providing irrigation water was Reclamation's bread and butter, but flood control garnered even wider public support. Montana residents may have been on edge following the severe June floods of 1952 in the lower Missouri River basin, a result of heavy mountain snowpack augmented by late blizzards in the Dakotas. Then, in early June 1953, a series of rainstorms swept across the Rocky Mountain front and sent the Sun River over its banks, washing out bridges, flooding low-lying areas in Great Falls and nearby communities, and causing an estimated $5 million in damages, according to Bureau of Reclamation officials. Kenneth Vernon, the bureau's regional director in Billings, told reporters that a dam at Sun Butte would have prevented the disaster. "The question seems to be whether you are going to have flooding in Great Falls or flooding in the mountain valley area where there is no human habitat," he stated.[15] Bob Cooney bristled at this, telling Charles Callison of the National Wildlife Federation, who was also watching these projects, that Vernon "omitted mentioning that ten inches of rainfall was recorded in the Great Falls area during the flood period. Every small side drainage from the foot hills to the Missouri (over 50 miles) was running at flood stage." Cooney obtained runoff data from the U.S. Geological Survey and from Zane Smith, a cooperative Forest Service supervisor in Great Falls, which corroborated his analysis. A hydrologist for the Northern Region office prepared a report blaming poor land use practices within the entire drainage for exacerbating runoff and permitting debris to accumulate and wash downstream, where it damaged bridges and culverts.[16]

Cooney passed the information along to Howard Zahniser, who was in Montana that summer and had occasion to discuss the project with Douglas McKay, President Eisenhower's new secretary of the interior, at a dedication ceremony held at Glacier National Park (the park had acquired some state of Montana lands in the North Fork Flathead drainage as part of its attempt to stop the Glacier View project). After meeting with McKay, Zahniser returned to Moose, Wyoming, where he was staying as a guest of the Muries. There he followed up with a letter taking strong issue with what he termed the Bureau of Reclamation's "propaganda" favoring the Sun Butte Dam. Using the data Cooney supplied, he pointed out that on June 4, when the lower Sun had crested at 17,600 cubic feet per second (cfs), only 2,650 cfs were coming from the river's upper forks, as measured four days earlier at the edge of the Bob Marshall Wilderness. As Cooney mentioned, heavy rainfalls of seven to twelve inches had occurred below Gibson Dam and were the main cause of the flood. Zahniser termed "reprehensible" the bureau's efforts to "mislead the public" by blaming the floods on conditions in the river's headwaters.

During the 1950s the Bureau of Reclamation and Corps of Engineers epitomized what historian Dominick Cavallo called "the managerial values and techniques of large-scale planning," in which "unelected experts" formulated and executed public policy.[17] In the Echo Park battle, conservationists learned that they must challenge the bureau's and the corps' cost-benefit analyses, which depended on extensive and often opaque calculations. It would be many years before groups such as the Wilderness Society could afford to hire their own experts; for the time being they had to rely on informed local citizens such as Bob Cooney and sympathetic agency officials such as Zane Smith.[18]

By the end of 1953 the conservationist coalition and its friends in the government had raised serious questions about both the Sun Butte and Glacier View projects. That year Glacier National Park superintendent John Emmert took strategic action by upgrading an old, rough road that ran through the southwestern part of the park and constructing two new campgrounds at Logging and Quartz Lakes—all conveniently located within the flood basin of the proposed Glacier View reservoir, so as to lay claim to an underutilized part of the park.[19] However, both the Corps of Engineers and the Bureau of Reclamation had many other possible sites for new dams, as outlined in their extensive reports on the upper Columbia and Missouri River systems. Murie, Zahniser, Cooney, and their colleagues needed some way to permanently forestall such projects, which were taking up an inordinate amount of their time and organizational resources. If the federal dam builders could not be persuaded to give up their dreams, perhaps Congress could instruct them to do so. Howard Zahniser, in particular, hoped that the new federal wilderness law he was contemplating would permanently seal off headwaters streams from such encroachments.

This would prove to be a difficult and elusive goal. Elk, deer, moose, and mountain sheep had their devotees in the Northern Rockies, but even by the mid-1950s there were not enough concerned sportsmen and wildlife biologists to overcome the American public's (and Congress's) love affair with huge reclamation projects. For now they would have to hope that federal budget constraints and the vagaries of Washington politics would break in their favor, and that plans for projects such as Sun Butte would remain on drafting tables and in bureaucratic reports.

4

The Battle of Bunker Creek
The Timber Salvage Emergency, 1949–1955

Despite its losses from the fires of 1910, the Northern Region of the Forest Service still had charge of a vast timbershed in northern Idaho and northwestern Montana, forming the headwaters of the Flathead, Kootenai, Priest, and Clearwater Rivers. Never content to take a purely custodial posture toward its lands, the region's staff sold as much as 123 million board feet of timber annually during the boom years of the 1920s. The Great Depression sank this output to less than 40 million board feet, but wartime demand allowed sales to reach new heights, and by 1946 the region's forests were producing 313 million board feet, a new record.[1] Much of this timber went to midsize producers such as the J. Neils Lumber Company in Libby, Montana, and Plum Creek Lumber, a Minnesota firm that opened a mill in Columbia Falls in 1946. These firms dominated the timber market in northwestern Montana, while dozens of smaller sawmilling operations each processed a few million board feet per year.

Regional forester P. D. Hanson and his lieutenants regarded the timber industry not as a client they had to supply with sawlogs, but as an ally in accomplishing their overriding goal of placing all forestlands under active management. By employing silvicultural tools such as thinning and clear-cutting, they hoped to replace old, slow-growing, disease-laden stands of Douglas-fir, western larch, and Engelmann spruce with thrifty new plantations. What they did not expect, and had difficulty comprehending when it happened, was that an entirely different forest clientele would emerge that would strenuously object to their management plans. Focused entirely on the timber resource, the officers of the Northern Region were as startled as an elk on a mountain logging road when significant numbers of sportsmen began to question their doctrine of intensive timber management—and proposed instead that certain forestlands be placed permanently out of reach of the agency's timber staff. The controversy over a single large timber sale on the Flathead National Forest highlighted the issue of "de facto" wilderness and set the stage for a long-running battle over forestlands on all sides of Montana's Bob Marshall Wilderness.

The chief aim of silvicultural doctrine as applied by the Forest Service was to substitute regular, periodic timber harvests for the natural agents that normally regenerated forest stands. Fire, disease, insects, and wind had molded the forests of the Northern Rockies for millennia; the raging wildfires of 1910 appeared unusual only because humans now intended to permanently occupy these lands. And despite the foresters' best efforts, nature's agents were still active. In November 1949 a severe Pacific windstorm toppled valuable sawtimber throughout a wide area of western Montana and northern Idaho. Salvage operations began the following summer and continued into the early 1950s, but as Forest Service crews fanned out into the woods to map potential timber sales, they noticed that the fallen timber had attracted the interest of yet another natural agent of regeneration—the spruce bark beetle. This quarter-inch-long insect burrows under the bark of downed trees, where it typically maintains its population at endemic, or resident, levels. With so much spruce lying on the ground after the '49 storm, beetle populations exploded and quickly spread into the surrounding live timber. The Northern Region countered with an emergency salvage program, offering timber sales at prices as low as a dollar per thousand board feet in order to attract qualified bidders. The first sales came in the North Fork of the Flathead River, where Plum Creek and other firms harvested nearly fifty million board feet of spruce and other, more desirable species that were offered as part of the package.[2]

Improved logging, skidding, and transportation methods, including specialized saws developed at the Forest Products Laboratory in Madison, Wisconsin, came into play as Hanson's crews raced to clean up the literal windfall. Hundreds of miles of timber haul roads, paid for with emergency appropriations from Congress, were punched into previously inaccessible backcountry stands. By 1955 timber harvests on the Flathead National Forest alone spiked to more than fifty million board feet.[3] By the end of 1956 Montana and Idaho firms had trucked out two billion board feet of spruce from the Flathead and nearby forests. Soon the light-colored wood was paneling dens and decking roofs in homes throughout America. Hanson praised the beetle control program as "one of the biggest jobs this region has ever tackled. The reputation of the Forest Service as an outfit that gets things done is directly at stake." The control effort took on the urgent language of a military campaign. This was, one agency memo stated, an "all-out battle . . . spread over a wide front . . . fast action is absolutely essential."[4]

The Forest Service requested $8.5 million in federal funds to build access roads in Idaho and Montana in what assistant chief Ed Cliff called "desperation measures to forestall the possibility of crippling timber losses." But the salvage sales did not "cure the conditions which made these epidemics possible," he told a convention of logging contractors in 1953. Only comprehensive management of backcountry timber stands could accomplish that, which required roads into every major drainage outside the region's designated wilderness and primitive areas. It was poor business, Cliff said, for logging crews to harvest low-elevation timber close to major highways during the summer; the outfits needed to be working the back ends of drainages high up in mountains, where only a few hikers, horse riders, and forest rangers ventured.[5]

The spruce salvage program allowed Flathead National Forest supervisor F. J. Neitzling to increase timber harvests from nineteen million board feet in fiscal year 1951 to nearly thirty-nine million board feet in 1952, principally in the North Fork drainage, but in order to fulfill his allowable cut of forty million board feet (which did not include salvage sales) he would need to expand logging into new areas.[6] The wild forests of the South Fork of the Flathead River looked like an ideal candidate: for miles on either side of the river, beginning at the road's end at the Spotted Bear Ranger Station to the boundary of the Bob Marshall Wilderness, the mountains were cloaked with fir, larch, and spruce, some of the latter showing the telltale reddish-brown needles of bark beetle infestation. Sales of live trees would help meet the forest's allowable cut as well as curtail the beetles' spread. District ranger Charles Shaw believed he could put together a single timber sale of a hundred million board feet in this drainage, which would supply a large sawmill such as Plum Creek's at Columbia Falls with a major portion of its needs for a decade or longer. His dream, according to one associate, was to have the biggest sale in the region—one that would extend from "ridgetop to ridgetop from one end [of the drainage] to the other."[7]

"Fritz" Neitzling may have appreciated Shaw's enthusiasm, but a sale that large would shut out all but the largest bidders. Early in 1953 he announced an offering of thirty-one million board feet from the South Fork, still the largest timber sale in the forest's history. The purchaser would receive a credit to build eleven miles of main haul road and reconstruct nearly twenty miles of existing roads, as well as blade twenty-seven miles of spur roads to the logging units, most of which were to be clear-cut. Sales of this magnitude served several purposes: they reduced administrative costs and permitted the winning bidder to make long-term plans and acquire needed capital improvements such as new saws and processing equipment. Sportsmen in the Kalispell area, however, were aghast when they saw the maps of the planned road layout. Two main haul roads would branch out from the Spotted Bear Ranger Station in the South Fork drainage, one following the Spotted Bear River almost to its source before looping north into the drainage of the Middle Fork of the Flathead and joining U.S. Highway 2 near the Continental Divide. The other would head up the South Fork to the boundary of the Bob Marshall Wilderness, turn west along Bunker Creek, reach the crest of the Swan Divide near Thunderbolt Mountain, and continue down to the Swan River Valley. The result would be a continuous road link from the Swan through the Middle Fork to Highway 2, lopping off a quarter million acres of predominantly wild country that happened to be outside the wilderness boundary. It had the appearance of a strategic encirclement, and members of the Flathead Lake Wildlife Association, a local sportsmen's group, took it as such.

By one report, six hundred angry sportsmen crowded into a meeting room in early February 1954 to protest the invasion of a mountain stronghold they held sacrosanct. Supervisor Neitzling, invited to explain his agency's plans, was stunned at the response to a single timber sale. He reportedly broke into tears as he stood outside the door at the end of the meeting, saying "How could you boys do this to me?"[8] All along he had assumed that the Flathead's hunters and anglers would welcome the chance to drive up to the edge of the "Bob" in much less time than a horse would take. Following the meeting Forrest Rockwood, a Kalispell attorney who enjoyed camping and hunting excursions in the Bob Marshall, drew up a resolution on behalf of the association asking Secretary of Agriculture Ezra Taft Benson to expand the wilderness boundary to include the threatened lands. Representative Ory Armstrong of Kalispell shepherded the measure through the Montana state legislature, but Secretary Benson rejected it. Similar petitions went to supervisor Neitzling and regional forester Hanson. The wildlife association, which up until now had concerned itself mostly with hunting and fishing regulations, was directly challenging the plans of the major federal land management agency in western Montana.

Unlike the Corps of Engineers, which had little public presence in the Flathead Valley, the Forest Service was woven into the fabric of local society. Its personnel enjoyed the same outdoor activities, shopped at the same stores, and sent their children to the same schools as the wildlife association's members. Supervisor Neitzling's reaction to the sportsmen's protest suggests that his logging plans were not a devious attempt to foreclose expansion of the Bob Marshall Wilderness, but rather a natural extension of resource development into an area that was clearly available for such purposes. This was normal procedure in an agency that was used to determining the best management policy for the public's good. What had gone wrong? The answer was there to read in the wildlife group's petition. The Flathead sportsmen regarded the "Bob" as the centerpiece of a great wild region encompassing several million acres. "Pack train travel moves into this primitive area from all sides," the petitioners stated, "not only from the north, but over passes on the west, over passes from the Missoula territory on the south, and over passes from the Augusta territory on the east." Each of these approaches lay outside the wilderness and would be contested in turn over the next few decades.

Meyer Wolff's "smoke of a thousand campfires" was not far from the mark; hunting parties came from all over the United States to pursue elk, bighorn sheep, and grizzly bear in this inspiring remnant of the frontier. Whereas the Forest Service estimated that 1,500 visitors made use of the "Bob" in 1947, trail traffic was rising rapidly and by 1959 was estimated at 5,000 visitors. Virtually all of this was from horse parties, half of which visited during hunting season.[9] Such use represented a significant economic asset and "far exceed[ed] the economic value (quoted as $5,600,000) to be realized from the timber within the area," according to the wildlife association. The value of fishing alone in the Flathead River's headwaters ran as high as $600,000 per year, the group stated, based on estimates of a trout stream's recreational value at $20,000 per mile per annum.[10]

This analysis appears to be the work of Clifton Merritt, who served as secretary of the Flathead Lake Wildlife Association. Clif (he insisted on the single *f*) grew up on a ranch in the Prickly Pear Valley north of Helena, where he enjoyed making horse packing trips into the east side of what would later become the Bob Marshall Wilderness. Merritt worked for the state of Montana's employment services division in Kalispell, from which he explored the Flathead side of the mountains. Merritt, whose soft voice and formal demeanor belied a bulldog tenacity when it came to public lands issues, soon drew in his fishing buddy Dallas Eklund, who was president of the Flathead Lake Wildlife Association. The group engaged the Forest Service in what became known as the "Battle of Bunker Creek," a conservationist campaign that would last more than two decades and would spread to involve every acre of wildland surrounding the Bob Marshall.

Resolutions of support for the Flathead sportsmen's petition came from the Western Montana Conservation Association and the Whitefish Rod and Gun Club. In a news story that appeared in the *Washington Post,* a dude rancher from Ronan, Montana, named Herb Toelke opposed the Bunker Creek sale. "'There's always been bugs in trees up here,'" he said. "'There's been bugs for thousands of years there, and nature takes care of it. . . . Shucks, let that country alone.'" [11] An outfitter from Ovando named Tom Edwards displayed similar sentiments in a cartoon he drew to alert his clients to the issue. It depicted the "US Forestry Department" at the controls of a bulldozer that was about to wipe out Bunker Creek and nearby pristine lands, all for the benefit of "Big Biz," which was funneling money to the agency. Edwards, who was known as "Hobnail Tom" to his clients, operated mostly in the southern part of the Bob Marshall and a little-known fringe area called the Lincoln Back Country. Edwards would have a great deal more to say (and draw) as the agency's development plans reached that area as well.

In May 1954 Merritt and Eklund approached Bob Cooney about getting the Montana Fish and Game Commission to pass a resolution opposing the logging plan. Cooney shared their concerns and drew up a resolution that the commission approved that month. It cited the importance of Bunker Creek and the Middle Fork of the Flathead as undisturbed grizzly bear range, linking the protected reserves of Glacier National Park and the Bob Marshall Wilderness. Logging on the west side of the Continental Divide would also impinge on the summer range of the beleaguered Sun River elk herd, adding to the possibility of an "undesirable firing-line type of hunting in the back country." Opening these drainages to road access would also increase pressure on the Montana black-spotted cutthroat trout, the department stated. [12] This was a new kind of critique, which extended the recreational arguments wilderness proponents historically used against backcountry roads. Such roads not only compromised the essential nature of a wilderness pack trip, as Aldo Leopold had argued in the 1920s, they also harmed its wildlife, and with it one of the backcountry's chief pleasures. For the Flathead sportsmen, the joy of horse travel was wrapped up in solitude, superb hunting and fishing, and the promise of limitless horizons. This was an argument about not only recreational preferences but the qualities of the land itself, and wilderness proponents such as Tom Edwards spent much effort attempting to define this elusive quality of unroaded landscapes.

The unprecedented opposition to a seemingly routine logging proposal clearly discomfited Forest Service officers in Kalispell and Missoula. Fritz Neitzling tried to lay out his reasoning in a letter to Howard Zahniser, who had become interested in the Montana controversy. The agency's entomologists had found spruce bark beetles in 10 percent of the trees in the Bunker Creek drainage, and logging the affected stands offered the best hope of control. If the beetle infestation were to spread, the dead trees would leave the entire drainage subject to wildfires that could threaten nearby Glacier National Park. There were close to one hundred million board feet of merchantable timber in the country above Spotted Bear, of which forty million consisted of at-risk Engelmann spruce. Neitzling scaled back the initial sale offering to twenty-three million board feet, which would still require thirty miles of new road. He told Zahniser that it might be possible to establish a separate wild area somewhere in the Middle Fork drainage under the 1939 U-2 regulation, which would allow the timber sale and proposed roads to proceed.[13]

The Flathead sportsmen, however, were unwilling to defer to the Forest Service's presumed expertise in the matter. In a letter to Olaus Murie, Clif Merritt pointed out the poor quality of timber in the upper reaches of the Flathead, where it "takes a sapling of the commercial species upwards of 150 years to become what might be called a sawlog."[14] The river's South and Middle Forks offered the last natural spawning habitat for the native black-spotted cutthroat trout in the entire Flathead River drainage, whereas the heavily logged North Fork had "declined almost to the point of being written off," Merritt said. Being "cold and comparatively infertile," the river's South and Middle Forks would not stand the fishing pressure that the network of access roads would bring.

Neither Zahniser nor Murie made any move to involve the Wilderness Society in the Bunker Creek battle. That summer Merritt and Dallas Eklund drove down to Missoula to join a dinner meeting between Zahniser and Northern Region officials, but the Wilderness Society leader was focusing on the impending Forest Service review of the Selway-Bitterroot Primitive Area and could offer the Kalispell men no immediate help. The wildlands of Bunker Creek and the Middle Fork did not enjoy even the limited protection of a primitive area, nor would they under Zahniser's contemplated wilderness law. Disappointed, Merritt and Eklund resolved to stop the Bunker Creek sale on their own.[15] To Merritt, the experience underscored the importance of grassroots action.

Fortunately for them, certain officials in the regional office in Missoula were having their own doubts about the Bunker Creek sale. The infestation in that drainage was one of the lesser in the region, and the project was near the bottom of their list of how to spend federal road construction dollars. Even some timber industry workers were not especially eager to see the sale go ahead, given the impact it would have on country they enjoyed using. In October 1954 Robert

Weller, the secretary of Montana's Lumber and Sawmill Workers Union, wrote to Senator James Murray in opposition to the sale, which he called "a dangerous encroachment upon the Bob Marshall wilderness area."[16] John Castles, a top operations planner who normally favored logging, acknowledged that the drainage was too distant from sawmills to make a good logging "chance" and that the sale should be canceled unless markets improved.

In January 1955 P. D. Hanson informed Howard Zahniser that although the latest field surveys disclosed a heavier insect infestation in Bunker Creek than before, he had decided to pull the sale because of lower-than-expected timber volumes and high road costs. He would instead use federal dollars to gain access to stands in other, less controversial, drainages. The spruce in Bunker Creek appeared to be "decidedly submarginal"—for now at least. Logging would continue apace in other parts of the Flathead National Forest, where 72 million board feet were harvested in fiscal year 1954 and 102 million in fiscal 1955 (with salvage sales making up the overrun above the forest's allowable cut of 40 million board feet).[17] The resistance of the Flathead sportsmen undoubtedly influenced Hanson's decision. The agency was entering a new era of resource management in which it would have to carefully weigh local and national sentiments for a wide range of forest benefits, not just the traditional (and easily quantified) measures of timber and forage.

Perhaps sensitized by the Bunker Creek debacle, Northern Region officials managed to avert another protracted controversy after Clif Merritt and a local outfitter named Bill Frederick raised protests over plans to construct a road and harvest timber in the Graves Creek drainage, part of the Swan Range east of Kalispell. In the summer of 1956 the two men learned that a new road had been flagged along the creek up to a cluster of attractive lakes below the crest of the range. Merritt named the area Jewel Basin and publicized it in an outdoors column he wrote for the Kalispell *Daily Inter Lake*. Tours with Forest Service officials followed, leading Fritz Neitzling to modify the sale and retain the area as a nonmotorized recreation destination. Merritt relished the victory, which led in 1970 to the designation of the Jewel Basin Hiking Area under the Forest Service's U-3 and U-6 regulations. It affected only fifteen thousand acres of the vast roadless lands adjoining the "Bob," most of which remained at risk from the Forest Service's timber program.[18]

Clif Merritt and his friends had won their battle for Bunker Creek, but time would show whether it would stay won, or whether more permanent means were needed to set forested lands off limits to logging. Shortly after Pete Hanson announced he was canceling the sale, Merritt told *Sports Afield* columnist Mike

Hudoba that "the biggest battle is still ahead. That is of course to get the primitive area on the north boundary included in the Bob Marshall Wilderness."[19] The Flathead Lake Wildlife Association's proposal remained in abeyance until Zahniser's new wilderness bill was enacted. This law would permit citizens to work directly with Congress instead of the development-oriented Department of Agriculture. Meanwhile Merritt and his friends would be forced to engage in a lengthy holding action until the umbrella of wilderness designation could be brought over threatened lands such as Bunker Creek.

5

Idaho's Lifeblood
The Clearwater River, 1948–1955

For thousands of winters Pacific air masses streamed over the grasslands of the lower Columbia River basin, feeding moisture to the Bitterroot Mountains of northern Idaho. Douglas-fir and true fir, Engelmann spruce, white pine, cedar, hemlock, and larch grew tall and thick boled on the steep slopes, mosses gathering about them in conditions resembling those in the rain forests of the Pacific Northwest. Hundreds of tributary streams crashed down from metamorphic crags to settle into the pools and riffles of the Clearwater and St. Joe Rivers, creating ideal habitat for cutthroat and bull trout. Elk and moose browsed in openings created by avalanches and fires, while black and grizzly bears foraged among the fog-shrouded slopes. These rivers and their surrounding forests would become a conservation battleground during the mid-twentieth century, pitting a handful of Idaho sportsmen against the Corps of Engineers, the timber industry, and the Forest Service. As in Montana's Flathead and Sun River basins, a dispute over dams would set the stage for a broader contest over the management of a river's headwaters. Here, too, conservationists initially found an ally in the Forest Service, only to break with the agency when it announced its own expansionist goals for the upper Clearwater.

As one of the Snake River's main tributaries, the Clearwater River played a major role in northern Idaho commerce. The river supported annual spring log drives beginning in 1928, one year after the Clearwater Timber Company, a Weyerhaeuser operation, opened a sawmill in Lewiston. Merged with two other Weyerhaeuser firms in 1931 to form Potlatch Forests, the company continued to hold log drives on the North Fork of the Clearwater for more than four decades—operations that required hand-selected crews of exceptionally skilled men.[1] Lewiston prospered during the timber boom following World War II, while upriver communities such as Orofino placed their hopes in the completion of the Lewis-Clark Highway, a water-level route connecting Lewiston with Missoula, Montana. Intended to replace the tortuous, ridge-hopping Lolo Trail roadway, it took until 1962 to engineer a passage through the cliffs along the Lochsa River. This brawling mountain stream emerged from the largely undeveloped headwaters at the crest of the Bitterroots, joining the Selway River at the village of Lowell to form the main Clearwater. Here the river settled into a long, delightful forested stretch in which deep pools invited anglers and picnickers to spend a summer afternoon.

The river could assemble its forces in fearsome and destructive ways, as Clearwater Basin residents learned in the late spring of 1948. The same warm rains that melted snowpacks in the Flathead River drainage also produced severe flooding along the Clearwater lowlands from Orofino to Lewiston. The disaster prompted the Army Corps of Engineers to advance its existing proposal to build two flood-control and hydropower dams on the river. The Penny Cliffs Dam was to be a rock-fill structure nearly six hundred feet high on the Middle Fork of the Clearwater, four miles above the town of Kooskia. Its reservoir would extend past the confluence of the Selway and Lochsa and at high pool would reach six miles into the Selway-Bitterroot Primitive Area. The Bruces Eddy Dam would extend across the North Fork of the Clearwater two miles above its confluence with the Middle Fork. Both were of interest to the Northwest Power Company of Spokane, which filed hydropower applications with the Federal Power Commission.[2] Potlatch also was interested in the Bruces Eddy project as a means of more easily rafting logs out of the North Fork basin.

Most residents living along the river welcomed the dams and the prospect of construction jobs and economic growth. Orofino mayor A. B. Curtis led the citizen campaign for both projects and lined up support from Idaho's congressional delegation, including Senator Henry Dworshak. Boosters saw the dams as a politically feasible alternative to the controversial High Mountain Sheep Dam on the Snake River, which was mired in a debate between private power interests and advocates for federally funded reclamation projects.[3]

Some Idaho sportsmen feared the dams would spell the end of the Clearwater's flashing runs of salmon and steelhead, which had already been severely compromised when Potlatch and Washington Water Power Company constructed a low, run-of-river dam at Lewiston in 1927. Originally serving as a millpond, with power generation facilities added later, the dam blocked virtually all of the migrating chinook salmon and steelhead (a sea-run rainbow trout) from reaching the upper Clearwater, despite the inclusion of a fish passageway. After the power company added two more fishways in 1939, the Idaho Fish and Game Department conducted experimental plantings from the Salmon River that allowed steelhead to increase to more than ten thousand by 1953.[4] Still, with many more dams planned for the lower Snake and Columbia, the future of these anadromous fish was highly problematic.

Much of the bottomland along the upper Clearwater, Lochsa, and Selway Rivers provided winter range for immense numbers of elk. Their populations exploded following the Bald Mountain and Pete King fires of 1929 and 1934 as browse species grew back in burned areas. Game managers struggled to prevent die-offs as the herds outgrew the available winter range on south-facing hillsides and along stream corridors. The Penny Cliffs and Bruces Eddy Dams together would inundate more than a hundred miles of these streams, removing tens of thousands of acres of winter range for elk and white-tailed deer. Both impoundments would pose major barriers to fish migration and would be too tall for fish ladders.

Colonel F. S. Tandy presented the Corps of Engineers' proposals to a crowd of four hundred Idahoans in Orofino's Veterans of Foreign Wars hall on November 20, 1953. Tandy said the benefit-to-cost ratios for the two Clearwater dams were among the best of any in the Columbia Basin. Twenty-seven representatives of civic and governmental organizations as far away as Spokane lined up in favor of the dams, with only five speaking in opposition. These included a representative of the Nez Perce Tribe and a member of Oregon's fish and game commission, who spoke of the deleterious effect of the lower Columbia River dams on salmon spawning runs.[5] Ross Leonard, the newly appointed director of the Idaho Fish and Game Department, testified that the dams "probably will annihilate the runs of salmon and steelhead from the Clearwater drainage suitable for spawning purposes." Despite this, he promised that his department would not oppose the project.[6]

There was also the matter of flooding an increasingly popular stretch of the Selway River within its primitive area. At the Orofino hearing, Frank Cullen of the Idaho Wildlife Federation stated unequivocally that the Penny Cliffs Dam would spell "goodbye to our primitive area for good." Frank Evans, an outfitter from Coeur d'Alene, Idaho, spoke against the dams on behalf of the Wilderness

Society, complaining afterward that "the only thing the opponents were not subjected to was physical torture." The Corps of Engineers had much experience in presenting the benefits of water projects and was disinclined to report objectively on their drawbacks, an approach Evans characterized as "trickery in every sense of the word."[7]

Stewart Brandborg, the son of Bitterroot forest supervisor G. M. Brandborg, took a strong interest in the Clearwater dams as part of his work with the Idaho Fish and Game Department. He met Ross Leonard at an Orofino hotel before the hearing and found his boss "as nervous as he could be, obviously because here was this juggernaut of support from all the commercial interests and the political conservatism of Idaho behind it," he recalled. Joining them was Les Pengelly, a wildlife biologist who was studying mule deer in the Coeur d'Alene area. Neither could speak publicly against the dams, so they pinned their hopes on Leonard, who before his appointment had represented the Wildlife Society, a major professional organization. "We wanted him to make a bold and strong statement against these proposals," Brandborg recalled, and while his testimony in Orofino was not a "bell ringer, it was a start."[8]

Regional forester P. D. Hanson also expressed concern for the Clearwater's steelhead in a letter to outdoor writer Jack O'Connor of Lewiston early in 1954. The Penny Cliffs Dam, he wrote, would "block much of the migration to and natural reproduction of steelhead trout in the Clearwater River. . . . Artificial propagation would be extremely costly and probably not feasible as a replacement function." It would also wipe out the winter range of an estimated 5,800 elk and 1,600 deer. "We believe that the lands which would be inundated in the Lochsa and Selway River drainages have far greater future capacities for game range and game production through habitat management than they do at the present time," Hanson wrote. At the same time, though, he cautioned conservationists that more than sixty miles of the Clearwater and Selway Rivers had been withdrawn for power purposes before the primitive area was established. "There may be some question concerning the Forest Service's ability to object to the construction of the Penny Cliffs Dam," Hanson informed the Wilderness Society's Howard Zahniser.[9]

Hanson's statement masked considerable dissension within the agency about the effect of the dam on the Selway-Bitterroot Primitive Area. Assistant regional forester Robert Harmon advised chief forester Richard McArdle early in 1954 that the Penny Cliffs project would contribute more to the local economy than would be lost in wildlife values, and that the primitive area boundary could

simply be redrawn to exclude the reservoir. Since Harmon was in charge of recreation issues for the region, his views carried some weight. John Sieker, who
was Bob Marshall's successor as recreation division chief in Washington, also
advised Hanson not to make an issue of the inundation of the primitive area.[10]

The most outspoken opponent of the Clearwater dams was a Potlatch sawmill employee and third-generation Idahoan named Morton R. Brigham. A
senior engineer at the company's Lewiston mill, he was responsible for its complex log-handling machinery. Summer weekends generally found him test-
ing the pools of the Clearwater with his fly rod or exploring the high basins of
the upper North Fork and the Selway. After attending the Orofino hearing (and
feeling rebuffed by what he took as the Corps of Engineers' indifference to
wildlife values), he resolved to stir up as much opposition as he could among
Idaho's sporting organizations. "There is utterly no reason for the Clearwater
dams except to pacify the Army Engineers' love of authority and special interests interested in handling logs," Brigham told Olaus Murie the following spring.
He had just attended a follow-up meeting in Lewiston of what would today be
called the stakeholders in the project, which included the Washington Water
Power Company. Colonel Tandy, according to Brigham, "came right out and
stated that the Selway wilderness was worthless except for a few rich people, and
that elk and deer hunting will get no consideration in his plans." Perhaps the colonel's actual words were not that harsh, but in appearing to dismiss the concerns
of Idaho's sportsmen, he gained Brigham's strenuous and lasting opposition.[11]

Brigham pointed out that the Penny Cliffs Dam would inundate a hundred
miles of highway, six bridges, and seventy-eight family homes; flood a vast amount
of arable land; and eliminate the historic Fenn and Selway Falls Ranger Stations.
At Bruces Eddy, expensive log-handling facilities would be needed to permit use
of the reservoir for log rafts, which would benefit a single company—the one he
worked for. Speaking against the interests of his employer seemed not to concern him, but later that year, after warning him not to continue organizing opposition to the dams, Potlatch fired him. Brigham made ends meet for a few years
by cutting firewood but soon reestablished himself as a consultant to sawmill
firms around the country. The independent income allowed him to continue his
outspoken advocacy for maintaining the wild Clearwater and its tributaries. He
rounded up resolutions of support from sportsmen's groups, including his own
Lewis-Clark Wildlife Club and the statewide Idaho Wildlife Federation, which
voted to oppose the two dams at its January 1954 convention.

In February 1954 Stewart Brandborg, who had recently been hired by the
National Wildlife Federation as an assistant to its director, Charles Callison,

testified along with Olaus Murie at a hearing in Washington, D.C., before the Board of Engineers for Rivers and Harbors, an internal Corps of Engineers review panel that passed judgment on its pending projects. Brandborg pointed out that northern Idaho contributed 10 percent of the nation's annual elk harvest and that losses of winter range could jeopardize this important economic asset. The dams would cause the "destruction of the major sport and commercial fishery resources of the Clearwater River," while fluctuations of two hundred feet or more in the reservoirs' pools would severely limit their usefulness for fishing and other recreation. But the conservationists' testimony had little effect. Following the hearing A. B. Curtis met with Corps of Engineers officials in Washington, who assured him that they had "been up against such tactics for a long time" and that the best thing would be to "let them run themselves dry and have their talk."[12] Federal dams were typically packaged into basin-wide authorizing legislation, which ensured support from the northwestern states' congressional delegations and their various chambers of commerce.

The Penny Cliffs project appeared the more problematic of the two dams, since it would require extensive rerouting of the projected highway along the Lochsa River. With the Forest Service objecting to the inundation of the Selway-Bitterroot Primitive Area and considerable private land at stake, the Corps of Engineers shifted its main thrust to Bruces Eddy, which would flood a relatively undeveloped tributary of the main Clearwater. Some dam proponents characterized the opposition as shortsighted and selfish, unwilling to place the greater good ahead of narrow recreational interests. John Corlett, the political writer for Boise's *Idaho Daily Statesman*, editorialized that "the several industries have a greater stake in Idaho than the sportsmen. Were it not for industry, including agriculture, there would be no sportsmen."[13] Jack O'Connor, who wrote for the national sporting magazine *Outdoor Life*, replied that the dams represented "a very grave threat to those of us who live in this area, who love the purple spruce-clad hills, the sparkling trout streams, the sleek whitetail and the handsome elk." Both dams would be deadly to migrating trout, O'Connor maintained. "Spawning fish can be got up over the dams by one means or another, but by no means known to man can the fingerlings returning to the sea be got down safely over dams of that height," O'Connor wrote.[14] Various expensive strategies, including construction of the world's largest salmon and steelhead hatchery at the confluence of the North Fork of the Clearwater and the main stem, would be tried to deal with the difficult problem of maintaining anadromous fish stocks in compromised rivers.[15]

Although no national parks or classified wilderness areas were at stake in the Clearwater, the dispute over the two dams encompassed many of the same issues that disturbed preservationists in the Flathead and Sun River basins. At its heart was the unacknowledged value of wild fisheries and undisturbed big game habitat. Boosters like A. B. Curtis saw few drawbacks to replacing steelhead and salmon stocks with hatchery-bred rainbow trout. Elk and deer harvests could be sustained if the Forest Service were allowed to clear-cut forests and conduct controlled burns to improve browse. The dams' opponents, on the other hand, could hardly envision a Selway wilderness without steelhead venturing upstream each summer, or a North Fork that floated logs rather than a dry fly.

The Clearwater had a well-placed defender in Stewart Brandborg, whose move to Washington allowed him to serve as unofficial congressional liaison for Mort Brigham and the Idaho sportsmen. Raised in the small towns of Grangeville, Idaho, and Hamilton, Montana, young Brandy (a nickname he shared with his father) gained an appreciation for Idaho's backcountry on family pack trips into the Selway and Salmon River country. As an undergraduate at the University of Montana he studied mountain goats in the Bob Marshall Wilderness in cooperation with the Montana Fish and Game Department. Subsequent studies of bighorn sheep along Idaho's Salmon River led him to appreciate the value of wild country for its native wildlife. After receiving a graduate degree in wildlife biology at the University of Idaho, Brandborg returned to his mountain goat studies as an employee of the Idaho Fish and Game Department, working at first in the Selkirk Mountains and authoring the first life history of this elusive high-country dweller. An exciting outdoor career lay in front of him, but in 1954 the renowned wildlife biologist Durward Allen, who was working as the assistant chief of wildlife research for the U.S. Fish and Wildlife Service, told him of an opening with the National Wildlife Federation back East. Charles Callison, the group's conservation director, was seeking an energetic young advocate with a wildlife background and connections to the western states. Brandy had never been to Washington, and his wife, Anna Vee, was caring for their young child at home in Moscow, Idaho. Still, the potential to make a difference in the emerging conservation movement persuaded him to leave the Rockies for the nation's capital.[16] He and Anna Vee experienced a degree of culture shock in Washington, but he quickly learned his way around Capitol Hill as he met with legislators and prepared the federation's monthly digest of conservation legislation.[17] As Callison's assistant conservation director, Brandborg worked closely with Howard Zahniser on the Dinosaur National Monument fight, learning firsthand how congressional interior and appropriations committees dealt with the many public works proposals emanating from the Bureau of Reclamation and Corps of Engineers.

Callison gave Brandborg license to try to kill the two Clearwater dams, and in May 1954 Brandy enlisted support from Michigan representative George Dondero, who chaired the House Public Works Committee that oversaw river basin legislation. Realizing that economic arguments would carry more weight than the concerns of sport anglers, he told Dondero that the Clearwater's salmon and steelhead were "of great importance to commercial fisheries of the Columbia, the primary salmon-producing stream in the United States." One in every three salmon and steelhead migrating up the Columbia turned right at the Snake River, and a significant number of those—historically at least—wound up in the Clearwater. With the Columbia's salmonids already in trouble, further dam construction would make ongoing recovery efforts that much harder.[18]

The Senate issued a favorable report on Bruces Eddy in 1955, which stated that the loss of salmon and steelhead spawning areas could be compensated through fish stocking. Inundating "relatively small areas of winter range" in the reservoir site was not believed to be significant, it said. Authorization for detailed planning, however, encountered delays from Oregon senators Richard Neuberger and Wayne Morse, who were angry that Henry Dworshak had failed to support the High Mountain Sheep Dam in Hells Canyon. In 1957 Dworshak, a Republican, was joined by a young liberal Democrat named Frank Church, who like Morse and Neuberger supported a federally built dam in Hells Canyon. Church agreed with Dworshak on the need for Bruces Eddy, however, and despite working in concert with conservation groups on many issues (including passage of the 1964 Wilderness Act and the 1968 Wild and Scenic Rivers Act), he would prove to be the driving force in the Senate for the Clearwater project. Mort Brigham attempted to inoculate Church against some of the dam supporters' claims before he took office, pointing out that actual damages from flooding over the past sixty years amounted to far less on an annualized basis than the figures the Corps of Engineers used in its benefit-cost calculations. Church, however, stood with the water project developers, having announced during his campaign that "water is our lifeblood" and its use an important right akin to the enjoyment of private property.[19]

In a letter to Neuberger, Mort Brigham characterized the Clearwater dams as "the beginning of a landslide of disastrous proposals." A consortium of private power interests in Washington was looking at a dam site on the Snake River below the confluence with the Salmon River, which would arrest salmon migration in both streams (as opposed to the High Mountain Sheep Dam, which would affect only the Snake). Another dam was being considered on the upper Snake River that would inundate part of Jackson Hole and its elk winter range, and there were still proposals to harness the Flathead and Sun Rivers in Montana.[20] In the face of this powerful concrete-laying coalition, Brigham hoped that his little band of concerned sportsmen could somehow carry the day. Support from national conservation groups was essential. He told Michael Nadel, the Wilderness Society's publications editor, "If you folks can keep up the struggle at that end of the line there appears little reason for us to surrender in this fight. The opposition is becoming slowly organized and we at last have some organized financing and have gotten together a few hundred dollars."[21]

Whether that pittance would be enough to counter the Corps of Engineers' publicity and lobbying budget, not to mention the strong support for more dams among the state's congressional delegation, was an open question. Idaho's conservationists were making their first tentative steps into the world of high-stakes political action. Stewart Brandborg hoped they would jump in farther, for he knew there were larger battles ahead. Organized constituencies of conservationists were needed in every western state if Howard Zahniser's proposed Wilderness Act, just introduced in Congress, was to have any chance of passage. Meanwhile, dams such as Bruces Eddy, Glacier View, and Sun Butte had to be stopped. To do this, the parochial concerns of anglers and hunters would need to be expanded into an effective critique of the reclamation "juggernaut," as Brandy put it. This would require scientific and economic studies that called into question the assumed congruence between technological progress, economic development, and the well-being of America's citizens. In the mid-1950s it appeared unpatriotic to raise such questions, but in formulating its wilderness defense campaign, the national preservation organizations and their local collaborators would search for an alternative view of progress that might appeal to a broader constituency.

6

Partitioning Eden
The Selway-Bitterroot Wilderness, 1937–1963

By the mid-1950s the Northern Region's wilderness program had barely pro-
gressed beyond the achievements of two decades earlier, when Evan Kelley and
his associates designated ten primitive areas in lofty landscapes ranging from
the Beartooth Plateau to the Bitterroot Range. One wilderness area, named fit-
tingly for Bob Marshall, had been consolidated in 1940 from three of those primitive areas, and the sole additional designation came in 1948 with the 28,600-acre
Gates of the Mountains Wild Area northeast of Helena. This consisted of several
steep-sided canyons leading down to the impounded Missouri River at the "dark
and gloomy" limestone cliffs Meriwether Lewis noted in 1805. Aside from this
limited set-aside, which involved few stands of commercial timber, no new initiatives to recognize wildland values or protect substantial areas of forest appeared to
be at hand in either Idaho or Montana. The impetus toward preservation, never
strong within the Northern Region, seemed to have died out with the passing
or retirement of Bob Marshall, Evan Kelley, Elers Koch, and Meyer Wolff. Their
replacements turned their attention to reclassifying the remaining primitive areas,
especially Idaho's Selway-Bitterroot, which held timber once thought to be value-
less and inaccessible. The resulting conflict would draw attention from the nation's
top preservation leaders and spur efforts to enact the nation's first wilderness law.
In the long-running battle for the upper Selway, fisheries and wildlife concerns,
not scenery and hiking trails, informed much of the preservationists' efforts.

Although the Forest Service had been administering the Selway-Bitterroot Primitive Area under its U-1 wilderness regulation since 1939, regional officials wanted to draw new boundaries to account for road intrusions, changing administrative needs, and the growing interest in making timber resources available to mills in western Montana. The Magruder Road sliced through the south-central part of the area, from which other truck trails branched out to various lookouts and guard stations deep within the Selway backcountry. There were calls to extend these and other roads even farther to permit hunters to harvest the area's burgeoning elk herds. Evan Kelley, whose enthusiasm for wilderness seemed to wax and wane, halted one plan to extend the existing road along the lower Selway River as far as Moose Creek, which would have placed much of the northern part of the primitive area within a day's walk. Another road was proposed from Paradise Guard Station downstream to this same point, along with a spur leading up Running Creek, which would have opened up the entire middle reach of the river. This scheme, to the relief of wilderness backers, fell prey to wartime budget cuts.[1] Meanwhile, on the eastern side of the Bitterroot Range, irrigators had built twenty-seven dams in headwaters canyons, many with primitive access roads, and a new fire protection road marched up Lost Horse Canyon to the Bear Creek divide at the crest of the range. By the end of World War II the primitive area's boundary appeared porous indeed.

Beginning in 1946 regional office staff met with field personnel to consider new boundaries for the Selway, but they seemed reluctant to open this potentially contentious issue to public scrutiny. The question was pushed aside as the Forest Service turned its attention to an immediate crisis: the appearance of large numbers of spruce bark beetles in the upper Lochsa River drainage. The 1949 windstorm that flattened forests in northwestern Montana also hit the upper Lochsa, providing the insects with fresh blowdowns in which to breed. Bud Moore, the district ranger on the Lochsa's Powell District, offered two timber sales of forty million and seventy-five million board feet each, which were sold in 1954 to the Missoula firm Tree Farmers, a subsidiary of the Intermountain Company, a midsize regional outfit. Moore called in the Bureau of Public Roads to survey and build the road network needed to develop these sales, and soon the first major timber development south of the Lochsa was under way.[2] These were huge sales; the larger of them, called Lower Powell, required approval from the chief of the Forest Service. Once road construction got under way, however, Moore was taken aback by the 12- to 14-foot-wide road cuts along steep hillsides and through stream bottoms. As he related in his memoir *The Lochsa Story*, construction workers brought "the junk of American industrialization into the freshness of the Lochsa's mountains where, like children tired of their toys, they dribbled trash whenever their mood changed or their attention shifted to some other interest."[3] More serious was the sediment he observed coming from the roads, which created a new gravel bar jutting seventy-five feet into the river.[4] Moore tried to ride herd on the cat skinners and mitigate the damage where he could; he also reined in the fire road program, halting a planned extension of the Elk Summit road down to Moose Creek, deep within the primitive area.[5]

Moore had joined the Forest Service when rangers patrolled the far reaches of the Selway on horseback and pack strings supplied lookouts and fire camps. The agency was eager to shed this past, however, and in the early 1950s the Selway's managers contemplated using small bulldozers to build a ridgetop trail system within the primitive area. Smokechasers could then ride Cushman motor scooters along these trails to reach lightning strikes before they erupted into large blazes. To test the new equipment, crews cleared eleven miles of trail outside the primitive area in the Bitterroot's West Fork, gouging four-foot-wide paths through ridgetop forests and blasting rock outcrops with dynamite. Jack Parsall, the ranger at Moose Creek, wanted to extend the project into the Selway wilds, since it was becoming harder to find workers who knew how to pack mules and use hand tools. The idea was finally abandoned for fear of angering sportsmen who might oppose what amounted to a system of backcountry motorcycle and jeep trails.[6]

The leaders of the Wilderness Society were made aware of the regional office's deliberations over the Selway-Bitterroot through inside contacts such as Meyer Wolff and G. M. Brandborg. Following the society's 1953 council meeting on the Sun River, George Marshall (Bob Marshall's brother) met Wolff for a quick tour along the northern boundary of the primitive area. After driving over Lolo Pass into the basin of Brushy Creek, they looked at some of the spur roads that led off the newly constructed Elk Summit road to ridges and lookouts overlooking the Moose Creek drainage. Marshall agreed that the roads would have to be excluded from any new wilderness boundary, but neither he nor his colleagues were prepared to render judgment on all 1,875,000 acres of this intricate mountain expanse, most of which they had never seen. Nor was he familiar with the other six primitive areas in Region 1. "All this adds to my uncomfortable feeling," Marshall wrote afterward to Olaus Murie and Howard Zahniser, "that we need much more information about our major wilderness areas than I believe we have—what they are, what are their major features, what are the major dangers facing them."[7] In February 1954 Zahniser met with regional forester P. D. Hanson to review possible boundaries for a new Selway-Bitterroot wilderness area, and two years later the Wilderness Society scheduled its summer field trip in the Selway to acquaint its council members with the nation's largest potential wilderness area.[8] G. M. Brandborg, who retired in early 1955 as supervisor of the Bitterroot National Forest, arranged for his successor, Thurman Trosper, to take the group on a four-day horseback ride in the Moose Creek drainage. Recounting the trip in his book *Faces of the Wilderness*, council member Harvey Broome expressed appreciation for the Forest Service staffers' knowledge of and affection for the area, yet he was disturbed that so many encroachments had been made for the sake of administrative convenience, including landing fields, backcountry telephones, and mechanical equipment to clear trails and fight fires. The result, he wrote, was "a whittling away of remoteness, of the great silences, of the subtle spell of the wilderness."[9]

The Wilderness Society council regrouped that August at Olaus and Mardy Murie's log cabin in Moose, Wyoming, to consider their options. They agreed that the new wilderness boundary should come all the way down to the Lochsa River in order to forestall roads and timber sales that the agency was promoting to improve elk habitat. The Elk Summit road, its guard station, and its main spurs would be excluded from the wilderness, but they asked that the few miles of road that led into the drainage of Moose Creek be returned to a foot and horse trail. The road down the Selway River to Paradise Guard Station should be extended no farther, they said, and some of the existing spur roads, such as a steep track leading up to Hell's Half Acre Lookout, should be closed. The council admitted that the Magruder Road was there to stay and should form the area's southern boundary, but south of that road they envisioned another great wilderness area that would take in the remainder of the Selway-Bitterroot that lay between the Magruder Road and the Salmon River, as well as the million-acre Idaho Primitive Area, which began at the river. They proposed to name this huge expanse after the Salmon River's old moniker–the River of No Return.[10] If the wilderness advocates could not excise the Magruder Road from the landscape, they at least hoped to draw boundary lines snug against it and thus prevent further intrusions into the surrounding country. The result, if they were successful, would be the largest wilderness region in the United States, stretching from the Lochsa almost to the Sawtooths, and broken only by one ten-foot-wide dirt track. It would take in two of the wildest rivers remaining in the country and an untold number of granitic crags, windswept ridges, and no small amount of timber growing on benchlands overlooking these rivers.

This was the vision of a handful of men who had spent barely over a week in the area. They drew on Elers Koch's and G. M. Brandborg's intimate knowledge of the Selway, and Mort Brigham of Lewiston weighed in with his desire to include the uncut Meadow Creek drainage west of the primitive area. Otherwise, there was little involvement from the citizens of Idaho and Montana who made the most use of this landscape. That would come later. The council passed its recommendations along to P. D. Hanson in June 1956, but to make this vision a reality would take nearly a quarter century of strenuous organizing and a major campaign before Congress. During that interval the Wilderness Society would be transformed from a small band of concerned outsiders into a sophisticated lobbying network that would help build an unprecedented grassroots movement for land preservation in the Northern Rockies. The Selway would be one of its first major tests.

The notion of a nationwide system of wilderness areas had been floating around preservationist circles ever since 1925, when Aldo Leopold called for protecting national forest roadless lands in which Americans with a yen to do so "could disappear into the tall uncut."[11] He had in mind a system administered by the Forest Service following the model of New Mexico's Gila Wilderness, which he had helped establish the previous year. By 1939 the Wilderness Society's Robert Sterling Yard was discussing with his colleagues legislation that would permit the president to establish a wilderness area by executive proclamation, as was the case with national monuments. A legislated federal policy would unify management of the various primitive, wild, and wilderness areas the Forest Service had established under the L-20 policy and the U regulations, as well as ad hoc withdrawals such as the Glacier Peak Limited Area in Washington.[12]

After a decade of internal discussion and growing frustration with the agencies' dithering over reclassifying its primitive areas, the Wilderness Society council took up the question of a federal wilderness policy at its 1947 meeting at Rainy Lake in the Boundary Waters region of Minnesota. The gathering proved to be a turning point for the 12-year-old organization. The council resolved to press for a unified system of wilderness areas managed under a single, congressionally mandated policy that would supersede the Forest Service's patchwork of regulations and would include other federal lands such as national parks. "This was a carefully discussed departure" from the agency-initiative approach, according to historian and wilderness activist Doug Scott. The council took this step, he writes, "with their eyes open to the challenges they faced in getting Congress to take such a proposal seriously."[13] Howard Zahniser, the society's executive secretary, enlisted help from the Legislative Reference Service, a congressional research arm, to help draft the new legislation. It circulated among various conservation leaders a questionnaire that helped lay out the rationale for Zahniser's initiative and draw in other organizations such as the Sierra Club, whose support would be crucial in the coming legislative campaign.

On June 7, 1956, after Zahniser circulated drafts of a proposed bill among his confidants, Minnesota senator Hubert Humphrey introduced S. 4013, the first of many versions of what would become the Wilderness Act of 1964. Pennsylvania's John Saylor sponsored a similar bill in the House.[14] As initially formulated, it would have designated as permanent wilderness all of the existing wilderness, wild, and primitive areas on the national forests, and it would have required other federal land-management agencies such as the National Park Service and Fish and Wildlife Service to review their lands and submit recommendations for further designations to the president. These would become law by presidential proclamation and would be subject only to a veto by the House or Senate. The wilderness bill would undergo significant alteration during its eight-year journey through Congress. Its sponsors were forced to jettison the provision for presidential proclamation and accept numerous compromises allowing continued livestock grazing, location of mining claims, and even such things as power lines and dams under presidential decree.[15] For the first time, though, preservation interests saw hope of ending the attrition of wildlands at the hands of development-minded federal officials.

The introduction of the first wilderness bill spurred the Northern Region to get on with the reclassification of its seven remaining primitive areas before their boundaries were locked in—and with them valuable timber stands, administrative sites, and road corridors. Axel Lindh, head of the region's timber branch, pointed out that the primitive areas contained 10 percent of the region's commercial-quality timber, which if placed under management could produce an annual harvest of 250 million board feet—half of the region's current total.[16] To take these volumes out of production would seriously compromise the region's plans for expanded timber cutting, he wrote. He was particularly interested in the estimated 7.5 billion board feet of standing pine, fir, and spruce in the Selway-Bitterroot Primitive Area, which heretofore had been considered too remote to harvest. The Magruder Road had changed that, and now it was time to bring such stands into production.

In 1957 the Northern Region circulated among its staff a preliminary recommendation for a 1,163,555-acre Selway-Bitterroot wilderness area. Nearly half a million acres of the original primitive area would be opened for general forest management, while 207,000 acres lying between the Magruder Road and the Salmon River would be retained as the Salmon River Breaks Primitive Area, to be examined at a future date along with the adjacent Idaho Primitive Area. The agency rejected the proposed Meadow Creek addition because of planned roads, while the airstrip at Moose Creek was to be lengthened to accommodate DC-3 aircraft for fire control. Firefighting needs led to a retraction of the proposed wilderness boundary along the steep slopes south of the Lochsa River, known as the Lochsa Face, and in the vicinity of a proposed road extension down Running Creek to the Selway River. The area's eastern boundary was redrawn to exclude irrigation dams and the road up Lost Horse Canyon. By far the most significant omission, though, was 310,000 acres of mostly timbered lands on either side of the Magruder Road in the upper drainage of the Selway, identified (with customary government flourish) as "Area E."[17] Howard Zahniser was shown the proposal during a two-day meeting of the Society of American Foresters at the Fenn Ranger Station in October 1957, but despite his recommendation that more lands be included, the Northern Region released substantially the same proposal to the public in August 1960.

Even so, the reclassified Selway-Bitterroot Wilderness would be the largest wilderness in the national forest system, encompassing the crest of the Bitterroot Range from Lolo Peak almost to Nez Perce Pass on the West Fork of the Bitterroot River. More than thirty miles of the Selway River from Selway Falls to Running Creek would be included, as would all of Moose Creek and much of the high country north and west of this drainage. Agency personnel believed that their proposal struck a balance between wilderness uses, resource development needs, and fire protection requirements. Hikers and horse packers could revel in the miles of deep canyons, cirque-bound lakes, open ridges, and spangled peaks on either side of the Bitterroot crest. By developing a significant road network in the headwaters of the Selway River, the agency could capture considerable timber volume, ensure better fire protection, and enhance elk winter range. Nearly twenty years of discussion went into their proposal; now the public would react.

Historian Donald Worster claimed that "the key American environmental idea, and at once the most destructive and most creative" is that the historical American landscape was a kind of Eden restored to the face of the Earth. Worster called this a "grand, mythic illusion" and believed that it was the "primary source of our self-confidence and our legendary, indefatigable optimism."[18] To the Anglo settlers of this continent, Eden was a vast storehouse of resources placed there expressly for their use, a God-given bounty that was not subject to the claims of kings, governments, or future generations. In twentieth-century Idaho, the remnants of this original patrimony had been pushed back to the most inaccessible mountain ranges. Why stop now? many of its residents wondered. A long and painful awakening was needed before a significant number of Americans agreed that controls must be placed on the miners, loggers, and cattlemen who had made the West what it was.

Beginning in 1905 the Forest Service interposed itself between those who sought to exploit the West's virgin forests in the customary manner and those who placed a high symbolic value on them as a last reservoir of Nature, untainted by humanity's basest drives to rip and tear the earth. Determined neither to exploit nor to preserve, the agency's rangers and foresters would instead create a new, tightly controlled and expertly managed version of paradise, one in which the most destructive American impulses would be channeled into productive harmony with the natural world. Informed by science, its rangers and supervisors would dole out access to timber, forage, and recreation for the good of all. Forest Service culture was built around this interventionist paradigm. What a forest ranger or timber-stand examiner could not abide was to watch an insect epidemic take root in blowdowns and wind-weakened trees, eventually turning whole hillsides into a sea of dead snags. Nor was wildfire accorded any functional role in a national forest during the 1950s; instead, powerful new methods of fire control were being tested in the Selway, including smokejumpers and retardant drops from helicopters and fixed-wing aircraft.

Wilderness, to many agency officials, was the antithesis of good forest management. Forest Service officers believed that if their personnel were restricted to the pack trails and mule strings of the 1930s, they could not fight wildfires effectively, improve browse for big game, or provide the varieties of recreational use the public expected. Land withdrawals might be countenanced among the high peaks of the Bitterroot Range or in other alpine strongholds such as the Cabinet Mountains, Mission Range, Spanish Peaks, or Absarokas, but to the men in green it was self-evident that no single user group had a unique claim to the vast Selway drainage. The key was to find the most suitable uses of each forest and mountain type, set lines and limits, and adjudicate whatever disputes might arise. The agency's proposal for the Selway-Bitterroot Primitive Area was probably as good a scheme as they could devise. It was a partitioning of a last frontier; a drawing of lots that they hoped would lead to satisfaction, not bitter dispute.

The Forest Service got itself into trouble because it failed to recognize the power of the Edenic idea itself. If wild country represented an untapped storehouse to timbermen and miners, it was also a symbol of the ineffable to others. The Bitterroot Range may have lacked the soaring peaks of Glacier National

Park and the glittering alpine basins of the Teton Range, but it had certain qualities that equaled or surpassed those places: a vast scale, the possibility of endless
wanderings, and the mysterious sense that deep within its valleys Nature might
be able, for once, to work out its destiny free from human interference. These
romantic ideals derived support from new concepts that had sprung up in the
sciences—that the human influence on forests, rivers, and grasslands was complex and profound; that we had already messed up too many rivers, streams, and
forests searching for gold and timber; and that a close look was needed into the
inner workings of natural ecosystems before loosing the bulldozers on the last
strongholds of wild country.

With these goals in mind, the Wilderness Society made the Selway a priority,
holding its 1960 summer council meeting at Shoup, Idaho, along the main Salmon
River and hearing a presentation by Ralph Space, supervisor of the Clearwater
National Forest, on the proposed wilderness boundaries. In January 1961 Howard Zahniser made a circuit through Montana, Idaho, and eastern Washington to
encourage supporters to appear at Forest Service administrative hearings on the
Selway proposal, which were scheduled for March in Missoula, Lewiston, and
Grangeville. The hearings were important in themselves, but Zahniser wanted a
strong turnout in order to persuade Idaho representative Gracie Pfost to support
the national wilderness bill. Pfost chaired the House Public Lands Subcommittee
and would hold hearings on the bill the following year.

Zahniser now had the help of an able young understudy who was familiar with
Idaho and its vast wildlands. Stewart Brandborg had helped Zahniser lobby for the
wilderness bill while working for Charles Callison at the National Wildlife Federation, and in 1956 he was invited to join the Wilderness Society's governing council. Four years later, after a shake-up at NWF left Callison without a job, Zahniser
created a position for the young Idahoan as his special projects director—a catchall for the lobbying and outreach work needed to pass the wilderness bill and deal
with the various primitive areas coming up for reclassification. In 1961 Brandy
made two trips to his home state, the first in March to organize the turnout at the
Selway hearings, and another in October to rouse local supporters ahead of Pfost's
congressional field hearings. On the latter trip he traveled with the well-known
outdoor writer Ted Trueblood, "meeting," as he recalled, "over breakfast, lunch
and dinner with every outfit we could" and showing slides from his mountain goat
studies as an entrée to the wilderness issue.[19]

Brandborg understood the high value Idahoans placed on wildlife and hunting; he had spent months roving the Bitterroot Range for his graduate studies
and in his later work for the Idaho Fish and Game Commission. This work put

him in touch with some of the leading wildlife biologists of the day, including Les Pengelly, John Craighead, Durward Allen, and Olaus Murie. He credited Murie, whom he met at a wildlife conference in Missoula in the late 1940s, with advancing his thoughts about the value of wilderness. He was taken at once, he recalled, with "this sweet, humble epitome of a fine biologist" who had worked throughout the West and the Far North for the Biological Survey. Beginning in 1956, as part of the campaign to designate the Arctic National Wildlife Refuge in Alaska, Brandy arranged meetings for Olaus and Mardy in the nation's capital with key representatives and senators, listening as the two explorers told of the sweeping distances and abundant wildlife in the Brooks Range. "It gave a framework for something deep in my psyche," Brandborg recalled in a 2003 interview. His work with the fish and game departments of Idaho and Montana had emphasized the harvest side of wildlife management, but he could see that in the "wild untrammeled setting" of the Muries' Arctic "we had things that far transcended the human experience of taking an animal or indulging in one kind of recreation or another." Here one arrived as an observer, traveling "quietly and unobtrusively . . . to savor it, to measure it, to watch it, and above all, to leave it untouched as much as humanly possible."[20] Brandy was eager to apply these concepts to the Bitterroot Range, which held one of the largest concentrations of elk and mountain goats in the Lower 48, not to mention the trout swimming in the unsullied waters of the Selway.

The region's timber industry was preparing for the March 1961 hearings as well. The Inland Empire Multiple Use Committee, a trade group representing Potlatch and other regional mills, issued a statement that February advocating an 862,000-acre wilderness that omitted a large part of the lower Selway drainage as well as Area E. The deletions would free up more than 1.7 billion board feet of timber, which would permit an annual harvest of some 66 million board feet, the committee estimated. This amounted to nearly $25 million in annual benefits to the surrounding communities through the logging, processing, distribution, and retail sale of wood products. "The value of wilderness country for recreation and spiritual stimulation is fully recognized," the timbermen granted, but these qualities must be "kept in balance with the other needs of local and regional citizens for the necessities of life." These included all the elements of a high standard of living—"good homes, churches, automobiles, television sets, sporting goods, camping equipment, a dinner out now and then," they stated.[21] Cliff Hopkins, another Potlatch official, stated that regional sawmills depended on prospective timber harvests from the Selway. "We must have access to all of the merchantable timber of the region for survival," he said. He decried as elitist those who could afford wilderness pack trips. "We are asked to mortgage the future economy of the region to purchase recreation for a handful of trophy hunters, utopian campers and individualistic hikers," he said.[22]

Hopkins touched a sensitive nerve among many Idahoans who resented out-of-state hunters and anglers, but the outfitting and guiding industry was more diverse than his statement indicated and it brought significant income to the Gem State. A 1953 survey disclosed that more than a hundred packers, plus an additional thirteen operating out of Montana, utilized Idaho's wildlands, principally within its three primitive areas (the Selway-Bitterroot, Idaho, and Sawtooth). Twelve hundred clients thus were able to experience the wilderness in the 1950 season, spending $400,000 in direct outfitter charges and presumably laying out even more before and after their trips. Numerous part-time outfitters who worked informally with friends or other clients added to this total.[23]

Despite Hopkins's call to arms, it would be Idahoans themselves who would express a preference for wild trout and elk. The upper Selway had never been a commercial forest, nor were timber sales scheduled in the area, so wilderness may have appeared less threatening to employees of the state's wood-processing firms. What it had, in abundance, was wild game and the allure of the primitive, and in the end that would trump volumes of economic statistics.

Conservationists made a strong turnout when the Forest Service opened its hearings on the Selway proposal in Missoula on March 7, 1961. Speaking for the Wilderness Society, Stewart Brandborg scored the agency for proposing to shrink the protected area in the Selway-Bitterroot by more than one-fourth, particularly in the 310,000-acre Area E along the Magruder Road and the 71,000-acre Lochsa Face. His father, G. M. Brandborg, who had traveled the Selway's trails since 1925 as assistant supervisor of the Nez Perce National Forest, spoke of meeting Bob Marshall in the 1930s to discuss boundaries for the primitive area. The elder Brandy worried that Forest Service officers and staff no longer frequented such places. "Maybe it was because we had spent many of our early years in the back country that we became apprehensive as we observed encroachments of roads and the other developments moving closer to the very heart of the back country areas. Whatever the cause, we knew we could see the end of our remaining wilderness within a generation if measures were not taken to protect them."[24]

The fate of the Selway's elk herd was a key issue at the Lewiston hearing, which followed on May 9. Mort Brigham spoke before a crowd of 250 on behalf of his local sportsmen's association. He still hoped to gain protection for the

Meadow Creek drainage, an "elk paradise" that compared favorably to hunting grounds he had visited in the Bob Marshall Wilderness and central British Columbia. "A system of proposed roads such as the Forest Service has planned would bring ruin to these fine wildlife scenes," he stated. He cited fish and game department statistics that showed hunter success ratios of 45 percent in the Selway Primitive Area, compared to only 26 to 29 percent in the more accessible roaded country in the river's lower reaches.[25]

During the 1930s and 1940s the Idaho Fish and Game Department favored better road access in the Selway so that hunters could cull surplus elk, and the Forest Service stood ready to oblige. Now Frank Cullen, the department's director and Brandborg's former boss, turned this policy on its head. In his testimony at Lewiston he examined the issue from the standpoint of the hunting experience itself, saying that "any replacement of the type of elk hunting available in wilderness country would only result in the cluttered type of hunter concentration which is already too prevalent in many easy access areas." This was the "firing line" argument that Cullen's counterparts in Montana worried about wherever roads impinged on prime big game habitat. "Wilderness conditions seem to be the surest way to maintain quality elk hunting for the future," he stated.[26] The department's turnabout reflected the strong influence of preservationists like Brandborg and the University of Montana's Les Pengelly, who placed inviolate habitat above the "take" of game animals.

Cullen's department also worried about the effect of roads on the Selway's fishery. Timber staffers in the regional office wanted to build an extensive road network in the Area E deletion to access millions of board feet of pine, fir, and spruce. The Magruder Road, a rough-and-ready "truck trail" that for three decades had been used for fire control and recreation access, would be widened and surfaced as a main haul road. Fish and game officials worried that rainstorms would carry sediment from these roads into the area's streams, which would have "a profound effect upon the aquatic environment and could jeopardize the Selway's cutthroat and steelhead trout fishery," Cullen stated.[27] This was perhaps the first time that resource professionals directly challenged the Forest Service's operating assumption that logging and road building could be done without significant harm to other multiple-use values. The fisheries issue in Area E quickly emerged as the centerpiece of the Selway controversy.

The framing of arguments for and against wilderness would occupy the representatives of public interest groups and trade associations over the next half century. The 1961 Selway-Bitterroot hearings were the first open public forums in the Northern Rockies where specific land allocations could be debated. There would be many more. What is notable about them is the emergence of scientifically informed testimony about the effect of resource development programs on fish and wildlife populations. Wilderness advocates appreciated the fine scenery and hiking trails of the Bitterroot Range, but they also expressed great concern for spawning beds, water temperatures, and escape cover. Stewart Brandborg spoke this language and made sure that his Montana and Idaho colleagues were present at each hearing. He knew that an emotional attachment to wild country would never carry the day against the Multiple Use Committee's economic calculations. Elk, mountain goats, salmon, and steelhead lent a practical and immediate value to this mountain Eden. These creatures gave the Selway wilderness an allure beyond any roaded and timbered landscape. In the coming debates Brandy and his friends would focus on the welfare of these animals and their habitat as much as on the needs of the human spirit. Indeed, perhaps they were closely connected.

7

A Book and Its Cover
The Madison Range, 1958–1967

At the conclusion of the September 1958 meeting between the Gallatin Canyon outfitters and Forest Service officials, Ken Baldwin spread out a forest map and with the outfitters' help outlined some 220,000 acres in the headwaters of the Gallatin River as an immediate target for protection. It contained much of the southern Madison Range, including Hilgard Basin and the Sage Peak–Monument Mountain area, along with Buffalo Horn Creek in the adjacent Gallatin Range. Ed Barry, the regional official in charge of recreation and lands, carried the proposal back to regional forester Charles Tebbe, who gave his approval for what became known as the Hilgard Hold Area in a letter to Baldwin that October. The designation made no reference to the protective U regulations that governed the region's wilderness and primitive areas, but Tebbe promised to withhold timbering and road building from the area pending a study of its wilderness qualities. Continued use of jeeps, motorcycles, and Tote Gotes would be allowed, however, and he could not be very reassuring about the ultimate disposition of the area. "We accept the proposal because you urge it, because we too are interested in delineating boundaries along proper and defensible lines, and because for the time being there are no pressing needs for non-recreational developments in the area," Tebbe wrote. "It must be recognized that no significance attaches to the lines as drawn."[1]

Tebbe's caveats must have filled Baldwin and his friends with anxiety, for much of Montana's high country was coming under claim not just for timber harvesting but also for new forms of motor-based recreation. Jeeps, trail scooters, and motorbikes gave unprecedented mobility to sportsmen and other trail users, making it possible to reach the remote subalpine lakes of the Madison and Gallatin Ranges in an hour's ride. The machines were easier to maintain, store, and transport than horses, and they brought an aura of excitement to backwoods travel. Forest Service officials themselves sometimes used scooters for trail patrols and maintenance and were not inclined to ban the machines. By 1960 Grace Miller of the Elkhorn Ranch in Gallatin Canyon was complaining to Ed Barry that scooter riders were buzzing past her cabins and through pastures on their way into the Hilgard Basin and Monument Mountain area. Correspondents for an outdoor magazine had shown up at her ranch and were enthusiastic about publicizing the Hilgard Lakes as a "scooter heaven."[2]

Ken Baldwin laid out a lengthy bill of particulars before Olaus Murie the week after their September 1958 meeting. Users of jeeps and trail machines were disturbing wildlife, interfering with traditional backcountry hunting, endangering hikers and horse users, and digging ruts into soft soils and steep slopes, he claimed. "Serious erosion" resulted, "which destroys watershed and downstream values for fish, wildlife and municipal uses," Baldwin stated. He wanted the Forest Service to halt all motor traffic off designated roads.[3] At the time, the Forest Service lacked a true multiple-use planning process through which it could identify such conflicts and segregate trail users. Delineating the Hilgard Hold Area was a start, but Baldwin and the outfitters hoped to place this and the rest of the Madison and Gallatin Ranges under more permanent designation—either as an administrative wilderness area under regulation U-1, or as a congressionally sanctioned wilderness under the new wilderness bill before Congress. To accomplish this, Baldwin knew he needed support from a wider circle of preservationists than the handful of outfitters living up the Gallatin.

Ken Baldwin was the son of a Methodist minister and often expressed his love of wild country in spiritual terms. He had grown up in Fort Shaw, a farming community on the Sun River west of Great Falls, while his wife, Florence, came from a homestead north of Choteau. The couple moved to Bozeman following their wartime work with the Air Force outside Great Falls. Their three children attended Montana State College while Ken managed a bulk oil distribution plant on the north side of town. Weekends found them exploring the trails and ridges of Hyalite Canyon, the Spanish Peaks, and the deeper wilderness to the south. While on a hunting trip in the Gallatin Range in the fall of 1946, they looked across the river to Lone Mountain, which presided over dozens of square miles of untrodden country. Exploring this range on subsequent trips, they found a tiny log cabin at the foot of the mountain. Though it belonged to the Crail family who had homesteaded in the West Fork of the Gallatin, Ken put a new roof on it and used it as a base for his and Florence's hunting trips. "We saw all of that country when it was virgin wilderness," he recalled in a 2002 interview.[4] But much of this mountain paradise belonged to the Northern Pacific Railway, which owned dozens of "checkerboard" sections interspersed among the national forest holdings. By the 1950s log trucks were hauling timber out of railroad lands in the West Fork basin while sportsmen and adventurers were beginning to visit the area on motorcycles and Tote Gotes. To Baldwin, these developments threatened the continued existence of the elk, grizzly bear, and mountain sheep that populated the mountains. "I began to see that it was necessary that some of the wild lands be set aside, to leave the habitat for these animals," he said. "You can't have them unless you have a place for them to live."[5]

Bob Cooney and his fellow biologists, including Les Pengelly and Eldon Smith of Montana State College's wildlife extension service, also saw wilderness areas as an essential component of habitat protection. As early as 1947 Cooney approached Olaus Murie about setting up a Montana affiliate of the Wilderness Society and was courteously rebuffed, but by 1958 he sat on the society's governing council and was a key cooperator with Murie on Montana issues such as the Sun Butte Dam.[6] With a bill in Congress to formalize the federal government's languishing and haphazard program of wildland set-asides, both Cooney and Baldwin believed it was time to form a new organization that would focus on these issues. Such a group could take stances that government employees could not, and it would serve as a liaison between the national wilderness preservation groups and Montana's sporting and conservation organizations, including the Montana Wildlife Federation. In March 1958 Baldwin sent a letter to his fellow conservation-minded sportsmen and other cooperators, inviting them to meet in Bozeman to form a "Montana Wilderness Society." Its purpose was to mobilize conservationists to resist the invasion of designated wilderness areas and to increase public awareness of what he termed "a valuable natural resource" that was "part of a balanced conservation program [that] is essential in the survival of our civilized culture."[7]

Twenty interested Montanans, including Gallatin Canyon outfitters Vic Benson, Jim Goodrich, and Howard Kelsey, showed up on March 28, 1958, for the group's organizational meeting, held beneath the polished wood beams and columns of Bozeman's venerable Baxter Hotel. Bob Cooney amplified the theme that had driven his and Ken Baldwin's years of effort: the need to protect habitat for wild creatures such as trout, grizzly bear, mountain goat, bighorn sheep, and elk. "The wilderness program should not be divorced in any way from the overall program of conservation," he stated. Wilderness areas helped protect the headwaters of streams and "constitute the best upstream soil and plant stabilization measures."[8] Both he and Baldwin would continue to emphasize habitat preservation as a central part of the wilderness program, establishing Montana as a leader in what would later emerge as the field of conservation biology.

There were particulars to discuss, especially the Gallatin outfitters' proposal to designate a quarter million acres of wilderness in the Madison Range. Forest supervisor George Duvendack assured the group of his agency's support for wilderness and said that such an area would be administratively set aside as soon as reasonable boundaries could be established—setting the stage for a field inspection trip and meeting that September. A Madison Valley rancher named Elliot Redman urged him to proceed with this designation, which would protect an area above his ranch in the drainage of Jack Creek. That afternoon Redman, Duvendack, and Cooney helped draft temporary bylaws for the new organization, now called the Montana Wilderness Association (MWA).

The new group held its first annual meeting at the Baxter Hotel that December, drawing sixty attendees despite unusually cold weather. Howard Kelsey described the September trail ride and meeting with Duvendack and other Forest Service officials that had led to the establishment of the Hilgard Hold Area, the first citizen-initiated land withdrawal in Montana since the establishment of the Gates of the Mountains Wild Area in 1948. An eleven-member council was chosen and Ken Baldwin was elected president of the group. After dinner the attendees sat back as Olaus Murie showed slides and spoke of his and Mardy's adventures in Alaska's Brooks Range.[9] Murie spoke again at the MWA's third annual meeting in 1960, apparently reconciled to its status as an organization independent from the Wilderness Society. His friendship with Bob Cooney and Ken Baldwin helped cement close ties between the two groups.

In January 1962 a Texas oilman named Phil Yeckel inquired of the Montana Wilderness Association whether there were any plans to expand the Spanish Peaks Primitive Area to include the forested drainage of Jack Creek, which connected this high mountain stronghold to the rest of the Madison Range. Yeckel owned a ranch farther downstream on Jack Creek where it spilled into Montana's scenic Madison Valley. The upper part of this drainage had seen a little timbering and railroad tie hacking in previous decades, mostly from the Gallatin side, but the greater part had been left to nature's devices, and extensive stands of Douglas-fir and spruce still lined an unroaded stream. As a result Jack Creek ran clear and cold down to Yeckel's irrigation ditches and on to join the Madison River, one of Montana's premier trout streams.

Rich men with cattle outfits were not a rarity in Montana, and now that the days of the open range were over, some latter-day land barons were acquiring spreads in the most beautiful portions of the state. Yeckel ran four hundred head of cattle from his Jumping Horse Stock Ranch up into the forests and meadows of Jack Creek during the summer, but unlike many stockmen who were wary of the Forest Service (and especially of preservationist organizations), Yeckel counted himself a wilderness supporter. For the past few years he had voluntarily let his grazing permits in the Spanish Peaks go unfilled, and the entire area, he told MWA president John Craighead, "is probably one of the most primitive and spectacular regions in southwestern Montana." He feared that if this area were not protected, it would "degenerate to a condition as bad as the Gravelly Range which has been really damaged by excessive use of power vehicles during hunting seasons."[10]

Yeckel's proposal gained little traction within the MWA, which counted few members in the Madison Valley. Obtaining the 220,000-acre Hilgard Hold Area had taken years of effort by local sportsmen and outfitters, and in the Spanish Peaks the organization was willing to settle for a modest expansion of the 49,800-acre primitive area. The Forest Service floated a 56,000-acre wilderness proposal for the area in September 1965, but regional forester Boyd Rasmussen finally settled on a 50,776-acre proposal in the spring of 1966. It included a significant expansion to the northwest in the upper reaches of Spanish Creek and a smaller expansion to the southwest, but it omitted lands in the drainage of Little Hell Roaring Creek on the north and above the Gallatin River on the east. These omissions alarmed Ken Baldwin, who noted that the cliffs above the river provided winter range for a sizable herd of bighorn sheep, and that Little Hell Roaring Creek was an integral part of the larger wild area.

The Forest Service viewed high peaks and alpine lake basins as the primary features of wilderness, so it favored proposals that excluded the lower approach valleys. In the eyes of Charles Tebbe, Ed Barry, and their associates, areas such as Hilgard Basin, the crest of the Spanish Peaks, and the Beartooth Plateau would suffice for the limited number of people who actually visited such areas. The result, if allowed to stand, would have been seven or eight wilderness and wild areas in the Northern Rockies comprising fewer than three million acres. Unwilling to acquiesce to the Forest Service's limited concept of wilderness, Ken Baldwin formed an ad hoc Spanish Peaks Wilderness Committee in July 1966 to draft a response. Clif Merritt and Bob Cooney attended, along with local ranchers, sportsmen, and fish and game officials. They agreed on a northern boundary along a line roughly from the Forest Service ranger station on Squaw Creek west to the upper reaches of Cherry Creek, which took in six intermingled sections of private ranchland whose owners were willing to exchange for lands lower on the mountain slopes. Overall, the conservationists' proposal would expand the primitive area by some thirty thousand acres, including the extensions the Forest Service suggested, but they decided not to include an outlying area of high forests and expansive meadows to the northwest of the primitive area, known as Cowboys Heaven for its excellent summer range.[11] Its steep western breaks overlooked the Madison River canyon and often stayed clear of snow, offering excellent winter range for deer and elk. Because it lacked the spectacular mountain terrain of the main Spanish Peaks, the conservationists felt it would be too difficult to classify as wilderness. It was a rare oversight for Merritt, Baldwin, and Cooney, who usually took pains to include areas of high value for wildlife. Cowboys Heaven would remain, along with Jack Creek, one of the main points of contention for a later generation of Bozeman-area preservationists.

With no support forthcoming from conservation groups, Phil Yeckel tried to enlist Senator Lee Metcalf in his Jack Creek campaign. The area was a favorite among dude ranchers from the Madison Valley and attracted hunting outfitters who set up camps in the area during the big game season. "The area is dotted with several trout lakes and two very good streams," Yeckel wrote, calling it "one of the few areas left in southwestern Montana that is not available to jeep and car travel." The timber in the drainage was of "dubious value," he claimed, with road-building costs likely to equal the price of the stumpage removed. The biggest conflict in Jack Creek, however, was the approximately nineteen thousand acres of Northern Pacific lands distributed throughout the basin in checkerboard fashion. Some of these sections lay practically at the foot of Lone Mountain. Nevertheless, Yeckel hoped that "with persistence a trade can be worked out."[12]

Metcalf forwarded Yeckel's letter to the Forest Service, but he appears not to have taken further action—even after Yeckel buttonholed him at a gathering in Billings that June.[13] Other developing controversies over forestland management, including the upper Selway River drainage and an area south of the Bob Marshall Wilderness called the Lincoln Back Country, were taking much of the senator's attention. He was unlikely to become deeply involved in a dispute where there were no active logging proposals, as well as a noteworthy lack of agreement among conservationists.

The Gallatin National Forest scheduled a hearing on its Spanish Peaks proposal for September 9, 1966. The auditorium of the Emerson School in Bozeman filled with 250 citizens, 50 of whom spoke in favor of the MWA proposal, with only 5 in opposition. In rare agreement with wilderness advocates, Intermountain Lumber Company president Horace Koessler noted that three-fourths of the area was classified as noncommercial timber and its preservation would have "little or no impact on forest management operations in the area." He opposed any expansion of the wilderness beyond the agency's proposal, however.[14] The MWA stuck to its call for a modest expansion of the wilderness area boundaries. Ken Baldwin told agency officials that leaving Little Hell Roaring Creek open to logging would "overlook the intangible loss that accrues from damaged watersheds, scenic beauty, and recreation potential." Similarly, he felt that the lodgepole forest that stretched west of Little Hell Roaring to Cherry Creek "sets off the beauty of the high peaks to the south." To exclude it from the wilderness "would be like taking the cover from a book."[15] In a statement submitted after the hearing, MWA president John Montagne called on the agency to "save some terrain, other than in National Parks, which can exist under its own natural devices, bugs, windfall, deadfall—even the risk of unusually heavy fire conditions."[16]

Unsatisfied with either the Forest Service or MWA proposals, several Madison Valley residents took their case for including Jack Creek in the wilderness directly to their senators. Pete Combs, a rancher on lower Jack Creek and chairman of the Ennis bank, told Lee Metcalf that "this area has had no commercial activity at all. . . . In the Southwestern part of Montana there is no area of this nature. This area should be saved for our children." Arthur Orr, also from the lower Jack Creek drainage, said that a road up the drainage would turn it into a "mountain slum."[17]

The Forest Service had its own idea of how to improve recreational access to Jack Creek: a new road transecting the Madison Range that would permit easy travel between the Gallatin and Madison Valleys. Around 1966 they came to an agreement with the Northern Pacific by which the Forest Service would acquire the railroad's holdings within the proposed Spanish Peaks wilderness, while the railroad would block up some of its timberlands in upper Jack Creek. Both outfits could then proceed with logging outside the wilderness. Phil Yeckel got wind of the plan and registered his objection with Lee Metcalf. The cost of acquiring the railroad land outright would run from $200,000 to $400,000, he said, hardly greater than the value of the timber that could be extracted. Metcalf was noncommittal, but Yeckel and Combs believed the issue important enough to meet with him in Washington in January 1967. They were evidently persuasive, for that afternoon Metcalf wrote to Agriculture Secretary Orville Freeman to ask that the Forest Service initiate a land exchange in Jack Creek. In a separate letter written that day, Metcalf told the chairman of the Ennis Commercial Club, "I agree with you wholeheartedly" about including Jack Creek in the wilderness. But a departmental spokesman offered only that the agency would restudy the primitive area boundaries in light of comments at the September 9 hearing.[18]

Nor would the Northern Pacific go along easily: its lands supervisor, R. N. Witter, informed Metcalf that it had developed a "joint access plan" with the Forest Service for a connecting road between the Madison and Gallatin Rivers through Jack Creek. The lure of a new road corridor through the range appealed to the timbermen in both outfits, who shared an interest in limiting wilderness to the high peaks.[19]

In April 1967 Yeckel traveled to Saint Paul, Minnesota, to press his case with Northern Pacific president Louis Menk. Menk preferred to complete the timber exchange already in the works, but if Congress would reimburse the $33,000 the company had spent on surveys and resource evaluations, he would consider Yeckel's Jack Creek proposal. Yeckel relayed this information to Metcalf and asked him to help grease the wheels within the Department of Agriculture. But Forest Service chief Edward Cliff informed Metcalf in July 1967 that any attempt to negotiate a new land exchange would delay the extant proposal for the Spanish Peaks.[20] Either Metcalf could go forward with a more limited proposal that had the administration's support, or he could open a can of worms by trying to extend the Spanish Peaks' boundaries into Jack Creek. Metcalf preferred the former, although Yeckel, whose wealth gave him ready access to the principal officials in the case, kept trying to find some way around the land exchange problem. Later that summer he and fellow ranchers Pete Combs and Ed Beardsley arranged a meeting in Billings with Arthur Greeley, the assistant chief of the Forest Service. Greeley refused to change course but suggested that the Senate Interior Committee attach language to Metcalf's forthcoming Spanish Peaks bill to facilitate a land exchange.[21]

The Jack Creek ranchers lined up an impressive show of support for their proposal, including the Madison Valley Cattle Ranchers Association and the Ennis Commercial Club, whose director, L. A. Chamberlain, tallied the value of outfitting and hunting trips taken into the area. Adding in the sales of cattle that ranged there every summer, some $150,000 to $200,000 in annual local income was thereby created, compared to the $250,000 value from logging, which he said would be finished in two or three years. "Why do people continue to come year after year to spend their vacations here?" he asked. "Because of the true beauty and scenic area. Great mountain peaks with outstretched arms to the sky welcoming all to come and enjoy what God has created." This beauty stood in contrast to the logging that was going on in the West Fork of the Madison River, which he said was leaving "great scars of bare acres that will not be useful to anyone for years to come."

Chamberlain closed with a quotation from Gifford Pinchot, who was not known for his preservationist tendencies. The Forest Service's founder, Chamberlain said, had visited Jack Creek almost annually while serving as governor of Pennsylvania and once proclaimed, "I hope the day will never come when the sound of an axe, the purr and putt of a gas vehicle will be heard to destroy the beauty and solitude of this beautiful creation." As it happened, Pinchot's agency would soon be engaged in negotiations designed to turn upper Jack Creek and the nearby West Fork of the Gallatin River into Montana's largest destination resort. Much more than an occasional car or truck was headed for the quiet slopes beneath Lone Mountain.

Ed Beardsley was the former president of Miles Laboratories, a pharmaceutical firm based in Indiana, and was well represented in the business world. One friend, an Indianapolis newspaper magnate named Eugene Pulliam, got in touch with the executive assistant to Vice President Hubert Humphrey, one of the original sponsors of the Wilderness Act. Humphrey offered to help, and his subsequent letter to Metcalf and Mansfield finally gained Jack Creek an audience. At the Montanans' behest, Henry Jackson, the chair of the Senate Interior Committee, asked Agriculture Secretary Orville Freeman to take another look at Jack Creek as part of its just-completed Spanish Peaks study. Committee action on the proposal would be deferred until negotiations could be held with the Northern Pacific Railway over the needed land exchange.[22] This was a direct rebuff to the administration's stated desire to keep the Spanish Peaks proposal unencumbered by controversy.

Freeman could not have appreciated the Interior Committee's interference; President Johnson had already transmitted the Department of Agriculture's report to Congress, and on April 9, Montana representative Arnold Olsen introduced the administration's wilderness proposal in the House. The secretary told Senator Jackson, in effect, that the Forest Service would study Jack Creek when it got around to it. "Our negotiating position is made somewhat less favorable because of the publicity which the Jack Creek area has received," Freeman added.[23] The department preferred to deal with the Northern Pacific in private, and on its terms—an approach that would not prove friendly to the wilderness supporters' aims.

The pro-wilderness contingent in the Madison Valley represented wealthy newcomers such as Beardsley and Yeckel as well as a number of longtime valley residents such as Pete Combs and L. A. Chamberlain. What united them was a resistance to change in the landscape they had come to love. The wide open, windswept valley of the Madison River was framed along its eastern length by the bold peaks of its namesake mountain range. The large ranches arrayed along the mountain front admitted the public at only a few points, Jack Creek among them, and dude ranch guests and hunting parties made up most of the recreational traffic within the range. Here was Montana's original Big Sky—the version that offered no chairlifts to its stunning heights. But a Gilded Age land-disposal policy burdened these mountains with an ownership pattern antithetical to preservation, as wilderness advocates were learning. The Forest Service would take a second look at Jack Creek only grudgingly, and after much badgering from Senator Metcalf.[24] Its personnel never embraced the notion that in the Madison Range lay one of the greatest opportunities for landscape preservation in the Northern Rockies—if only the government could undo the tangle created by the land giveaway of 1864.

8

Wild River
The Middle Fork of the Flathead, 1957–1964

On the morning of July 15, 1957, a single-engine Fornaire Aircoupe crested the 7,000-foot rampart of the Swan Range and proceeded east over Hungry Horse Reservoir. Twenty miles beyond lay the mountain-hemmed basin of the Middle Fork of the Flathead River, where a slim avenue of bright green split the spruce forest. This was the primitive landing strip at Schafer Meadows, from which the Forest Service supplied trail crews and firefighters working in the wild country that stretched in all directions. Approaching the airstrip, John Craighead gazed intently at the surrounding meadows, where at least fifteen elk were browsing the lush forage. As a professor of wildlife biology at the University of Montana, he was used to making census flights to survey big game herds, but today's count was performed more out of habit: this flight marked the start of a week's exciting vacation. A second plane soon landed, carrying his friends Clifton Merritt of Kalispell and Dr. J. Frederick Bell of Hamilton. Together they unloaded a small mountain of gear and hauled it five hundred yards to the banks of the Middle Fork. For the next six days the men would have their hands on oars and ropes as they guided their two rafts down Montana's wildest stretch of river.[1]

"Fritz" Bell worked at the U.S. Public Health Service's Rocky Mountain Laboratory, where he conducted research in infectious diseases. He would be Craighead's bow man while Clif Merritt soloed in the other raft. Craighead and Merritt had made the descent the previous year with local fishing legend Dallas

Eklund, during which they had encountered difficulties among the river's many boulders and cliffs. The stream was even lower this summer, and soon after launching, Craighead's overladen raft was scraping bottom. The pursuit of wild trout, not the thrill of running rapids, had drawn them to this remote locality, but Craighead's experience on many of the world's great rivers would come in handy. He and his companions found both adventure and trout in abundance on the Middle Fork—a river that, like too many others in the Northern Rockies, faced its own uncertain future.

During their first afternoon Craighead and Merritt kept busy maneuvering their rafts around rocks, but after making camp Clif walked downstream to a deep pool below a rapid where he caught a three-pound Dolly Varden, as the Flathead River's native bull trout (actually a char) was known. Craighead soon joined him and landed a ten-pounder, which they filleted and salted for later use. In all they caught eighteen fish before dinner, including the Middle Fork's native black-spotted cutthroat trout, a strain that had not been genetically contaminated by downstream populations. Most of these they tagged and released, hoping to demonstrate that this was a migratory population that returned to Flathead Lake after spawning in the gravel beds of the upper Middle Fork.

The "cutts" gave plentiful sport throughout their float trip, with as many as sixty attacking the anglers' flies each day. The men kept a few twelve-ounce fish for meals as well as a sampling of three- to five-pound Dolly Varden, while several larger specimens avoided their creels. The superb fishing on this little-traveled river compensated for the rocks and rapids that in places gave them serious trouble. On the second day Craighead asked Bell to walk one difficult stretch to lighten the unwieldy raft, but even so he broke an oar on a rock. Later that day they encountered a section where the river dropped thirty feet over the space of several hundred yards. The current propelled their boat onto a rock, where it tipped and quickly filled with water. Merritt, following in the second raft, pulled over and waited.

Craighead was an experienced whitewater man and with his twin brother, Frank, had recently written a survival manual for the U.S. Navy. Their situation was not life threatening, but with the raft pinned to the rock and their gear starting to take off downriver, he knew he had to act quickly. He and Bell unloaded gear bags onto the rock, then attempted to open the flap valves to deflate the raft. These were held shut under the water's pressure. Finally Craighead took out his knife and slashed the main compartments, whereupon they pulled the sorry-looking carcass to shore. Bell helped Merritt portage the second raft while Craighead repaired the incisions. They pulled into camp that afternoon drenched and near exhaustion. Craighead wrote in his log that "a hot bourbon and some hot soup gave us new strength and we soon felt much better."

No further mishaps befell them, but they pulled over each afternoon tired and soaked from the unrelenting rapids. "Water getting deeper and rougher," Craighead wrote at the end of their fourth day. The fishing remained superb, though, yielding as many as a dozen in a quarter hour of casting. They saw a black bear cross the river and observed beaver, harlequin ducks, and mergansers navigating the waters. Storms threatened, but at the end of their fifth day a brilliant double rainbow framed a magnificent sunset. All three men enjoyed wilderness travel, and Merritt, an avid horseman and hiker, had spent much of his free time trying to organize support for protecting the unbroken forests of the Swan Range and the upper Flathead. The river's wilderness setting accounted for its outstanding fishing. Logging had not yet damaged the river's headwaters, nor was there some gigantic human-made obstacle in its path.

That could easily change, as Craighead and his companions knew. At 3:30 in the afternoon of July 20, after spying a dozen big Dolly Varden in a deep pool, they reached Spruce Park at the head of a narrow gorge. Here, in just a few years, there might stand an earthfill dam 350 feet high against which the rushing waters of the Middle Fork would pile up and grow still. A tunnel would shoot pressurized water from the 11-mile-long reservoir clear through the mountain rampart to the west, supplying a projected power plant on the bank of Hungry Horse Reservoir in the adjacent South Fork drainage. The Spruce Park project, which the Bureau of Reclamation and local boosters touted as an alternative to the unpopular Glacier View Dam, was not nearly as large as Hungry Horse, but it would irrevocably alter the Middle Fork's downstream hydrology and pose a barrier for migratory cutthroat and bull trout. The dam would not flood the Bob Marshall Wilderness, but many sportsmen considered the Middle Fork country its natural extension. Besides flooding bottomland habitat, the project would open up the rest of the Middle Fork region to further development, which posed a significant risk to the elk, grizzly bear, and mountain goat that flourished in this unprotected drainage.

All this was on Craighead's mind as he contemplated the fierce whitewater and somber spruce forests of the Middle Fork. Why not recognize wild rivers as a resource in themselves? On the previous year's trip he had proposed to Clif Merritt that Congress enact a law to protect the great wild rivers of the West. Elaborating on this idea in a letter to Ken Baldwin, Craighead proposed to inventory and classify the recreational potential of free-flowing streams, much as Bob Marshall had tried to classify wilderness and recreation areas to facilitate planning. Rivers such as the Middle Fork that ran through roadless wild regions would be called "wild," while others that had road access would be considered "semi-wild." Streams that had been channelized, diverted, or dammed might be listed as "semi-exploited" or "exploited." He believed that it was time for conservationists to "sharpen our wilderness objectives" and focus attention on the rivers, "the most fragile portion of wilderness country."[2] Twelve years later, his idea would reach fruition in the Wild and Scenic Rivers Act of 1968.

Frank Craighead joined his brother in promoting the wild rivers concept in articles and at scientific conventions. In 1961 he requested of newly appointed Interior Secretary Stewart Udall that "some constructive action be taken in the near future or there will be few, if any wild rivers left in the United States."[3] Although Udall supported dam construction on many western rivers, he grasped the importance of the Craigheads' idea. Under his direction the Bureau of Outdoor Recreation examined all three of the Flathead's upper branches as part of a nationwide study of free-flowing rivers.[4] These would eventually be protected from dams and impoundments under the 1968 act, but there were hurdles in the way. Forest Service chief Ed Cliff informed Lee Metcalf in 1962 that his agency would not oppose the Spruce Park project so long as it did not flood its airstrip and administrative site at Schafer Meadows. He also opposed a study of the upper Middle Fork as a wild river, calling such a move "impracticable as long as the Bureau of Reclamation is planning a major reservoir on it."[5] Ed Cliff's predecessors had adamantly opposed dams that threatened to flood portions of the Bob Marshall Wilderness and Selway-Bitterroot Primitive Area, but Spruce Park lay outside any protected area. With the Forest Service rapidly extending roads from Highway 2 toward the Middle Fork, he foresaw no conflict with the project. Instead, he offered to maintain the river canyon in its primitive condition "until or unless a dam is built."

The U.S. Fish and Wildlife Service, another Interior Department agency, objected to the Spruce Park Dam in a letter to the Bureau of Reclamation. The dam would flood "one of the few remaining natural spawning areas for cutthroat and Dolly Varden trout," an official from its Portland, Oregon, office stated, as well as entail the loss of winter range for mule deer and elk. Road access for the project, furthermore, "would contribute materially to the decimation of the last major grizzly bear population in the United States."[6] The strong objections from wildlife interests led the Army Corps of Engineers in 1961 to terminate its engineering studies for the Spruce Park Dam, although the Bureau of Reclamation continued to seek its authorization.[7]

Then, in June 1964, nature intervened. Heavy rains in western Montana soaked the spring snowpack and sent rivers on both sides of the Continental Divide into sudden flood. The Middle Fork tore out part of Highway 2 and the Great Northern rail line, washed away homes farther downstream, and caused $28 million in damage in Flathead County. East of the divide the Sun River overtopped Gibson Dam, while farther north several smaller dams collapsed, killing twenty-eight people. The disaster led to immediate calls for additional flood control measures, and the Department of the Interior reactivated its studies of both the Spruce Park and Sun Butte dam sites. Lee Metcalf, now Montana's junior senator, requested the Public Works Committee to "provide any reasonable appropriation necessary" for the Army Corps of Engineers to review water storage projects in the Flathead and Clark Fork drainages "with a view to achieving maximum water use benefits."[8]

As a friend to the conservation movement, Metcalf found himself in the middle of another unwanted dispute over dams. Reclamation commissioner Floyd Dominy pointedly reminded him that summer that the flood discharge at Columbia Falls would have been 40 percent higher without the storage in Hungry Horse Reservoir. Spruce Park was the most attractive reservoir site on the Middle Fork, although Dominy acknowledged it would lead to "significant losses for migratory fish." This point was amplified by Bob Sykes of the Montana Wildlife Federation, who told Metcalf that "the tributaries and the Lake are one complete integrated unit in so far as our trout fishery is concerned. The tributaries are the spawning areas, the Lake is the Mother Body for the continued life cycle of the trout, and the establishment of their growth." Spruce Park Reservoir would offer relatively little in the way of flood storage, he added.[9]

Metcalf's sympathies remained with the reclamationists. In a reply to Dominy, he took note of the $9 million in direct damages from the 1964 flood on the Flathead and Sun Rivers and added that its "full impact" was "unmeasurable either in dollars or personal grief." Some means must be found, he said, "to eliminate forever the periodic menace to life and property" from these unharnessed rivers. He assured a West Glacier rancher who had lost cattle and buildings to the flood that he was working with Representative Arnold Olsen to obtain funding for new dams. Preservation advocates were showing considerable political muscle, however. "I went through a fight with the conservation people when I was in the House over the Colorado River Project and Echo Park," he told his constituent. "They are able to marshal support from all over America. This does not mean that your congressional delegation is not going to try to get you some relief. But it will take time."[10]

National groups such as the Sierra Club and Wilderness Society could indeed bring pressure on western legislators. Many of Metcalf's constituents, however, favored reclamation projects such as Spruce Park and Sun Butte. Opposition to the Glacier View Dam led Metcalf to mute his support for that project, but he remained wedded to a dam on the Sun River. Following the 1964 floods he pressed the Montana Wilderness Association, then six years old, to endorse a flood control dam somewhere in the upper Sun River basin. John Montagne, the group's president and a professor of earth sciences at Montana State College in Bozeman, believed that sites farther downstream would prove more efficient at capturing floodwaters. Through his university connections he brought in two professional engineers to buttress his case. They reported that of sixteen major floods in the Sun drainage since 1864, only two—the recent 1964 disaster and one in 1916—appeared to have originated from storms in the upper drainage. Based on historical storm patterns, Montagne claimed that an upper-basin reservoir would "materially reduce a Great Falls flood not more than 25 percent of the time." An alternative plan devised by the Bureau of Reclamation in 1956, consisting of canals and laterals that would divert some Sun River water to the Teton drainage, would be "fully capable of supplying the needs of irrigation development" in that drainage without the Sun Butte project.[11]

Building a solid case against the upper basin dam helped bolster concerns about wilderness and big game habitat. After the Cascade County soil conservation district came out against the upper Sun dam sites, Brit Englund, Metcalf's press secretary, advised him to shift his support to a site forty miles farther downstream. He noted that conservationists had "whipped up" so much opposition to the Sun Butte project that it had become "a dirty word." The upper-basin project even drew the opposition of Governor Tim Babcock, Metcalf's opponent in the coming senatorial election, who Englund suspected was looking for a campaign issue.[12] The opposition to the dam, while vocal, hardly represented a significant portion of the electorate; Metcalf learned from an opinion poll he commissioned during the 1966 election that that only one in five Montana voters listed conservation, including the development of water resources, as a serious concern. Conservation ran roughly equal in his poll with civil rights, although Metcalf, a long-standing Progressive, took such issues seriously.[13]

Metcalf continued to work with the preservation and wildlife groups in cases that did not directly oppose reclamation and public-power interests in his state. In March 1965 he cosponsored Idaho senator Frank Church's bill to establish a national wild rivers system—the first legislative attempt to enact John Craighead's river classification and protection scheme. Metcalf assured the president of the Upper Flathead Valley Flood Control Association that the bill did not include the Flathead River, leaving room for Glacier View, Spruce Park, and the Paradise or Knowles Dams on the lower part of the river.[14] But as opposition continued to mount to any new impoundments on the Flathead River, Metcalf agreed to a provision in the final wild and scenic rivers bill, enacted in 1968, which provided for a study of its upper forks. The Forest Service conducted the study of the three forks and in 1973 issued a report recommending that their upper reaches be classified as wild rivers—reversing chief Cliff's earlier stand.[15]

Preservationists defeated the Bureau of Reclamation at Echo Park in Utah largely because of a nationwide outpouring of concern for scenic beauty and the sanctity of the national park system. Glacier View was derailed partly for the same reasons, whereas the Sun Butte and Penny Cliffs Dams came under fire in part because they would inundate designated wilderness or primitive areas. Concern for wildlife habitat featured strongly in all of these controversies, however. In his memoirs, Clif Merritt recalled trying to convince the fisheries supervisor of the Montana Fish and Game Department that the Dolly Varden, or bull trout, made long spawning runs from Flathead Lake up the Middle Fork to gravel beds in the river's pristine headwaters. The supervisor argued that the fish likely moved no more than a mile or so up and down the stream, based on what his biologists had found in other rivers such as the Madison, one of Montana's most highly prized trout streams. Merritt pointed out that the Middle Fork had a steeper gradient and its runoff flushed out the river bottom each spring and summer, allowing for much less aquatic life than in the gently graded Madison, where trout could forage happily all year long within a limited area.

Merritt urged the department's fisheries biologists to do a simple tag study by placing a fish trap in the Middle Fork below the Spruce Park dam site. There the biologists tagged and released a small number of bull trout. "A month later, in October [Merritt wrote], a sportsman caught one of the tagged bull trout at the southern end of Flathead Lake and reported it. . . . The fish had traveled at least 80 miles." More returns confirmed this finding, and the Fish and Game Department changed its position to one of strong opposition to the dam.[16]

Merritt would not forget the lesson. It took more than claims of great beauty and outstanding recreation to halt development projects and gain support for wilderness proposals; science must be brought to bear as well. Equally important, such experiences helped him understand the complex workings of a riverine ecosystem. He was not a trained biologist, but he quickly grasped the central concepts of what became known, many years later, as conservation biology. Fish such as the Dolly Varden were confined to flowing water of a certain temperature and clarity. Place a dam in their way—even one supplied with a fish ladder—and the ancient link between spawning bed and feeding ground was broken. The principle applied as well to the elk and grizzlies that roamed the Middle Fork country.

John Craighead's wild river concept was a start toward protecting this ecosystem, but Merritt wanted to significantly broaden the protected area around the Middle Fork. The Forest Service was pushing a road up the adjacent South Fork from Spotted Bear toward the Bob Marshall Wilderness boundary. Other roads were being built south from Highway 2 into the Middle Fork drainage, and Flathead Forest supervisor F. J. Neitzling confirmed that his ultimate goal was to extend these as far as Schafer Meadows.[17] In May 1964 Merritt proposed to Craighead that they seek a designated "wild area" taking in much of the Middle Fork drainage, which he noted was "at least 60 percent true wilderness-type country."[18] Later he expanded this into a proposed 170,000-acre "Flathead Wilderness Area" encompassing part of the upper South Fork as well. This became the basis for later conservationist proposals linking the Bob Marshall to protected lands in Glacier National Park. The germ of an idea was taking hold in Merritt's mind: that the fate of grizzly bears, mountain goats, and wild trout in Montana depended on preserving more than isolated recreation areas among the high peaks. The entire headwaters of major rivers such as the Flathead must be set aside, along with all the unroaded country they subtended. This approach would guide his work for decades and help give rise to a new approach to protecting wilderness—one that tried to recognize whole ecosystems instead of remnant parts.

9

Full Use and Development
Timber and the De Facto Wildlands, 1956–1963

When Charles Tebbe assumed command of the Northern Region from P. D. Hanson in November 1956, he inherited a timber program that was in danger of outrunning demand. The region's national forests were offering 1.1 billion board feet of timber annually to purchasers in Idaho and Montana—more than three times the amount at the close of World War II.[1] Spruce was saturating the market in western Montana, yet salvage sales alone could not form the basis for a long-term forest management program. Millions of acres of remote, unexploited timber, chiefly smaller-diameter lodgepole pine, were still subject to high mortality from fire, insects, and disease, so Tebbe turned to his timber staffers, Axel Lindh of the timber management branch and John Castles of the operations branch, to devise a bold new program to help modernize the region's timber industry and begin to tap this underutilized resource. By encouraging mills to adapt their equipment to handle smaller trees and capture more wood waste for manufacture into specialized construction products such as particleboard, their agency could extend harvesting operations far into the backcountry. Their report, titled *Full Use and Development of Montana's Timber Resources*, was presented to the state's congressional delegation on the last day of 1958. It signaled the transformation of western Montana's de facto wilderness into a working forest, placing wood fiber production ahead of the traditional activities enjoyed by hunters, anglers, and trail users.

In prefacing the *Full Use* report, Tebbe announced that the burgeoning nationwide need for specialized wood-fiber products "augurs well for those sections of the country with large reserves of virgin timber."[2] Backcountry timber stands "need to be harvested and brought under management," Tebbe said. To do this Lindh and Castles sought to institute a program of *extensive* as well as *intensive* timber management throughout the national forests in the western part of Region 1. They singled out Montana's lofty, isolated Big Hole Valley for particular mention: surrounded by a million acres of lodgepole pine belonging to the Beaverhead National Forest, and for a century home to large ranches that drew on the forest for irrigation water, fence posts, and barn poles, the valley now needed a full timber development program, according to their report. Fifteen million board feet of timber and much additional salvage material could be harvested annually from this high-elevation basin, but first a network of timber haul roads and a railroad for long-haul shipment would have to be constructed. Local mills were too small and inefficient to utilize all this timber.[3]

Extensive timber management would by no means be confined to the Beaverhead's high-elevation pineries. On the adjacent Gallatin National Forest lay vast stands of lodgepole pine that could supply stud mills in the Bozeman area as well as cordwood for a prospective pulp mill. The latter would use materials from forest thinnings to enhance growth in managed stands. The anticipated growth increment would then be captured in higher allowable cuts. Similar efforts would be undertaken all across western Montana and northern Idaho. The *Full Use and Development* report was predicated on the need to efficiently manage forest stands, not on any current demand for timber in such a sparsely populated area. "The timber is here, good and plenty of it," the report stated, "but it is not moving satisfactorily. Great areas and volumes of it are not moving at all."[4] This represented an unconscionable waste of the productive potential of the state's timberlands.

The access road network needed to develop these remote mountain basins would far surpass the region's existing (and haphazardly planned) system. Tebbe's staff laid out long-range plans for some thirteen thousand miles of new timber haul roads within the national forests of Idaho and Montana, some of which could be built by timber purchasers using credits against stumpage prices, but most needing federal dollars appropriated by Congress.[5] The *Full Use and Development* report envisioned a forest development program as ambitious as any river-basin scheme put forth by the Corps of Engineers or Bureau of Reclamation. Its publication marked a decisive break with the agency's past. Improving forest productivity was now the goal, not just maintaining existing sawmills through a desultory and market-dependent timber sale program. This required that much greater acreage be put into production. What the *Full Use* report did not say was that in order for this to happen, there could be no substantial expansion of protected wilderness lands within Region 1.

Montana's congressional delegation was already on record in support of expanding the Northern Region's timber program and had been meeting with Charles Tebbe and his staff to expedite the *Full Use* program. Lee Metcalf, notwithstanding his conservationist credentials, regarded timber development as an integral part of the overall multiple-use program. The national forests were "'use' forests, not preserves," he stated at a field hearing held in Missoula in 1957 on forest development matters. Speaking on behalf of the entire delegation, he noted that Montana's national forests were harvesting only two-thirds of the 900 million board feet of timber they could potentially supply. Many backcountry timber stands were being "preyed upon by insects and disease" and were "threatened by the ravages of fire because they are inaccessible," he said.[6] In 1959, with Tebbe's report in hand, Metcalf urged the House Appropriations Committee to approve a $13 million line item for this purpose. He presented the request as a jobs issue, telling the committee that "in view of the drastic unemployment in Montana and other western states it is of the utmost importance that the maximum amount of road money be available to the Forest Service."[7]

The *Full Use* report generated little public controversy, but the Montana Outfitters and Guides Association was concerned that the road network needed to supply the new mills would displace its traditional use of the backcountry. Shortly after the report was released, Ovando outfitter Tom Edwards, a member of the association, sent a heartfelt letter to Lee Metcalf explaining his concerns. "You turn our Montana mountains into a maze of industrial development feeding sawmills, plywood factories and pulp mill plants with access roads going east, west, and crooked and you will be going a long way toward destroying the second largest industry in Montana," he wrote. Guides and outfitters, he said, "make our living selling living tree resources to the tourist as surely as the lumberman makes this dollar by cutting down the tree and selling boards." Edwards understood that Montana must develop its timber resources, but "please," he pleaded with Metcalf, "don't do it at the expense of strangling another industry."[8]

Metcalf replied that the Northern Region was undertaking a study of recreation needs and that "in this program, recreation will have the place it merits." In 1955 he had sponsored legislation to fund national forest recreation programs through a percentage of the agency's gross receipts, similar to how reforestation and timber stand improvement were handled. It did not pass, and the agency's recreation expenditures continued to lag behind its timber-related programs.[9] But to Edwards, the problem was not the lack of funds; it was the Northern Region's emphasis on developed recreation in conjunction with logging and road-building programs. He offered his guests a far different experience than could be provided in drive-up campgrounds. He tried to explain this distinction in a talk he gave to forestry professionals in Missoula in 1959, shortly after the *Full Use* report was released. "Perhaps the biggest conflict between recreationists and the forestry [service] is this building of roads. We know the road kills the primitive value of an area. We feel this poses a constant threat to the solitude idea—and to millions of Americans the value of our forests for recreational purposes is lost when the road comes in."[10]

A 1960 survey of users of the Bob Marshall Wilderness backed up Edwards's assertions. Lawrence Merriam, a forestry professor at the University of Montana, found that clients taking guided trips in the area desired an experience closer to nature (and farther from crowds) than was possible in developed parts of the forest. Out-of-state visitors to the wilderness tended to be highly educated, Merriam found, and when asked about a hypothetical extension of roads and timber cutting into the area, they expressed overwhelming disapproval. Most summertime visitors felt it was "very important to get away from the sounds, sights, and smells of civilization," he reported, and even a majority of those who came during the hunting season gave as their uppermost reason the desire to "observe the beauties of nature."[11] Tom Edwards's erudite, nature-focused approach meshed well with this clientele—but his goals would soon run headlong into the Northern Region's contrasting vision for the wildlands surrounding the "Bob."

The *Full Use* program comported with policy coming from the agency's Washington office as presented in the 1958 *Timber Resources Review*, the latest in the Forest Service's periodic surveys of national timber needs and development goals. Chief Richard McArdle noted that it called for "an intensity of forest practices that will startle us."[12] The Montana study also anticipated, and in some ways served as a template for, a service-wide program called Operation Multiple Use. Unveiled in 1960, it called for increased congressional appropriations for all phases of national forest management, including timber, recreation, wildlife, and environmental protection. Historian Paul Hirt demonstrated in his book *A Conspiracy of Optimism* that while Operation Multiple Use was intended to restore balance to these programs, Congress continued to funnel money mostly to timber, since it generated the most Treasury revenues. Instead of reducing allowable cuts to match the pace of reforestation—just one example where the timber program had outrun basic land protection and restoration measures—the Forest Service instead increased cutting levels still further. By 2000 the agency anticipated more than doubling the nation's 150,000-mile network of timber haul roads, primarily in the Northwest and Northern Rockies. The consequences for forest soils and biota, as Hirt noted, would be "incalculable."[13]

The expanding road system would also "spell multiple tragedy for millions of hikers, family campers, and sportsmen," according to David Brower, the Sierra Club's executive director, who was turning his attention to forestry issues after having successfully challenged the Bureau of Reclamation's proposed dams within Dinosaur National Monument. Shortly after Operation Multiple Use was announced, he complained to Olaus Murie that the fifty-five million acres of roadless lands that L. F. Kneipp identified in his 1926 survey of the national forests had shrunk to a mere seventeen million acres. "That's *38 million acres* gone in the short time you and I, just two mortal conservationists, have been interested in the cause. More than two thirds of what we had as boys!"[14] A further eight million acres would be lost under the road-building program envisioned in Operation Multiple Use, Brower said. "The Forest Service refuses to give the public a voice" in these decisions, he told Murie. "We just can't get through the Sawdust Curtain."

Brower's challenge to the Bureau of Reclamation's benefit-cost calculations during the Dinosaur campaign had attracted national attention, but conservationists also needed to challenge the Forest Service's assumed expertise in matters of forest policy, he told his colleague. "I rebel at the pervasiveness of Management," he said. "One trouble is that the managers have corralled all the experts; leaving no one on the outside, free of professional conflict, to tell the managers when to restrain their compulsion to manage."

The managerial paradigm that Brower and Murie objected to was a product of Democratic and Republican administrations alike. The New Deal's activist government agencies, run by presumed experts in their fields, merged seamlessly with the Eisenhower administration's program of promoting extractive industry. The western states' congressional delegations were united in support of these programs. Idaho's Frank Church, a liberal Democrat, responded to Brower's critique of Operation Multiple Use by pointing out that mortality stole seven hundred million board feet of Idaho timber annually. "We need to push roads into the *commercial* forest areas rapidly," he insisted. Unless this were done, he believed that "the very thing we seek to preserve—the present wilderness system of our forests" would be in jeopardy.[15] As he stated in a Senate report on the wilderness bill, "The Wilderness Preservation System can be established without affecting the economic arrangements of communities, states or business enterprises since the areas are already withdrawn. . . . There will be no withdrawal of lands from the tax base of counties or communities, no withdrawal of timberlands on which lumbering operations depend, nor any withdrawal of present grazing or mining rights."[16]

These were the terms under which Senators Church and Metcalf offered their support for the Wilderness Act. Their strategic agreement with Brower and Zahniser envisioned a wilderness system encompassing no more than about 2 percent of the nation's land area, leaving prime timberlands to be managed intensively for maximum wood fiber production. It would include the Forest Service's existing wilderness and wild areas along with most of the primitive areas, with the possibility of expanding the latter to include some of their surrounding wildlands. Outside these areas, there was no expectation that the wilderness bill would provide blanket protection for roadless lands on the national forests. The bill must not threaten timber supplies—on this everyone agreed. At a hearing on federal timber sales policy held in Redding, California, in 1955, one year before Hubert Humphrey introduced the first version of the wilderness bill, Brower made it clear that conservationists were not talking about reserving the entire national forest system from development. "I hope you understand the distinction," he emphasized. "The vast area of national forests . . . we think should be cropped, used for tree farms, sustained yield." Only the fourteen million acres designated as wilderness and wild areas at the time—a "tiny piece" that was "relatively insignificant," he said—would be set off limits to timbering. And the merchantable timber within those areas constituted "a very small part of a small part"—on most of the wilderness lands there were, in fact, "probably more rocks than trees." Brower acknowledged that he would not want to preclude the possibility of including some additional areas outside the current system of wilderness and wild areas, but he gave the representatives the distinct impression that these would be few in size and number.[17]

Howard Zahniser made similar comments to a conference of agency and timber industry officials in 1961, as the final version of the Wilderness Act was taking shape. He noted that less than 7 percent of national forest land was then preserved as wilderness, wild, or primitive areas—some 14.8 million acres by his reckoning—whereas on the remaining 93 percent of the national forests "we can obtain the forest products we need and on these lands enjoy the forest recreation with roads and other conveniences."[18] Under this tacit agreement, legislators from timber-rich states could support the wilderness bill, which was facing an uncertain future in Congress. By this time, however, Brower was coming to realize that much more undeveloped land was at stake in the national forests and that the rush to control forest mortality would spell the end for many of these areas. In 1960 he advised the Sierra Club's board of directors that the nearly four hundred thousand miles of new forest roads planned by the year 2000 under Operation Multiple Use "would be initiated and completed solely on administrative discretion, without opportunity for public hearing. . . . This is a small sample of the enormous threat posed to the nation's as-yet undeveloped wilderness."[19]

These were early warnings of a developing storm that would transform wilderness politics in the West. The genteel discussions that Brower, Zahniser, and others were having with their allies in Congress would broaden into a raging battle involving the entire western timber industry. The preservation movement's national leadership maintained that proposed land withdrawals under the Wilderness Act posed little or no threat to timber supplies or wood-processing jobs, but in the Northern Rockies, the extensive forest management envisioned in the *Full Use* report was at complete variance with this assumption. One of the most significant clashes over national forest wildlands was already brewing in the upper Blackfoot River drainage, where Northern Region officials were at work on a plan to construct a major road network in the undeveloped backcountry south of the Bob Marshall Wilderness. In reacting to this plan, Tom Edwards and a handful of concerned residents in the town of Lincoln were about to initiate one of the key battles of the modern wilderness movement. The precedent they set would help determine the future of millions of acres of national forest throughout the Northern Rockies and propel a little-noticed Montana senator to the forefront of the preservation movement.

10

The Storekeeper and the Kleinschmidt Hoss
The Lincoln Back Country, 1957–1964

In the summer of 1957 a University of Montana forestry student named Arnold Elser took a job at the White Tail Ranch, Tom Edwards's outfitting operation located at the edge of the Helena National Forest northeast of Ovando, Montana. Behind the ranch's rustic log buildings rose a forested ridge flanking the North Fork of the Blackfoot River, along which ran a well-used trail leading through miles of undeveloped forestland into the Bob Marshall Wilderness. Elser had left his home in Ohio three years earlier to find work in just this kind of country— either as a forest ranger (as he hoped to be one day) or as a wrangler for an outfit such as the White Tail. Edwards was willing to take a chance on the young student, especially after he offered to try out for a couple of weeks at no pay. His job was to supply and run the backcountry kitchen, but Edwards first put him to work moving a fence—an unusual task in an area where property lines had been settled decades ago. The Forest Service wanted to make use of an old right-of-way that came up from Kleinschmidt Flat and ran along the western edge of the 160-acre ranch. The following summer saw the construction of a 32-foot-wide road, graded and crowned to accommodate heavy traffic. It led into the adjacent national forest and ended at a substantial concrete bridge across the North Fork. Progress, it appeared, had arrived in the upper Blackfoot.[1]

Elser recalls that one evening Edwards's business partner, Howard Copenhaver, suggested that the three of them go have a look at the new bridge. There they discovered a four-by-eight-foot plywood sign announcing the "Lincoln Back Country Scenic Highway" and bearing the Forest Service's logo along with a schematic map depicting how motorists soon would be able to drive through the mountains and come out at the town of Lincoln, fifteen miles to the southeast. "This would be terrible," Copenhaver announced to his companions. Edwards agreed: he had been watching the Forest Service push new roads into the South and Middle Forks of the Flathead River, getting closer each year to the northern boundary of the Bob Marshall Wilderness. Now the country south of the wilderness, a magnificent portal through which he had taken horse parties for two decades, was about to be opened to log haulers and Sunday drivers.

Tom Edwards was perhaps the most highly educated outfitter in the "Bob," having received his MFA from the University of Illinois with further graduate studies at Stanford. He founded the White Tail Ranch in 1938, when he and his family lived in Cerro Gordo, Illinois, where he served as superintendent of schools. Having grown up on a dryland homestead outside of Choteau, Edwards longed to return to the Montana he remembered, and in 1944 he and his first wife, Eila, brought their family to Helena, where he taught art and biology at Helena High School. Summers found them at the White Tail, adding cabins and corrals when not guiding parties into the wilderness. In 1955, following Eila's death, Tom retired from teaching and with his second wife, Helen, moved to the ranch to live full time, building it into one of the premier guest ranches in the region.

Wiry and small in stature, Edwards hardly fit the image of a rugged western outfitter. Yet his enthusiasm for the woods and meadows of the upper Blackfoot was contagious, and he built a loyal clientele ranging from upper-crust easterners to school groups and excited teenagers. He affected a corny western idiom in the annual newsletters he and Helen sent to their guests each year, filling its pages with humorous drawings of life on the trail and paeans to the beauty of the outdoors. He sometimes described himself as "just an old Kleinschmidt hoss," referring to the broad prairie at the edge of his ranch, but most everyone knew him as Hobnail Tom, a sensitive and genial artist and student of nature who could bring the wilderness alive for his guests. Lawrence Merriam, who made a study of horse users in the Bob Marshall Wilderness, recalled that Edwards's interest in natural history stood out among his fellow outfitters.[2]

Besides trying to make their operation pay, Edwards was growing concerned about changes that were rumored to be coming to the national forests ringing the Bob Marshall. The planned scenic highway up the North Fork would intrude on the long approach valleys he and his wranglers regularly used on their trips into the wilderness. This landscape, known locally as the Back Country, contained its own delights. From the vantage point of Red Mountain, located a dozen miles north of Lincoln, the twin forks of the upper Blackfoot reached around the peak in a huge embrace to meet at a low divide above Parker and Webb Lakes. Farther north rose the limestone ramparts of the Continental Divide, atop which the alpine bulk of Scapegoat Mountain exerted a mysterious pull.

To Duncan Moir, supervisor of the Helena National Forest during the 1940s and 1950s, Scapegoat Mountain overlooked the grandest country of all. A friend of Edwards, Moir knew the Lincoln Back Country as a superb horse packing destination. He sometimes took business and civic leaders from Helena into the area to promote it as a so-called protection forest—a concept that still had some credence within the agency.[3] State fish and game officials, too, wanted to maintain the area's superb hunting opportunities and, in solidarity with the outfitters, passed a resolution requesting the Forest Service to keep the area in "trail access" status. Edwards went a step further; in late 1954 he wrote to Montana representative Lee Metcalf to request that the Lincoln Back Country and adjacent lands in the North Fork drainage be added to the Bob Marshall Wilderness—particularly the lofty Scapegoat Mountain area, which served as a scenic highlight for many of his pack trips. "Our interest in the preservation of our back country far exceeds our business interests believe me," he told Metcalf. Edwards also made the request to regional forester P. D. Hanson, but no action was forthcoming.[4]

Edwards was occasionally asked to speak on recreation topics at Forest Service meetings, which gave him an opportunity to promote wilderness travel as a viable economic activity on a par with timber and livestock grazing. In his notes for a talk he gave in 1959, he pointed to the "esthetic value, intangible and difficult to describe, that you can harvest at this very moment as truly as the timber." He was careful to distinguish this resource from hunting and fishing, although many of his clients enjoyed these activities. This was, rather, "a Something hard to define but no less real—a delicate fragile something that does exist in the Back Country. It is as definite as the sacred hush of a great cathedral—and this is a recreational forest resource that millions of Americans feel the need for today." He would go on to call this quality "the hush of the land," an amalgam (it seemed) of the stillness of a forest-rimmed meadow at dusk and the whispered sounds of the wilderness. By following the measured pace of a horse, it was possible to immerse oneself in this stillness; it could be enjoyed in company, but perhaps most easily in solitude.[5] Edwards claimed that three-fourths of his income came from the "sale" of this esthetic value, which could be found only in the absence of motors and car traffic. "The disturbing thing to me," he told the foresters, "is that with the grazing fee or the timber sale you can see the shekels roll in but in the sale of the recreation resource you are removed."[6]

His words seemed not to strike a chord with the Northern Region's staff, who were not about to halt their resource development programs to accommodate an outfitter's need for solitude. The Forest Service saw important values in its wilderness areas, certainly, but new policies and new personnel mandated a different approach. In 1958 supervisor Moir retired and was replaced by Vern Hamre, whom one observer described as "ambitious" and a "comer." The Northern Region was moving beyond the protection forest concept, and building up a timber program was considered the surest route to advancement.[7] Hamre had his staff draw up a new management plan that placed thousands of square miles of forest within the cutting circles. An allowable harvest of some twenty million board feet per year was planned, which would permit the entire working circle to be cut over within seventy-five years. Ed Barry, the region's staff officer in charge of recreation and wilderness, viewed timber roads as an asset to recreationists as well. As noted in the new timber plan, the roads contemplated for the Lincoln Back Country would give greater access for hunters and fishermen, which was "one of the essential phases of good game management."[8] The new road up the North Fork of the Blackfoot was a portent of major changes in the Back Country.

Arnold Elser, who gained the nickname "Smoke" from summer jobs fighting fires, worked for the White Tail Ranch for six years before acquiring an outfitting business of his own. He recalls that around 1960 Tom Edwards invited the owner of the general store at Lincoln, a young North Carolinian named Cecil Garland, to come over for Sunday dinner and discuss the changes that were coming to the mountains north of their homes. Garland supplemented his income by working for the Lincoln Ranger District as a construction foreman, supervising the building of campgrounds and other improvements. A conservative Republican who held a deep mistrust of the federal government, Garland was not shy in voicing complaints about bureaucratic inefficiencies. The new timbering plan met with his strenuous disapproval as well. What it meant for the Back Country was clearly depicted on a map he obtained, which displayed dozens of roads reaching into nearly every valley. Garland likened the map to a plate of wet spaghetti tossed against a wall. Yet from his experience cruising timber on the Lincoln District, he knew the Douglas-fir, lodgepole pine, and subalpine fir found in those remote drainages could never sustain the volume of timber harvest his bosses anticipated. In one sale area he had cruised for the agency, he found not the projected ten million board feet but something closer to three—"if," he said, "you built a road to every tree." Garland recalled that the owner of a local logging company came to him with tears in his eyes upon discovering the poor quality of timber he had just bid on. "The Forest Service is swapping the nation's timber for a system of dirt roads," Garland stated in a protest to supervisor Hamre.[9]

Garland and a retired Texas oilman named William Meyger, who owned a cabin near town, founded the Lincoln Back Country Protective Association in 1960 to fight the Forest Service development plans. The following year Garland left the agency in what was clearly a mutually agreeable decision. He assumed leadership of the association following Meyger's death in 1962 and proved to be an articulate and charismatic spokesman. That January he spoke with Vic Reinemer, Lee Metcalf's top aide in Washington, about the Lincoln Back Country and received a cordial response, but no commitment of action. A long letter to regional forester Boyd Rasmussen brought the response that with "some of the state's finest scenery, mountains, lakes and rivers" already included in wilderness areas, "there must be some limitation on how much wilderness is set aside in relation to other demands for land use."[10] Garland was unwilling to accept the agency's assurances of the benefits coming from its logging and road-building program. "There was at the time," Garland recalled a few years later, "a great arrogance with[in] the U.S. Forest Service. It was as though they were all-knowing, even omnipotent. That their word was sacrosanct and the mistakes that they were about to make were not apparent to them. Clear cutting was just beginning and on every forest you could see huge patches of timber being removed as though some great force had ripped it off like patches of hide had been skinned off a living thing." In challenging the cult of expertise that was commonplace in federal resource agencies, he helped carve out a new role for the concerned local citizen as critic as well as beneficiary of forest management policy.[11]

In March 1963 the Lincoln Back Country's transition from protection forest to working timbershed became official when Vern Hamre released an ambitious proposal for recreation and timber development in the northern half of the Lincoln Ranger District, an area comprising some seventy-five thousand acres and most of the Back Country area. The plan called for an annual timber harvest of 4.5 million board feet, to be hauled out on a new road system extending up the Landers Fork past Heart and Webb Lakes and continuing down into the North Fork of the Blackfoot River, where it would tie in with the recently developed road coming up from Kleinschmidt Flat. A second road would branch off to follow the upper Landers Fork over the Continental Divide and into the Dearborn River drainage, creating another loop drive. Spur roads—Garland's "wet spaghetti"—branched off these main lines, some going to campgrounds and fishing access sites to provide "family-type recreation opportunities adapted to the physical and financial abilities of most families," the plan stated. Outfitters and backpackers would be shunted to the proposed 19,000-acre Red Mountain Scenic Area and the adjacent high country, where a new trail system would "provide a semi-wilderness experience for those wishing a one- or two-day hike or horseback trip."[12]

As in Bunker Creek a decade earlier, the plan failed to draw the expected accolades from hunters, anglers, and car campers. Instead there came the most serious public outcry the Northern Region had experienced to date, orchestrated by individuals with strong ties to the status quo. Tom Edwards, Cecil Garland, Clif Merritt, and many other outfitters, hunters, and hikers who had long used the Lincoln Back Country would not be satisfied with a "semi-wilderness experience" of a few days' duration. To them, roads and clear-cuts spelled the end of a mountain region where wind, birdsong, and bugling elk formed the audible background. Garland tried to express this feeling of impending loss in letters to the nation's chief wilderness advocates. "It seems that everywhere you look out here in our country, there are forces eating away at what few miles of true wilderness we have left," he wrote to Howard Zahniser shortly after Hamre's plan was released. He suggested to the Sierra Club's David Brower that "there seems to be something more behind this drive to open this area now than the Forest Service is admitting publicly. It seems to be a sort of test. They know that if they can beat down public opposition here, they can do it most anywhere else in the West."[13]

A few weeks after announcing the new plan, district ranger Bert Morris invited discussion at a meeting of the Lincoln Lions Club. Garland and representatives of several western Montana sportsmen's groups showed up to voice their complaints. Hamre afterward told Boyd Rasmussen to expect "a deluge of letters" opposing the development plan.[14] More than clear-cuts alone, the prospect of high-standard recreation roads leading everywhere in the Back Country seemed to arouse the greatest ire. Garland heard from a general contractor from Billings who had built the original secondary highway through Lincoln in 1939 and had recently resurfaced a long stretch of it. "I do not want to see another foot of road built in the Lincoln area if we ever expect to have any kind of decent fishing in that country," he wrote.[15]

The Forest Service, however, was working on a tight schedule. Garland learned that a bulldozer was parked at the end of the Copper Creek road northeast of town and the operator was waiting for the go-ahead to blade the first road into the area. A local logger told him, "I'll be in Heart Lake in ten days and I won't have to walk to get there." A Forest Service road engineer took Garland aside in his store and said that instead of performing a full survey in advance of construction, he had been ordered to simply flag the route with tape in order to expedite the project. Garland wondered where he could turn for help. A phone call to Arnold Olsen's office in Butte was met with a stone wall, he recalled. Governor Tim Babcock refused to get involved. Republican James Battin had just been elected to Montana's eastern district House seat, and out of "sheer desperation," Garland recalls, he pleaded with him to help. Battin was sympathetic and phoned Boyd Rasmussen; after some argument, the regional forester agreed to halt the bulldozer for ten days. Battin also asked his Montana field representative, Lou Aleksich, to look into the controversy; Garland arranged for Gene Youdarian, a local outfitter, to take him into the Back Country that summer.[16]

At Garland's request, supervisor Hamre scheduled an open meeting in Lincoln on April 19 to air the issue. Garland made sure his friends among western Montana's sporting and conservation organizations were there. Some three hundred people attended, many favoring some form of protection for the Lincoln Back Country. Once again Forest Service officials appeared to be taken aback by the vociferousness of the opposition, which they blamed on Garland's antigovernment attitude. Boyd Rasmussen opposed what he termed the "indiscriminate or patchwork 'setting aside' of undeveloped land," which would decrease allowable cuts and inhibit the coordinated management of the whole forested region.[17] Yet as Garland observed years later, "People all over were becoming alarmed at this new ugly way to log and at the enormous waste associated with it. Yet the U.S.F.S. could not see the 'fire coming over the mountain.'"[18]

As it had in the upper Selway River controversy, the Montana Wilderness Association offered measured support to the local activists. Following the meeting in Lincoln, John Craighead, the group's vice president, wrote to Boyd Rasmussen to ask that the development plans be reconsidered. "We do not advocate that this area be set aside as wilderness," he assured the regional forester, "nor, on the other hand, do we support a full scale development program." He recognized the need to harvest timber from the district as well as provide "mass and family type recreation areas," yet he favored leaving the area north of Red Mountain in its present condition for backcountry recreation and watershed protection. The Montana Wildlife Federation also stopped shy of recommending wilderness for the Lincoln Back Country. Its director, Leland Schoonover of Polson, requested that the area north of Red Mountain "be left in its primitive state as much as possible and remain as much of a roadless area as it is now."[19] He and his fellow leaders believed that a cautious approach stood the best chance of changing minds in the Forest Service.

Garland may have realized that his cause was only as strong as his friends in the MWA and MWF were willing to espouse. Instead of pressing for wilderness designation, he requested a ten-year delay of any logging and road building in the Lincoln Back Country. Timber sales could proceed farther downstream in the Landers Fork drainage, he said, which would release more than one hundred million board feet to sustain the local mill. The rest of the area would remain in reserve, "with a view to eventual logging" if demand existed. It was "imperative," he said, that nothing "upset Lincoln's already too-unstable economy at this time."[20]

Hamre would not agree to abandon his plan at this early juncture, but in June 1963 he and Boyd Rasmussen came up with a modified plan that would terminate the planned road up the Landers Fork near the mouth of Middle Fork Creek, some four miles short of the Continental Divide. An additional road coming up the East Fork of the Blackfoot would be halted one mile west of Webb Lake for the time being.[21] Clif Merritt, who was familiar with the Lincoln Back Country from boyhood trips with his grandfather and his twin brother, Don, advised his fellow leaders in the MWF that the compromise was "a hollow victory" intended only to "stop some of the hollering and allow the Forest Service to get the road started through the back-country, so that it can no longer be considered or fought for as wilderness." He believed that the area was "true wilderness-type land that should be given some appropriate designation to preserve it as much as possible in its natural condition."[22] Merritt assured Cecil Garland that "you have more support than you perhaps realize" and said he would "do all I can for a cause that is just."

Tom Edwards took a less public stance on the issue, instead using his connections to help finance Garland's committee and draw in influential friends. George Weisel, John Craighead's colleague in the University of Montana's biology department, had ridden with Edwards and brought his expertise to the controversy as president of the Western Montana Fish and Game Association, a local MWF affiliate. In July 1963 he joined fellow activist Don Aldrich for a five-day pack trip into the area with Gene Youdarian. In a subsequent report to Forest Service chief Ed Cliff, they noted that logging and road construction would degrade the area's fragile streams. The area was hunted to near capacity, they reported, and while new clear-cuts might produce more forage for elk, any possible gains "would be offset by the probable alteration of natural migration routes and ensuing winter game range problems." The proposed road bisecting the area would increase hunting pressure and bring thousands of new visitors to Heart Lake and Meadow Creek, which they noted were already suffering trampled shorelines.[23]

Weisel, Aldrich, and Craighead sought an agreement that would maintain the status quo in the Lincoln Back Country without the controversy that wilderness designation would bring. But the national conservation lobby was also taking an interest in the area, and Stewart Brandborg, Howard Zahniser's assistant at the Wilderness Society, brought a political perspective to the issue. He asked Craighead to take a close look at what was happening in other states such as Oregon, where the Forest Service was vigorously pushing timber roads into lands removed from the recently reclassified Three Sisters and Eagle Cap Primitive Areas.[24] Forest Service administrators had "wide latitude and discretionary power" over some seven million acres of unclassified and unprotected wildlands, Brandborg noted. This was one of the first times that a national conservation leader acknowledged the unfinished work of preserving what would come to be known as "de facto wilderness"—a concern that would intensify even after the Wilderness Act passed.

Supervisor Hamre and regional forester Rasmussen undoubtedly believed they were representing a broad public interest in proposing to build a road past Heart Lake and on over the Continental Divide, lining it with attractive campgrounds and trailside hitching racks. That this road would also help remove timber was another public good, expressed in local payrolls and shipments of processed studs to railheads in Missoula or Great Falls. Neither Hamre nor Rasmussen reckoned with the passionate sense of ownership that a handful of users of the Lincoln Back Country expressed in the spring of 1963. Cecil Garland had left his native North Carolina while still a young man, in dismay over the pollution of waterways, erosion of farmland, and the pervasive loss of open space. He recalled later how towns like Deerfield and Trout Creek were named after creatures long vanished from the surrounding hills. Before moving with his family to Lincoln he had worked as a casino employee in Las Vegas, sampling the polar opposite to rural life. His dissatisfaction with the more flamboyant manifestations of American culture may have primed him for a stirring encounter with the wild in the land north of Lincoln. At a Senate field hearing held in 1968 to consider the fate of the Lincoln Back Country, Garland expressed the wonder he had experienced on his first pack trip to the country below Red Mountain.

We camped that first night on a small bench above Ringeye Falls. Taking down our tent from an old frame that the pack rats had been using as a home, we made a secure camp, cooked our supper, fed our stock, and then turned our complete thoughts to our whereabouts. We took from our duffle an old reed elk bugle and as the chill air fell with the sun we shattered the calm of that September evening with a blast . . . above us on Red Mountain a bull elk bugled his challenge that this was his territory and over on the Webb Lake Hill another bull called back that this was his home. All through the frosty air the calls echoed back and forth and I knew that I had found wilderness. I would not sleep that night for I was trying to convince myself that this was really so; that there really was wild country like this left and that somehow I had found it.[25]

Tom Edwards expressed similar sentiments about the landscape he had been visiting for the past quarter century. As he revealed in a letter to George Weisel, "I feel almost alone with my deep inner feeling for the majesty of the eternal mountains." He was impelled to "cry out in my puny attempt to block the reckless rush for progress in its ruthless crushing and defiling of the haunts of the hermit thrush and water ouzel and forever slamming a discordant note into the music of the Wilderness." He acknowledged that this amounted to a religion with him, but he objected to how the "builders of civilizations and empires" looked down on such "long-haired Thoreaus" as he.[26]

Edwards was not as alone as he feared; many of his guests shared a deep love for the wilderness and were willing to help. Soon letters were arriving in congressional mailboxes from across the country, protesting the development of this obscure mountain stronghold. After Lou Aleksich made a favorable report to James Battin, the representative assured Stewart Brandborg that the agency's development plan "would serve no useful purpose even from a lumber point of view. You may, therefore, be assured of my opposition to this project." Mike Mansfield received so many letters on the subject that he asked his legislative aide, Teddy Roe, to interrupt a Montana field visit and interview Edwards and Garland about the issue. Roe found Garland to be something of a know-it-all, but he advised his boss that a serious dispute was brewing that involved many members of the local community.[27]

Cecil Garland's arguments appealed to the independent, antigovernment streak found among many rural Montanans, whereas Tom Edwards's clientele included many out-of-state residents who valued Montana's mountains for the contrast they offered to city life. The participation of fish and game groups from Missoula, Helena, and Great Falls broadened the campaign's appeal among hunters and anglers. The diverse support from ordinary Montanans made it easier for politicians such as Mike Mansfield to enter the fray. Lee Metcalf, however, still had close ties to the Forest Service and was not eager to jump into a direct confrontation with the agency. He informed Garland in June 1963 that he was "inclined to believe that there is considerable merit in the compromise proposal" for protecting only the northernmost part of the Lincoln Back Country. He requested a meeting with associate Forest Service chief Art Greeley to air the issue. Mansfield, who was less conspicuously allied with the Forest Service, dispatched an aide to the meeting with instructions to demand a postponement of the road-building plans. Greeley assured the senators that no action would be taken until Boyd Rasmussen visited the area in July.[28]

Rasmussen, however, was determined to resist this unaccustomed challenge to his agency's expertise and autonomy. That October he issued a five-page decision that affirmed the original development plan for the north half of the Lincoln Ranger District, along with the phased-in road development he had offered as a compromise that summer. In his view, enough land had been reserved as wilderness or national parks in the Northern Rockies to meet the need for primitive recreation. Without the 4.5-million-board-foot harvest from the Lincoln Back Country, the local sawmill with its 115 employees could be in jeopardy.[29] But to those affiliated with Garland's group, the language of timber-working circles and site productivity took a backseat to concerns over resource damage and the loss of cherished solitude. They suspected that agency planners were marching ahead more out of bureaucratic momentum than from any identifiable need. They now had the ear of the Montana congressional delegation, and in November 1963 Mike Mansfield asked the chairman of the Senate Agriculture and Forestry Committee to hold field hearings on the Forest Service's plan, which he said "has stirred a bitter controversy which has lasted for months and shows no signs of abating."[30] The committee was not yet ready to travel to the Montana wilds to investigate a Forest Service development plan, but the strong interest Congress was taking in the issue foretold difficulty for the agency.

Boyd Rasmussen's 1963 statement was his last on the Lincoln Back Country controversy; that fall he was promoted to an assistant chief position in the agency's Washington office. Vern Hamre, too, transferred to Washington and in 1970 became the head of the Intermountain Region in Ogden, Utah. His replacement, Bob Morgan, arrived in late 1963 from the same office. He was not a stranger to Montana, however, and while working on the Flathead National Forest he had helped Clif Merritt draw the boundaries for the proposed Jewel Basin Hiking Area. After taking some trail rides into the Lincoln Back Country, he cautiously raised a red flag about rushing ahead with the development program and sought to open a dialogue with the sportsmen and wilderness groups.

Arguments over strategy threatened to divide the Back Country enthusiasts, however. George Weisel drafted a resolution calling on the Forest Service to delay timber sales in the area for ten years and manage it as a roadless recreation area. He advised Cecil Garland that this approach would avoid the controversy of wilderness designation, for which "Smokey would have a lot of arguments against."[31] Clif Merritt had little enthusiasm for Weisel's proposal, which would involve building footbridges, shelters, toilets, and similar facilities to aid hikers and horse users. "To me this position is absolutely untenable," he told fellow activist Loren Kreck. "It is either wilderness and should be so classified—or it isn't and should receive multiple-use treatment."[32] Garland seemed to waver between Weisel's development moratorium and Merritt's more aggressive approach. The key players decided to talk things over in Lincoln on February 22, 1964, when winter still held its grip on the frigid valley of the upper Blackfoot.

Representatives of six sportsmen's groups from as far away as Butte and Great Falls attended, as did Frank Dunkle and Bob Cooney of the state fish and game department. Supervisor Morgan was present in his self-appointed role as the agency's moderate facilitator. Merritt reported afterward to Stewart Brandborg that Morgan would not go along with the proposed ten-year delay and that the issue was one of either preserving the area as a wilderness or proceeding with development.[33] Morgan's words seemed to galvanize the attendees, who realized that their only remaining option was to seek a wilderness or wild area designation for the Lincoln Back Country. But how large an area? The Cascade Sportsmen's group from Great Falls wanted to include the headwaters of the Dearborn River on the far side of Scapegoat Mountain, while some of the Missoula sportsmen wanted to take in the headwaters of the North Fork of the Blackfoot River on the Lolo National Forest. Garland's original notion of administratively protecting a 75,000-acre roadless area in the northernmost part of the Lincoln Ranger District had suddenly more than trebled in size, to 240,000 acres of national forest land. By resisting the proffered compromise, the Forest Service now faced a national political battle over this once hidden landscape.

The conservationists' new proposal emboldened advocates within the MWA, MWF, and Garland's Lincoln Back Country Protective Association. Howard Zahniser and Stewart Brandborg favored the expansive new approach and asked

Merritt to pin down its boundaries for prospective legislation.[34] These advocates, like those in Gallatin Canyon years earlier, were riding into unfamiliar territory: with the Wilderness Act yet to pass, no formal process existed for the Forest Service to consider citizen-nominated wilderness proposals. One option was to seek an expansion of the Bob Marshall Wilderness southward to include Scapegoat Mountain, with a separate wild area designation for the Blackfoot River country. Merritt favored this approach and asked Brandborg to make a field visit that summer to ascertain boundaries. Brandy, however, was occupied with the final legislative maneuvers needed to pass the Wilderness Act. Tom Edwards and Cecil Garland's dream of protecting the wild country south of the "Bob" needed a unifying voice, and most important, someone in Congress who was willing to carry legislation that would take the game out of the Forest Service's hands.

11

Rumblings along the
Magruder Road
The Battle for "Area E," 1962–1967

Of the seven primitive areas awaiting reclassification in the Northern Rockies during the early 1960s, preservation interests were most anxious to hear word of the Selway-Bitterroot, which at 1,875,000 acres was the largest protected landscape in the national forest system. At Forest Service hearings held in March 1961 they focused their criticism on the agency's proposal to exclude 310,000 acres from the so-called Area E in the Magruder Corridor—the connecting link between the main Bitterroot Range and the Salmon River country to the south. On December 28, 1962, after nearly two years of internal debate, regional forester Boyd Rasmussen released a proposal for a 1,239,840-acre Selway-Bitterroot Wilderness, with an additional 216,870 acres in the rugged breaks of the Salmon River to be retained in primitive area status pending a study of the adjacent Idaho Primitive Area.[1] Area E, comprising much of the headwaters of the Selway River, was to be opened to timber development under the plan. Chief forester Richard McArdle transmitted Rasmussen's recommendation unchanged to Secretary of Agriculture Orville Freeman, who signed it in January 1963. Writing in *Living Wilderness* following Freeman's announcement, George Marshall characterized the proposal as wilderness "splinterization," which he said had been going on for several generations "despite the growing realization that the preservation of a considerable number of large tracts of wilderness in their natural state is essential to American life and culture."

Little controversy attended the reclassification of the Cabinet Mountains and Anaconda-Pintlar Primitive Areas, both of which were expanded slightly when the chief of the Forest Service announced their designation in the early 1960s under administrative regulations.[2] The dismemberment of the Selway-Bitterroot, on the other hand, met with sharp disapproval from preservationists. Sigurd Olson, Marshall's colleague on the Wilderness Society's governing council, met privately with Secretary Freeman following his Selway decision and came away believing that Area E would be studied further before any road or timber development occurred. But Boyd Rasmussen and his local forest supervisor, Harold Andersen, had already arranged for timber inventories in Area E and were turning the efficient machinery of the agency's timber management branch toward full utilization of the pine, fir, and spruce growing on benchlands above the Selway River. Helicopters were requisitioned, aerial photos taken, and Abney levels and increment borers unsheathed in an effort to utilize what Andersen called "a 182,000 acre multiple use management area." He promised to submit a full development plan to Rasmussen by February 5, 1963—less than one month after Freeman's decision.[3]

Wilderness supporters were especially angry that they had so little say with Freeman, a New Frontier Democrat who they hoped would usher in a renewed period of conservation activism. Former Bitterroot National Forest supervisor G. M. Brandborg complained to Arnold Olsen, Montana's western district representative, that the agency's approach "casts aside all semblance of democratic processes" and showed the urgency of passing the Wilderness Act, which would leave the final decisions on establishing new wilderness areas to Congress. The Montana Wilderness Association and Flathead Wildlife Association lodged similar protests with Olsen and with Lee Metcalf, Montana's junior senator, but no help was forthcoming.[4]

Secretary Freeman, in fact, was responding to the clearly stated position of Democratic Party leaders in the western states. In March 1962 Lee Metcalf sent Freeman an eight-page letter calling for an immediate policy review to determine whether allowable cuts on the western national forests could be increased still further. The Forest Service, Metcalf said, needed to increase its road building, reforestation, and timber stand improvement activities in order to "market the optimum amount of timber consistent with sustained yield."[5] Sales might need to be modified in places to protect scenic and recreation values, but Metcalf implied that this could be done as part of normal multiple-use planning. He was reiterating what regional forester Charles Tebbe had spoken of when he had met with Metcalf and the rest of the Montana congressional delegation in 1958 to outline the "Full Use and Development" timber program. Tebbe had made it clear at that time that timber management would be extended into the headwaters of the Flathead, Blackfoot, Clearwater, and Selway Rivers—areas that many outdoor enthusiasts considered to be natural candidates for wilderness designation. In seeking to protect such areas, the preservation lobby would expend considerable effort trying to pry Metcalf out of the Forest Service's arms.

Freeman was happy to oblige the senator; no new policies were needed to boost the Forest Service's timber program, only more dollars from Congress. He assured Metcalf that allowable cuts were on the rise and noted that "special attention should be given to setting forest development road authorizations at substantially higher levels than now prevail"—bureaucratese for more road money.[6] His approval of a circumscribed Selway-Bitterroot Wilderness Area, limited mostly to high peaks and sparsely timbered ridges, comported with the doctrine of extensive timber management that held sway at all levels of government, including Congress.

The signs of impending timber development showed up along the Magruder Road in August 1963, when a Forest Service engineering crew flagged a new road location in the Deep Creek drainage. G. M. Brandborg heard about the project from his contacts in the agency and began calling his friends. Tom Ford, a member of the Ravalli County Fish and Wildlife Association, protested to Lee Metcalf, who as a courtesy asked chief forester Ed Cliff to look into the matter. He was told that "it was not the Secretary's intention in establishing a boundary for the Selway-Bitterroot Wilderness Area to provide for the same type of management outside the boundary as inside."[7] This curt response served to extinguish any action from Metcalf that year.

The preservation groups gained unexpected help from a Hamilton, Montana, couple who had been vacationing in the upper Selway for the past dozen years. Doris and Kelsey Milner had moved from New Orleans to the Bitterroot Valley in 1951 after Kelsey received his doctorate in microbiology at Tulane. He obtained a research position at the Rocky Mountain Laboratory, a Public Health Service facility originally set up to investigate the tick-borne spotted fever endemic to the eastern Bitterroot Range. For Doris, the move was a return to the country life she had known during her farm upbringing in Maryland. She would eventually gain statewide recognition as an outspoken preservationist, one of a relatively new variety that did not have a connection to wealth, a university, or an elite upbringing.

While camping at a favorite spot along the Selway River in the late summer of 1964, the Milners heard the growl of a bulldozer firing up before dawn.

They returned home wondering what was in store for the personal paradise they assumed would always remain unchanged. Doris alerted G. M. Brandborg, who already knew that a major development plan was in the works. When Clif Merritt, newly hired by the Wilderness Society, stopped by the Brandborg home in Hamilton to offer his services, Brandy was ready. Merritt recalled how this "big, powerful Swede . . . had a hand on him about twice my size and plopped it on my shoulder. 'What can you do for us? Well, you can protect the upper Selway.'" Merritt pointed out that the national conservation organizations had failed to stop the deletion of Area E in 1961 and now it was up to local activists. They could start by organizing an ad hoc committee to halt the logging in Area E. There followed a minute's pause, Merritt recalled. "'All right, we'll do her,'" Brandborg said.[8]

Brandy saw the makings of a leader in Doris Milner, and under his prodding she agreed to chair a "Save the Upper Selway Committee." She posted letters to the heads of every conservation and wildlife group in Idaho and Montana, warning that impending road construction and logging in the Magruder Corridor would "begin the processes of erosion, silting, and pollution that will turn the unequalled clear and beautiful Selway River into another ugly product of man's greed, stupidity, and shortsightedness." Stewart Brandborg came up with money to print a brochure, written by Milner, which called for a stay of development in Area E.[9] Soon the Northern Region's leadership realized that they had a second wilderness battle on their hands, led by another determined Montanan who refused to give in to the inevitability of progress.

The strong opposition to the agency's logging plans made an impression on incoming regional forester Neal Rahm, who had served as associate deputy chief in Washington and was well versed in the political nature of resource decision making. Rahm was simultaneously dealing with the blowup over the Lincoln Back Country and would hardly have wanted to deal with a second crisis. In the fall of 1964 he drove over Nez Perce Pass on the Magruder Road with members of his staff to confer on-site with Harold Andersen and his associates, who agreed to delay any timber sales in Area E for several years. Rahm okayed the initial road work, however, and in September Andersen let a $350,000 contract to realign and improve a 6.5-mile segment on the Montana side of Nez Perce Pass. Eventually the entire route would be widened and oiled to permit log truck travel.[10] The Milners had witnessed the road builders' vanguard; soon most of the upper Selway would hear the bellow and clank of bulldozers at work.

Stewart Brandborg's contacts in the nation's capital gave Milner's committee an inside track to the Montana and Idaho congressional delegations. Arnold

Olsen was the first to offer help. In February 1965 he asked Secretary Freeman to delay the logging plans, but without a unified voice from Montana or support from Idaho's delegation, he made little headway. Such inquiries were routinely referred back to the agency for reply; Ed Cliff told Olsen that "Mrs. Milner presents no new factual information that has not been reviewed in previous correspondence with you about this situation."[11]

Kelsey Milner took issue with both the necessity and the expense of the Magruder Road project. The segment currently under contract, he stated in a letter to Mike Mansfield, amounted to an entirely new road along a new grade. Costs would mount correspondingly with its continuation into Idaho. He doubted that the total value of the timber to be harvested in Area E would pay for all the needed roads and maintained that such roads should not be entered on the ledger as benefiting recreation. He cited an example from the South Fork of the Skalkaho Creek drainage east of Hamilton, where a road that had been built up Weasel Creek "destroyed my old hunting camp site, took away the livelihood of one of the better-known outfitters and guides of our community, and permanently scarred a beautiful high mountain ridge that formerly abounded with game." Milner preferred to leave the Magruder route unimproved as a "picturesque mountain road."[12]

Supervisor Andersen tried to reassure conservationists that development would not ruin the upper Selway. He said that Area E fit into a multiple-use framework that would yield benefits for many users—an approach the agency promoted throughout the controversies of the 1960s. Reconstructing the Magruder Road, he told Idaho activist Mort Brigham, was necessary for public safety and the enjoyment of recreationists. "The existing road was built in the 1930's by the CCC's. It has grades of 20 percent and is narrow and crooked. Each year there are a number of accidents and near misses. . . . As this road is reconstructed, it will become increasingly important as a recreation route." He did not mention that the road improvements were required for logging trucks as well. As for concerns about stream damage—Brigham's perennial worry—Andersen noted that his multiple-use plan contained a mile-wide riverbreak zone along the Selway in which special consideration would be given to streamside values. The logging would provide "some urgently needed forage for the declining elk herd in the area. Big game forage has decreased in the old burns in this area due to natural plant succession."[13]

Stewart Brandborg talked up the Magruder Corridor at the North American Wildlife and Natural Resources Conference in Washington, D.C., in the spring of 1965, which several of his old friends from Idaho, including Frank Cullen and

Ernie Day of the Idaho Wildlife Federation, also attended. Afterward Brandy told Doris Milner to undertake an "all-out campaign" to alert their friends in Idaho and press Senators Frank Church and Len Jordan to intercede with Secretary Freeman. Mort Brigham and Boise attorney Bruce Bowler lined up resolutions of support from the IWF, whose leaders had been split on whether Area E merited full wilderness status. Bowler's wife, Beth, had raised funds for Church's election campaigns and obtained assurances of his support at a meeting in March 1965. Church took the step of adding the upper reach of the Selway to his bill establishing a Wild and Scenic River system, which also included stretches of the Salmon and Clearwater Rivers.[14] This designation extended only one quarter mile on either side of the stream and gave no protection to the benchlands that were slated for logging.

Idaho conservationists made less use of the Magruder Corridor than Montanans, who would have their work cut out to get Church to take on an issue that materially affected his state's powerful timber industry. Milner faced similar difficulties rounding up support within Montana conservation circles; incoming MWA president John Montagne confided to Clif Merritt that he was not familiar with Area E and disliked having to fight the Forest Service on what seemed like a technical forestry issue.[15] Without a united front from conservationists in both states, there was little chance of their representatives or senators intervening.

The eight-year campaign for the Wilderness Act was nearing its culmination in May 1964 when conservationists learned of the death of the bill's chief architect, Howard Zahniser, of a heart attack. His loss followed that of Olaus Murie, who had passed away the previous October after a lengthy illness. The Wilderness Society council appointed Stewart Brandborg as its new executive director, who in turn recruited Mardy Murie to informally carry on some of Olaus's outreach work, hoping this would help assuage her grief over losing her life's companion. She gave freely of her time, and their Jackson Hole home became a pilgrimage stop for many young conservationists and wildlife biologists. She also appeared on behalf of the Wilderness Society at numerous public hearings and during the 1970s took part in some of the society's volunteer training workshops, helping inspire a new generation of activists.

Zahniser had been working with Brandborg to augment their small staff with effective grassroots organizers. Clif Merritt, who had helped stave off the Bunker Creek timber sale in 1954 and was closely involved with the Lincoln Back Country issue, approached Zahniser in early 1964 about working for the Wilderness Society in some kind of field position. "We shall be very fortunate to have you as one of us," Zahniser wrote in March 1964, two months before his death. That June, Merritt resigned from the Montana Employment Service to begin work under Brandborg in the Wilderness Society's Washington headquarters.[16] Two years later Brandy hired Ernie Dickerman, a Tennessee native, to head the society's outreach campaigns in the East. Merritt preferred to live in the West and several years later opened the society's first field office in Denver. His primary job was to turn out supporters at local hearings on primitive area reclassification, but he continued to take a close interest in de facto wildlands in Idaho and his native Montana.

The Wilderness Society's strategy was to establish a firm precedent of legislative oversight for Forest Service decisions regarding such areas. For decades the agency's leaders believed themselves to be the most qualified and knowledgeable arbiters of land-use allocations on the national forests. Their rangers and field staff dealt on a daily basis with the intricacies of forest administration, from initial resource inventories to timber sales and road construction standards. When it came to leaving lands unmanaged, however, Forest Service attitudes meshed closely with those of its constituency of resource users. The result was an unyielding knot that Brandy was determined to untie. As he told Doris Milner partway into the Selway battle, "I don't know whether you, Don [Aldrich], Morton [Brigham], Bruce [Bowler] and some of the rest realize how much you have accomplished through your effort, but from where we sit we feel that the future outcome of much more than the Selway-Bitterroot issue is involved. Through this issue we can set a pattern for the things that lie just ahead in implementing the Wilderness Act, resolving the Sun Butte dam and Lincoln Back Country controversies as well as some of the challenges to be found in getting a strong Wild Rivers Bill."[17]

Milner, for her part, was acting out of a deep sense of frustration at what she believed to be Forest Service stonewalling. Composing letters to bureaucrats and legislators, telephoning supporters, accompanying reporters on field trips, appearing at public meetings, arranging meetings with news editors and congressional aides—all this took hours out of days in which she also cooked, cleaned house, and kept the children in clothes. The higher-ups in the Forest Service replied to her letters with maddeningly bland assurances that they had considered all the options and were acting in the public's interest. As she told her friend Mavis McKelvey in 1975, "Something hit a nerve, a raw nerve, that said 'you'd gone too far on this.'"[18]

Her sense of humor served as a blowoff valve. In March 1965, tired of writing one temperate and constructive letter after another, she drafted a note to

Ed Cliff that laid out the situation. "You must be about as tired and bored with letters from me as I am from you," she began. "I represent a lot of citizens who wish to keep Area E in protected status. You are the head of a large dept. which has made recommendations to the Secretary and, by the gods, you are going to stay with them, do or die." Cliff had assured her in a previous letter that his agency would limit road development and protect watershed conditions in the Selway, but Milner thought otherwise. "For Heavens sake how stupid and G. D. dumb do you think we are," she exploded. "When you are out with a woman, do you stop with the kissing?" The agency's handiwork throughout the western forests led her to believe that nothing would be left in the Selway once the loggers were done. She challenged him to "show me a case of your delicate touch."[19]

Doris presented the draft to Kelsey, who advised against sending it; after some argument, he phoned G. M. Brandborg to referee. Old Brandy drove up the hill that evening and read the letter in Doris's absence, enjoying a good guffaw with Kelsey over her invective. His opinion of chief Cliff was, if anything, even more cynical, but the game had to be played by the rules. As consolation, Doris sent her thwarted missive to Stewart Brandborg, after adding a purported carbon-copy list that included Mike Mansfield and Orville Freeman. Doris could fight the fight as hard as anyone, but she would not relinquish her quintessentially Irish sense of humor.

Milner's frequent entreaties to Lee Metcalf finally paid off in June 1965 when the senator met with Ed Cliff to discuss the conservationists' concerns. Cliff replied in writing with a defense of his agency's development plans, expressing the hope that "we can get on with the work and the controversies such as the one about 'Area E' do not unduly divert the manpower and budgets away from the mainstream effort needed to get the job done"—a clear reference to the supportive relationship his agency had long enjoyed with Metcalf. But Mort Brigham heard from a sympathetic agency staffer that privately, Cliff had agreed to hold off on development activities in the area for two years.[20] Although Metcalf was far from endorsing wilderness for Area E, a delay in the logging plans would cool tempers without materially affecting the local timber industry. Harvests from the Bitterroot National Forest were at record levels at the time, thanks to new road-building and clear-cutting programs Metcalf and the rest of the Montana congressional delegation had funded.

Bitterroot National Forest officials knew, however, that timber harvests in the readily accessible "front country" could not be sustained without eventually tapping reserves in the Magruder Corridor. To shore up their position they held a two-day field trip in Area E in early August 1965 to show eighteen conservation leaders from Idaho and Montana, including the Milners, G. M. Brandborg, Clif Merritt, Frank Cullen, and Bruce Bowler, how they planned to implement timber harvesting. Magruder district ranger Bob Shackelford told the participants that the development plan would reserve streamside corridors from logging and identify areas of unsuitable soils. Most of the attendees were not mollified. Jim Keating, a fisheries biologist with the Idaho Fish and Game Department, pointed out that his agency was coordinating an expensive long-term project to restore chinook salmon runs in the Selway and that any siltation of spawning beds could retard its success. He cited disastrous erosion in the South Fork of the Salmon River during the winter of 1964–65 as a foretaste of what the upper Selway could suffer if it were logged.[21]

Not all of the fish and game officials saw wilderness preservation as the answer. Ken Reynolds, head of the Idaho Wildlife Federation, wrote to Frank Church following the tour to say that the lands in question were not even especially scenic. He noted that among his companions, which included Idaho Fish and Game director J. R. Woodworth, "it was pretty close to being unanimous that the existing road building would not hurt the area in any way. The facts are that the new road is far from being a paved highway, but it will open up the area to more people with the sense of seeing and using the country." Reynolds believed that "it is a great mistake for citizen conservation groups to put themselves against federal and state agencies when it comes to experience and skills directly related to management."[22] Curiously, Reynolds also told Church of his pleasure at seeing some young chinook salmon in the Selway River during the field trip. He said these were the first to be seen since 1925, the result of an experimental planting of eggs in the lower river. He did not mention, as Mort Brigham had reminded Church in an earlier letter, that the very reason the Selway had been chosen for the salmon reintroduction was its clear water and pristine forest environment.

With the MWA also wavering on the Selway issue, Stewart Brandborg pressed John Montagne to take a firm stand against the logging. "Those who wish to eliminate the Upper Selway wilderness will play on the indecisiveness of any of us, even though our hearts may be in the right place," he advised.[23] Doris Milner and Mort Brigham shared no reservations about rejoining Area E to the adjacent Selway-Bitterroot Wilderness. "We can imagine no sound reason for making great haste to develop this area," they wrote in a joint letter to the two states' congressional delegations. "Development can be initiated at any time, but it can never be undone."[24] They sent copies of their statement to every participant in the annual meetings of the MWA and the Montana and Idaho Wildlife

Federations, hoping to strengthen these groups' commitment to fighting what promised to be a long and difficult battle.

In March 1966 one of G. M. Brandborg's agency contacts showed him a map of planned road locations and timber sales in Area E. Brandy passed it along to Mort Brigham, who traced and returned it. It showed that every bench above the Selway River from the Paradise Guard Station to the Magruder Ranger Station would be subject to logging, as would the entire drainage of the Little Clearwater River and sizable areas to either side of the Magruder Road east of Deep Creek. "I think the Forest Service would like to know where I got hold of that logging map of the Selway," Brigham told Brandy. "I would suggest that you forget what you know."[25]

Brigham circulated the map among conservation leaders, calling it "a blueprint for the destruction of the Selway watershed . . . nearly the whole Magruder corridor is slated for logging, the exceptions being a few mountain tops and some strips along a few of the streams." He drew up a fact sheet under the auspices of his North Idaho Wilderness Committee, which compared the timber volumes and growth potential in Area E with more productive sites in eastern Washington. The Selway, he wrote, could produce "about one-half as much as a good east-side cut, and one-seventh of a good west side cut. In short, it looks really marginal." Drawing on his background as a sawmill designer, Brigham figured that the 12-million-board-foot annual harvest from the upper Selway would supply only about three months of sawlogs for a modern stud mill with one headrig, operating on two shifts. To him such a cut would never compensate for the loss of a treasured wild landscape. "One thing can be said about the buffalo hide hunters," Brigham told Rodger Pegues of the Federation of Western Outdoor Clubs. "At least they got some good hides."[26]

Some of Rahm's field staff seemed to have doubts about the sale program as well. Ranger Shackelford reported to forest supervisor Andersen in early 1967 that two of the three sales planned in the Magruder Corridor would lose money for the government. He described the Kerlee Creek sale as "a very tough chance" owing to "very poor quality timber on steep sidehills." The projected stumpage value of five dollars per thousand board feet covered only $15,000 of the anticipated road cost of $27,500, while the Wilkerson Creek sale was projected to run a deficit of $16,310. A third sale would cover its costs only because a portion of the road construction would be paid for by the government. Shackelford did not recommend withdrawing the sales, but it was an indication of the difficulty of extending full-scale timber harvesting far into the backcountry.[27]

Economics aside, logging opponents fundamentally objected to opening a still-wild region to increased traffic and human activity. Potential losses to fisheries remained a major concern, as Don Aldrich pointed out in a joint meeting of the Montana Wildlife Federation and the Save the Upper Selway Committee in early 1967. "As sportsmen, we are not attempting to put a price on the timber resource, but we do know the value of clean streams enough to provide good trout, steelhead and salmon habitat," he reported afterward. "We have learned [this] by losing most of them."[28]

With the issue at a stalemate, Stewart Brandborg explored the possibility of a blue-ribbon study that might nudge Lee Metcalf off the fence. In early June 1966 he met with Dr. George Selke, a former chancellor of the Montana state university system, to urge him to intervene with Secretary Freeman. Selke was willing to help; when Freeman was governor of Minnesota, Selke had chaired a study committee to examine the management of the Boundary Waters Canoe Area. He brought up the Selway issue at a breakfast meeting with Freeman, who afterward phoned Metcalf and said he was agreeable to a study that would address concerns about "soil fragility, ecological relationships, and effect on down stream fisheries." Freeman meanwhile directed the Forest Service to continue the hold on its development plans.[29]

Selke called on five resource professionals to assist him with the Magruder study. The committee made field visits to the area during the summer of 1966 and held public meetings in Missoula, Grangeville, and Boise in early December.[30] The Save the Upper Selway Committee turned out a strong majority of supporters in the two larger communities.[31] Selke's report, which Freeman released in the spring of 1967, called for a new management plan that would minimize siltation and protect the area's fisheries. Timber harvesting and road building should be deferred pending new resource studies, it said, although the agency could proceed with reconstruction of an eight-mile section of the Magruder Road over Nez Perce Pass. Freeman gave the report his cautious endorsement and directed the Forest Service to maintain the area's "wild land conditions . . . without resorting to special designation or classification."[32]

The Save the Upper Selway Committee had won time, but Milner and her friends understood that a permanent resolution would be achieved only through an act of Congress. Blue-ribbon studies were a useful expedient, but the preservationists would not be satisfied with changing the design of cutting units or extracting promises to log more carefully. They would settle for nothing less than reserving the entire watershed of the upper Selway as a wilderness area, which would require the active assistance of historically protimber congressional delegations. In the mid-1960s timber was still king in western Montana and northern Idaho, although Milner, Brigham, and their allies were working feverishly to show how these forests might provide a wholly different set of values.

12

The Green of Our Forests
The Clearwater Mountains, 1936–1970

In the summer of 1936 Mort Brigham, then a forestry student at the University of Idaho, stood watch at Needle Peak Lookout in the headwaters of the St. Joe River. Virtually the entire drainage had burned in the fires of 1910, leaving little to guard except brushfields and young trees that clung to the slopes. On Surveyors Ridge to the west of his station, the pioneering lodgepole pine stood only ten feet tall. He could see a few pockets of real timber up on the Bitterroot Divide far to the east, while other patches had survived to the south of his lookout in the deep valleys of the St. Joe and upper Clearwater.[1] Other times that summer Brigham manned the lookout on Sawtooth Peak, the westernmost high point of Surveyor's Ridge, which afforded views into the deep valley of the Little North Fork of the Clearwater, where more forest remnants grew. Between these assignments he wielded shovel and mattock on a trail crew under the supervision of Paddy McIntyre, a colorful figure who spent his winters trapping furs and, it is said, never used a tent and practiced only the most cursory forms of personal hygiene. Little matter; in those days the Forest Service wanted men who were comfortable in the backcountry, not in an office chair. Major Kelley's crews had built a main road up the St. Joe River to Red Ives Ranger Station and had bladed truck trails up and over some of the principal ridges, but blowdowns and steep hillsides still limited travel, which is perhaps why a solitude-seeking renegade named William Moreland took up residence in the area in the 1930s, raiding cabins and helping himself to supplies at fire lookouts.[2]

Brigham returned often to this country to fish and hunt, later boasting that he had bagged his elk in twenty-six out of twenty-eight years since the start of World War II. Spike camps in the headwaters of the Selway River also yielded many elk, fattened on ceanothus, red alder, and other shrubs that colonized the scorched Selway timberlands. These animals wintered on south slopes and along the narrow drainage bottoms in the main river valleys and their principal tributaries. It was an elk paradise, a gift of the unruly forces that had blasted away and then restored the lush mantle covering these mountains. It was paradise as well for a young man who found something ineffable in the Clearwater and Selway mountains, and over the next four decades Brigham would try mightily to hold on to the wild country that bred so many elk, moose, trout, and salmon.

The landscape was changing, however, in both its biological patterns and its human uses. Seedlings planted in the years following 1910 became young stands of timber, and although by the 1950s they were still far from maturity, Forest Service crews measured their productive potential and entered calculations in logbooks and on punch cards. These, in turn, were transformed into sustained-yield figures for what the agency called "working circles"—areas of analysis that might contain several ranger districts. Under this system the remaining older trees could be harvested rapidly on the promise of vigorous new growth in sapling- and pole-sized stands. In 1952 regional forester P. D. Hanson told an audience in Sandpoint that once all the forests of the region were made productive—that is, opened up to logging and their old growth removed—they would "provide enough wood to obtain the full measure of benefits that we envision, and the green of our forests will match the gold of our fields forever."[3] No fires would again be allowed to converge in such terrifying fashion, nor would the timber barons be permitted to strip the cover from the land. Under Hanson's watch the national forests of northern Idaho saw a combined timber harvest of 176 million board feet in 1952, but his foresters expected to substantially expand this in the years ahead.[4] Within a decade, harvests from these national forests more than doubled as new methods of clear-cutting, broadcast burning, and replanting replaced selective cutting. Hanson's managed forest began to override the wild paradise that had grown up in the wake of natural catastrophe.

Mort Brigham felt a deeply personal connection to the upper Clearwater and St. Joe, for it was in these woods that he had rehabilitated devastated muscles after an attack of polio when he was nineteen. He developed a sense for the habits of wild creatures and for the forest itself, knowing when to take shelter before a windstorm struck or how to spot a motionless elk in a thick spruce grove. By the mid-1950s, however, he could see how roads were reaching into the remote headwaters of these streams. He began plotting planned road locations and prospective clear-cuts on maps and calling his friends in the Idaho Fish and Game Department to see what could be done.[5] In 1957 he sent a personal plea to Richard McArdle, his former professor at the University of Idaho, who was now midway through a ten-year term as chief of the Forest Service. "We are nearing the day when the only recreational areas we will have will be the public domain, and a modern logging operation leaves much to be desired in the way of recreational resources," Brigham wrote. "If the remaining wild areas are not preserved as such, future generations of young Americans will be driven from wholesome outdoor recreation into the beer halls."[6]

Hunting and fishing could be enjoyed from roads as well as on trails, despite Brigham's stated preference, and road-based recreation figured into a "coordinated resource study" of the upper St. Joe drainage that the Forest Service undertook in 1960. Intended to identify suitable timber development prospects as well as opportunities for improving recreation access, the plan resulted in roads being extended throughout the river's headwaters, including on Surveyor's Ridge and into the deep valley of the North Fork of the Clearwater River. Once completed, this network would nearly encircle the country Brigham had long treasured for its hunting and solitude. Idaho fish and game biologist John Morrison identified the upper Clearwater as supporting "a virtually untouched population of elk" that provided "a high-quality type of hunting, a quality that vanishes wherever the roads penetrate."[7]

In the summer of 1961 Brigham heard that a spur road was to be built from Surveyor's Ridge to Snow Peak, where a resident herd of mountain goats maintained its own watch over the surrounding forests. Brigham sent a letter of protest to forest supervisor Ray Hilding, pointing out that increased human use on this road would jeopardize these denizens of remote crags. Ever since his lookout days, he wrote, "I have returned many times to this fine country and each time my admiration for its scenery and wildlife seems to increase. I have always hoped that a way might be found to prevent such intrusions as would damage these resources."[8] Brigham knew that Stewart Brandborg had conducted studies of the mountain goat in central and northern Idaho and asked him for help. Brandborg had seen goats use steep terrain above the busy Salmon River road, but the small population on Snow Peak was much more vulnerable. Road construction and the human traffic it would bring would doom this herd, he believed.[9] With the Idaho Fish and Game Department also expressing concern, the road plan was dropped and the Snow Peak population became a source for transplants to many other localities in the West.

Successes such as these were few as the Forest Service pushed ahead with its full-development program. By 1969, 726 million board feet of federal timber were being hauled to sawmills in Coeur d'Alene, Lewiston, Sandpoint, Palouse, and Bonners Ferry. For the agency's working-circle plans to succeed, each national forest in Region 1 needed to keep all of its commercial timberland available for harvest. When citizen advocates went to Congress to try to halt logging in the Magruder Corridor, or when they drew up new wilderness proposals for the Lincoln Back Country and the upper Flathead, the agency's foresters were forced to look elsewhere. The headwaters of the Clearwater–St. Joe were a logical place to turn. Once again, however, the foresters would have to reckon with a persistent advocate who claimed a kind of ownership of this rich and evocative landscape.

The wildlands of the North Fork suffered their greatest loss on October 23, 1962, when Congress authorized construction of Bruces Eddy Dam on the North Fork of the Clearwater. Idaho's congressional delegation reached agreement in May 1961 to include the project in an omnibus public works construction bill, with Frank Church announcing that "on balance, the damage to fish and wildlife values would be less consequential than the definite economic gain that would come from completion of the dam." Representative Gracie Pfost, with support from the Kennedy administration, maneuvered the bill through an economy-minded House of Representatives, and when the House-Senate conference committee that reconciled the two measures looked as if it might drop the project, Church threatened a filibuster.[10]

Mort Brigham had spent the better part of a decade fighting the dam and felt the loss acutely. "It was a black day" in their home, Brigham's daughter, Janet, recalled when news came of the dam's final approval.[11] Opponents of the project "failed to document their extreme claims of potential elk damage," according to one newspaper editorial, and "refused to concede that Bruces Eddy planners were working earnestly and well to minimize and compensate for" losses to salmon and steelhead.[12] Ironically, the *Lewiston Morning Tribune* ran an editorial that December praising the removal of the Washington Water Power dam at Lewiston, which in 1927 had decimated the fish runs of the Clearwater. The low numbers of salmonids in the North Fork had permitted boosters of Bruces Eddy to claim that it would have little effect on migrating fish.

One year later, Potlatch Forests president Benton R. Cancell announced that Bruces Eddy would increase log transportation costs in the North Fork drainage, jeopardizing the company's Lewiston operations to the extent that further capital investment "may not be justified." This was a turnabout from the company's earlier support for the project, which was based on the Corps of Engineers maintaining higher water levels and constructing a complex log haul system around the dam. Brigham, who had lost his job at Potlatch owing to his opposition to the dam, hoped that the company's change of heart would prompt Congress to reconsider the dam, but to no avail.[13] Site preparation work for what was renamed Dworshak Dam commenced the following year and in 1966 work began on the dam itself. The long battle to save the partially restored salmonid runs of the North Fork was over.

In a further irony, in March 1965 Church introduced his bill to establish a national system of wild and scenic rivers, which included the main stem of the Clearwater above Kooskia. Although the Wild and Scenic Rivers system eventually grew to include nearly nine hundred miles of Idaho's streams and represented a major step toward curbing the "folly" of unrestricted river-basin development that Winton Weydemeyer had identified in 1948, the North Fork represented the price Church was willing to pay to further water development in northern Idaho.

Both Mort Brigham and Stewart Brandborg resolved to protect what they could of the higher reaches of the North Fork, where there remained a native cutthroat trout fishery as well as significant elk winter range. Clear-cutting and road building were planned throughout this drainage as well as on the Lochsa Face, the steep slopes above the Lochsa River that the Forest Service had removed from the old Selway-Bitterroot Primitive Area. Brigham let his frustration show in a letter to a supporter, whom he advised "not to look at a map showing new roads on their five year plan. It would give you nightmares for a week." Brigham claimed that the Forest Service "has in recent years become an entrenched bureaucracy," and while it had "many dedicated and competent people . . . this kind seems to have less and less to say about policy matters." Conservationists had little recourse, he said, except to appeal to the secretary of agriculture or obtain action from Congress—both of which had led to significant results in the upper Selway. "Nothing else does any good," he complained. "An appeal to their sense of what is right and wrong is like asking a bear to stop eating huckleberries."[14]

There was a wide gulf between activists such as Brigham and supporters of the Forest Service's full-development policy. Keith Thompson, the supervisor of the Clearwater National Forest, told a state forestry association that conservation groups were "violently opposed to building roads of any kind in the forests" and constituted a new "menace to forestry" in northern Idaho.[15] The timber and recreation planners in his agency believed that the 1963 designation of the Selway-Bitterroot Wilderness should have settled the issue of wilderness lands in northern Idaho—yet the conflict merely jumped the river, flaring up in an arguably less scenic set of mountains to the north. They had difficulty recognizing that the conflict over the Clearwater wildlands hinged more on fish and wildlife than on scenery.

In late 1968 Brigham circulated an ambitious proposal for a new wilderness area to encompass the headwaters of the Clearwater River and the slopes below his old fire lookout in the upper St. Joe. By proposing closures for some lesser-used roads and drawing intricate boundaries around existing clear-cut lands, he was able to outline 160,000 acres of undeveloped national forest land stretching from Goat Mountain in the west to Illinois Peak in the east. Complicating matters were some thirty-five sections of land belonging to the Northern Pacific Railway within its boundaries.[16] While his proposed "Upper St. Joe Wilderness" was a tenth the size of the Selway-Bitterroot, it encompassed lush and varied forest stands that were largely unrepresented in the Selway.

The publicity that Mort Brigham almost single-handedly generated in northern Idaho pushed the Forest Service into what was likely a preemptive strike in the spring of 1969. Regional forester Neal Rahm signed off on a new classification for the higher-elevation roadless lands in the headwaters of the Clearwater River. The 30,500-acre Mallard-Larkins Pioneer Area was a collection of minor mountain peaks and attractive subalpine basins on the high divide between the North Fork and Little North Fork of the Clearwater, twenty-five miles southeast of Avery, Idaho. Established under the agency's U-3 regulation, the area would be maintained for nonmotorized recreation, with no timber harvesting allowed.[17] Outside this area, however, lay forested lands that were "exceptionally productive and fully suitable for sustained yield production of wood products," the agency stated. The Mallard-Larkins designation was supported by Outdoors Unlimited, a pro-timber-industry group based in Coeur d'Alene. The group circulated a flier attacking Brigham's St. Joe wilderness proposal as the work of "selfish individuals who have . . . enjoyed this area for their almost exclusive use for many years."[18] By this categorization the timber industry and its supporters hoped to shift the debate away from concerns about big game winter range and siltation of trout streams—issues that had dominated the debate over the upper Selway.

In rebuttal, Mort Brigham pointed out that the main timber haul road in the Little North Fork would run directly through an elk winter range. Here the animals were confined to a narrow canyon, a situation he said had occurred on the

Lochsa River when Highway 12 was built. "Elk are rugged animals that can survive snow depths that would starve a deer," he told Jim Calvert, a professor at the University of Idaho who had recently helped form the Idaho Environmental Council. "They can give a herd of moose rough competition. But they cannot stand to be around people, and when their winter range is occupied by humans part or all of the time in the winter, they pass out of the picture."[19] Instead of logging, Brigham advocated controlled burning as a means of perpetuating winter range and summer foraging areas, a practice he believed should be allowed in wilderness areas.

Field biologists with the Idaho Fish and Game Department shared Brigham's concerns about new roads in winter range and increased access to high mountain streams and lakes. There was a fine balance between the ecological needs of wild creatures and the demands of hunters and anglers who wanted a full creel or game bag. The department usually came down on the side of "quality hunting" and "quality fishing," concepts that eluded precise measurement. Usually this favored a wilderness-based or semiwild experience over that available from the roadside. Brigham applauded this approach and often cited statistics that showed higher hunter success ratios in the deep backcountry. A new road, he said, "chases the [elk] away and makes them harder to sneak up on. They bugle less, and are generally more alert." He observed that the elk harvest in the Lochsa River canyon dropped by one-half the year following construction of Highway 12, and by 1967, five years after the road was opened, the harvest was less than one-third what it had been in 1961. Calving success was down, too, indicating a stressed herd.[20]

Such figures could be read in different ways. Was it better for fewer hunters to enjoy success in the backcountry, when this often favored guided, out-of-state clients? Or should state policy favor local residents who roved the roads in pickups? Brigham had his answer. He told Jim Calvert about Cook Mountain, a favorite area on the Clearwater National Forest that two decades earlier "was a paradise; a large meadow with unlimited grass for pack animals, abundant elk nearby in areas where they were easy to hunt, and no competition from road hunters. It was too good to last, and the Forest Service decided to raise timber instead. A vast road building program has riddled this area."

Not every Idahoan owned a horse and trailer or felt like pursuing game far from roads, and the fish and game managers were acutely aware of who paid their salaries. The same charge of elitism came from some anglers after the department considered closing the Little North Fork of the Clearwater River to fishing in order to ease the pressure on the native cutthroat trout, whose populations had declined after the main North Fork disappeared under Dwor-shak Reservoir. Brigham supported this move and believed that other creeks should be closed as well.[21] It was this kind of uncompromising attitude regard-ing the hunting and fishing experience that led to the charge of selfishness from Outdoors Unlimited and its supporters.

Brigham tried to build interest in his wilderness proposal among sports-men's clubs in small towns around northern Idaho. He reported to Clif Merritt in the spring of 1969 that "our opposition is bitter, but a little at a time we do seem to be making headway." That March the local district of the Idaho Wild-life Federation voted to support his St. Joe wilderness proposal. His measured and factual (if colorfully written) critiques of the Forest Service's road-build-ing and logging program were having an effect. In the fall of 1970 Brock Evans, the newly appointed regional lobbyist for the Sierra Club, addressed a group of Idaho Democrats meeting in Pocatello to raise funds for a promising guber-natorial candidate named Cecil Andrus. It was six months after the first Earth Day, and party activists were hoping to boost environmental protection to a sig-nificant campaign issue. "What's at stake was brought home again to me on my flight to Pocatello today," Evans said. "We flew from Spokane to Lewiston, and off in the distance were the splendid wild forests and mountains of the St. Joe and upper Clearwater River country. It's still there, still wild—200,000 acres of the finest of North Idaho; the last living remnant of the great white pine forest, the superb hunting and fishing. But they're logging there every day, further and further, over our protests."[22]

The protests would continue, even though regional forester Neal Rahm appeared to be more sensitive to environmental concerns than his predecessors had been. He pulled plans for a controversial road up Collins Creek and another that had been laid out along the Little North Fork of the Clearwater. The follow-ing summer Brigham announced to his little band of northern Idaho wilderness supporters that a major timber sale in the Foehl Creek drainage had been called off after Forest Service engineers ran into slopes that appeared ready to slide.[23] He remained concerned for the integrity of this biologically rich mountain land-scape, whose value transcended scenery and recreation. Most hikers and anglers might have been satisfied to visit the high country of the Mallard-Larkins area, but he had witnessed a forest regrow in the upper St. Joe to once again shelter abundant wildlife within its deep valleys and rushing streams. This old-timer could see no tree farm taking its place.

The peaks of the Madison Range frame the scenic Hilgard Basin in this 1939 photo by Forest Service photographer K. D. Swan. Typical of the spectacular high country the agency viewed as suitable for wilderness, the area was not designated until 1983 owing to land ownership conflicts elsewhere in the range. Photograph from USDA Forest Service, Northern Region.

To the north of Hilgard Basin lay the roadless drainage of Jack Creek, a locus of conflict over the disposition of intermingled Northern Pacific Railway timberlands. In 1970 the Big Sky ski and real estate development occupied lands to the left of this photo. Fan Mountain is shown in the center. Photograph taken in 1936 by K. D. Swan; from USDA Forest Service, Northern Region.

Wilderness management in 1957. For a short time the Forest Service employed D-2 Caterpillars to blade access trails for firefighters within the Selway-Bitterroot Primitive Area. Wilderness advocates sought legislative designation of such areas to halt what they regarded as the agency's pursuit of administrative convenience. Photograph of Bear Creek Trail in the Moose Creek Ranger District by A. W. Blackerby; from USDA Forest Service, Northern Region.

View from Surveyors Ridge on the Clearwater National Forest, August 1953. The northern Bitter-root Range burned extensively in 1910, but following World War II Forest Service officials slated much of the area for timber harvest. Photograph by E. C. Slusher; from USDA Forest Service, Northern Region.

Bargamin Creek, a tributary of the Salmon River, in 1938. Controversy erupted here and in the adjacent Selway River drainage in the mid-1960s after the Forest Service announced plans to harvest timber in their headwaters. Preservationists feared logging and road building would damage these rivers' pristine waters. Photograph by K. D. Swan; from USDA Forest Service, Northern Region.

Logging road construction on the Kootenai National Forest, 1960. Conservationists raised concerns about sedimentation from roads such as these. Photograph by I. E. Sanderson; from USDA Forest Service, Northern Region.

J. Neils Lumber Company mill, Libby, Montana, in 1936. Photograph by K. D. Swan; from USDA Forest Service, Northern Region.

Aerial view of the North Fork of the Clearwater River at the site of the proposed Bruces Eddy (later Dworshak) Dam, 1963. Photograph by A. B. Curtis; from Special Collections and Archives, University of Idaho.

Olaus Murie in the Teton Wilderness, 1952. Photo by James Gilligan; from U.S. Fish and Wildlife Service.

Morton Brigham of Lewiston, Idaho, led efforts to set aside wild areas in the upper Clearwater River basin of Idaho. Photograph courtesy of Janet Brigham Rands.

Doris Milner of Hamilton, Montana, on Idaho's Selway River. During the 1960s Milner led a citizen campaign to protect the upper Selway drainage and went on to become one of the state's most effective wilderness advocates. Photograph from Clifton Merritt Collection, Archives and Special Collections, Mansfield Library, University of Montana.

Dr. John Craighead, a noted wildlife biologist from the University of Montana, pulls a native cutthroat trout from the Middle Fork of the Flathead River in 1957. Craighead and his brother Frank originated the concept of protecting such rivers through the Wild and Scenic Rivers Act, which was enacted in 1968. Photograph by Clifton R. Merritt; from Clifton Merritt Collection, Archives and Special Collections, Mansfield Library, University of Montana.

Picnic Lake in the Jewel Basin Hiking Area, the scene of an early conflict over road access in the upper Flathead River region. Photograph by Clifton R. Merritt; from Clifton Merritt Collection, Archives and Special Collections, Mansfield Library, University of Montana.

Montana member of Congress Lee Metcalf meets with national conservation leaders in Washington around 1959. Seated, from left: Stewart Brandborg of the National Wildlife Federation (later with the Wilderness Society), Anthony Wayne Smith of the National Parks Association, Metcalf, Howard Zahniser of the Wilderness Society. Standing, from left: Joseph Penfold of the Izaak Walton League, Daniel Poole of the Wildlife Management Institute. Lot 31 B5/13.03, Montana Historical Society Research Center, Archives.

Idaho senator Frank Church, sponsor of the Wilderness Act, the Wild and Scenic Rivers Act, and the Central Idaho Wilderness Act, on a float trip in 1965. Photograph from Special Collections and Archives, Boise State University.

Idaho's Bitterroot Range became a wilderness battleground in the early 1960s when the Forest Service attempted to implement a timber harvesting plan in the Magruder Corridor. Looking east from Elk Track Lakes over the upper Selway River drainage. Photo by Ernst Petersen. Photograph from Special Collections and Archives, University of Idaho.

Loren Kreck of Columbia Falls, Montana, was active for many years in efforts to protect the Middle Fork of the Flathead River as a wilderness. Photograph by and courtesy of Bill Cunningham.

Outfitter Arnold "Smoke" Elser on a fire line in the Scapegoat Wilderness, Montana, June 1988.
Photograph by and courtesy of Bill Cunningham.

The massive escarpment of Scapegoat Mountain, the scenic culmination of the Lincoln Back Country, gave its name to the first wilderness area designated as a result of grassroots citizen action. Photograph from USDA Forest Service, Northern Region.

Cecil Garland, the outspoken hardware store dealer who led efforts to set aside the Lincoln Back Country and Scapegoat Mountain area as a wilderness. Photograph from Clifton Merritt Collection, Archives and Special Collections, Mansfield Library, University of Montana.

Outfitter Tom Edwards contemplates the wild country of the Bob Marshall–Scapegoat Mountain region. "Hobnail Tom" aroused concern for protecting this area among his clients and fellow outfitters. Photograph courtesy of Edwards family.

THE BATTLE FOR OUR BACK COUNTRY

Tom Edwards's 1954 cartoon expressed his fear that the Forest Service would open the road-less lands surrounding the Bob Marshall Wilderness to logging and road building. Note the pail labeled "bug dope," a reference to the insect epidemics the agency felt must be controlled through logging. Photograph courtesy of Edwards family.

Clifton Merritt of Kalispell, Montana, organized Flathead Valley sportsmen in the 1950s to halt timber sales in roadless areas and went on to coordinate the Wilderness Society's grassroots advocacy program in the West. In 1977 he cofounded the American Wilderness Alliance, which worked on issues of wildlife habitat protection. Photograph by and courtesy of Bill Cunningham.

Clif Merritt photographed the track of a grizzly bear beneath Scapegoat Mountain in 1964. Merritt believed that the great bear could survive only within large protected landscapes. Photograph from Clifton Merritt Collection, Archives and Special Collections, Mansfield Library, University of Montana.

The Montana Wilderness Association sponsored "wilderness walks" each summer into country such as the Mission Mountains to draw attention to the state's scenic high points. Photo by Thad Lowry, August 1964. Photograph from USDA Forest Service, Northern Region.

Montana wilderness activists Joan Montagne (left), Patsy Culver, and Frank Culver in the Beartooth Mountains. Photograph courtesy of Joan Montagne.

Butte, Montana, activist Al Luebeck on the North Fork of the Blackfoot River. Photograph courtesy of Al Luebeck.

The West Big Hole proposed wilderness from Twin Lakes. Photograph by and courtesy of Steve Luebeck.

The rugged canyon of the Middle Fork of the Salmon River in 1937, six years after the Forest Service designated a million acres of the surrounding landscape as the Idaho Primitive Area. Photograph from USDA Forest Service, Region 4 History Collection.

Boise, Idaho, activist and photographer Ernie Day on the Middle Fork of the Salmon River in 1968, just as the battle for this huge wild area was about to begin. Photograph from USDA Forest Service, Region 4 History Collection.

Moscow, Idaho, activist Dennis Baird beneath Elk Mountain at the edge of the Selway-Bitterroot Wilderness. Photograph by and courtesy of Eric Barker.

Bill Cunningham, longtime Montana wilderness activist. Photograph courtesy of Bill Cunningham.

13

The Hush of the Land
The Lincoln Back Country, 1964–1968

When Lyndon Johnson signed the Wilderness Act on September 3, 1964, in an outdoor ceremony at the White House, the Forest Service lost exclusive control of the undeveloped lands under its jurisdiction. The new law, according to historian Dennis Roth, "marked the end of an era in which both the Congress and the public depended entirely on the Forest Service to determine how National Forest lands should be classified."[1] The act ratified the boundaries of the existing wilderness and wild areas on the national forests, reserved for Congress the sole power to classify new wilderness areas, established permissible uses of such areas, and established a ten-year review period for reclassifying the remaining primitive areas.

Howard Zahniser's early drafts of the wilderness bill provided that the primitive areas would become wilderness upon passage of the act, but Colorado representative Wayne Aspinall, the head of the House Interior Committee, insisted that every addition to the original slate of wilderness areas would have to run the gantlet of congressional committee action and be brought to the House and Senate floors for a vote. Stewart Brandborg, who with Zahniser had originally opposed this proviso, eventually came to regard Aspinall's hurdle as a blessing, for it spurred citizens to build an effective lobbying force that would prove useful on many conservation issues. At first, though, the need to bring each new wilderness proposal before Congress appeared daunting. Brandborg recalled that the day after the act was signed, he was riding in a taxicab in downtown Washington when it struck him how great a challenge still lay ahead. Dozens of primitive areas would be coming up for review in the next few years, each requiring a strong conservationist response. Soon afterward, he bought an open-ended ticket on Frontier Airlines and, as he put it, "barnstormed around the West" to speak with as many Wilderness Society members as possible and lay the groundwork for what would be an arduous and time-consuming campaign.[2]

His itinerary did not include Montana, where citizens had already mobilized to protect the Lincoln Back Country—an area for which no review was mandated under the Wilderness Act. Cecil Garland and his friends faced uncharted territory in bringing a de novo proposal before Congress, and with the Forest Service determined to push roads into the far reaches of the area, he did not have the luxury of a ten-year review period. Here was an issue the framers of the Wilderness Act had not fully taken into account, arising from the grass roots that Brandborg was so interested in cultivating. The Lincoln-Scapegoat area would set a crucial precedent for the disposition of millions of acres of de facto wilderness throughout the West.

Some in the agency disputed whether the Wilderness Act even applied to areas such as the Lincoln Back Country, but Garland was not about to defer to the bureaucrats he had been fighting for years. Following Brandy's and Clif Merritt's advice, he continued to plead for help from Montana's congressional delegation. By late 1963 his entreaties, backed by letters from Tom Edwards's clients and many others, led Mike Mansfield to ask the chairman of the Senate Agriculture Committee to hold a hearing on the issue. Lee Metcalf, however, refused to join his colleague in what he termed an "extraordinary proceeding" to examine an administrative agency's decision. In a letter to Tom Calvert of the Cascade County Wildlife Association, he suggested that the sportsmen back off for a while and let the Forest Service demonstrate good faith in its promise not to develop the area for a few years.[3]

It was going to take an extraordinary grassroots effort to overcome the Montana delegation's high regard for the Forest Service and its timbering programs. In the spring of 1964 Garland invited Lou Aleksich, Representative Jim Battin's district aide, to his association's Memorial Day weekend dinner at the 7-Up Ranch east of Lincoln. Aleksich owned a cabin near Lincoln and proved to be sympathetic to the group's goals. That summer Garland took Vic Reinemer, Lee Metcalf's longtime aide, and his two sons on a pack trip into the Lincoln Back Country and the wildlands surrounding Scapegoat Mountain. "We toughed it out in some pretty bad weather," Garland recalled. After enduring days of soaking rains, they reached the Forest Service cabin on the North Fork of the Blackfoot River, for which Garland still had a key from his days of working for the agency. After enjoying a hot meal and a good night's sleep, Reinemer returned to Washington with a glowing report on the area.[4]

Meanwhile, Clif Merritt prodded other wildlife clubs into action. The Helena-based Prickly Pear Sportsmen's Association paid for an advertisement in a weekly sporting newspaper urging wilderness status for the Lincoln-Scapegoat, with a coupon for readers to mail to congressional members and the chief of the Forest Service. Jim Riis, the group's president, stated that "as areas of mass recreation become crowded, there is also an increasing number of people who get fed up with such crowds."[5] Merritt had been making trips into the area for many years, and in late June of 1964, before leaving for Washington to begin work with the Wilderness Society, he returned for a last look, accompanied by outfitter Gene Youdarian. Merritt observed numerous grayling spawning in the shallow outlet of Heart Lake and caught and released "many brightly colored specimens" of the native westslope cutthroat trout.[6] While climbing a ridge beneath Scapegoat Mountain, Youdarian's horses alerted them to an animal presence. A lone grizzly was heading up the other side of the ridge, but it disappeared into the mists before Merritt could change his camera lens. He settled for a photo of its massive paw print in a snowbank. "The grizzly is the epitome of wilderness," he wrote in his memoirs. "In fact, the grizzly cannot live without undisturbed wild country."[7] Not far from where they encountered the great bear lay the pass over which the Forest Service hoped to build a scenic highway.

Merritt apprised the leaders of state and national wildlife federations of the significant natural values found in the entire Lincoln-Scapegoat area. Its remote plateaus and meadows appeared to harbor an even denser population of grizzlies than the Bob Marshall. Merritt pointed out that little sawtimber could be found in this basin, but if it were logged the elk and grizzlies would move out.[8] It was a theme he and his friends would repeat every time the Forest Service proposed to develop timber stands in a roadless headwater area. Backcountry hunting was the ultimate Montana adventure, one that drew natives and out-of-staters alike to areas such as the Scapegoat. The support of sportsmen and other outdoors enthusiasts would be essential if Garland's little band of concerned citizens was to make any headway in Congress. Clif Merritt's wider contacts with sporting and wildlife clubs, along with Tom Edwards's ties to the outfitting industry and its well-placed clients, gave the tiny Lincoln Back Country Protective Association the political clout it needed. But it was these individuals' ability to frame the issue in terms that had wide appeal that ultimately brought it success.

In January 1965, after sustained lobbying from the wildlife and wilderness groups, Lee Metcalf and Mike Mansfield introduced a bill to establish a wilderness area "not to exceed 75,000 acres" in the Lincoln Back Country—roughly equivalent to Garland's original proposal. The bill came as a surprise to Edwards and Garland, who by this time were lobbying for a much larger area. Clif Merritt reassured them that although the bill fell well short of the conservationists' latest proposal, it was a step in the right direction. He advised Garland not to "clobber Lee for not asking at the start for the whole area. Otherwise, he and Mike may wash their hands of the whole matter." To ask Congress to designate a new, quarter-million-acre wilderness just months after the Wilderness Act passed, Merritt said, "could arouse instant nationwide opposition from single interest groups and cause much damage in Congress to wilderness preservation efforts."[9] Merritt may have been right; Lee Metcalf recalled years later that most members of Congress expected that additions to the wilderness system would be limited to the primitive areas that were undergoing their ten-year reviews, and that "the exceptions in the future will be few and the subject of extensive study."[10]

Even with its limited boundaries, the Metcalf-Mansfield bill was far from a sure thing, and meanwhile Cecil Garland remained skeptical of Forest Service intentions. The lengthy battle with its community-wide divisions was wearing on him and causing difficulties within his family. In March 1965 he penned an anguished letter to Elizabeth Smith, an activist friend from Missoula who had taken pack trips with Tom Edwards. Foreseeing the demise of his favorite wild country, he asked Smith, "How do you say goodbye to a wilderness? How do you turn around and walk out and say 'come on in, crushing, rumbling, gouging machines'?" He lashed out at agency officials who insisted that wilderness was only for the strong and the rich. "Would they have been there to see my daughter 5 years old, legs too short for any stirrup, in the heart of our country. They were not there to see our good friend of this wilderness 73 years old sitting straight in the saddle on a mountain cayuse, a twinkle in his eye, litterly [sic] absorbing energy from our wilderness." Writing from some place of darkness, Garland concluded, "My friend the wilderness when you die perhaps we all die. Perhaps you will again rise like the bird out of the ashes and our ashes will be among your ashes."[11]

Whatever doubts Garland had about his group's ultimate success, he chose not to express them in public. He took his leadership role seriously, and according to reporter Dale Burk (who observed his speeches on many occasions), he would often stand in the back of a room and size up his audience before delivering another stirring appeal for action. He continued this role as head of the Montana Wilderness Association from 1972 to 1974, with Elizabeth Smith as the group's vice president. Although he was a relative newcomer to Montana, his words—and his antigovernment viewpoint—struck a chord in many people who valued the state's wild places.

Tom Edwards had grown up in the lee of the Rockies and had been enjoying trips into the Bob Marshall Wilderness since 1932. He brought the folksy, outgoing persona of "Hobnail Tom" to the Lincoln Back Country affair, drawing in supporters with his homespun descriptions of the wild country that lay behind his and his wife Helen's mountain lodge. His affinity for the wilderness verged on the religious, as he wrote in a 1954 newsletter they sent to their guests:

> When you drop through the notch in the pass and down into Alpine Park—you look back—great Arrastra Peak has in some mysterious way closed in and blocked your retreat—you look to your right and there is that mighty Red Mountain that keeps even old Sol at bay till well into the forenoon. And on your left Bugle Mountain admits none except those that know the game trails. Night comes on—the night hawks cry—the hatch comes out on the lake and the trout make rings all over the surface of the water. To some, yes, I guess to most of us who camp here there comes a time of sacred meditation never to be forgotten. In the cool of the evening in this campfire valley so full of hush we seem to feel His presence and we wonder why we miss it on the other side of the mountain.[12]

Edwards's paeans to the beauty of the Lincoln Back Country deepened its mystique among his clients, many of whom brought useful political connections and financial backing for the Protective Association. Although he guided hunting trips in the area during the fall, Edwards stressed that the key value of the Back Country did not depend on bagging game or catching fish. Simply being attentive to the moods of the wilderness was restorative. His was a romantic attachment to the land, one shared by many of his clients, who (he said) enjoyed "a very deep soul-satisfying experience of finding their relationship with living things and the eternal mountains." Edwards distilled these experiences into the memorable phrase "the hush of the land," a quality he believed would vanish once the roads came in. The prospect of cars and trucks disgorging their occupants at Meadow Lake or Danaher Meadows provoked in him a deep sense of impending loss.[13]

Edwards was not the first to try to describe the stillness that fell over the mountains at day's end or lingered at daybreak by a mist-shrouded pond, but he pioneered new ground in trying to link this landscape property to dollar-and-cents concerns. His clients, he told Forest Service leaders, shelled out twenty dollars a day or more for the privilege of experiencing the all-enveloping silences along forest trails and at evening campfires. It was difficult to place a price tag on quietude, yet Edwards and his fellow outfitters knew they were competing for the use of this land with industries that could point to the payrolls and taxes they paid. Edwards claimed that the twenty outfitters who guided in the Lincoln-Scapegoat area produced an annual gross income of $125,000, while outfitter R. H. Hultman of Condon, who was elected president of the MWA in 1968, estimated that his guests spent $150 per visit on "licenses, clothes, equipment, whiskey, gifts to take home, etc." With additional expenditures on gasoline and travel, he calculated that his fellow outfitters brought more than a half million dollars annually into local coffers.[14]

As important as economic considerations were in the political sphere, it seems doubtful that the guides and outfitters using the Bob Marshall or Lincoln-Scapegoat had chosen their arduous and barely remunerative line of work as a means to get wealthy. Cecil Garland's experience of hearing the returning bugle of an elk above Webb Lake was freighted with more than the promise of meat in the freezer. Nor was he indulging in a mere romantic attachment to a lost nineteenth-century world. The land brought silence, solitude, stillness— yet it included the cries of wild creatures, the murmur of a breeze in the lodgepoles, the roar of wind unloosed on the stony ridges. These men were pointing to a world where humans did not run affairs; where no technicians implemented their management schemes; where different purposes reigned than those that people imposed upon the land. It included wild creatures but encompassed more than the quest for sport.

What the Forest Service's planners did not seem to realize was the attraction of a world where people traveled and camped in such small numbers that they were a mere ripple upon its waters. Edwards, Garland, and their friends had touched on an unspoken ideal that lay close to the hearts of many Americans. This was a last opportunity to hold back a culture that was bent on destroying the things they most valued, including the chance to observe wild creatures engaged in lives utterly apart from humans. In places such as the Lincoln Back Country, the Magruder Corridor, and the Madison Range these enthusiasts, as Olaus Murie had prophesied, would attempt to take a little higher view of things that could barely be named.

The Metcalf-Mansfield bill drew a protest from Robert Delaney, whose sawmill depended on the estimated 245 million board feet of timber that lay within the Lincoln-Scapegoat area. He wanted the Copper Creek road extended all the way to the North Fork of the Blackfoot to enable his firm to bid competitively on timber sales in that area.[15] Delaney found support for his views among many Lincoln-area residents. Leonard Lambkin, whose father had opened the town's first tourist lodge in 1918, told a reporter that "we can't go back to the old days" when Lincoln was an isolated community in the midst of the wilderness. Its future lay in recreation, he believed—particularly car camping and snowmobile outings, which were becoming increasingly popular in the area. "There can be a compromise," Lambkin said.[16]

Lee Metcalf hoped as well to find a compromise, and following the disastrous flooding of June 1964 in the Sun River drainage, he floated an unusual proposal to expand his Lincoln-Scapegoat bill in exchange for conservationists dropping their opposition to the Bureau of Reclamation's proposed dam on the upper Sun. An ardent reclamationist, Metcalf believed that preservationists too often opposed necessary hydroelectric and flood control projects. Helena National Forest supervisor Bob Morgan, who was showing sympathy with the logging opponents, apprised Clif Merritt of "vague rumors of conservation (sportsmen's) groups advocating trades of this for that country; dam here—more wilderness there, etc. This sort of thing would have no end except mental chaos. I hope it goes no further." Cecil Garland opposed the idea and asked Metcalf, rhetorically, whether the nation would continue to "chip away at our newly created wilderness system, or shall we really hold on to these areas and strive to find suitable alternatives to their destruction."[17] Merritt and Ken Baldwin agreed and kept the pressure up on both fronts. Wilderness proponents were coming to believe they could decisively influence congressional politics without resorting to onerous compromises.

Despite his discouragement with intransigent Forest Service officials, Garland's discussions with Lou Aleksich led him to press Jim Battin for a new bill covering the entire 240,000-acre conservationist proposal. At Battin's request Garland and a couple of friends, including a supportive Forest Service employee, drew up boundaries over a bottle of whiskey in a back room of his store. Ken Baldwin took the map to Washington, where he was to attend a National Wildlife Federation convention, and presented the proposal to the representative in early March 1965. The eastern district Republican introduced the bill on April 7.[18] Tom Edwards paid a visit to Washington soon after to press Metcalf and Mansfield to support the Battin measure. He reported to Garland that although Lee seemed to be in the dark about the proposal, the senator appeared willing to amend his bill.[19] The two men urged their cooperators to write still more letters to Mansfield and Metcalf. Dozens filled the senators' mailboxes, far outnumbering those supporting the Forest Service's development plan. Many of the Protective Association's supporters had ties to industry and agriculture and had personal experience with the area from hunting and horse-back trips. Letters from Tom Edwards's out-of-state clients and mass mailings coordinated by the Wilderness Society added to the pressure.[20]

In 1968 Forest Service leaders in the Northern Region office made a last attempt to regain the initiative in the Lincoln-Scapegoat battle. In a brochure titled *Patterns for Management, Blackfoot-Sun River Divide Area*, they offered a remarkable exposition of the philosophy that had guided their treatment of backcountry areas since the early 1950s. Pointing out that timber stands south of the Bob Marshall Wilderness could contribute 17.5 million board feet per year to the local economy, they warned that "the time is rapidly approaching when either these stands must make their contribution or the sustained yield for the three Forests be revised downward." As agency officials had argued in places such as Bunker Creek and the Magruder Corridor, the road network needed for timbering the Lincoln-Scapegoat would give better access to "relatively unused sections of the Bob Marshall Wilderness and the High Country." A road that would cross a pass south of Scapegoat Mountain would provide an overlook of the peak's "massive vertical escarpments." Marked snowmobile routes and a pos-sible ski area at the head of Dwight Creek would augment backcountry trails. The plan would "give opportunities to families, students, scouts, hiking clubs, and similar groups for short-distance hiking to areas of special interest or that will permit short-term experience in primitive surroundings." The foresters con-cluded that "this proposal makes a much better contribution to the needs and desires of the whole public."[21]

Cecil Garland took strong issue with these statements, claiming that the Forest Service had overestimated timber volumes on a regional basis and that allowable cuts must be "revised downward in any event." There was enough tim-ber in the Lincoln-Scapegoat to run a small to medium-sized sawmill for three to four months a year, he said, but the cost to build the necessary access roads could reach over $30 million—far more than the value of the timber itself. "There can be no doubt that the present system of growing trees is a direct sub-sidy to the lumbering industry," he maintained.[22]

The Forest Service had simply lost the confidence of many western Mon-tana residents who wanted the agency to recognize and maintain wildland val-ues. In turn, these citizens increased the pressure on Lee Metcalf, bringing about a shift in his thinking. Safely reelected to the Senate in 1966 and cognizant of the growing nationwide interest in environmental values, he began to reconsider his longtime allegiance to the Forest Service and the reclamation and hydropower bureaus. He arranged for a field hearing in June 1968 on S. 1121, his and Mike Mansfield's latest Lincoln-Scapegoat bill, which now encompassed the entire 240,500-acre citizen proposal. Rescheduled for September following the assassination of Senator Robert Kennedy, the hearing drew statewide attention. Tom Edwards wrote to four hundred of his guests to ask for letters to be submitted at the hearing—and for funds for the trips to Washington that would follow. "Money or no money, you must give us a hand," he insisted, "or the next time you visit Meadow Creek it may be in a limosine [*sic*] on a 30 minute ride—or a stop among beer cans for a picnic. The game and the fish and above all the tranquility and hush will be gone forever."[23]

On September 23, 1968, Metcalf, James Battin, and Quentin Burdick of North Dakota sat down at the head of a crowded third-floor courtroom in the Cascade County Courthouse to open the subcommittee hearing on S. 1121. They listened to eighty-two citizen witnesses testify for and against the bill; government witnesses would be heard in a subsequent session in Washington. It was the first public hearing held in the Northern Rockies since the Wilderness Act was passed and was an important test of the preservation groups' strength. Many in the crowd of three hundred wore green-and-white badges announcing "I'm for wilderness," distributed at the door by local MWA members.[24] The hearing brought out many of Montana's conservation stalwarts, including Doris Milner, who presented sixty statements in support of the Lincoln-Scapegoat from her contacts in the Bitterroot Valley. Tom Edwards once again brought up his yearning for the tranquility of the wilderness, which to him even outweighed the value of the area for fishing and hunting. "How can you stand on that great Scapegoat Mountain looking down at its foot at bulldozers, trucks and cars, at the head of Dry Fork, Cabin Creek, and Tobacco Valley, listening to the hideous noises of modern devices and kid yourselves that you are enjoying the wilderness and partaking of its goodness?" he asked.[25]

Support for wilderness designation also came from Leonard Lambkin, who had previously sided with the Forest Service, and from other local residents. Governor Tim Babcock, a Republican, had a spokesperson deliver his endorsement of the wilderness proposal, an indication of the bipartisan support for protecting the area. Sportsmen from clubs in Butte, Great Falls, Helena, Missoula, and Kalispell insisted that building roads into the Lincoln-Scapegoat area would make it more difficult to maintain viable wildlife populations, including grizzly bear, elk, and the native cutthroat trout. Frank Dunkle, director of the Montana

Fish and Game Department, observed that "we have roads and mass recreation opportunities in quantity. Untouched and undisturbed areas for present and future generations are in short supply." John Craighead maintained that roading and logging would be a "direct threat" to a small grizzly population centered in the Scapegoat Mountain area. Craighead's colleague George Weisel, whose connection to the area was long and personal, said the agency's road-building program would have fishermen "standing shoulder to shoulder" along the area's streams, eliminating native fish and replacing them with "expensive put-and-take fishing" of hatchery-bred trout.[26] To these sportsmen, the quality of hunting and fishing in the wilderness outweighed ease of access—a contention that fish and game advocates would continue to make even as the popularity of motorized access grew by leaps and bounds.

For Cecil Garland the hearing was the culmination of eight years of effort to raise public awareness of the Lincoln Back Country. In his own statement, he drew on memories of his North Carolina boyhood—and the contrast he had felt on his first soul-stirring day in the Lincoln Back Country at Ringeye Falls when he heard the elk bugling from distant hillsides.

> That night I made a vow, that whatever the cost, for whatever the reason, I would do all that I could to keep this country as wild as I had found it. . . . Sleep came then and for 8 wonderful days thereafter I caught many trout, killed a big bull elk and whetted an appetite for wilderness that has not yet been satisfied. Never again would I be satisfied with my former home that had names like Elkmount, but had no elk, Deerfield, but no one could ever remember seeing a deer there, Trout Creek that had only minnows, Beaver Dam that had no beaver and East and West Buffalo that one could not even find the remains of an old skull. . . . My people had been careless with their land and water and wildlife resources, and we found that it could be destroyed.[27]

Supporters of the Forest Service's timber development plan were outnumbered at the hearing, but local mill owners and timber industry spokesmen pointed out the potential economic value of timber production from the area. Horace Koessler, president of the Intermountain Lumber Company (which had mills in Missoula and Darby) objected to the preservationists' aims for backcountry lands such as the Selway and Lincoln-Scapegoat. "Foresters, executives and managers in all facets of the wood industry are deeply concerned at the rapid and continuing erosion of the land base on which to grow the required raw material for this great industry," he said. "The set-asides for national parks and wilderness areas continue to take their toll." Robert Helding, chairman of the Montana Forest Industries Council, told the committee that "the sincere concern of this industry is that the rural economy of western Montana be preserved and that the jobs and associated businesses be sustained." He said that there were 1,500 year-round employees working in his industry within the immediate area, producing lumber worth $4.8 million in annual gross value. Allen White of Missoula's Van Evan Company, a medium-sized lumber mill, pointed out that 2.5 million acres of wilderness had been designated on national forests in western Montana and northern Idaho. How many people could be expected to use these areas in the foreseeable future? he asked. In contrast, the Lincoln-Scapegoat could supply twelve million board feet of timber annually to the ten mills in the surrounding area, each of which was producing at less than capacity owing to limited log supplies.[28]

For the past sixteen years Lee Metcalf had been closely identified with the Forest Service and its timber policies, but in Great Falls he signaled that he would not always follow the development agenda. When an industry forester from Spokane suggested that the public would be better served by road access into the Lincoln-Scapegoat area, Metcalf replied that the area "is of such a nature that it couldn't survive the influx of weekend campers and Sunday afternoon picnickers. So in order to save the special and unique qualities that are alleged to be there, we have to set it aside as a wilderness." It would be better, he said, to "look into other areas of the national forest that are sturdier and more susceptible" to logging.[29]

Metcalf's statements throughout the hearing reveal a man who was beginning to question the prevailing multiple-use doctrine, which held that disparate land uses such as backcountry recreation and timbering could be made compatible with proper management. It was an important distinction. In virtually every case, agency and industry spokesmen argued that active management could do a better job of providing public benefits. Elk numbers could be boosted through judicious logging and prescribed burning; recreation could be enhanced by providing trailhead facilities and backcountry toilets; active fire suppression prevented wildfires from denuding whole watersheds. Wilderness designations, on the other hand, benefited uses that could be found nowhere else: the chance to stand on a high ridge and watch a grizzly disappear into the mists, or to make camp at the edge of a meadow and know that no truck was going to pull up in the middle of the night. Cecil Garland argued strenuously for the cultural significance of such experiences, Tom Edwards for their spiritual worth, and George Weisel and Clif Merritt for their biological importance, but these men must have known in their hearts that a majority of Americans would be satisfied with something less than pure wilderness. The Lincoln-Scapegoat was, as Garland knew, a test case for forest policy and for the Wilderness Act. It is a measure of these advocates' eloquence and persistence that they were able to dislodge a U.S. senator from his long-standing allegiance to the multiple-use concept, and thereby set him on course to become one of the best friends the wilderness would have in Congress.

14

One Powerful Senator
The Battle for the De Facto Wilderness, 1967–1972

In April 1967, less than three years after the Wilderness Act became law, Stewart Brandborg delivered a progress report to the Sierra Club's tenth biennial wilderness conference in San Francisco. He noted that seven years remained for federal agencies to complete their reviews of some 150 potential wilderness areas, encompassing the remaining primitive areas on the national forests as well as roadless portions of national parks and national wildlife refuges. If each of these areas were recommended for wilderness classification and approved by Congress (as Brandy hoped), the National Wilderness Preservation System would make up "no more than two to three percent of the nation's land area"—approximately fifty to seventy million acres. "This will be nearly all the wilderness land we can expect to set aside in the future," he predicted. "Additions of any remaining unprotected federal wild lands will depend on the increasingly improbable escape of de facto wilderness from development."[1]

A year and a half later, Brandborg congratulated Montana activists for accomplishing just such an escape. The strong turnout at the Great Falls hearing on Lee Metcalf and Mike Mansfield's Lincoln-Scapegoat bill foretold the demise of the Forest Service's logging and road-building plan for the area. But more was at stake than a single roadless area, as Brandy reminded MWA president Buff Hultman. Montanans were setting "an important precedent at a time when the Forest Service is dragging its feet and telling everyone that there can be no de facto wilderness designations until the end of the Wilderness Law's 10-year review period in 1974."² Congress had yet to take up any national forest wilderness proposals outside the primitive areas and their contiguous lands, so the Lincoln-Scapegoat set an important precedent for de facto wilderness throughout the West.

The Forest Service understood this dynamic as well. Bob Morgan, who as supervisor of the Helena National Forest was quietly trying to sidetrack the unpopular development plan for the Lincoln Back Country, called the Great Falls hearing "disastrous" for his agency.³ He hoped instead that some alternative designation short of wilderness could protect the area while salvaging a degree of autonomy for his agency. The issue came to a head at a tense meeting of his fellow division chiefs the following March, during which regional forester Neal Rahm objected to citizens tying their hands as far as properly managing the Lincoln-Scapegoat area. "We have lost control and leadership in the sphere of wilderness philosophy," Rahm lamented. "Why should a sporting goods dealer in Lincoln, Montana, designate the boundaries of the Lincoln Back Country addition to the Bob Marshall Wilderness? If lines are to be drawn, we should be drawing them."⁴ His agency had pioneered the wilderness concept on public lands and Congress should defer to its expertise, he insisted.

In response, supervisor Morgan ventured some misgivings about going ahead with road building and logging in the Lincoln Back Country in the face of mounting citizen opposition. Bud Moore, now head of the region's fire control division, decided to add his two cents, telling Rahm that "if the people want this to be wilderness, why, let's go ahead and give it to them—we can manage the hell out of it." There was a stunned silence for a moment, he recalled, whereupon Bill Worf, the new head of the region's recreation division and a friend of Moore's, added, "I'm with Bud."⁵

Morgan, Moore, and Worf were avid wilderness travelers who understood why some forest users might be upset about high-standard roads climbing over the Continental Divide next to the Bob Marshall Wilderness. Their defection from the development-minded old guard spelled the end of the Forest Service's ambitious plans for the Lincoln Back Country. Neal Rahm was not ready to embrace wilderness designation, however, and testified at a hearing held in Washington that month that the area should be classified as "backcountry" so that shelters, picnic tables, and fire grates could be constructed for visitors' use. "People could come up for a weekend, or for a one-day trip," he said. "They could park, and then they can walk in to the lakes for fishing." A similar designation was in the works for the Jewel Basin area on the Flathead National Forest;

both Rahm and Worf saw these as useful alternatives to wilderness designation that offered greater latitude to manage visitors.[6]

Rahm's subordinates, however, sensed the shift in the popular mood. A broad cross section of Montanans was in favor of leaving the Lincoln-Scapegoat country alone. A letter from a former Lincoln district ranger, one of hundreds that Metcalf and Mansfield received on the issue, told the story as clearly as any. James Uttley had served on the district in 1936–37, when he recalled watching bears bathe in its crystal streams and eagles snatch fish from its lakes. During subsequent assignments he had seen "virgin areas that were pack trail country . . . opened up and gutted with roads. The fish and wildlife that were once abundant just seem to dissolve. They were not able to compete with the automobile."[7]

Wilderness advocates had won the initial battle; now they would have to persuade the Department of Agriculture and congressional committeemen to drop their opposition to the Lincoln-Scapegoat bill. Cecil and Barbara Garland, Tom Edwards, Don Aldrich, and F. M. Gannon of the Helena Wilderness Riders group traveled to Washington to testify at the March 1969 Senate Interior Committee hearing, after which they spoke with key legislators, including Idaho's Frank Church, who assured them that he would shepherd the Metcalf-Mansfield bill through his committee. This was accomplished on May 29, with approval by the full Senate following in early June. The biggest hurdle now lay in the House, where Colorado representative Wayne Aspinall sat as head of the corresponding Interior Committee. "He will be tough," Gannon reported to his fellow backcountry horsemen.[8]

The term fully described the representative from Colorado's rural western slope. Aspinall had serious reservations about allowing a "wildcat" wilderness proposal to take precedence over his committee's orderly review of the primitive areas. Stewart Brandborg took a head count of House Interior Committee members and determined that fifteen would probably vote for the companion bill carried by Arnold Olsen and James Battin, with two members likely to vote against it and seventeen unknown. But Aspinall was angry over the pressure he was receiving, and Brandborg reported that he "probably would not support it." Aspinall also insisted on examining the Scapegoat's mineral resources before moving the bill through his committee, but the U.S. Geological Survey field teams that normally conducted these surveys were already occupied in the Bob Marshall Wilderness.[9]

The delays dismayed supporters of the bill. Clif Merritt objected that there were few mineral resources in the Bob Marshall and that the USGS should give the Lincoln-Scapegoat higher priority. But what finally moved the bill was the show of popular support for the area within Montana. Cecil Garland recalled how during a visit with Mansfield following the Senate hearings he was unable to hide his tears over the lack of progress. Mansfield "listened quietly, leaning back in his chair, his fingertips touching gently as he moved his hands together again and again. And then he said, 'Cece, you go back to Montana and tell the folks back there that we'll get the bill passed, that there'll be a wilderness there some day.' And he went on to say, 'Some day there will be something that Mr. Aspinall will want, and we'll be there.'"[10]

Mansfield was as good as his word. In late October 1969, after the measure had cleared the Senate, he wrote to Aspinall to urge that early hearings be scheduled before the House Interior Committee. The slender possibility of significant mineral resources in the Scapegoat area did not justify holding up the bill, in his view, and Congress would be "perfectly justified" in proceeding without the usual study. At the bottom of the letter he added a handwritten note: "Wayne, I've just come back from Montana and talked to the folks in the Lincoln area & they really want this. So do I as I think it is badly needed. Thanks, M.M."[11] The Senate majority leader's words had the intended effect. With a little shuffling of priorities (and a letter from Senate Interior Committee chairman Henry Jackson) the USGS scheduled the requisite field work for the summer of 1970. It showed little prospect of economically significant mineralization in the area.[12]

Other members of Congress were beginning to take notice of this unusual lands battle. Albert Quie, a Minnesota representative who had cosponsored the original Wilderness Act, made a visit to the Scapegoat with his son, Fred, who worked summers on the Lincoln Ranger District and rented a cabin from Cecil Garland. Albert quickly became entranced with the area and appreciated Garland's forthright approach to the issue. He recalled this "rough outspoken individual" chewing tobacco and telling of his experiences in the backcountry in eloquent language. Although Quie was not on the Interior Committee, he worked closely with fellow Republican Jim Battin to advance the bill in the House. He also included the area in a nationwide omnibus wilderness bill he introduced that year. These actions helped clear the way for final action on the bill.[13] In late 1971 Wayne Aspinall added the bill to the Interior Committee's calendar. Cecil Garland later asked him why he had changed his mind. The representative replied, "Son, you've got one powerful senator."[14]

Garland and Edwards returned to Washington in March 1972 to testify at hearings held before Representative Walter Baring's Public Lands Subcommittee, the first step in moving the bill through the House Interior Committee. Tom Edwards had sold the White Tail Ranch two years previously and no longer had an economic stake in the battle; this was about his feelings and those of his guests, whose letters he noticed lying on the desks of many House members. One member told him, "'You fellows from Montana are one of the most influential conservation groups we've seen in Washington.'"[15] Baring's committee issued a favorable report and on August 20, 1972, the House passed the measure establishing the 240,000-acre Scapegoat Wilderness. President Nixon signed it that day. Tom Edwards sent a congratulatory letter to his friends and clients that featured his drawing of an exultant cowboy shouting "We've done it!" He told his friends that "the fight to save these majestic mountains began over twenty years ago. From the bottom of my heart I want you to know what a part you have played in this victory."[16]

The Scapegoat was the first national forest wilderness designated as a result of citizen pressure instead of a mandated agency review. Adjoining the existing Bob Marshall Wilderness, it substantially increased the protection afforded to iconic creatures such as grizzly bear, elk, and native trout. Its advocates not only presented heartfelt tales of encounters with a great wilderness; they had assembled impressive testimony from biologists on the importance of this primeval landscape to the free movement of wildlife. Those who stood to lose from this campaign—the Delaney brothers, their contract loggers and sawmill workers, and the owners of larger mills in Missoula—entered statements on timber volumes and employment figures into the record, but they had not yet come up with a compelling narrative of their own to counteract the eloquence and sheer volume of testimony that conservationists, sportsmen, and outfitters had managed to elicit. That balance would shift in the years ahead as the preservation groups, building on their successes in the Lincoln-Scapegoat and Magruder Corridor, dramatically expanded their goals to include virtually every roadless tract remaining on the national forests of the Northern Rockies. In doing so they managed to stir up an equally powerful grassroots opposition among timber industry workers and motor vehicle users. For now, however, the testimony of Garland, Edwards, and their friends held sway with a freshness and power that commanded attention.

The Lincoln-Scapegoat controversy forced Northern Region officials to defer harvesting timber stands south of the Bob Marshall Wilderness, but they had no intention of relinquishing the more productive sites north of the wilderness in the upper Flathead River drainage. Here arose the next great contest between production-minded foresters and their opponents among Montana's sporting and wildlife organizations. Beginning in 1965 the Flathead National Forest built roads south of U.S. Highway 2 into the drainages of Skyland, Dodge, and Morrison Creeks, which permitted the sale of more than thirty million board feet of timber. Further sales followed in 1968 and early 1969 that extended the road network into Challenge, Lodgepole, and Puzzle Creeks, while another timber development road was pushed up the Spotted Bear River from the South Fork side as far as Big Bill Mountain. Local sportsmen learned that plans were in the works to take the road as far as Silvertip Guard Station, a remote backcountry outpost, and build a spur partway up the side of Dean Ridge, a high rampart dividing the Spotted Bear drainage from the Middle Fork of the Flathead. This was not all: a sympathetic Forest Service employee leaked a planning map to *Missoulian* reporter Dale Burk, who was an avid hunter and angler with a personal stake in the Middle Fork country. The map confirmed his worst fears, showing a collector road extending from Spotted Bear clear to the Middle Fork at Schafer Meadows, then continuing north to join the logging roads coming down from Highway 2.[17] It was the mirror image of the road network that Tom Edwards and Cecil Garland had fought in the Lincoln Back Country, and once it was built it would end any hope of preserving the wild interior of the Flathead north of the Bob Marshall.

Burk publicized the map and the Dean Ridge road controversy through articles in the *Missoulian, Sierra Club Bulletin,* and other periodicals and would go on to write a self-published book titled *Great Bear, Wild River,* which extolled what he and his fellow activists were calling the Great Bear Wilderness. Burk was no stranger to controversy, and his 1969 series on clear-cutting in Montana's Bitterroot National Forest made national headlines, but his behind-the-scenes work drew criticism for exceeding the objectivity expected of a reporter. He had the support of the *Missoulian's* editor and publisher, however, both of whom were eager to erase the paper's former image as a mouthpiece for Montana's corporate interests.[18]

With Burk stirring up controversy over the road plans, Flathead Forest supervisor Joseph Pomajevich issued a statement promoting the Dean Ridge road as "a scenic recreational drive with panoramic views of the mountains to the south and the headwaters of the Spotted Bear River. Provisions for parking areas and vistas have been included in the construction plans."[19] This was the same rationale the Northern Region used in the Lincoln-Scapegoat area, and it did nothing to alleviate the sportsmen's concerns. They viewed the Bob Marshall as a complete ecosystem stretching from Glacier Park to the Blackfoot River—more than two million acres of predominantly wild country, not just the 950,000-acre wilderness the Forest Service set aside in 1940.

The Montana Fish and Game Department had been following the Bunker Creek controversy and now weighed in against further road building and timbering in the Spotted Bear drainage. According to director Frank Dunkle, elk congregated in the fall below Dean Ridge and Big Bill Mountain before heading to lower country along the Spotted Bear—what he termed "one of the longest migration patterns from the Bob Marshall wilderness to a winter range outside the wilderness boundary." He feared that increased road access would disrupt this migration and "seriously deplete" the herd. Dunkle reiterated his concern in a letter to Lee Metcalf, asking the senator for a "calm and rational . . . examination of this country to see what is the appropriate use of the land in light of changing public values."[20]

Dunkle was alluding to a significant shift in public opinion regarding forest management in the Northern Rockies, driven in part by a controversy that had been brewing since 1968 in Metcalf's native Bitterroot Valley. The senator had been hearing from numerous citizens and retired Forest Service officers (including G. M. Brandborg) about the rapid pace and environmental effects of timber cutting on the Bitterroot National Forest. In late 1969 Metcalf asked Arnold Bolle, dean of the forestry school at the University of Montana, to look into the issue, perhaps hoping that a blue-ribbon panel of the kind George Selke had chaired on the Selway would defuse the controversy. Instead, Bolle and six fellow faculty members issued a broad denunciation of Forest Service management policies on the Bitterroot. A particularly scathing critique came from forest economist Robert Wambach, whose analysis showed how the Bitterroot National Forest was losing money by clear-cutting and terracing tree plantations.[21]

The Bolle report gained worldwide circulation and indelibly associated Metcalf with criticism of the agency he had long supported. Lee was persuaded that the Forest Service's timber program needed greater environmental safeguards, and with Frank Church he set about crafting guidelines to restore a more balanced program. Coming on the heels of the Lincoln-Scapegoat and upper Selway issues, the Bitterroot clear-cutting controversy was the wedge that preservation groups had been seeking in order to disengage Metcalf from his support of Forest Service timber programs. By 1970, with his constituent mail running heavily against clear-cutting and wilderness-busting road development, Metcalf swung firmly over to the preservationist camp. That May he sent a letter to Forest Service chief Edward Cliff, consigned by Mike Mansfield and Arnold Olsen, questioning whether the Dean Ridge road should be given high priority.[22] This was a considerable turnaround for Metcalf, who until then had advised conservationists in the Flathead Valley to go along with Forest Service plans for orderly development of the national forest.

Metcalf appears to have been influenced more by ordinary Montanans who used the Flathead than by professional lobbyists in Washington. An outfitter from Marion, Montana, named Norman Hanson wrote to Metcalf in June 1970 to object to the imminent extension of the Dean Ridge road. "I have outfitted in this area for 20 years," he wrote. "I have watched the steady growth of the roads and the steady decline of the Elk herd. . . . I believe we should see what can be done to help them survive; not be a party to creating tougher problems for them."[23] Dozens of such letters arrived that month, which attracted the attention of Metcalf's aides and made it easier for lobbyists such as Clif Merritt and Stewart Brandborg when they called on the senator.

Metcalf and his colleagues received little satisfaction from Ed Cliff, however. The Dean Ridge road was first "flagged out" in 1963, the chief replied, and had been brought up in annual public meetings held since. He assured Metcalf that the road would not be extended into the Middle Fork drainage, despite the engineering map Dale Burk had obtained. "If problems should arise, we feel a cooperative action consisting of road closures, season adjustments, and other steps to protect wildlife can be taken. . . . In most instances the habitat of elk, especially, can be improved by timber harvest which generally results in increased forage." Cliff noted that elk populations within the Bob Marshall were declining, the "result of protection, which has created a dense forest cover containing little game food."[24]

To attempt to settle the issue, the Northern Region entered into a cooperative agreement with the Montana Fish and Game Department and the University of Montana to study the effect of logging and road building on elk herds in western Montana. Various studies would be produced over the next ten years that showed that road densities affected elk herds more than logging itself, chiefly by increasing hunting pressure and dispersing animals.[25] Meanwhile, preservationists wanted the northern outliers to the Bob Marshall closed off to new roads and logging as soon as possible. As they feared, once the Dean Ridge road was constructed (it did not actually extend onto the top of the ridge), the Flathead National Forest turned its attention once again to the Bunker Creek drainage, where a 30-million-board-foot timber sale had lain in abeyance since 1955. Clif Merritt, who was watching events from Washington, chided Montana conservationists for not organizing stronger opposition as in the old days. "You know the procedure," he advised Loren Kreck, a Columbia Falls dentist who had been working with Dale Burk to try to stop the sale. "Letters, statements, and resolutions, beginning now." This time the wildlife groups were unsuccessful and the road and associated logging crept up the slopes of Bunker Creek.

The loss stung Merritt badly, and he warned Kreck that unless conservationists in the Flathead organized soon, the rest of Dean Ridge would also be opened to road traffic.[26] Two years after the Bunker Creek sale was completed, a young biologist named Douglas Chadwick reported that with the improved road access, hunters had "all but wiped out the [mountain] goats, taken several grizzlies, trapped out most of the wolverine, and decimated the elk."[27]

In the summer of 1967 the opponents of logging in the Magruder Corridor—the controversial Area E south of the Selway-Bitterroot Wilderness—were celebrating the moratorium on development that followed the release of the Selke committee's report. Shortly afterward, Don Aldrich asked Lee Metcalf to introduce a bill to add Area E to the Selway-Bitterroot Wilderness, but Brit Englund, Metcalf's press secretary, replied that the mandated studies would accomplish the same purpose. In early 1969, however, Mort Brigham learned that surveyors had run flagging tape for a new road through the Little Clearwater River drainage, a major tributary of the upper Selway located north of the Magruder Road. Brigham passed the news to Doris Milner, whereupon (as he told a friend) "the war was renewed right there."[28] Milner informed Metcalf and Frank Church of the agency's evident breach of its agreement to stay out of the upper Selway. The senators made inquiries of the Agriculture Department and were told that the work was merely a preliminary flag line designed to assist resource studies and did not signal new logging plans. But to Brigham and Milner the tape was evidence enough. Brigham informed Frank Church that "a little bit of logging and road building in this country is like a little bit of cancer—it keeps spreading. The road to stop is Number One."[29]

Wilderness advocates gained scant comfort the following year when Bitterroot Forest supervisor Orville Daniels released the first of his agency's resource studies of the Magruder Corridor, which were mandated under the Selke agreement. The study team recommended against logging in the "high alpine zone" or on lands with a high erosion hazard, but on another sixty-six thousand acres, soils were considered stable enough to permit regular harvests that would yield 6.4 million board feet of timber per year.[30] Milner's response was to recruit an attorney named Loren Knudson, who submitted a 41-page brief to an advisory committee Daniels had set up for the Magruder study. Knudson cited research by Dr. Ted Bjorn of the University of Idaho showing that spawning of chinook salmon dropped off "precipitously" when streambeds accumulated more than 30 percent in fine materials. The bed load of the Selway was already at that level, making any increase owing to logging and road-building activities highly problematic.[31]

Knudson's involvement portended the strong role environmental attorneys would play in determining how de facto wilderness lands would be disposed. He raised a legal precedent brought about in a Colorado lawsuit over the disposition of the Gore Range–Eagles Nest Primitive Area—the so-called *Parker v. U.S.* decision, which had broad implications for how the Forest Service treated de facto wilderness adjoining the primitive areas. The previous year the federal district court in that state had ruled that the Forest Service was required to include roadless lands contiguous to a primitive area in its reclassification studies before proceeding with logging or other development projects.[32] Area E had been part of the Selway-Bitterroot Primitive Area before the area was reclassified, so Congress (Knudson argued) had not had a chance to consider its value as part of the overall wilderness.

Milner chose not to pursue a lawsuit under *Parker*. Instead she focused pressure on Lee Metcalf, approaching him at public gatherings and keeping a stream of letters coming from her committee. At the time, the senator was embroiled in the Bitterroot clear-cutting controversy and could hardly have wanted to take on another contentious wilderness campaign. Stewart Brandborg recalled visiting Metcalf in Washington around this time, only to hear him deliver a tirade about Milner's incessant pleas.[33] Metcalf was known on Capitol Hill for his volcanic temper, but to his credit, he did not dismiss Milner's concerns. In early December 1970 he agreed to introduce a bill for a 250,000-acre "Upper Selway Wilderness."[34] A "by-request" measure, it had little chance of passage so late in the session.

The Magruder controversy reemerged in June 1971 when Orville Daniels released his management proposal for Area E. Carefully couched in the language of agency planners, it amounted to a blueprint for timber development. Watershed and recreation values would be emphasized in the upland areas while still developing the "secondary values" of timber and wildlife. New roads branching off the Magruder Road would feature pulloffs so that summertime visitors could enjoy scenic vistas. In winter these roads would open up new territory for snowmobilers, the report stated. Secondary roads would be closed after logging, while thinning of "wild and managed stands [would] provide quality timber stands for the future." Concerns about erosion and sedimentation would be addressed by minimizing road widths, avoiding large sidehill cuts, and surfacing the main collector system with gravel. The hope was that any sediment generated in the uplands would not make it into the Selway's prized spawning beds.[35]

In a politically astute move, Daniels proposed to delay implementation of the plan for five years so that additional studies of the Selway's soils and fisheries could be completed. The offer, predictably, pleased no one; Milner told her supporters that the plan "gives little, if any, real recognition to the wilderness resource. . . . Roading and logging the area cannot be thought of as reflecting or maintaining wild land conditions, even by the wildest stretch of the imagination." The Federal Timber Purchasers Association of Denver, on the other hand, called for an end to the delays. The industry group believed that logging could be conducted without damage to streams and cited 10 percent unemployment in Ravalli County as reason to press ahead with development of the upper Selway.[36] But Daniels realized that the stakes in the game had grown considerably and that Congress would ultimately pass judgment on the logging-versus-fisheries question.

It did not take long for Church and Metcalf to react. A month after Daniels released his management plan, the senators announced that they would introduce new legislation to designate 205,000 acres in the Magruder Corridor as wilderness. As Church stated for the record, "I, for one, do not want to gamble on the future of the fishery in the Selway River."[37] Action on the measure ultimately would be subsumed into the fight over reclassification of the two primitive areas that lay to the south of the Magruder Road. Further delay would result from a new Forest Service study of roadless areas on the national forests—the so-called RARE program, which included four areas within the Magruder Corridor. In the meantime, wilderness advocates could count on vigorous advocacy from Frank Church and Lee Metcalf. Although Mike Mansfield, the hero of the Lincoln-Scapegoat, was nearing retirement, preservationists in the Northern Rockies now had two powerful senators on their side.

15

Wilderness Made Rational
The First Roadless Area Review, 1967–1972

The preservationists' success in derailing the development plans for the Lincoln-Scapegoat and upper Selway areas made it clear to Forest Service officers that any undeveloped tract on the national forests might become a new wilderness battleground. Rather than acquiesce in the loss of their prerogatives, agency leaders strove to reassert their authority. One approach, which remained unofficial and largely under the radar, involved defining wilderness in the strictest terms and offering an alternative "backcountry" type of designation for lands that they believed were less than pristine. A related effort sought to identify all remaining undeveloped lands on the national forests so that their uses might be determined once and for all. This evolved into the endlessly contentious Roadless Area Review and Evaluation (RARE) program of the 1970s. While the Forest Service did not succeed in redefining wilderness to its liking, RARE largely reset the terms of the wilderness debate in ways that neither the agency nor preservationists anticipated.

Officers of the Northern Region of the Forest Service played key roles in developing both the "backcountry" policy and the RARE program. Regional forester Neal Rahm, upset over the Lincoln-Scapegoat and Magruder Corridor debacles, sought to sidetrack further battles over de facto wilderness by promoting alternative designations such as the Mallard-Larkins Pioneer Area and the Jewel Basin Hiking Area. These, he and his staff hoped, would satisfy most recreational users while still permitting a level of resource management not allowed in wilderness areas. Parallel to this effort, several of his officers and research staff helped promulgate the so-called wilderness purity doctrine, by which new wilderness designations would be limited to outstanding examples of alpine country free from major timber conflicts. Rahm's assistants also helped lay the groundwork for the first nationwide roadless area review, which changed the course of wilderness politics in the post–Earth Day era.

Forest Service leaders warned that designating an area as wilderness would attract so many visitors that solitude would be lost and campsites overused. Areas managed under the backcountry concept, in contrast, opened up "exciting possibilities for enhancing recreation opportunities in ways ruled out in wilderness," according to researchers Robert Lucas and George Stankey, who were stationed at the Montana Forest and Conservation Experiment Station in Missoula. They envisioned such measures as clearing trees to improve views, harvesting timber in limited amounts to promote the growth of desirable browse species, and in certain areas even constructing "natural looking earthen dams" that could be stocked with fish. Backcountry areas would thus lessen the recreational pressure on wilderness lands, which could be devoted to true preservation. "If we water down our wildernesses to make them more inviting recreational areas," Lucas wrote in 1979, "natural ecological processes will be substantially altered. The chance to experience a wilderness as wilderness and to find outstanding solitude will slip away."[1]

The backcountry concept gained impetus from a Forest Service task force convened in late 1964 to formulate new regulations implementing the Wilderness Act. Richard Costley, head of the agency's recreation and lands branch (and heir to the seat once held by Bob Marshall) headed the panel; Bill Worf, who had field experience managing the 383,000-acre Bridger Wilderness in Wyoming, played a leading role in determining what standards to employ in managing wilderness areas. Could outfitters leave permanent hunting camps in them? Could irrigators use trucks and heavy equipment to maintain high-country dams? Should state wildlife agencies be allowed to plant fish or transplant big game by helicopter? "Hardly a week went by without some new and different challenge," Worf noted.[2]

To head off such dilemmas, Costley's committee set a high standard for the management of wilderness areas. No motorized or mechanized equipment— even chainsaws for clearing trails—could be used in them except in serious emergencies. Outfitters and temporary permit holders were to leave no evidence of habitation. Range permittees and irrigators would have to use horses to maintain their improvements. As Worf wrote, "Specific and consistent policy guidelines were necessary to prevent gradual erosion of the wilderness resource."[3] High standards of management were one thing, but the Costley committee adopted a corollary to the so-called purity doctrine, which held that nonconforming uses must be excluded from *candidate* areas as well. Not only would temporary intrusions such as outfitter camps and administrative vehicle use count against a proposed wilderness, so would signs of former resource management activities such as salvage sales (as had been conducted in the Mission Range in the 1950s), active and former mining areas like those in the Cabinet Mountains, and remote airstrips such as the one at Schafer Meadows in the Middle Fork of the Flathead. Such areas would be better suited for backcountry designation, they argued. As Costley put it in a 1972 article for *American Forests* magazine, "The standards for wilderness classification and the standards for management must be the same." He promised that the Forest Service (which had set up the first wilderness areas in the West) would resist "attempts to dilute or warp these basic standards." According to agency historian Dennis Roth, Worf and Costley "foresaw that the Forest Service would encounter many, perhaps intractable, problems in protecting wilderness unless high standards were used in creating them."[4] For an agency that desired autonomy of management above almost all other considerations, the backcountry concept had great appeal, with Worf, Stankey, and Lucas actively promoting the idea at meetings and conferences during the 1970s.

Some wilderness advocacy groups toyed with the backcountry concept during the 1960s as a way of stopping timber sales in roadless areas such as the Lincoln Back Country and Oregon's French Pete Creek. The idea seemed easier to sell to the public than wilderness, but the leaders of the national preservation groups insisted that only full wilderness designation would prevent the agency from slipping timber sales into roadless lands under the guise of controlling insects or improving wildlife habitat. They saw the agency's purist approach as an attempt to disqualify generally undeveloped forestlands that bore the odd mineral prospect, irrigation ditch, or old tie-hack road.[5] Such intrusions were "substantially unnoticeable" in the context of thousands of acres of wild country and hence met the criteria of section 2(c) of the Wilderness Act.[6]

Bill Worf and his colleagues no doubt found it ironic that they were incurring the wilderness advocates' wrath for insisting that wilderness areas be a shining example of preservation, unsullied by chainsaws, helicopters, old lookout stations, and fire roads. But the purity doctrine, however well intentioned, played into a common prejudice among Forest Service officers: the belief that a wilderness area should feature impressive mountain peaks, beautiful lake basins, and outstanding hiking and pack trails. The high country constituted what many in the agency called "quality wilderness" as opposed to the heavily forested approaches to the peaks, which in their view were best suited to intensive resource production. The Lincoln-Scapegoat, upper Selway, and Clearwater areas all came under this criticism. Were unbroken forests of stagnant, close-growing lodgepole pine really that valuable? forest rangers asked. The preservationists, it seemed, wanted broad buffer zones around their favorite high lakes and peaks—a scenic viewshed, perhaps, but not real wilderness, and not something the nation could truly afford.

All of these considerations—the Forest Service's desire to maintain its management prerogatives, the quality of candidate wilderness areas, and the need to keep resources available for development—converged in the mid to late 1960s as the agency contemplated the serious challenges to its authority that had emerged in the Lincoln-Scapegoat and Selway controversies. Neal Rahm and his staff had invested much effort in drafting management plans for these areas, only to see them evaporate under the preservationists' offensive. They speculated that by undertaking a comprehensive survey of potential wilderness lands, they could determine once and for all which areas should be preserved and which could be made available for resource management. Richard Costley's wilderness task force endorsed such a survey and called on forest supervisors to identify "all new potential wilderness areas" by December 1966. The idea gathered momentum, and in January 1967 Ed Cliff asked each regional forester to recommend new roadless study areas to the Washington office by June 30, 1970. Two years passed with little action, whereupon Cliff issued a Forest Service Manual directive that set out procedures and extended the deadline to June 1972.[7] Most of the regions did not get under way with their studies until early 1971, after Dick Joy, Neal Rahm's deputy from the Northern Region's recreation division, spent several weeks in the Washington office talking up the idea of a comprehensive examination of roadless lands.[8] Additional impetus for a roadless area study came from the newly formed Council on Environmental Quality, a Cabinet-level group that had been engaged in discussions with the Wilderness Society and Sierra Club over a possible executive order to examine the de facto wilderness question. But it was not until Cliff issued a third directive in February 1971 to all nine regional foresters that the service-wide roadless review process got under way in earnest.[9]

Willing or not, Forest Service offices nationwide soon were embroiled in the first systematic review of potential wilderness lands since L. F. Kneipp's broad-brush inventory of 1926. Initially given the cumbersome title of "Selection of New Study Areas from Roadless and Undeveloped Areas," it was better known by the name given its second phase, Roadless Area Review and Evaluation, or RARE.[10] Agency administrators believed that RARE's systematic planning process could ameliorate conflicts over roadless lands and allow forest administrators to get on with the business of managing forests.

Their optimism was badly misplaced. Probably no one in the agency, from Bill Worf on up to Ed Cliff, realized the nature of the storm their roadless area survey would unleash. Until that time, wilderness enthusiasts in the Northern Rockies had focused their limited resources on a handful of key areas such as the Lincoln-Scapegoat, upper Selway, Spanish Peaks, Middle Fork of the Flathead, and the headwaters of the Clearwater River. But the new roadless survey laid a wide table: once it became public, wilderness advocates set about marshalling public support for hundreds of additional tracts, few of which had previously appeared in their fliers and newsletters. The Forest Service intended to foster a deliberate and systematic planning process that would bring an end to the debilitating controversies over wilderness. Instead it managed only to paint a huge target on itself.

The environmental policy revolution symbolized by the first Earth Day in 1970 brought swelling memberships and budgets to the nation's wilderness advocacy groups, permitting them to substantially expand their staffs in response to the new roadless area reviews. That year Stewart Brandborg hired Harry Crandell, a career biologist with the U.S. Fish and Wildlife Service, to oversee the Wilderness Society's field programs. He joined Ernie Dickerman, Clif Merritt's counterpart for the eastern states, while Merritt moved to Denver to recruit volunteer activists to help with the primitive area reviews.[11] To rouse activists to take part in the often exhausting rounds of agency meetings, Merritt hired minimally paid field organizers (termed "consultants" to avoid having to pay them benefits) in each western state. The volunteer network they helped create would prove indispensable in the new set of roadless area reviews.

The RARE study presented preservation groups with an unprecedented opportunity to protect de facto wilderness on the national forests, but the program appears to have taken some of its leaders by surprise. The Sierra Club's Brock Evans acknowledged the new inventory in an August 1971 letter to Steve Yurich, who had replaced Neal Rahm as Northern Region forester. Doug Scott, who was then working as Brandborg's chief assistant at the Wilderness Society, learned of the program that November at a lunch with a Washington office division chief.[12] Both organizations scrambled to turn out supporters in small western communities where the Forest Service held many of its public meetings on RARE. Assembling comments on the new survey nearly swamped wilderness advocates, who were unfamiliar with many of the roadless areas. By June 30, 1972, the Northern Region had identified 283 areas comprising some 7.6 million acres, exclusive of the primitive areas that were already undergoing review.[13]

In the analysis phase of the program that followed, forest-level and regional office staff employed three highly subjective criteria to determine which of the inventoried roadless areas should proceed to a further, more formal, study. To the preservationists' chagrin, the criteria involved resource management considerations not found in the Wilderness Act—thereby imposing a narrow bottleneck in the process. To be considered *suitable* for classification as wilderness, in the Forest Service's view, a roadless area needed to be virtually free of human imprint, to the point of excluding large blocks of forestland if they contained so much as a single logging spur traversing a portion of the area. Each area also had to be *available*; that is, not subject to timber harvesting plans or other agency management activities. Finally, there had to be a demonstrated *need* for preserving the area.[14] If there was already a designated wilderness nearby, the agency generally saw little purpose to further protective designations.

These initial screens appeared wholly unjustified to lobbyists such as Brock Evans, who reminded Steve Yurich that the Wilderness Act did not require that candidate areas be unsuitable for any other use.[15] This was for Congress to determine, with the Forest Service limited to assessing the areas' physical characteristics and passing its analysis along to the secretary of agriculture's office. Forest Service officers, however, believed that only they had the expertise to make the difficult choices between competing land uses. In February 1972 the Northern Region developed an internal list of "tentative candidate study areas" for further examination. Not released to the public until the following January, the list included eighteen areas totaling 1,580,000 acres. Several had previously attracted interest from conservationists, including the 240,000-acre Hilgard area in the Madison Range, the 420,000-acre Continental Divide area surrounding the Middle Fork of the Flathead River, and several areas in the Magruder Corridor totaling 138,000 acres. Conservationists in the Spokane, Washington, area promoted the 35,000-acre Salmo-Priest area in the Idaho panhandle, while a batch of roadless areas surrounding the Beartooth and Absaroka Primitive Areas attracted attention from Billings-area supporters affiliated with the Montana Wilderness Association.

The RARE study brought to the fore a number of areas that were relatively unknown to conservationists, including the Pioneer Mountains north of Dillon,

Montana, which formed two geologically and botanically distinct areas. Farther west, the high peaks along the Continental Divide were clustered in an area known as the West Big Hole. Bozeman-area MWA members called attention to the roadless areas along the Gallatin Range south of Hyalite Reservoir. Reviewing these and hundreds of other areas at one time served the Forest Service's planning needs and made it possible to quantify the economic cost of setting them aside. At the same time, it forced the preservation interests to divide their attention among many areas, unlike the focused campaigns they had conducted in the Selway and the Lincoln-Scapegoat. The MWA had members in many parts of the state, and the Wilderness Society hired Don Aldrich to help coordinate the response to RARE, but an unprecedented show of support would be needed if any but the least controversial areas were to be selected.

The case of the Hoodoo roadless area was instructive. A relatively unspectacular mountain expanse arrayed along the Montana-Idaho state line between Lookout Pass and Lolo Pass, the 160,000-acre area had received one of the highest "quality index" ratings in the country. The area formed the headwaters of a half dozen good-sized streams on the Lolo and Clearwater National Forests and was popular with hunters, but it received little attention from hikers and backpackers. That changed in 1971 when a group of students at the University of Montana adopted the area as a focus of a one-year, foundation-supported independent study program. The loosely organized group had been traveling around western Montana in a purchased school bus, meeting environmentalists such as Don Aldrich and Doris Milner and learning about the intricate web of administrative and political procedures that governed the public landscape. That summer the group embarked on a three-week trip into the Hoodoo area, caching supplies at different points. The fires of 1910 had swept through the entire area, stripping trees from the high ridges and leaving the valleys choked with deadfall. Sixty years later the land was still healing: heather and shrubs covered the exposed ridgetops while dense forests, not yet ready for harvest, cloaked the lower drainages. The trip, according to participant Dale Harris, "was about wind and water." Hiking up Fish Creek with his young friends, he was enchanted to find clear rushing streams flowing through deep woods of cedar and fir.[16] Up on the Montana-Idaho divide, clouds sped over the naked ridges. Impressed with the area, Harris and his friends founded the Great Burn Study Group, giving the area a more resonant name and developing a well-documented wilderness proposal for the Forest Service's consideration. Harris went on to graduate from the University of Montana's forestry school and cofounded the Wilderness Institute, a research unit that fielded student study teams in many of the RARE areas in western Montana and northern Idaho.

Despite the Hoodoo–Great Burn's high RARE rating, many forest officers opposed its inclusion on the new study area list, since it would not be long until its blanket of young trees reached commercial maturity. Harris and his group played their cards unusually well for a student-run group, adopting a relatively nonconfrontational approach and cultivating friends among community leaders and sympathetic Forest Service officials. The Great Burn made it through the RARE reviews, unlike many others that lacked the close attention of concerned individuals.

In tying the roadless area review to its planning mandate under the Multiple-Use Sustained-Yield Act of 1960, the Forest Service sought to assess wilderness no differently than other forest uses it was charged with providing. Multiple-use planning was then in its infancy in the national forests, but already the compunction to quantify wildland values was evident. No other aspect of the RARE process drew as much derision as the "quality index" that was applied to each of the 1,449 roadless areas identified nationally. Ranger district personnel were asked to assign numbers to various criteria, the sum of which was intended to measure an area's scenic quality, degree of isolation, and variety of possible outdoor experiences. For obscure reasons, scenic quality was weighted 1.33 times as heavily as isolation and recreation. The scenic rating was boosted if a candidate area possessed "numerous lakes and streams," whereas isolation was scored higher if the area had "numerous and well distributed campsites." Areas larger than one hundred thousand acres received higher ratings, while those with "varied fishing and hunting" also gained high marks. Areas were also rated on their uniqueness, with preference given to those that displayed "climatic, elevation, and ecological changes" and that provided "contrast with non-wilderness areas in the region."

The result was that wilderness attributes were skewed toward conventional notions of recreational and scenic value, with more ordinary forest landscapes (especially those with "monotonous" expanses of uncut timber) downrated severely. A case in point was the West Pioneer Mountains in southwestern Montana's Beaverhead National Forest, which lacked the spectacular, glacially sculpted peaks of the nearby East Pioneers, a selected candidate area. The West Pioneers did possess a number of unusual ecological features, including refugial populations of arctic grayling in scattered lakes and the country's oldest known stand of lodgepole pine.[17] Yet in the agency's eyes, the area's subdued topography and unbroken forest cover meant that it was unsuitable as a wilderness area. Similarly downrated was a 68,000-acre area of deep, forested valleys in the upper

Clearwater and St. Joe River drainages, named Bean-Bacon after two headwaters creeks. Adjacent to the Mallard-Larkins Pioneer Area, this forest appeared more suitable for timber management than for the enjoyment of the occasional hiker or horse party; thus it was deemed "not available" for wilderness.

Other measures gauged the opportunity cost of wilderness classification to timber or mineral production. Areas were downrated if they were located next to an existing wilderness area or if they lacked public support, as determined during a public comment period held during the late winter and early spring of 1972. Still other roadless lands were dropped from the inventory if they straddled administrative boundaries, which caused them to be evaluated as separate, smaller units. Only 274 roadless areas representing 12 million acres nationwide made it through this gantlet, 3.4 million acres of which lay in Idaho and Montana. These were designated as New Study Areas, presumably to be winnowed still further before they gained the secretary of agriculture's approval and were sent to the president and Congress.

Protests by preservation groups over the subjective nature of RARE had little effect, and in August 1972 the Sierra Club's legal arm filed suit against Secretary of Agriculture Earl Butz, alleging that development activities in the roadless areas required an analysis under the National Environmental Policy Act (NEPA). After winning a temporary injunction, the club accepted a Forest Service offer to perform NEPA analyses in the multiple-use plans then underway on most national forests.[18] This won time for the preservationists, but roadless areas would not gain any kinder treatment under the unit plans than they had received under RARE. The Forest Service, for its part, was now looking at another time-consuming round of planning and environmental analyses before timber sales in many of the roadless areas could proceed. The rational planning process Ed Cliff had called for was devolving into a legal battleground, the result (in part) of Congress not having specifically addressed the de facto issue when it passed the Wilderness Act.

With RARE already in serious jeopardy, the Forest Service issued a draft environmental impact statement (DEIS) on the overall program in January 1973, followed shortly by a final statement that October.[19] The document laid out 235 roadless areas comprising eleven million acres for tentative wilderness study, 45 of which lay within the Northern Region. Many of the areas on the previous year's list had been pared considerably: the Middle Fork–Continental Divide roadless area on the Flathead National Forest shrank from 420,000 acres to 302,700, the Hilgard area on the Gallatin National Forest was reduced from 240,000 acres to 79,000, and the West Big Hole on the Beaverhead National

Forest from 50,000 to 38,500. Even the lofty North Absaroka area south of Big Timber was reduced from 290,000 acres to 221,000. Areas that survived the process, such as Hyalite (22,300 acres) and Scotchman Peak (37,000 acres) were limited mostly to alpine and subalpine reaches. Other areas, such as the 145,000-acre Meadow Creek drainage that Mort Brigham had long advocated, the Sapphire Mountains, and the 88,000-acre Middle Fork of the Judith River in central Montana's Little Belt Mountains, were missing entirely. The agreement in *Sierra Club v. Butz* also did not apply to an additional seven million acres of undeveloped forestland in the Northern Rockies that were left out of the initial roadless inventory. Activists dissected the draft study recommendations and assembled data showing that timber values in roadless areas were likely exaggerated, but RARE seemed to absorb data and comments like a sponge. This was no longer the direct advocacy of Cecil Garland addressing a crowd in Lincoln, Montana, or Mort Brigham displaying incriminating photos of road landslides in the Clearwater. Public anger had become public input, tallied as statistics instead of as a cry from the hinterlands.

From his second-floor office overlooking Seattle's university district, Brock Evans kept track of the roadless area reviews for the Sierra Club and the Federation of Western Outdoor Clubs, which shared his salary costs. A former Marine, compact and powerfully built, Evans expressed himself forcefully on the need to combat the Forest Service's depredations. It appeared to him that the agency was offering "tokens, with as few trees as possible in them, in areas where we had been fighting the longest and the hardest."[20] He cautioned preservationists not to get sucked into the whirlpool of administrative procedure. They needed to monitor the RARE program, but he felt they were going to be "drowned in an avalanche of paper." Instead, they must stay on the attack. "We must never be in a position of reacting to what the Forest Service is doing," he warned his fellow staff members. "We must always be acting first; the power of initiative is one of the few basic strengths that the environmental movement has." That had been proven in the Lincoln Back Country, where the Forest Service had lost control of its plans. If sponsors for wilderness legislation could not be found, Evans suggested that representatives from other states introduce omnibus bills, as Pennsylvania's John Saylor had done in 1970.[21] "Let us go to the political level," Evans concluded. "It is the only way that we can ultimately prevail."

Indeed, preservation groups had few successes to celebrate when the Forest Service released its final list of study areas in October 1973. Thirty-nine additions were made that brought the nationwide acreage to 12.3 million, a third of which already had that status from earlier reviews, as Evans pointed out. Most other areas were unchanged; no studies were proposed for the Bean-Bacon area in the upper Clearwater, Meadow Creek, the Sapphire Mountains, most of the Gallatin Range, or the Elkhorn Mountains south of Helena, among many others.[22] Don Aldrich, who compiled the comments of various Montana and Idaho conservationists on the RARE study, prefaced the lengthy document with some harsh words intended for Forest Service chief John McGuire. It was a manifesto of frustration.

> Statements such as "no unique characteristics," "doesn't warrant wilderness consideration," "other values are dominant" were made by men who spend their workweek in forested land and can't wait until Friday night so they can get to the home, beer parlor or sporting event. Their agency responsibility is providing raw materials for local industry so establishing areas closed to roading and timber harvesting complicates their assignment. One cannot expect understanding or enthusiasm for wilderness from these people. Wilderness is not a tangible thing that can be measured in yards, weighed in pounds, or expressed in volume. It is a philosophy and an emotional response to beauty, serenity, [and] uniqueness that is found in places where the plant and animal communities are not disturbed and the atmosphere and topography are unaltered by Man. It can be quantified only by those who feel these things. You have it or you don't.[23]

As RARE wound toward its conclusion and was replaced by the mandated analyses in multiple-use plans, Aldrich and his friends faced multiple challenges in dozens of roadless areas on the national forests of the Northern Rockies. Timber sales were proposed for Moose Creek in the Sapphire Mountains, the South Fork of Swan Creek in the Gallatin Range, Tizer Basin in the Elkhorn Mountains, the Ten Lakes and Mount Henry areas on the Kootenai National Forest, the West Pioneers on the Beaverhead, and the Blue Joint drainage on the Bitterroot. Aldrich, Doris Milner, and Clif Merritt knew they had little time to act and once again sought a legislative remedy—this time as a bill mandating a full wilderness study for these and twelve other roadless areas that had not made the cut during RARE. Merritt presented the nineteen areas to Teddy Roe, Lee Metcalf's legislative aide, in February 1974. When Roe showed the list to his boss, Metcalf exclaimed, "Oh my God, I can't do that, tell 'em to cut it to ten."[24] Merritt pared the list, and on October 1, 1974, Metcalf introduced S. 4066, the Montana Wilderness Study Act.

It required the Forest Service to refrain from developing the ten study areas during a five-year study period, after which the secretary of agriculture was given another two years to file a report on their suitability as wilderness.

Significantly, the bill extended protection for the study areas until Congress made a final determination.[25] This ensured that the areas would not fall prey to timber cutting and road construction in the event the agency once again decided they were unworthy of designation. At Metcalf's request, Forest Service chief John McGuire postponed timber sales in the proposed study areas, lopping ten million board feet off the Northern Region's six-month sale roster.[26] This raised the stakes to a new level: unlike in the Lincoln-Scapegoat, where relatively little timber was at stake, the immediate reductions meant that industry would mount a coordinated attack on the Metcalf bill. Opposition would also come from newly organized groups of snowmobilers and off-road vehicle users who saw a threat to areas where they enjoyed riding.

RARE may not have resolved the roadless area issue as Ed Cliff and Neal Rahm hoped, but in one important respect it succeeded: in attempting to substitute a rational decision-making process for what had been an emotionally charged issue, the agency recast the wilderness debate for years to come. De facto wilderness, in all its diverse landforms and habitats, was given over to the soulless heart of the computer with its opportunity cost calculations and public input algorithms. Quantification counted for everything, which gave timber, minerals, and recreation visitor-days additional importance. The preservation lobby responded with its own analyses of timber values, wildlife habitat needs, and soil and watershed issues, all of which gave their cause better scientific grounding, but increasingly the debate would hinge on acreage tallies and allowable-cut figures. Wilderness supporters would have a difficult time keeping the public's attention on the traditional benefits of wilderness, which were much harder to quantify: the chance to experience real solitude, to seek unfettered hunting and fishing, and to experience a world untrammeled by machines and management schemes. The preservation movement was in danger of losing its central story—one that featured ordinary citizens working to protect the West's most resplendent and soul-stirring landscapes.

16

The Organization of Spirited People
The Salmon River Wilderness, 1970–1975

The rustic home of Doris and Kelsey Milner in Hamilton, Montana, served as a favorite meeting place for conservationists during the 1960s. Situated in the evening shadow of the Bitterroot Range, surrounded by fragrant pines, its location reminded visitors of the wild country that stretched for dozens of miles to the west. Drinks and banter flowed as longtime activists such as Ernie Day, Mort Brigham, Don Aldrich, and G. M. Brandborg laid bare their frustration with the Forest Service. On the first weekend of September 1969, these men and women met with seven other activists to deal with the impending reclassification of the two primitive areas lying to the south of the Selway-Bitterroot Wilderness, which together formed the greatest expanse of wild country in the Lower 48. Joining them were Sierra Club lobbyist Brock Evans, who was touring the Bitterroot that week in the elder Brandborg's company; Clif Merritt of Denver, representing the Wilderness Society; Laney Hicks, a Sierra Club activist from Wyoming; Jerry Jayne, a computer programmer at the government's nuclear facility west of Idaho Falls, who represented the Idaho Environmental Council; Dr. Walt Blackadar, a whitewater river runner from the town of Salmon; Jim Calvert of Moscow, representing the Idaho Wildlife Federation; and Ruth Brandborg, who added her calm and thoughtful presence to the intense discussions that followed.

Jayne, Day, Brigham, and others in Idaho's overstretched preservation ranks faced a daunting task in trying to secure protection for the million-acre Idaho

Primitive Area, which the Forest Service had designated in 1931, as well as for the smaller Salmon River Breaks Primitive Area, a holdover from the reclassified Selway-Bitterroot Primitive Area. Separating the two areas was the canyoned course of the main Salmon River, itself a recreational treasure of national importance. The Magruder Road had sundered the Selway-Bitterroot in the 1930s, but an enormous wild region still stretched almost from the Sawtooths to the Lochsa River. How much of this land could be permanently designated as wilderness? The Forest Service was embarking on separate studies of the two primitive areas, but as Jim Calvert noted in his summary of the meeting, the entire region from the headwaters of the Salmon's Middle Fork north to the Lochsa was historically a single wilderness, and "the very act of giving it three names was the first move to break it up. We will not be a party to this fraud."[1] The two remaining primitive areas must be studied together, the group insisted, and while the Magruder Road was fact, they would not accept wholesale deletions around it such as the Forest Service had done in Area E. This was a "mountain wilderness big enough to maintain forever its individual ecology," and they hoped that "a more enlightened age will have the opportunity to eliminate" the intruding road. They proposed that the reclassified area be named the River of No Return Wilderness.

The strong position for a unified wilderness probably reflected Brock Evans's attendance at the Hamilton meeting. The previous year he had urged conservationists to form the Idaho Environmental Council, an umbrella group under Jayne's and Calvert's direction that pressed Idaho politicians to protect its public lands and waters. Evans saw his role as stiffening the resolve of local wilderness supporters in the timber-rich Northwest and Northern Rockies. A gifted speaker, his presence at meetings could be electrifying, and he reminded activists that the law and national public opinion were on their side. In his absence, however, the obstacles often appeared insurmountable. Two months after their initial meeting, many of the same activists met again at the Milners' home, this time without Evans, to discuss boundaries for the River of No Return Wilderness. Ernie Day—a legend among Idaho sportsmen and conservationists—persuaded them that studying the two primitive areas separately would give their opponents less opportunity to attack.[2] A unified River of No Return Wilderness remained their goal, but reaching it in increments instead of one colossal battle appeared prudent to some. The "disgruntlement" that Jim Calvert recorded at this meeting signaled the difficult strategic decisions facing preservation groups in the Rockies. They managed to agree on additions to the Idaho and Salmon River Breaks Primitive Areas that would yield a new wilderness area of some 1.5 million acres—the largest yet proposed in the country.

One fear was that the Forest Service would develop the Salmon River corridor separating the two primitive areas. Only three years earlier Neal Rahm, then working as an assistant regional forester with the Intermountain Region in Ogden, had announced that he was open to the idea of completing the road down the main Salmon River as part of what he termed "long-range multiple-use management planning for this mighty river canyon."[3] A road linking the towns of Salmon and Riggins had been a fever dream of boosters for years. In 1962 their counterparts in northern Idaho had succeeded in blasting a paved road through the cliffs along the Lochsa; the Salmon presented no difficulty dynamite could not overcome.

Nor was the Idaho Primitive Area itself a shoo-in for wilderness status. Forest Service administrators had shown considerable antipathy toward the area ever since its designation in 1931. In 1956 the supervisors of the four national forests encompassing the area proposed that less than one-fourth of it—a mere 235,000 acres—be retained as a wilderness. The remainder would be treated as a recreation area under regulation U-3, which allowed for administrative development and some road construction.[4] Part of the rationale for improving access came from wildlife managers who wanted to cull more of the area's growing elk herds. As in the Selway, elk had benefited from increased browse resulting from large wildfires in 1910 and 1934 and were making heavy use of winter ranges along the Salmon River and its tributaries. This led to spring die-offs and also a reduction in the forage available to bighorn sheep, which suffered serious declines beginning in the 1920s. Horse packers took many hunters deep into the wilderness, but most congregated around its edge, staying close to existing roads and enjoying relatively less success.[5]

There were many nonconforming features in the primitive area as well, including a half dozen airstrips that had been built on private inholdings. These, too, tended to concentrate hunters. In 1947 Eugene Wilson, a Connecticut sportsman who happened to be a prominent aircraft manufacturer, complained to chief forester Lyle Watts that during his much-anticipated horse packing trip into the Middle Fork country, others had come in the easy way. One hunter had "killed a deer right on the landing field, had dressed it out and flown back home before the meat could cool." Wilson, who was president of the Aircraft Industries Association of America, found it "incredible" that with so much of the West's backcountry open to aircraft, the Forest Service could "permit such a violation of the spirit of a wise law which set aside a few primitive areas."[6] The Forest Service, however, viewed the airstrips as a substitute for roads: in a letter to Howard Zahniser, Lloyd Swift of the agency's wildlife division pointed out that the landing fields were needed to retrieve smokejumper crews. It was either the airstrips or a "network of motor ways," Swift wrote.[7]

Idaho conservationists were also worried about Chamberlain Basin, a series of plateaus and low ridges in the northwestern part of the Idaho Primitive Area. At 6,500 feet in elevation, blanketed with open meadows, it formed ideal elk habitat and drew hundreds of hunters each fall. A Sierra Club survey team in 1963 described the basin as "a wilderness for the wanderer and the dreamer, and for the young and the very old." Subsequent surveys noted how ancient lakes had left peaty bogs that supported many varieties of wildflowers, while the surrounding forest was a fire-created patchwork of lodgepole and ponderosa pine.[8] These trees had grown to merchantable size since the earlier conflagrations and now looked promising to sawmills outside the primitive area on the Payette River.

During the late 1960s Forest Service officials from the regional offices in Ogden and Missoula debated how to proceed with their studies of the two central Idaho primitive areas, as required under the Wilderness Act. The Northern Region's Ed Barry, author of the controversial highway development plan for the Lincoln Back Country, proposed a national recreation area that would permit road and highway construction. Other officials pointed out the "vast amount of non-conforming uses" in the Idaho Primitive Area, including airstrips and numerous mining claims.[9] But J. M. Herbert, Barry's counterpart from the less timber-dependent Intermountain Region, was cool to the idea of opening this wild expanse to vehicle-based recreation, proposing instead to regional forester Floyd Iverson that "we gear our thinking to what is the best long-range management, taking into account the needs of the people as well as protection of the fragile country involved."[10] The two primitive areas should remain roadless, he said, even if they were not formally classified, and some adjacent undeveloped lands should be examined as well.

In March 1970 in the sleepy riverside town of Salmon, the Intermountain Region opened the first of numerous public meetings to consider the reclassification of the Idaho and Salmon River Breaks Primitive Areas. Whitewater recreation was beginning to boom in Idaho, but many of the two hundred attendees were more concerned about an assured log supply for the local sawmill. Preservationists wanted to add the Clear Creek–Garden Creek area, an important bighorn sheep winter range east of the Idaho Primitive Area, to the overall study. Testimony split narrowly in favor of preserving this area, reflecting a strong effort from Clif Merritt and Stewart Brandborg to turn out Wilderness Society members and other cooperators from eastern Idaho and southwestern Montana.[11] The agency followed with "informational" meetings during April 1971 in Boise, McCall, Grangeville, Challis, Salmon, Idaho Falls, and Hamilton, at which it explained its goals for the primitive area studies and took comments from the public. By then preservation groups were casting their gaze on far more land than the 1.3 million acres under study in the two primitive areas.

In 1972 a young Sierra Club activist named Peter Morrison assembled the club's various wilderness surveys in central Idaho into a report that called for designating a 2.4-million-acre wilderness encompassing both primitive areas and the canyons of the main Salmon and its Middle Fork, plus a million acres of surrounding national forest land. In the Salmon River Mountains, Morrison wrote, "a sweeping expanse of deeply dissected wild land extends to all horizons. Here is finally a land where you will not find roads, towns, or clearcuts beyond the next ridge."[12] With this benchmark established, Idaho and Montana activists met in February 1973 at Walt Blackadar's home in Salmon to settle on a wilderness boundary they could all support. Jerry Jayne, Carl Hocevar, and Pete Henault represented the Idaho Environmental Council, while Montanans Doris Milner and Don Aldrich were veterans of the Magruder Corridor battle. Ralph Maughan of Pocatello and Richard Smith of Salmon represented a younger generation, as did Dave Pavelchek, who hailed from the Sierra Club's office in Seattle. With a large map of the Idaho and Salmon River Breaks Primitive Areas pinned to the wall, each of them took turns describing contiguous roadless lands they believed should be part of a single great wilderness. By the end of the meeting they had settled on what Jayne called a "very large, many lobed, and highly asymmetrical amoeba" that represented 2.3 million acres of wild country. Taking in the long-disputed Area E of the Magruder Corridor, it was the boldest move yet for a statewide citizen organization. Still, as Ernie Day pointed out later, their proposal fell considerably short of the three million acres of roadless land he believed could be found in these mountains.[13]

The group formally organized as the River of No Return Wilderness Council, with Tom Davis, an environmental engineer from Boise, as chairman. Its directors included many of Idaho's best-known conservationists, including Day, the outdoor writer Ted Trueblood, Boise attorney Bruce Bowler, and Mary Lou Reed, an activist from Coeur d'Alene. Most were also active in the Idaho Environmental Council or the Idaho Conservation League, a new organization formed that year, and had taken leading roles in the long-running battle to keep dams out of Hells Canyon. Trueblood, an associate editor of *Field & Stream*, had been using the backcountry airstrips in Chamberlain Basin for years and regarded the area as one of the country's premier hunting grounds, while Day professed that he was never happier than when he was floating the Middle Fork of the Salmon. Both men had met Howard Zahniser during the campaign for the Wilderness Act, when they formed the Idaho Wilderness Committee with Bowler, Mort Brigham, and Franklin Jones. "We felt very lonely out there," Day recalled in 1979 of their early efforts to raise support for wilderness in Idaho.[14]

One of the most difficult questions the wilderness council dealt with was the use of powerboats and aircraft in the area, along with the existence of permanent outfitter camps deep in the backcountry. The subject engendered "heated discussion" at the meeting in Salmon, according to Don Aldrich's notes, leading to an agreement that banning them "would alienate commercial outfitters" and "assure formidable opposition."[15] There was nothing in the Wilderness Act that excluded these "historic and traditional uses," the group stated in a press release following its February 1973 meeting. "This extreme purity interpretation is strictly an invention of the Forest Service and in no way reflects the intent of Congress."[16]

Doug Scott, who replaced Brock Evans as the Sierra Club's northwest representative that spring, worked closely with the River of No Return Wilderness Council to define the central issues of the campaign. He intended to dig a deep hole for the Worf-Costley purity doctrine, which held that designated wilderness should be free of noncomforming camps and evidence of past mining and timbering. He encouraged the Idaho group to accept continued jet boat use on the main Salmon, whereas on the Middle Fork, a cascading whitewater stream locked in an otherwise impassable canyon, all motors would be banned, allowing rafters and kayakers to enjoy their sport amid the sounds of nature. The River of No Return seemed big enough to hold all its various admirers.

That summer, after folding the Clear Creek area back into the primitive area study, Floyd Iverson released a proposal for a 1.5-million-acre wilderness, encompassing the two primitive areas and some adjacent acreage.[17] Anticipating this, the River of No Return Wilderness Council distributed a tabloid touting its 2.3-million-acre proposal. The Boise Cascade Corporation countered with a proposal for a 579,000-acre roadless recreation area along the main Salmon and its Middle Fork, which it said would "closely approximate pure wilderness classification." The company took out a full-page advertisement in Idaho newspapers, calling its proposal a "middle ground" between total preservation and total development. The recreation classification would permit "primitive camping facilities along these rivers whose waters are dirtied by the thousands of people who float and boat" them. Local mills were facing log shortages due to Forest Service cutbacks, the company warned. "In Idaho we are fully utilizing our own lands and no other timber is available.

Without replacement timber, Boise Cascade and other forest product companies in southern Idaho will be forced to shut mills."[18]

Boise Cascade's high-profile campaign, coupled with its threats to close mills, alarmed the wilderness council. Doug Scott assured them, however, that the company was so development oriented that few people outside local mill towns would take it seriously. When the Forest Service held another round of public meetings in November 1973 to take testimony on its proposal, wilderness supporters turned out in force. At meetings in Boise and Pocatello, a majority of those speaking favored wilderness designation for at least the two primitive areas, whereas in small towns such as Salmon, McCall, and Grangeville witnesses with ties to the timber and mining industry, as well as users of jeeps and trail bikes, predominated. Overall the Forest Service reported a four-to-one plurality of statements favoring a substantial wilderness designation. Clif Merritt congratulated the Idaho activists, telling Mort Brigham, "It must be most heartwarming to you, who fought so hard and with so little help for the conservation cause in central Idaho, to see such demonstrations of overwhelming support."[19]

If the two primitive areas seemed secure, much controversy remained over designating the surrounding wildlands. Lumber interests were especially interested in the so-called Dixie Tail, a 36,000-acre area on the Nez Perce National Forest that lay to the south and east of the Red River–Dixie road. Carl Hocevar of the River of No Return Wilderness Council called it "steep beautiful country which is essential habitat for bighorn sheep."[20] As in the Clear Creek drainage, wilderness activists were unwilling to relinquish even small areas that offered important wildlife habitat, believing that the integrity of the larger area was at stake. Water quality was also at issue: Ted Trueblood described how you could count the spots on a trout twenty feet beneath the surface of the Middle Fork, warning that its superb clarity could be lost if the Forest Service were allowed to pursue its road-building and logging ambitions.[21] He feared a repeat of the environmental disaster that had befallen the heavily logged South Fork of the Salmon River during the winter of 1964–65. Heavy rains and snowmelt on the steep, friable slopes of the Idaho Batholith had caused numerous logging roads to wash out, sending 1.5 million cubic yards of sediment cascading into the river. Spawning beds were buried, snuffing out salmon runs for years.[22] The Forest Service placed a moratorium on logging in the drainage, but the stream's slow recovery came too late for runs already compromised by downstream dams. No assurances that future logging would be conducted with more care would set wildlife and wilderness activists at ease.

Some of Clif Merritt's professional colleagues disputed the importance of the Forest Service meetings, which were not formal public hearings as required under the Wilderness Act. Harry Crandell pointed out that wilderness advocates "could fall into a carefully laid trap" of debating wilderness with the managing agency when the real action was before Congress. But Merritt felt strongly that the agency hearings were a crucial test of preservationists' strength in the areas where it mattered most—deep within the huge mountain landscapes they wanted to protect. "I have been around too long and spent too many years working with, for, and against government agencies . . . not to know that such public meetings, no matter how informal or unofficial, are used as 'sounding boards' by the agency," he told Crandell. What he called the "failure of conservationists for so many years to appear in reasonable numbers" at such meetings gave bureaucrats the excuse to make minimal wilderness recommendations, and this was why they "have had such big battles later, at formal administrative and Congressional hearings."[23]

The preservation movement was still casting about for a strategy that might overcome the Forest Service's strong antipathy toward placing timber or mineral reserves off limits to use. Merritt's insistence that the action began in local communities reflected his long experience working in western Montana, helping leaders such as Cecil Garland and Doris Milner rouse opposition to the agency's logging and road-building plans. In doing so they managed to gain acceptance of wilderness designations among some conservative rural residents, including the outfitting, guiding, and hunting fraternity that was held in high regard among politicians and decision makers. At the time, the Idaho Outfitters and Guides Association favored a "recreational back country" classification for the two primitive areas to permit construction of sanitation facilities, corrals, and high-standard trails. "Designation of the areas as wilderness would put the outfitters' camp facilities out of business," according to Norman Guth, an outfitter from Salmon who owned a rustic camp on the main Salmon river.[24]

The wilderness advocates took pains to cultivate the outfitters' support. Richard Smith of Salmon, who was both an outfitter and vice chair of the Sierra Club's Northern Rockies chapter, helped persuade Guth and his colleagues that wilderness designation would not prohibit reasonable outfitting practices in the backcountry. Ted Trueblood's contacts in the sporting media helped bring along the average hunter and angler as well. In a *Field & Stream* article written in 1975—one of many he wrote on the issue—he criticized the Forest Service for burning several old homesteads along the Middle Fork and for imposing burdensome standards on backcountry outfitters. Under the purity doctrine,

Trueblood claimed, "I would have broken a rule every time I tied my horse within 300 feet of a lake."[25] As one of the country's most respected outdoor writers, his message was crucial to overcoming sportsmen's suspicions of wilderness and its advocates. Their support would be essential in dealing with Idaho's deeply divided congressional delegation.

The Idaho activists had a sympathetic senator in Frank Church, who in 1973 informed his constituents that the Wilderness Act "always contemplated the inclusion of the designated Primitive Areas. . . . This can be accomplished without the least impairment of our working forests." Even James McClure, a conservative Republican who was elected to the Senate in 1972, indicated that he might support classification of the two central Idaho primitive areas. Replacing McClure in the House, however, was a young apple grower from Caldwell named Steve Symms, who ran on a platform of reducing the size of the federal government. His district took in most of western Idaho, including Nampa, Caldwell, and part of the Boise metropolitan area, but also the rural counties reaching to the state's northern panhandle. With Republican Orval Hansen holding onto his eastern district House seat, the stars were not well aligned for a major expansion of the primitive areas. Church stated in 1973 that when it came to new additions to the wilderness system, he intended to apply a "simple test: if the new area recommended is multiple-use ground, it is not suitable for single-use administration. Therefore, it should not be designated as wilderness."[26] This gave considerable pause to the leaders of the River of No Return Wilderness Council, who hoped to add substantial "multiple-use" (i.e., timber) lands to the two primitive areas.

Idaho governor Cecil Andrus was the only other bright spot for wilderness advocates in Idaho's political landscape. Elected in 1970 in part because of his opposition to a large molybdenum mine in the White Cloud Peaks east of Stanley, he retained his seat in 1974. He called conservation "an element of our survival," although he (like Church) took pains to not identify himself too closely with environmental advocates. A fishing and hunting buddy of Ernie Day, Andrus liked to tell how he once pulled his friend out of the Clearwater River after Day fell off a rock, saying "I should have practiced catch and release that day."[27] Day and his fellow council members were disappointed when Andrus recommended only a 300,000-acre expansion of the Forest Service proposal for the central Idaho wilderness. Marty Morache, a biologist with the state fish and game department, described these additions as "the critical minimum needed to protect the integrity of the Middle Fork watershed." Among them was the drainage of Big Creek, a 29,000-acre exclusion from the administration recommendation, which Morache described as "the finest resident fishery of the Middle Fork system" and "an exceedingly valuable nursery stream for all fish species."[28]

The governor's support proved important when the outgoing Ford administration delivered what appeared to be a serious blow to the wilderness lovers' hopes. Agriculture Secretary Earl Butz surprised many observers when he pared nearly 400,000 acres from the Forest Service's 1.5-million-acre proposal in his final recommendation, released in late 1974. To the horror of the Idaho preservationists, most of Chamberlain Basin, long thought to be a certain component of the new wilderness, was missing. The basin contained enough timber to support an annual harvest of 23.5 million board feet, and its removal was a sign of Boise Cascade's influence within the administration. Cecil Andrus quickly dismissed the timber company's claims as "a club being held over the public" and promised to seek reinstatement for the basin.[29]

Andrus's 1.8-million-acre proposal may have lent some credibility to the preservationists' aims, but their primary target was Frank Church, who as a ranking member of the Senate Interior Committee (and chair of its Public Lands Subcommittee) would make or break the River of No Return proposal. Several years earlier he had introduced a bill for the Magruder Corridor area in the upper Selway drainage and was now engaged in the debate over wilderness areas in the East, a campaign with major ramifications for the Forest Service's purity doctrine. With a difficult reelection contest looming, he appeared reluctant to challenge his state's powerful timber and mining interests, and his campaign statements stayed clear of endorsing the River of No Return proposal. Doug Scott, who was working closely with Church to craft a policy statement on the purity issue, urged him not to "wallow in the 'intellectual shallows' of multiple-use versus single-use with regard to the Idaho Primitive Area discussion." Scott circulated a memo to the Idaho leaders advising them to hold the senator's feet to the fire. "It is most important for Church to understand that we will not tolerate any excessive demagoguery on his part, while appreciating his current problem," he wrote. "We [must] keep Frank from entering into any implied or explicit commitments that will make it impossible for him to do the right thing later on."[30]

Church's support became all the more essential after Steve Symms endorsed a 1.4-million-acre central Idaho wilderness. The representative voiced many Idahoans' dislike of federal wilderness designations, claiming that "too much land has been dedicated to this restrictive classification. . . . We are finding wilderness to be not especially attractive to families with very young children, to the elderly, or to the casual camper who can only snatch brief times away from his job."[31] Church, however, announced that he had "no intention of presiding over the dismantlement" of the Idaho and Salmon River Breaks Primitive Areas. Congress would hold field hearings and make the final decision, he assured his constituents.[32]

The prospect of losing Chamberlain Basin so worried Idaho's conservation leaders that some wondered whether it was time to accept a strategic compromise. This set off alarms in the national offices of the Sierra Club and Wilderness Society, which were heavily invested in gaining the largest possible wilderness in Idaho. Clif Merritt and Doug Scott flew to Boise to buck up the local leadership, assuring Trueblood and his friends that the administration's proposal was merely a recommendation and that Chamberlain Basin would remain secure until Congress acted.[33] Conservationists were losing valuable time agonizing over the basin, Merritt complained to Mort Brigham, when they "should have been organizing support all over Idaho and the Nation." The protests induced President Ford to reinstate the basin to the administration's recommendation. Two days after the November 1976 election, which saw Jimmy Carter defeat Ford on a platform that included strong environmental protection, Frank Church announced to his constituents that "Chamberlain Basin has always been safe" and that he was confident that an "overwhelming majority" of Idahoans wanted the complete primitive area included in the new wilderness.[34] He was careful not to commit himself to including the roadless lands surrounding the primitive area, which was where the greater issue lay.

Doug Scott, too, took every opportunity to remind grassroots leaders that however much they had to deal with conservative rural politicians, their eyes needed to be on the national game. This was why wilderness advocates had fought for such a law in the first place, and why Wilderness Society staffers took pains to hold wilderness workshops and attend strategy sessions in so many western cities. In the end it was not Floyd Iverson, Neal Rahm, or even Earl Butz who would determine the fate of places such as Chamberlain Basin or the Magruder Corridor. The size and shape of Idaho's wilderness depended on whether it would be Frank Church or Steve Symms who had the last word in disposing of these incomparable lands.

17

Lee Metcalf and the Politics of Preservation
The Montana Wilderness Study Act and the Great Bear Wilderness, 1974–1977

When Clif Merritt submitted his list of ten proposed wilderness study areas to Lee Metcalf in early 1974, the senator was already working with Flathead Valley conservationists on a bill to designate the Middle Fork of the Flathead River drainage as wilderness and was involved in the ongoing review of the Spanish Peaks Primitive Area. By this time Metcalf had established his environmental credentials with enactment of the Scapegoat Wilderness, his inquiries into clear-cutting practices, and his consistent support for national parks and wildlife refuges. Conservationists were fortunate to have him in the Senate, for in 1972 he had contemplated retiring at the conclusion of his second term. In declining health and suffering from painful knees, Metcalf let it be known that he and Donna wanted to return to their home in Helena. He had amassed an important legacy of progressive legislation in the fields of education, labor, Indian affairs, public power, and the environment, but Montana's wilderness activists could turn to no one else to carry controversial legislation. Cecil Garland, then president of the Montana Wilderness Association, applied some extraordinary pressure the night before a hearing on the Spanish Peaks Primitive Area. "The Senator looked very tired," he recalled, "and told us that he was not well and we talked about his not running again for the Senate. I was stunned and pleaded with Lee that he must if he could at all, retain his Senate seat."[1] Metcalf stayed in the race and won reelection against Republican Henry Hibbard, a Helena sheep rancher and state legislator. In his final term he would take the lead on numerous environmental issues, including strip mining control legislation, energy policy, and wild river classification for the upper Missouri River. Wilderness legislation in his home state, however, would engender some of the sharpest controversy.

After seeing Bunker Creek and the lower slopes of Dean Ridge fall to timber and road development, Flathead Valley conservationists were determined to halt further encroachments on the wild country north of the Bob Marshall Wilderness. In 1970 Loren Kreck and Chris Roholt, a graduate student at the University of Montana's School of Forestry, organized a Middle Fork Preservation Committee and put together an ambitious proposal for what they called the Great Bear Wilderness. Named for its most emblematic animal, it would shelter "one of the last natural, free moving grizzly populations in the continental United States," according to Kreck, and would form an important bridge for these animals between the Bob Marshall and Glacier National Park.[2] The Great Bear proposal took in most of the drainage of the Middle Fork of the Flathead River as well as a long extension to the northwest along the divide between the river's Middle and South Forks, along with additional lands east of the Continental Divide in the drainages of Badger and Two Medicine Creeks. It was, Kreck said, "one of the last great unspoiled mountain-top to mountain-top drainages of a major river system in the United States that man hasn't loused up."

The Great Bear offered the best of recreational experiences, according to Jean Warren of Missoula, who headed a local Sierra Club group. She recalled "exhilarating moments scrambling hell-bent-for-leather down the slopes of Great Northern Mountain with wide-eyed respect for a lightning storm all about myself and my companions. And quiet, gentle moments in another area of dark, moist forests, photographing huge, orangish Alice-in-Wonderland-like mushrooms." Yet for her, the area's greatest value was found in its rare and endangered species. These represented "more than inspirational creatures for our national heritage or someone's calendar. They are a statement of the evolutionary process of life to which we all belong."[3]

Achieving wild river status for the Middle Fork was also a priority for Kreck, Roholt, and other preservationists. In 1973 the Flathead National Forest recommended that fifty-one miles of the Flathead's South Fork, from its headwaters to the Spotted Bear Ranger Station, be classified as "wild," with the remaining nine miles down to Hungry Horse Reservoir to be classified as "recreational" owing to road and timber development. It also recommended wild river status for nearly forty-seven miles of the upper Middle Fork, with the remainder to be classified as recreational. Dams would be prohibited on these streams and on the Flathead's North Fork.[4] This represented a likely victory over the Spruce Park Dam and gave added impetus to the wilderness proposal.

In July 1974 Lee Metcalf introduced the first of several bills that would ultimately establish the Great Bear Wilderness Area. By this time there was general agreement that the main valley of the Middle Fork should be preserved in some form, but the roadless lands to either side of this drainage were still subject to ongoing timber sales and other development projects. Snowmobilers were making use of trails south of Marias Pass, and the Bonneville Power Administration wanted to reserve a power line corridor through the heart of the area. The Forest Service had recommended a 240,000-acre study area in RARE, but this left out most of the conflicted lands. At a May 20, 1975, hearing on his 393,000-acre Great Bear bill, Metcalf agreed to amend it to provide for a wilderness study to resolve these and other conflicts, including treaty claims by the Blackfoot Tribe to timber cutting rights on 20,000 acres in the eastern part of the area.[5] The bill was reported out of the Senate Interior Committee in late 1975 and passed the Senate in the spring of 1976. Action in the House would depend on John Melcher, the state's western district representative, who shared Metcalf's party affiliation but was known for putting his own stamp on natural resource legislation.

In January 1975 Metcalf reintroduced his Montana wilderness study bill, now designated S. 393. At the bill's first hearing before the Senate Public Lands Subcommittee on May 9, he stated that "it does not take a genius to discern a connection between the headlong rush of the Administration to cut timber and its foot-dragging in implementing the large-scale studies mandated by the Wilderness Act." He called his bill "an attempt to pull the Administration back on the course originally intended by Congress."[6] By asking for nothing more than intensive studies of what were now nine roadless areas, he hoped there would be less opposition to the bill, but it was clear that he (and environmentalists) had misjudged the opposition as industry representatives mounted a major attack. National lobbying groups such as the Federal Timber Purchasers Association and the National Forest Products Association opposed the bill, as did regional players such as the Inland Forest Resource Council. Royce Satterlee of the F. H. Stoltze Company feared for the future of his Dillon sawmill if the West Pioneers area, which was included in the bill, was removed from the cutting circles. The Forest Service had already placed the rugged East Pioneers area off limits to logging as a result of the RARE program, and Satterlee was counting on the ten to twelve million board feet of annual cut from the more heavily forested western range. "We feel it is a very tough situation for us," he told the subcommittee. His mill had a two-year supply of logs under contract from national forest and private lands, but unless additional timber were made available from roadless areas, it would have to close, he said. The Dillon mill employed 120 people, a major employer in a town of fewer than 4,000.[7]

The story was repeated by owners of mills in Belgrade and White Sulphur Springs, which drew timber from relatively sparse east-side forests. Mills west of the Continental Divide had access to larger supplies of national forest timber, but the rope was drawing tighter as new environmental restrictions on clear-cutting and road building—a result of Lee Metcalf and Frank Church's collaboration on forest practices reform—added to the impact of wilderness withdrawals. Max Baucus, Montana's newly elected western district representative, pressed witnesses at the May 9 hearing on whether the loss of timber from the S. 393 areas would "absolutely" cause their mills to shut down. None would confirm this, yet they pointed out that their industry depended on log supplies from both public and private lands, and if one source was compromised the other would be overcut.[8]

Metcalf was also taking heat from snowmobile enthusiasts, who in recent years had been making use of a high-line trail through the Madison and Gallatin Ranges. At the May 9 hearing he agreed to amend his bill to allow motorized recreation to continue in the nine areas until they were classified as wilderness. "It was never my intention to diminish their winter enjoyment of these areas," he announced.[9] It was a significant concession, for although the snow machines left no permanent tracks in the high country, their use steadily increased in many of the areas and became an obstacle to wilderness classification.

Opposition to S. 393 also came from the Montana Power Company, which was proposing to build electric transmission lines in two of the proposed study areas. A 69-kilovolt line through the Taylor-Hilgard area in the Madison Range was needed to upgrade service to the growing Big Sky Resort, the company said, while a 161-kilovolt line running from Anaconda to Hamilton would cross the Sapphire Mountains. Both lines would require road access for maintenance, effectively splitting the areas in two. It appeared that only the highest crags and most remote basins of the Northern Rockies were free from "resource conflicts," as the Forest Service called them. Modern industrial society laid claim to most forestlands outside designated parks and wilderness areas, leaving no place in which new designations came cheaply. Following the subcommittee hearing, Clif Merritt advised Montana conservationists that "from now on there won't be any easy tasks to get areas considered for wilderness, let alone to obtain instant classifications."[10]

Six Montanans testified in favor of S. 393 at the May 1975 subcommittee hearing, including Doris Milner and Tom Horobik, a Great Falls science teacher. They reiterated concerns over the mishandling of the RARE review and pointed out the significant ecological, wildlife, and recreational values found in the proposed study areas. Hap Kramlich, a rancher and former sawmill owner from White Sulphur Springs, testified in favor of a study area called Big Snowies in the Big Belt Mountains. In earlier years he had clear-cut timber from the area under Forest Service direction, but now he wanted it kept inviolate for campers, hunters, and Boy Scout troops. "We are very much against going in on four-wheel-drives," he told the committee. "There is nothing more provoking than to be hunting and after you have been walking 4 or 5 miles and you are practically on top of your game to have a Honda or a snowmobile come by and scare your game away."[11] Kramlich appeared to be a lone voice in rural central Montana, however. The relatively small areas included in S. 393 attracted less support from hunters, anglers, and hikers than the huge Lincoln-Scapegoat, Selway, and Great Bear areas—or the dramatic Absaroka Range and Beartooth Mountains, which Montana activists also hoped would get their day before Congress.

Following the hearing various sawmill owners placed fliers opposing the bill in workers' paycheck envelopes and sent a delegation to meet with Governor Tom Judge. Labor representatives joined them, leading Judge, a liberal Democrat who had supported the Scapegoat Wilderness proposal while serving as lieutenant governor, to remark that "it's not every day that we see labor and industry on the same side of the fence."[12] This was an ominous development for Metcalf, who had depended on workers' support throughout his congressional career. Word of the meeting reached Doug Scott, who tried to allay the governor's fears of job layoffs. His calculations showed that the maximum impact on annual allowable cuts in Montana's national forests would amount to less than 3 percent. Timber supplies were restricted as a result of "severe overcutting of private industrial lands, increased overcutting of public forestlands, and a gross failure to assure restocking of productive cut over lands in all ownerships," he said.[13] But former practices, good or bad, did not change the situation for the mill owners, who based their plans on the Forest Service's assurances that new stands would be opened up in remote parts of the national forests. This was the legacy of the Northern Region's full-development program, which was predicated on building up mill capacity to utilize the highest possible yield of timber from the region's national forests—a policy Metcalf had consistently supported earlier in his career.

Five years earlier, when Metcalf had been faced with polarized opinion on the Bitterroot clear-cutting controversy, he had turned to his friend Arnold

Bolle for answers. Now, under pressure from industry over S. 393, he asked Robert Wambach, Bolle's successor as dean of the University of Montana's forestry school, to examine the timber supply issue.[14] Wambach agreed with "trepidation," no doubt recalling the angry reaction that greeted his analysis of timber sale economics in the Bolle report. In the summer of 1975 he sent teams of students into the field under the direction of Dr. Hans Zuuring, a forest mensurationist, to perform rough-and-ready field checks of timber volumes in selected study areas. The results indicated to Wambach that the Forest Service had overestimated both the amount of standing timber and the growth potential in these areas. In his report he observed that "some commercial timber does now exist in several of the areas, as a gift of nature, but it is old, small in size, generally of poor quality, and it occurs in small volumes per acre in remote areas where access is difficult. With present markets most of the timber is virtually unmerchantable, unless the government elects to subsidize the timber industry by way of minimum stumpage prices or by building roads with appropriated money."[15]

In marked contrast to these findings, Wambach stated that many of the areas in S. 393 did not meet the minimum requirements of a wilderness and contained "dozens of cases of conflicting uses such as on-going timber sales, powerline rights of way, microwave installations, snowmobile trails, active mines, etc." He called for most of them to be managed as "unroaded back country"—the same concept that Bob Lucas and George Stankey had been promoting through the Montana Forest and Conservation Experiment Station, a Forest Service research facility affiliated with the university.

Wambach's critique, which he defended in a stormy public meeting on campus, threw Metcalf's supporters off balance. Clif Merritt and Doug Scott tried to repair the damage in a meeting with Max Baucus, who had thus far remained on the fence regarding Metcalf's bill. Nonconforming intrusions could be excised, if necessary, during the wilderness study, and they took exception to "backcountry" designation as a valid alternative. Merritt reminded Baucus in a subsequent letter that wilderness was not primarily a recreational resource but a means of protecting watersheds and wildlife habitat, particularly for species that needed distance from people. "The fact that the grizzly bear and the wolf are found in at least three of the nine areas should speak for itself," he wrote. "These threatened and endangered species represent the epitome of wilderness." Elk, bighorn sheep, mountain goat, moose, mountain lion, and wolverine also numbered among these wilderness-dependent species, Merritt added. "I deeply feel that this is the trail we must travel in the public interest," he concluded.[16]

Despite Merritt's pleadings, biotic conservation was slow to make inroads within the Forest Service. One voice for a less utilitarian approach to land management came from a recent agency retiree. In 1974 Bud Moore left his position as the Northern Region's director of fire control to pursue his interests in trapping and woodsmanship. He entered the S. 393 fray with a commentary on wildlife values in the Sapphire Mountains, a heavily forested series of ridges and domed mountains east of the Bitterroot Valley. This range had none of the jutting peaks or lake basins that made the Anaconda-Pintler or Selway-Bitterroot Wilderness areas so popular with recreationists. Instead it offered a glimpse into the workings of a relatively undisturbed ecosystem with a nearly full complement of native game animals, furbearers, and some predators. In a journal he kept during a week-long hiking excursion along the crest of the range in the summer of 1974, Moore looked closely for signs of how the land functioned, seeing it as neither a purely economic resource nor a recreational getaway but as a complex web of relationships between land, humans, and animals. "The area is obviously prime habitat for small birds and mammals of the boreal forests, and there are no indications that its natural ecological processes will soon degrade their habitat," he wrote. "Martens, fishers, wolverines and lynx must find a good living here in the habitat of blue grouse, Franklin's grouse, snowshoe hares, squirrels and other small wildlife important to their survival."[17] Moore carried no rifle or traps on this visit, but in his regular haunts in the Lolo National Forest he inserted himself into this web by taking animals for pelts. Trapping, like hunting, was permitted in wilderness areas, yet in the Sapphires he concluded that "of all the resources found along this divide, and there are many, the most significant for me was isolation and wilderness." The range was a significant water producer, its seeps and springs "vital—perhaps basically essential—to all the other values" found there. The trail he followed was itself an important historical resource. Moore concluded that he would "plan from the interior's high values outward, not from the exterior's values inward." His viewpoint would today be termed biocentric, but he made room for humans as participants in the landscape. The key was to replace our species' predilection for ownership and control of resources with a more observant and careful relationship. As Moore trudged over the stony Sapphire ridges and made camp in mosquito-filled spruce glades, he noted how even his malamute companion seemed less inclined to leave territorial marks on the trees.

Near the end of his trek Moore entered the area of the 1962 Sleeping Child burn, an occasion of some heartache for this former fire control officer. The fire had been, he wrote, "a tough test for those who controlled it and strong men must have cried to see the potentially commercial forest land consumed by flames." Yet the bulldozers that were brought in to scrape out fire lines "did more damage in one pass than is possible to do on these pack trails in years, even with heavy use." Fire was always going to be present in these woods, and depending on one's viewpoint was an agent of either destruction or ecological renewal. Two years earlier Moore had helped devise an innovative fire management plan for the Selway-Bitterroot Wilderness, and he knew that a mosaic of burns was normal in this forest. If wildfire were allowed to return, the abundant dead windfall that choked the slopes and threatened a catastophic blowup might be partly consumed.[18]

Moore's observations carried little weight with his former employer, whose staff had its own plan for reducing the fire hazard in the Sapphire Mountains: a network of timber haul roads and clear-cuts to remove mature timber before it could burn. Two months previously, the Bitterroot National Forest had let a contract to the Intermountain Lumber Company of Missoula for the Moose Creek timber sale in the upper East Fork of the Bitterroot River. The sale especially worried John Firebaugh, the state fish and game biologist for southwestern Montana, because of its incursion into forests that provided escape cover for elk. Three hundred miles of logging roads had been constructed in hunting district 270 in the East Fork of the Bitterroot, known as one of the best in the country for trophy deer and elk. The increased hunter access "has been a very significant factor in the 50 percent reduction in the either-sex elk season length from an annual average of 82 days from 1960–64 to an annual average of 41 days from 1965–74," Firebaugh wrote. Farther north in the Sapphires, the Stony Mountain roadless area was home to around a thousand elk during the summer and fall, making it one of the largest herds in west-central Montana. Firebaugh wanted the Sapphires kept as roadless backcountry but noted that "probably the only way to ensure that no roads are built is to have the area designated as wilderness."[19]

Doris Milner, as president of the MWA, made a point of keeping communication open with government employees such as Moore, refraining from the blanket condemnation that some environmentalists engaged in. In turn, concerned individuals within the Forest Service would pass along useful information and advise her on tactics. Stu Burns, a wildlife biologist on the adjacent Deerlodge National Forest, regarded the Sapphires' deep forest cover and high mountainside meadows as essential habitat for elk, bighorn sheep, and mountain goat. These herbivores, he told Milner in 1978, followed the summer growth through succeedingly higher elevations, putting on fat that would sustain them through the winter. Disturbances from gunfire, motorized vehicles, and to some extent foot traffic displaced them from this habitat. The high productivity of the Sapphire elk herds was due "in large measure to the amount and kind of undisturbed habitat available to the elk," he explained.[20]

Burns, an agency maverick whom Milner appreciated as a kindred spirit, lamented that it was difficult to get the average forest user to take an interest in the land's long-term welfare. In a talk to a local sportsmen's club in 1973 he observed that Americans "have built an entire society around resources that seemed endless. And where we have worn these resources thin we have satisfied our distress with imaginings that we could re-create what we have lost." The reality, he said, was that we merely "patch up the thin spot," turn our attention toward another resource, "and continue with our dream."[21]

In his letter to Milner, Burns related the ineffable charm of this overlooked mountain range. "When I've been able to spend some time in an area such as the Sapphire Crest," he wrote, "I have sensed a belonging to something far greater than just our poor human kind. And when I have to leave, and take that one last look around, I say out loud for the rocks and the trees and the wind to hear, 'Goodbye this lovely place! May you always be!'"[22]

Burns had one last question for Doris Milner: "Why is it always such an uphill struggle to do for people that which tomorrow they will be happy for, and so very easy to do for people that which tomorrow they will be sorry for?" The undulating ridges and open meadows of the Sapphire Mountains provided excellent habitat for many four-legged creatures, but they were also a refuge for wandering trappers and soulful biologists who looked at the land not for what they could take from it, but for what it might freely give.

Lee Metcalf carried an enormous load of environmental legislation during his last term, including bills to control strip mining, set a national energy policy, and preserve wildlands in Alaska. All were high priorities for environmentalists, and Montana's contentious wilderness issues added to the burden. If Metcalf was at times disheartened by environmentalists' endless wish lists, he was also growing impatient with wilderness opponents—and especially with the perceived interference of Representative John Melcher, who in 1976 was running for the Senate seat about to be vacated by Mike Mansfield. Metcalf had tangled with Melcher on many occasions, but particularly over S. 393. Metcalf regarded his bill as ready for passage, but Melcher took note of continued strong opposition from timber and off-road vehicle interests and insisted that additional hearings be held in Montana. Metcalf held off on Senate action to accommodate Melcher's wishes, even taking the unusual action of recalling the bill after

Mike Mansfield inadvertently placed it on the "consent calendar," by which non-controversial measures are approved without debate or amendment. It finally passed the Senate on August 23, 1977.

Harry Crandell, a former Wilderness Society employee who now worked for the House Interior Committee, asked Melcher's office if they would schedule a hearing in Washington before the end of the Ninety-Fourth Congress.[23] An upset Melcher refused to honor the request. He believed that too many of the areas contained evidence of human activities or were better suited for motorized recreation. Instead he scheduled a field hearing on the Elkhorn Mountains, a proposed study area southeast of Helena that was popular with hunters. Support for the area was strong, but Melcher was able to remove it from S. 393 with the proviso that the Forest Service manage it for its wildlife values. Congress adjourned before the remaining areas in S. 393 could be considered.

Now it was Metcalf's turn to display the parliamentary acumen for which he was known. He reintroduced S. 393 the following January (waiting for the same bill number to come up), after removing Mount Henry from the bill and substituting the Hyalite–Porcupine–Buffalo Horn area in the Gallatin Range. Support for this area had been strong in the Bozeman area for many years, while Mount Henry was fraught with difficult timber conflicts. Metcalf once again managed to get the bill on the Senate consent calendar that May over the protests of Melcher, who was now Metcalf's colleague. After it passed that body, action turned to the House Interior Committee, where freshman representative Ron Marlenee took his turn as the bill's primary opponent.[24] Marlenee's efforts to remove or shrink some of the study areas were beaten back by Max Baucus, his western district colleague, who had finally come off the fence. Morris Udall, a strong wilderness supporter and chairman of the House Interior Committee, also provided crucial leadership. Passage in the full House was far from certain, however. An attempt to have it placed on the consent calendar in September 1977 failed, forcing wilderness lobbyists to mount a last-ditch lobbying offensive. Bill Cunningham, whom Clif Merritt had hired as the Wilderness Society's Northern Rockies representative, spent days on the telephone asking supporters in Montana and other states to send telegrams and call their representatives. Baucus gave the bill his full attention, helping it clear the House on October 18 with the Mount Henry area reinstated.[25] By this time Metcalf was seriously ill and learned of the study bill's passage while in Walter Reed Army Medical Center. He was greatly pleased to gain this long-sought victory. Although S. 393 did not designate a single acre of wilderness, it prevented the Forest Service from proceeding with its timber plans in the

nine study areas and specified that motorized vehicles and other nonconforming uses were to be kept at their 1977 levels.

With the passage of S. 393 the Northern Region's timber program was stymied on many fronts, especially on the Bitterroot National Forest, where the
Sapphire, Blue Joint, and Magruder Corridor study areas were now off limits to
logging. Doris Milner's success in these campaigns reflected her skill in recruit-
ing grassroots supporters and her dogged persistence with Lee Metcalf, who did
not always appreciate the pressure. Notwithstanding Metcalf's broad interest in
environmental protection, he would not have emerged as a champion of wilderness legislation had he not believed that a significant cross section of Montanans
favored protecting public forestlands. Milner and her colleagues in the Montana
Wilderness Association had shown that federal timberlands held broader values than stumpage or even recreation and scenery. Withdrawing the S. 393 study
areas from timbering, however, placed even greater pressure on developed forestlands. Metcalf and his staff were warning of a future reckoning, but to many
in the timber industry, that day had already arrived.

18

Timber and the Mountain Fortress
The Contest for Roadless Land, 1977–1978

On the last day of February 1977, five executives representing the forest products industry in northern Idaho and western Montana appeared before the House Public Lands Subcommittee, chaired by Wyoming representative Teno Roncalio. These men operated sawmills, plywood mills, and particleboard plants that employed some nine thousand workers, many in small towns such as Libby, Plains, and Polson. Timber harvests from Montana's national forests had declined by nearly one-third during the past seven years, the lobbyists said, owing to Forest Service planning requirements, wilderness and other land use designations, Lee Metcalf's wilderness study bill, and new restrictions governing clear-cutting. Four sawmills had already closed and five thousand timber and sawmill workers were drawing unemployment; more closures were expected owing to uncertain supplies of federal timber. Smaller mills in the region had as little as one year's supply of logs under contract and were overcutting private lands to get them, according to a spokesman for the Pack River Company of Sandpoint, Idaho.[1]

The timbermen wanted no further reductions in available sawlogs, as would happen under H.R. 3454, known as the Endangered American Wilderness Act. This was an omnibus bill sponsored by Arizona representative Morris Udall, but conceived and largely written by the Sierra Club's Doug Scott. Frank Church was carrying a companion bill, S. 1180, in the Senate. The bills would designate thirteen wilderness areas in nine western states, including Welcome Creek, a small area southeast of Missoula that had been overlooked in the Forest Service's first roadless area review. In its initial version the bill also designated seven new wilderness study areas, including the heavily forested Mount Henry and McGregor-Thompson RARE areas in the northwestern part of the state. All three areas figured in the agency's allowable cut calculations and had timber scheduled for sale. Each had a modicum of local support, though nothing like the popular and highly visible Lincoln Back Country and upper Selway areas. None offered the gorgeous high peaks and expansive lake basins normally associated with wilderness, as the industry representatives reminded Roncalio's panel. John McBride, a forester for St. Regis Paper (which operated the former J. Neils sawmill in Libby), described Mount Henry as "a blah wilderness in an area that already has spectacular and properly protected wilderness. There is absolutely nothing spectacular about Mount Henry. Mount Henry is a hill. It's a big hill, it's surrounded by smaller rolling hills, the whole thing is timbered."[2]

McGregor-Thompson was considerably larger, but it, too, was slated for conversion into a managed forest. One-fourth of this area, a stretch of uncut forestlands reaching south from McGregor Lake to and beyond the modest summit of Thompson Peak, consisted of "checkerboard" land holdings of Burlington Northern, heir to the Northern Pacific Railway's nineteenth-century land grant. The company intended to harvest timber from these blocks during the next few years, while the Forest Service planned to offer seven timber sales within the remainder of the area.[3]

These were remnant roadless lands, not entire mountain chains or river basins; in the case of Mount Henry, previous logging and road construction reached within a half mile of the peak itself, and no part of the area was more than two miles from the edge of a clear-cut. The Forest Service had laid out two additional timber sales and sold them to St. Regis, only to have them appealed by the Sierra Club. Doug Scott wrote the appeals as a test case demonstrating the inadequacy of the Forest Service's multiple-use plans, which were supposed to take a closer look at roadless areas rejected in the RARE review. Local forest officers had dismissed Mount Henry as a wilderness candidate once during RARE, and again in their East Fork Yaak unit plan, which was released in 1973. Scott's appeal gained a rehearing of the area, but in September 1974 the agency rejected a wilderness study for the third time and instead scheduled the North Vinal and Turner Creek timber sales in the area. Scott's subsequent appeal to the secretary of agriculture failed to reverse the decision, and in March 1976 the Sierra Club joined the MWA and two local plaintiffs in filing suit to block the sales. Now this isolated, overlooked "hill" was joining the McGregor-Thompson area in Scott's latest effort to circumvent the Forest Service's logging plans. "Our purpose," he informed Montana wilderness activists, "is to serve notice on this particular national forest that they may not escape harrowing oversight from conservationists if they persist in superficial, lousy planning and NEPA compliance, followed by 'business as usual.'"[4]

Scott envisioned the Endangered American Wilderness Act as a way to pluck areas such as Mount Henry, McGregor-Thompson, and Welcome Creek out of obscurity and bundle them in a multistate package, bypassing recalcitrant representatives from timber- or mineral-rich districts. Scott also crafted language in the act that he hoped would be Congress's final word on the Forest Service's purity doctrine. One of the areas in the Udall-Church bill was Lone Peak, a spectacular 11,000-foot granite massif that rose directly above Utah's heavily urbanized Salt Lake Valley. The Forest Service had rejected the area in RARE because of noise from aircraft overflights and from the city itself. Scott opposed this "sights and sounds" argument, pointing out that wilderness quality was governed by what was found within the area, not the lands surrounding it. In the case of the 8,847-foot Mount Henry, the surroundings happened to be mile upon mile of clear-cuts. That this lonely eminence, bump, or hillock lacked expansive lakes or thrusting crags was no matter: it still had trees, and the handful of wilderness activists living in Montana's Yaak River Valley happened to like uncut forests.

Two of those activists, the actor John McIntire and his wife, actress Jeanette Nolan McIntire, fit the definition of "outsiders," even though John had grown up in northwestern Montana. Both were veterans of numerous Hollywood westerns and now lived on the ranch John had purchased in 1937, located in the evening shadow of Mount Henry along Basin Creek, a tributary of the East Fork of the Yaak River. They had become concerned about widespread logging all around their ranch, which they said was causing heavy siltation and had snuffed out three-fourths of the native trout in the creek. Speaking at an earlier hearing on Lee Metcalf's Montana Wilderness Study Act (S. 393), which at the time included Mount Henry, Jeanette presented letters of support from other Yaak Valley residents, including Forest Service employees who objected to current logging practices. "Those who choose to live in the wilderness, who build their homes from logs and who survive from and within the limitations of its wildlife have an innate love and respect for their surroundings," she said.[5] "Their knowledge and judgments must be used." While these individuals could not speak out directly, the McIntires had no such limitation and were parties to the Sierra Club–MWA lawsuit on the North Vinal–Turner timber sales.

Uncut timber was both the attraction and the downfall of places like Mount Henry and McGregor-Thompson. The massive cedars, firs, and hemlocks growing in the lowland forests of northwestern Montana had supported an active timber industry for nearly a century; in Lincoln County, the J. Neils Company, St. Regis's predecessor, held an almost complete lock on the economy of Libby. During the prewar years Forest Service officials foresaw economic ruin if the heavy cutting of private lands continued. Regional forester Evan Kelley warned his forest supervisors in 1940 that unless they stepped in, the county faced "depleted forests, workless people, no plan for doing any better in the future than has been done in the past."[6] Kelley's plan consisted of merging uncut public timberlands with the cutover private forests, placing both on a sustained-yield footing. The result was to transfer the heavy cutting to the Kootenai and Kaniksu (later Idaho Panhandle) National Forests. By the 1970s only a few remnants of virgin forest existed in the Kootenai and Yaak Valleys, including the Ten Lakes area northwest of Eureka that was part of Metcalf's S. 393.

Douglas Chadwick, a wildlife researcher who was conducting studies of mountain goats in Glacier National Park, noted at the February 1977 hearing on H.R. 3454 that "the thing we don't talk about in these areas are the grizzly bear, the mountain lion, the lynx, wolverine, fisher, marten, all these species. . . . Mount Henry is good habitat for these critters." Challenging John McBride's characterization of the area, Chadwick said that "if this were really blah country . . . we would not have the grizzly on the threatened list, the mountain goat would not be declining and our elk and deer populations also going down." The recent logging in Bunker Creek (Chadwick's former mountain goat study area in the upper Flathead) remained a bruise in his memory. He told Roncalio's subcommittee that the goat's "recent, drastic declines should cause all of us to wonder: what are we doing so far back into the mountain fortress? If there is already enough protection of wildland resources; if we indeed have too much wilderness; if we are only taking resources such as timber from optimum sites in accordance with sustained yield principles; then what are we doing forcing even the mountain goat from its rocky home?"[7]

Protecting wildlife also figured in the Welcome Creek proposal. It was included in the Endangered American Wilderness bill because of a conversation Bud Moore had with Bill Cunningham, the local Wilderness Society representative.[8] Moore identified it as one of the few roadless tracts remaining in the northern Sapphire Mountains, where it offered sanctuary for elk during the heat of summer and in hunting season. It was also a tributary of Rock Creek, a well-known trout fishing stream. Wildlife biologists from the University of Montana were using parts of Welcome Creek as a baseline area for examining the effect of logging and road building on elk herds through a cooperative project with the Forest Service and the Montana Fish and Game Department. The study disclosed that elk avoided active logging operations and tended to congregate in the roadless area during the summer and fall.[9]

John Melcher, who replaced Mike Mansfield in the Senate in 1977, objected to all three of the areas in S. 1180, but he seemed to be especially exercised about Welcome Creek. Earlier the Forest Service had offered a timber sale in the area that had not yet been logged, and although the bidder had relinquished the sale, Melcher now wanted to resurrect it. Lee Metcalf, on the other hand, was personally familiar with Welcome Creek, which happened to lie a dozen miles from his boyhood home of Stevensville. Upset with Melcher's opposition to so many of his initiatives, he employed another legislative stratagem. Arranging for Frank Church to remove Welcome Creek from the bill, he then appeared before the conference committee that met to reconcile the differing House and Senate bills. After hearing Metcalf's stirring plea for preserving the area, Church (who sat on the committee) moved that the area be reinstated. The conferees agreed, leaving Melcher, who was not present, stymied.[10] Metcalf's last-minute maneuver ran out the clock and enabled Welcome Creek, at 29,135 acres, to become Montana's newest and smallest national forest wilderness area when President Carter signed the Endangered American Wilderness Act in February 1978.

That Metcalf was willing to argue on behalf of this obscure side drainage was remarkable given that he was already towing a heavy raft of legislation through the Ninety-Fifth Congress. This included S. 393 as well as bills to designate the Great Bear Wilderness, reclassify the Spanish Peaks Primitive Area, and a new bill, S. 1671, which would designate a 913,500-acre wilderness in the Absaroka Range and Beartooth Plateau. Metcalf also took the lead on several other environmental issues of nationwide importance, introducing legislation to control strip mining, protect national interest lands in Alaska, establish an organic act for the national wildlife refuge system, and implement a measure aimed at protecting biological diversity that, had it passed, would have required each state to submit plans for identifying, maintaining, and monitoring "elements of natural diversity" within its borders.[11] Nevertheless, Metcalf called the Endangered American Wilderness Act "the most important wilderness legislation in the Congress" since it would help settle the long-festering purity debate and would reestablish Congress's authority in the RARE issue. He concurred with removing Mount Henry from the bill, since it was already in S. 393 as a study area, and he hoped that the McGregor-Thompson area would be given a fresh examination in a new round of wilderness reviews recently announced by Assistant Secretary of Agriculture Rupert Cutler. Nonetheless, it would remain difficult to secure protection for what Metcalf called "a representative sample of what the great inland forest from northwestern Montana to northeastern Washington was once like."[12]

Another sample of the Northern Rockies' inland forest clung to the steep slopes north of the Clark Fork River along the Montana-Idaho border, where three rocky spines mounted nearly five thousand feet to join at the aptly named Vertigo Ridge. Logging had left its mark on most of the surrounding valleys, but in 1971 the Forest Service identified a 37,000-acre roadless area named for the 7,000-foot summit of Scotchman Peak. It was virtually devoid of timber and thus survived the winnowing parameters of RARE, but two Clark Fork Valley residents believed that a much larger roadless area containing many more trees was at stake. Linda and Mike Comola, both natives of England, had settled outside the roadside hamlet of Noxon where, like dozens of other newcomers, they sought to create a modern American homestead. Linda tended a bountiful garden while Mike, a veteran of U.S. military operations in Indochina, employed his mechanical skills at a local garage. Spiritual cousins of Cecil Garland and Doris Milner, they liked to explore the lush forests of Spar Creek and Ross Creek, where giant hemlock and cedar grew.

Elk, mountain goat, drifting bands of bighorn sheep, even an occasional grizzly moved up and down the rocky slopes of Scotchman Peak and its outlying ridges. By the end of 1975 the Comolas and a nearby homesteader friend, Cesar Hernandez, had outlined a 106,000-acre roadless area consisting of the Forest Service's new wilderness study area, two additional RARE units not selected for study, and 43,000 acres of contiguous roadless lands. The Comolas and Hernandez announced the formation of a new citizen group based in the lower Clark Fork Valley, named (in tribute to government bureaucratese) Northwest Citizens for an Expanded Scotchman Peak Candidate Study Area. Over the next few years the three homesteaders would take a highly creative approach to federal land law in defense of their adopted area.

MWA leaders were happy to have dedicated local volunteers working to protect a little-known area, but they were especially surprised when the Northwest Citizens group took on the mining giant ASARCO in a contest for the minerals underlying Scotchman Peak. Hernandez and the Comolas learned from government reports that high-grade deposits of lead, molybdenum, and other minerals were likely to exist in the Star Gulch area above the lower Bull River, so they took the unprecedented step of locating their own claims to the deposit. As Mike related later to fascinated MWA members, he and Cesar were marking their claims on a rocky slope when a helicopter appeared and began dropping lengths of PVC pipe containing ASARCO's own claim notices. The two men bundled up the pipes and delivered them to the company's exploration office in Spokane, along with a notice of trespass. Linda informed the company that any requests for information about their claims needed to be made "in writing, preferably in triplicate."[13]

The would-be miners announced their intention to develop their claims using the pick-and-shovel technology in place at the time of the 1872 mining law that granted them rights to the minerals. They noted that designation of the entire area could proceed under the terms of the 1964 Wilderness Act, which allowed claim location until 1984. ASARCO officials were flummoxed and, despite threats of legal action, were unable to dislodge the enterprising prospectors. Hernandez owned a couple of mules and used them to pack out ore samples, all in the spirit of the law that gave hard-rock miners nearly unlimited access to the riches of the West.[14]

At the same time, ASARCO was intent on developing a different copper-silver deposit on Mount Vernon at the eastern edge of the roadless area. Environmentalists were concerned about the mine's effect on water quality in the drainage of Lake Creek, a tributary to the Bull River, and asked the Montana Department of State Lands to prepare an environmental impact statement on the project.[15] Cesar Hernandez and Bill Martin, a California refugee who had built a cabin on Lake Creek, gathered other local residents to form the Cabinet Resource Group, a watchdog organization. ASARCO's patented claims predated the Wilderness Act, so no preemptive strike was possible, leaving Martin's group few options. The state of Montana conducted its review but went ahead and approved the project. Both citizen groups feared the changes that could come to the Cabinet–Clark Fork region with the influx of hundreds of miners and their families. Designating more wilderness offered some hope of securing a refuge for the area's wild creatures, as well as for former city dwellers who were seeking solitude in a remote part of northwestern Montana.

Timber was less of an issue east of the Continental Divide, where conservationists saw an opportunity to designate a large wilderness area in the Absaroka Range and Beartooth Plateau, two geologically distinct areas separated by a historical wagon trail leading from the former mining town of Independence on the Boulder River to Cooke City. The immense granitic tablelands of the Beartooth Primitive Area were a backpacker's and mountain climber's paradise, while the scenic lake basins of the Absaroka Primitive Area were popular with horse packers and anglers. Each was designated in 1932, when the only signs of human occupancy consisted of Forest Service patrol cabins and the relicts of nineteenth-century mining operations. Unlike in the Madison and Gallatin Ranges, land ownership remained primarily federal, although some Big Timber residents wanted to resurrect the abandoned wagon trail, known as the Slough Creek corridor, as a snowmobile route. The Forest Service, too, expressed interest in the more than half million board feet of timber in the corridor.

During the summers of 1967 and 1968 the MWA fielded eight teams of volunteers to examine conflicts in and around the two primitive areas—an indication of the importance it placed on this mountain landscape. Ruth Koch, an avid backpacker from Butte who spent her summers crisscrossing the Beartooths, coordinated their work and came up with enlarged wilderness boundaries for both areas but left them divided by the Slough Creek corridor. At the same time, Sierra Club field volunteers working under Francis Walcott, the head of the club's wilderness study committee, made a bolder recommendation—to join the Absaroka-Beartooth into a single 850,000-acre wilderness, eliminating the corridor and any possibility of building a road from Big Timber to Cooke City.[16]

Clif Merritt sharply disagreed with this approach in a report he filed with the Wilderness Society's Washington staff. Joining the two areas "would result in gaining solid opposition of local conservation and other civic and business groups" that supported the prospective road.[17] Stewart Brandborg at first sided with Merritt, recommending to regional forester Neal Rahm that the road corridor be left open, "as it is needed for the proper development of all resources in Southwest Montana."[18] Their reluctance to endorse a dramatically enlarged wilderness in south-central Montana may have reflected their close ties to the MWA. Only four years had passed since the Wilderness Act had become law, the Lincoln-Scapegoat and Selway controversies were far from resolved, and to many activists it appeared politic to work with the Forest Service in order to gain incremental expansions of the existing primitive areas. All this changed by the early 1970s as a younger generation of activists—many recruited through the Wilderness Society's outreach programs—saw no reason to be limited by the managing agency's wilderness recommendations. One of these activists, a Montana State University graduate student named Bob Anderson, grew up in the railroad town of Livingston and spent summer vacations exploring the northern Absaroka Range and Beartooth Plateau. In 1971 he completed a report for the MWA in which he called for a unified wilderness of about nine hundred thousand acres. He recommended that "eco-logical principles form the basis for making management and use decisions" and rejected what he called "a compromise which trades areas of high wilderness val-ues for areas with developable resources in an attempt to please the most people (or offend the fewest)." Slough Creek contained important grizzly habitat and was a productive fishery, Anderson said, and combining the two areas would increase the overall diversity of the wilderness.[19] The MWA, now headed by the fiery Cecil Garland and Elizbeth Smith, adopted Anderson's proposal. It was the largest in Montana to that date, reaching from the Beartooth Highway on the east to Para-dise Valley on the west.

By that time Congress was about to enact an expansive Lincoln-Scapegoat Wil-derness, the Forest Service was stymied in the upper Selway and was reeling from the Church-Metcalf clear-cutting hearings, and membership in preservation and environmental organizations was soaring. Clif Merritt lauded the new Absaroka-Beartooth proposal, satisifed that there would be sufficient local support to make it a reality. The Wilderness Society scheduled a summer pack trip into the area, led by Elizabeth Smith and accompanied by Ann Sutton, a noted naturalist and author. Ruth Koch jumped on the bandwagon, calling for "wilderness classifica-tion of the largest possible extent of this unmodified and natural land."[20]

Significant hurdles remained, however. In 1974 the Forest Service released a proposal to reclassify the two primitive areas separately for a total of 540,000 acres of wilderness. Sawmill owners in Livingston opposed both the MWA and Forest Service proposals, as did snowmobile clubs from Bozeman to Billings. Ed Carrell Jr., the mayor of Livingston, claimed that this and other pending wil-derness proposals had severely restricted the supply of timber from the Gallatin National Forest. With seven mills in the Bozeman-Livingston area depending on this timbershed, the "90 percent cut in timber sales can only mean a shut-down or phasing out of the major mills which will inflict a tremendous eco-nomic loss to Livingston," he stated. George Domasco of the Sweet Grass County Recreation Association told Metcalf that closing the Slough Creek cor-ridor "would result in an economic impact from the loss of trade to snowmobile dealers, motels, restaurants, resorts, guest ranches etc." But Hank Rate, a former forest ranger from Corwin Springs, said that "Slough Creek is as pure wilder-ness as anyplace in the world today. . . . If it's not included, the wilderness, as we natives know it, is gone!"[21]

Four Republican representatives, led by Arizona's Sam Steiger, introduced the administration's proposal for the separate Absaroka and Beartooth areas in February 1975. Unsatisfied with confining wilderness to the high treeline,

Montana preservation groups asked Lee Metcalf to introduce their unified Absaroka-Beartooth proposal. At the time, Metcalf was focusing on a controversial strip mining bill that had been vetoed by President Ford, and he also wanted to move S. 393, his stalled wilderness study bill. He promised to look into the issue—especially the thorny question of the Slough Creek road. In July 1976 the Agriculture Department's Office of General Counsel issued an opinion that "there is no evidence of the existence of any road. . . . If a road from Cooke [City] to Boulder ever did exist, parts of it have been abandoned and ownership has reverted to the United States."[22] Satisfied that he was on firm legal ground, Metcalf introduced the MWA's 913,500-acre Absaroka-Beartooth proposal in June 1977.[23] The bill provided that if a federal court determined that a right-of-way existed through the corridor, it would be excluded from the wilderness.

Both John Melcher and Ron Marlenee, a Republican who replaced Melcher in Montana's eastern congressional district, favored leaving the Slough Creek corridor open. "Wilderness loses its usefulness if it is not accessible to those who would like to enjoy the area," Marlenee told Hank Rate. Additional opposition came from the mining company AMAX, which wanted to protect access to its platinum-palladium claims in the Stillwater River drainage.[24] The opponents were in the minority, however. The MWA and its supporters in Livingston, Big Timber, and Billings pressed the Carter administration to expand its earlier wilderness recommendation. Working through Assistant Secretary Rupert Cutler and other officials, they gained an endorsement for a unified wilderness of 886,500 acres, including the contentious Slough Creek corridor as well as a smaller block of forested land on the western side of the Absarokas in the drainages of Cedar and Bassett Creeks. Undeveloped lands in the upper Boulder River drainage, parts of the mineral-rich Stillwater Complex, and about ten square miles of the Beartooth Plateau in the Goose Lake basin were added to the proposal. Max Baucus added his support when Metcalf's bill came before the Senate and House Public Lands Subcommittees in October 1977. Metcalf wanted to pass S. 393 first, however, which had recently failed a House vote.[25] With little time remaining in the congressional session, action on his Absaroka-Beartooth bill was postponed for the following year.

On January 12, 1978, near the end of the holiday recess, Lee Metcalf died at his home in Helena. His death shocked wilderness advocates in Montana who had depended on his strenuous advocacy and knowledge of Senate procedures to pass a significant legacy of public lands and environmental legislation. The *Washington Post* called him "one of the last of the traditional western populists" who favored "consumers over coal companies and power companies; wildlife and wilderness over economic interests."[26] Perhaps the most telling tribute came from the green archdruid himself: David Brower, who had worked closely with Metcalf on the issue of dams in Dinosaur National Monument, recalled his welcome presence at Senate committee hearings dominated by hostile reclamation interests. "Your voice steadies, your manner eases, and your hopes rise," Brower wrote of seeing the Montanan sitting on the panel. "There will be good questions to emphasize the points you did not stress well enough."[27]

Hoping to enact the remainder of the Metcalf legacy, wilderness advocates lobbied Governor Tom Judge to appoint Metcalf's widow, Donna, to fill out his term, but to their disappointment he named state supreme court chief justice Paul Hatfield. He joined John Melcher, Max Baucus, and Ron Marlenee in agreeing to pass Metcalf's Absaroka-Beartooth bill, which gained House approval on March 14 after the rejection of Marlenee's amendment (on a tie vote), which would have allowed continued snow machine and summer vehicle access to the Slough Creek corridor.[28] Two days later President Carter signed into law the 904,500-acre wilderness, the second largest located entirely within Montana.

Action on Metcalf's Great Bear Wilderness bill, which Morris Udall was carrying in the House, followed that fall with a hearing in Teno Roncalio's Indian Affairs and Public Lands Subcommittee. The bill passed the House on October 3, 1978, and the Senate on October 6; differences between the bills were resolved in conference committee and the president signed the measure on October 28, expanding the protected lands north of the Bob Marshall Wilderness by 285,771 acres. In one year Montana had gained three new wilderness areas ranging from the intimate drainage of Welcome Creek to the windswept plateaus of the Absaroka-Beartooth. Lee Metcalf had been at the center of all three battles.

For Montanans such as Dale Burk and Bob Anderson, securing protection of the Great Bear and Absaroka-Beartooth Wilderness areas fulfilled a decade-old dream. It was a bittersweet victory, for none of Lee Metcalf's and Mike Mansfield's immediate successors displayed much enthusiasm for wilderness, especially if it brought the displeasure of the state's timber industry or its growing number of off-road vehicle users. Bill Cunningham recalls that shortly after Metcalf's death, Doug Scott told him, "Now you'll find out what it's like in the real world." That world included a richer and more diverse system of wilderness areas, thanks to Lee Metcalf and his colleagues, but it was also home to a growing political movement that intended to halt any more such withdrawals.

19

RARE Redone
RARE II and the Coalescing Opposition, 1977–1980

The Endangered American Wilderness Act allowed preservationists to make an end run around unfriendly representatives from resource-rich western states, but with every political action there came a reaction. In August 1977, shortly before Morris Udall's measure passed the House, Idaho representative Steve Symms introduced the "Endangered American Natural Resources Act," which directed the secretary of the interior to convey an equal acreage of public land to any state in which Congress designated a new wilderness area.[1] The bill was more statement than substance and did not receive a hearing, but it foretold the growing resistance to public land withdrawals and environmental regulations that came to be known as the Sagebrush Rebellion. Ron Marlenee, Symms's colleague from Montana's eastern district, was a rancher with a similar antipathy to restrictive federal land designations. As Lee Metcalf's wilderness and wilderness study bills made their way through the House, Marlenee stated, "While I strongly believe in preserving the natural beauty of Montana, I also believe that Montanans need access to the bountiful sources of jobs, energy and recreation we are so lucky to have."[2] Both Symms and Marlenee seemingly wanted a return to the wide-open West of the 1950s, when ranchers, prospectors, timbermen, and oil companies could count on a friendly and responsive federal bureaucracy.

The Sagebrush Rebellion came in reaction to President Carter's attempts to circumvent these traditional power structures, culminating in the infamous "hit list" of western water projects that Carter vowed (unsuccessfully, as it turned out) to deauthorize in March 1977.[3] M. Rupert Cutler, Carter's assistant agriculture secretary in charge of the national forests, added fuel to this cauldron that May when he appeared before Teno Roncalio's Public Lands Subcommittee to offer virtually unqualified support for Morris Udall's endangered wilderness bill. His stance was unsurprising; as a former aide to Stewart Brandborg and a friend and mentor of Doug Scott, he had a keen appreciation for the federal government's role in protecting wilderness. Cutler and Scott stayed in close touch as a carload of important wilderness measures made its way through the Ninety-Fifth Congress.

Scott had been laying the groundwork for the Udall-Church bill by challenging the Forest Service's unit plans, which were to reconsider roadless areas not selected for wilderness studies under the 1973 RARE decision. He took special interest in the Kootenai National Forest, where he filed an administrative appeal of a sale that would impinge on roadless lands surrounding the Northwest Peak Scenic Area. Supervisor Floyd Marita agreed to pull back the sale boundary, but Scott informed regional forester Steve Yurich that the Sierra Club would challenge *any* timber sale that invaded roadless lands, whether or not those areas had been inventoried and properly evaluated in RARE. He sought a broader commitment from the agency to identify and protect such lands, taking his case to Zane Smith Jr., the agency's assistant director in charge of recreation and wilderness issues. Smith, whose father had aided Montana conservationists during the Sun Butte Dam issue of the 1950s, had helped break a logjam over Oregon's French Pete Valley in the 1970s and was among a small number of Forest Service officers whom conservationists trusted. He prepared a directive requiring that noninventoried roadless areas receive the same consideration in multiple-use plans as inventoried RARE areas.[4] This cannot have reassured agency officials who hoped to dispose of the roadless area question through those plans. Their unease, along with Scott's continued challenges, likely contributed to Cutler's determination to clean up past mistakes in RARE and start anew.

At the same time, industry representatives objected to the seemingly interminable resource studies that tied up productive timberlands in the Northwest and Northern Rockies. Unbeknown to the environmentalists, Cutler met with industry lobbyists in early 1977 and agreed with them that the case-by-case approach to designating wilderness was taking too long. He promised industry greater certainty in allocating forestlands to development or preservation— what one Forest Service officer later described as "a stable commercial forest land base and timber inventories to facilitate long-range planning and capital investments." With some sixty-five million acres of identified roadless land available nationwide, Cutler assured the timbermen there was "enough for everyone"—if those lands were allocated fairly.[5]

To the surprise of Doug Scott and nearly everyone in the House hearing room that May, Cutler told Teno Roncalio and his subcommittee that at his direction, the Forest Service would take "another complete look at the roadless and undeveloped lands in the entire National Forest System."[6] Cutler hoped this would resolve the uncertainty plaguing the timber industry as well as meet new wilderness acreage goals under the 1974 Resources Planning Act (RPA). This law was intended to rationalize Forest Service budgets by setting production targets for all forest resources, not just timber and forage as had traditionally been the case. The RPA goal was for a national forest wilderness system of twenty-five to thirty million acres outside of Alaska, which would require fifteen million acres of new wilderness. "This Department will pursue that goal with a new sense of urgency," Cutler told the subcommittee. He promised that the new review, which was quickly dubbed RARE II, would be broader in scope and more objective than the first RARE program and would be completed in "seven to nine months, or perhaps a year."

In a press conference held in Missoula to unveil the new program, Cutler told reporter Dale Burk that he wanted to put a finish to the "endless debate" over the roadless area question. That made sense to Burk, who was both an observer and participant in many of the region's toughest public lands battles. "The debate could go on for 20 more years," he wrote. "Cutler would like to have it over in two or three."[7] Neither man could foresee that two decades later, the battle for national forest roadless areas would be running just as strong.

Forest Service chief John McGuire and his associates viewed the new program with "distaste," according to Ray Karr, an agency insider who examined the RARE II program for his 1983 doctoral dissertation. In 1969 Karr succeeded Bill Worf as head of the agency's wilderness programs and later was posted to Missoula as head of the Northern Region's public affairs office. He believed that Cutler allotted too little time for the review and usurped the chief forester's prerogatives by taking personal charge of the program. This was "very unusual practice" for a Cabinet-level officer, according to Karr. Nonetheless, McGuire and his staff proceeded in "good faith," hoping to "get the thing over with."[8] The lack of enthusiasm for RARE II was mirrored on the individual ranger districts and forests where the initial inventories and analyses were performed. Cutler assured environmentalists and industry officials that the mistakes and biases of the first RARE program would not be repeated, but in the end the agency managed to reprise most of the conflicts, uncertainties, and biases of its original review, with an added dose of high-level political maneuvering thrown in.

John McGuire tapped Zane Smith to head the RARE II project, with two of Smith's recreation division staff assisting him. They were George Davis, who like Rupert Cutler was a former Wilderness Society staffer, and Tom Griswold, who came from the National Park Service.[9] These appointments alone might have worried timber industry officials, but in November 1977, when the agency released its final inventory of roadless areas under RARE II, the scope of the potential land withdrawals became clear. They encompassed 2,919 individual areas in thirty-eight states, for a total of sixty-two million acres—one-third of the entire national forest system, not including existing wilderness areas. The Northern Region alone made up almost nine million acres of this total, with an additional three million acres in Idaho's portion of the Intermountain Region.[10] RARE II would decide the fate of some of the region's most outstanding wildlands, including the Big Horn–Weitas roadless area in the upper Clearwater Basin, the Lemhi Range, the Meadow Creek drainage on the western edge of the Selway-Bitterroot Wilderness, more than 140,000 acres of unprotected land surrounding the Bob Marshall Wilderness, the West Big Hole in the southern Bitterroot Mountains, and dozens of others that a decade earlier were on no one's radar.

Cutler and McGuire explicitly ordered that "purity" issues such as the presence of adjacent roads and highways or a lack of scenic lakes and mountaintops not be considered in the analysis. Smith and his staff added measures designed to improve the representation of ecosystems and compute effects on allowable cuts and local economies. All these factors made their way into a draft environmental impact statement released in June 1978, which showed (among other things) that the classification of all inventoried roadless lands in the national forests of Idaho and Montana would result in a net loss of more than 3,600 jobs—a staggering total that no doubt motivated the timber industry's sharp response to the program.[11] The prospect of massive economic dislocations in timber-dependent regions led timber and motor-vehicle interests to turn out in force at hundreds of public meetings the Forest Service held on RARE II during the latter half of 1977. Their response, along with subsequent petition and form letter campaigns, largely overwhelmed environmentalists, who relied on their supporters to write formal letters with detailed comments on each area.

Idaho and Montana conservationists who were familiar with the areas drew up a list of priority wilderness candidates in each state, which they called Alternative W. In northern Idaho, Mort Brigham and seven of his friends organized Citizens for North Idaho Wilderness, which recommended a 150,000-acre wilderness centering on the Mallard-Larkins Pioneer Area. They also called for an expanded 261,900-acre Big Horn–Weitas area in the Clearwater River headwaters along with 193,000 acres in Meadow Creek. In all, activists identified more than 1.2 million acres of new wilderness designations in northern Idaho's national forests—a compromise, they insisted, since it would release more than 1.5 million acres for development. That the timber industry did not see this as sufficient merely demonstrated the tight confines in which the parties found themselves. Environmentalists were trying to stake out part of a territory industry had long believed was its own.

In Montana, Bill Cunningham and Mike Comola (who was now president of the Montana Wilderness Association) assembled a separate Alternative W from recommendations submitted by a few dozen activists around the state. They came up with 2.2 million acres of new wilderness, not counting the 1.4 million already under study through the recently passed S. 393, Great Bear, and Elkhorn Mountains legislation. At an August 1978 news conference called to announce the package, Doris Milner spoke for the newly formed Montana Coalition for Wilderness, which consisted of twenty-one supporting groups. "Montana is an oasis in the nation today, largely free from the urban sprawl, decay, congestion and noise that curse much of the nation and world of 1978," she said. "A large part of Montana's grandeur and free open space lies in her mountains." The coalition was willing to see nearly 1.6 million acres released for timber and road development—far less than the timber industry believed it needed to sustain its operations.[12] The Inland Forest Resource Council identified a mere 272,000 acres that it could accept as new wilderness, exclusive of the legislatively mandated study areas, while its close political ally, the Western Environmental Trade Association, was willing to accept only 173,000 acres. The gulf between the industry and preservationist positions appeared to be unbridgeable, although the Forest Service recommended 594,000 acres and Governor Tom Judge weighed in with 483,000 acres.[13]

Agency analysts treated this "input" as part of a ten-step decision-making process designed to ensure that their recommendations included areas with high wilderness attributes (as determined by field and office evaluations) and met predetermined targets for ecosystem representation, landform diversity, accessibility to population centers, and habitat for wilderness-dependent wildlife. Other steps adjusted the recommendations to better meet RPA goals while at the same time excluding highly timbered and mineralized areas. Finally, leaders from the regional and Washington offices made subjective additions and deletions, culminating in a review by the chief of the Forest Service, Assistant Secretary Cutler, and other Agriculture Department officials.[14]

For three-quarters of a century the Forest Service had prided itself on taking a systematic, rational approach to allocating forestland uses. RARE II was a culmination of this approach, but aggregating roadless areas into statewide and nationwide lists emphasized the potential losses to timber, grazing, and mineral production, while at the same time obscuring the esthetic and biological virtues of individual areas. Up until the RARE studies, preservationists had advanced their proposals one by one, calling attention to an area's value as a recreational and spiritual refuge and to its abundant (or perhaps scarce) wildlife. RARE II bypassed this avenue of public discourse, replacing the successful models of the Lincoln-Scapegoat and upper Selway campaigns with a new kind of political negotiation—a drawing of lots based on the fear of losing important resources. The program sparked much anger among resource interests, but in the end they were better able to exploit its parameters.

In January 1979 the agency released its final environmental impact statement on RARE II, which called for designating 15 million acres of new wilderness nationwide and releasing 36 million acres for nonwilderness uses, while retaining 10.8 million in the further planning category. In Montana the agency recommended a mere 600,000 acres for wilderness designation, much of which consisted of sparsely timbered alpine and subalpine areas such as the East Pioneers, the heart of Scotchman Peak, additions to the Cabinet and Selway-Bitterroot Wilderness areas, and a handful of popular wilderness gateways such as Monture Creek at the edge of the Bob Marshall Wilderness. An additional 1.2 million acres were recommended for "further planning," a catchall category that included ongoing wilderness studies under S. 393 and other laws. More than 3 million acres would be released to development and vehicular uses.[15]

In Idaho the agency recommended nearly 2.2 million acres for wilderness designation, including significant additions to the Idaho Primitive Area, a 137,000-acre wilderness centering on the Mallard-Larkins Pioneer Area, and nearly 100,000 acres as part of the Hoodoo or Great Burn area, matching a 65,000-acre proposal on Montana's Lolo National Forest. Borah Peak, the state's highest, was included, but the remote Lemhi Range to the east was not. Much of this range fell into the further planning category, which came to 1.2 million acres in all. The preponderance of Idaho's RARE II areas, 4.3 million acres in all, was allocated to nonwilderness uses, including great swaths of roadless country in the upper Clearwater drainage where timber development was deemed necessary to the economy of Clearwater County and towns in western Montana.[16]

Bill Bishop, the new president of the MWA, characterized the recommendations as "severely imbalanced" and said that this latest agency program had failed to resolve the problems with the original RARE.[17] The Inland Forest Resource Council, on the other hand, warned that even these limited recommendations would "add to critical timber supply problems in a number of communities which are dependent upon national forest timber," including Seeley Lake, Superior, Darby, Salmon, and Elk City.[18] Bill Turnage, the Wilderness Society's new executive director, labeled the agency's recommendations "among the most negative decisions in the history of public land management," while Ted Snyder, the president of the Sierra Club, vowed that "controversy will increase significantly" on lands not allocated to wilderness.[19] They had one more card to play, however. Under the Wilderness Act it was the president, not the chief forester or even the secretary of agriculture, who transmitted wilderness recommendations to Congress. These groups presented a list of areas to Jimmy Carter that they wanted him to recommend as wilderness or move from the nonwilderness category to the further planning category. Rupert Cutler was key to these changes, so in April 1979 Doug Scott, who was visiting Doris and Kelsey Milner at their home in Hamilton, composed a lengthy telegram to his friend that laid out the environmental community's dissatisfaction with the procedures used in RARE II and its results to date. With Cutler's support, the final list was modified to include wilderness recommendations for the Lemhi Range, the West Big Hole, and Scotchman Peak. Industry had its say, too, and the final list demoted several small areas from wilderness to further planning and some from further planning to nonwilderness.[20]

The acreage proposed for wilderness was within the range Rupert Cutler had specified for meeting the 1975 RPA target—and some preservationists believed that figure had served as a ceiling from the start. Many in the timber industry feared just the opposite: that environmentalists would consider the new wilderness recommendations as a floor and press Congress to designate as many of the nonwilderness and further planning areas as possible. Doug Scott and his colleague John McComb, along with the Wilderness Society's Tim Mahoney and John Hooper, realized that expanding the RARE II recommendations risked significant political backlash. They stated in a January 1979 press release that "much of the roadless inventory is, in fact, resolved and need not be part of any continuing controversy." Although many of their cooperators were upset with the nonwilderness recommendations, they observed that "this does not involve all, or even most" of the thirty-six million acres to be released for development.[21] They feared that if environmental groups at the state and local level agitated for too many areas—or worse, brought a lawsuit challenging the validity of the RARE II decisions—Congress would respond with legislation declaring the final EIS legally sufficient and direct the Forest Service to make available all nonrecommended roadless areas for development, notwithstanding the new forest plans.

The prospect of such "release language" loomed like a rumbling thundercloud over all subsequent discussions of roadless areas on the national forests and helped generate a serious split among formerly united wilderness proponents. The national environmental groups knew they could probably mount a successful court challenge to the RARE II EIS, but they believed the political reaction would nullify their gains and make it harder to designate any new wilderness areas. But in 1979 an activist official with the state of California broke ranks and filed a RARE II lawsuit against Secretary of Agriculture Bob Bergland, winning reconsideration of forty-eight roadless areas in that state through additional site-specific environmental reviews.[22]

In the wake of the decision in *California v. Bergland*, the Wilderness Society and Sierra Club released an analysis stating that although they were "gratified" by the judge's "tightly reasoned decision . . . that the RARE II process was poorly executed," they were at the same time "pleased with its limited scope." Solving wilderness designation issues, according to the two organizations, "lies with the Congress, not the courts. Environmentalists do not now, nor have they ever, desired to halt the process of land management decisions. . . . Plans for the majority of non-wilderness land management decisions under RARE II may proceed and are proceeding without interference."[23] Their assurances did little to calm the storm that RARE II stirred up in the western states.

Rupert Cutler envisioned RARE II as a way to settle the issue of roadless lands and provide the timber industry with a predictable forestland base. Chief John McGuire and some industry leaders went along with the program on that basis, but in the end it accomplished neither objective. Nearly thirty million acres of national forest land in the Lower 48 were allocated to nonwilderness uses, but environmental appeals, the state of California's lawsuit, and new wilderness legislation limited timber production in many of these areas.[24] The western timber industry maintained that having an assured log supply from roadless areas was critical to its continued health. Indeed, forest industry employment in Montana peaked in 1978 after nearly a decade of steadily increasing harvests from the national forests, much of which came from newly opened roadless lands.[25] Four years later, some four thousand timber industry workers in that state were out of a job as a nationwide recession and soaring interest rates caused a collapse in housing demand, bringing an end to a decade of high lumber prices. Companies that had bid on and won federal timber sales now found them unprofitable to harvest. Timber harvests from the region's national forests declined in like fashion until the economic recovery of the mid to late 1980s brought a rebound in housing and lumber demand. At this point the question of log supplies from roadless lands again became critical—and a new generation of environmental activists would employ new laws and regulations to try to achieve the protections that had eluded them under RARE II.

RARE II not only brought a strong response from the timber industry, it galvanized motorized vehicle users who feared they would lose access to trails and jeep roads they had been using for years. Dave Foreman, who helped coordinate the grassroots response to RARE II for the Wilderness Society, warned its governing council in 1977 of a "brewing anti-wilderness offensive" that was bringing together timber, mining, off-road vehicle, ranching, and rural development interests. He predicted a "wilderness Armageddon" unless its supporters mounted a campaign to "present the logical and reasonable arguments in favor of a large and representative National Wilderness Preservation System." Merely fighting "brush fire wars," as the movement had for years, would lose the war, he said.[26] Foreman hailed from rural New Mexico, where the Sagebrush Rebellion was particularly intense, but by 1980 the movement was established throughout the West. In Montana, Bill Cunningham and Mike Comola called for "tapping every possible source of support for wilderness in order to successfully meet the enormous challenges of RARE II in Congress." With Lee Metcalf gone, they warned their grassroots network that "each additional acre of wilderness will be increasingly difficult to designate."[27]

One problem was that wilderness designation had become a game of aggregates—this many acres of wilderness against that many jobs lost; so many petition signatures stacked alongside so many personal letters. The clash of organized interest groups bore little resemblance to lone activists working out of a store in Lincoln, a living room in Lewiston, or a kitchen table in Hamilton, from which they spoke and wrote of a landscape they knew intimately. The Forest Service did not resolve the roadless issue with its two RARE programs, but it was now clear to all concerned that there was much more potential wilderness land in the western states than almost anyone realized, and that virtually none of those lands came without serious resource conflicts. American society had ratcheted up its use of public lands tremendously since the days when Leon Kneipp and Evan Kelley first delineated the huge primitive areas in the upper

Flathead, Stillwater, Salmon, and Selway. In that era of custodial management, it was relatively easy to draw a line around remote mountain tracts and defer decisions on their use for another generation. Those bills were now coming due. Wilderness—at least outside the high peaks—was no longer a free good in an industrialized and heavily mechanized society.

20

Negotiating a Wilderness
The Gospel-Hump Agreement, 1976–1977

By the mid-1970s Idaho's preservation groups had stalled timber sales in the upper Selway River and elevated the Salmon River wilderness to national prominence, but timbering and road building were proceeding apace in the Clearwater River drainage to the north and west of these areas. Mort Brigham was first to sound the alarm about a cluster of mountains and lake basins southeast of Grangeville in the headwaters of the South Fork of the Clearwater. He described this 450,000-acre area in a letter to Frank Church as having "more wildlife than is to be found in most of the Selway Wilderness. Its waters sustain vast resources of anadromous fish and resident trout. There are moose that stand several feet taller than my horse, and my horse is no colt. . . . It's too good a place to receive the butchering that [forest supervisor Don] Biddison has scheduled for it."[1]

Heretofore overlooked in Idaho's conservation battles, this landscape of rugged breaks and ridges was topped by the 8,000–9,000-foot summits of Gospel Hill and Buffalo Hump. The Forest Service had divided the area into eight planning units and nine adjoining RARE areas, ostensibly in order to analyze smaller land units, but Brigham and his friend Dennis Baird, a librarian at the University of Idaho, took this as a divide-and-conquer strategy. Timber sales were scheduled throughout the area, including one that involved building a road through an elk calving ground, Brigham said. A sympathetic biologist with the Idaho Fish and Game Department affirmed that the roadless area supported a substantial elk harvest for those who desired a remote backcountry hunt. The opportunity for such experiences was "decreasing at an alarming rate nationwide," he wrote. Joseph Greenley, the department's director, expressed "serious concern" in a letter to Frank Church over Forest Service plans for the Mill Creek and Rainy Day planning units, which called for an extensive road network to access the area's timber stands. This, Greenley believed, would bring in heavy human use that could disrupt elk migration patterns and damage pristine lakes and streams.[2]

The pressure on roadless areas such as Gospel-Hump was not likely to relent. Recent directives from the regional office made it clear that each national forest in northern Idaho and western Montana was expected to meet its timber sale goal. There had been a "very poor showing" in the previous fiscal year's timber sale program, deputy regional forester Lawrence Whitfield warned in the summer of 1976. "We plan to hold rigidly to both the first half goal and the yearend sell goals," he insisted. Some staffers were becoming nervous that regional forester Robert Torheim was abandoning "quality management"—the term for the environmental safeguards that Neal Rahm and Steve Yurich had adopted in the wake of the Bitterroot clear-cutting controversy. The memo made it clear where the agency's priorities lay.[3]

Brigham and Baird sought a full wilderness study of what they called the Gospel-Hump roadless area, not merely a "regurgitation of the old RARE data which understated the wilderness values involved," as Brigham put it in a letter to supervisor Biddison. Working with Doug Scott and his assistant, Dave Pavelchek, they filed administrative appeals of each multiple-use plan as it was finalized, beginning with Little Slate Creek in February 1974 and Kelley-Bullion in June 1974. These took in the westernmost portions of the roadless area, while the Rainy Day and Mill Creek plans, released in 1976, covered the northern part. The appeals called for "a thorough, professional study of the relatively little-known wildlife resources and habitat relationships in this immense area, and a single, comprehensive wilderness study for the total area."[4] Their critique got the attention of officials in Washington, and in March 1977, after the Forest Service's Office of General Counsel looked at the case, chief John McGuire remanded both plans to the supervisor's office with instructions to examine the entire roadless area as a single unit. This had the immediate effect of blocking five timber sales totaling 70 million board feet and reducing the overall allowable cut on the Nez Perce National Forest by 22.5 million board feet. Mill owners in Grangeville were shocked and approached Frank Church and Idaho governor John Evans to see what could be done.[5]

Church took a close interest in this developing controversy, which only added to concerns about timber supplies in central and northern Idaho. After meeting with Torheim in Washington, he released a statement calling it "essential to Idaho's economy" that the unit plans be completed. In late March 1977 he met with a delegation of sawmill owners and civic leaders from Grangeville who pressed their demand for opening the roadless areas to harvest. Donald MacKenzie of Wickes Forest Industries, a medium-sized sawmill and one of the town's larger employers, pointed out that with so much commercial timberland tied up in appeals, the remainder of the Nez Perce National Forest was being severely overcut.[6] Unlike in the wilderness controversies of a decade ago, there were no other uncut drainages available for harvest.

Doug Scott intended to do more than tie up timber sales in northern Idaho and western Montana; he was looking for political leverage to jump-start wilderness legislation that had been stalled for years in Idaho's timber belt. The appeals of the Rainy Day and Mill Creek plans had the desired effect. When the owners of the Wickes mill and their backers in the Grangeville Chamber of Commerce met with Frank Church in March 1977, they raised the possibility of a deal: Would environmentalists be open to releasing some timber around the periphery of the Gospel-Hump roadless area in exchange for wilderness designation of its core? They especially wanted to go ahead with the so-called Honker timber sale, which had been held up by the chief's recent decision. Church broached the idea with Doug Scott, who immediately got in touch with Mort Brigham, Dennis Baird, and Dan Lechefsky, the new Wilderness Society field representative based in Boise. In a confidential memo, Scott noted that the interest on the part of the Grangeville delegation for a settlement left the preservationists in a strong position. He proposed that they ask for a sizable "instant" wilderness area, either through the Endangered American Wilderness Act or separate legislation, plus a surrounding wilderness study area. In exchange they would agree to release the Honker sale and certain other timber tracts around the periphery of the area. Frank Church would be directly involved in the negotiations, as would Larry LaRocco, his aide in northern Idaho.[7]

This was an unprecedented approach to wilderness legislation in the Northern Rockies. The Gospel-Hump area had not figured strongly in RARE or in any of the Idaho wilderness advocates' publicity campaigns, so Baird and Brigham could not count on a groundswell of support for preserving the area. Their negotiating position was based on the legal leverage they held through their appeals of the unit plans. It was new territory for these advocates, but as Baird recalled recently, the Grangeville business interests were less ideological in their opposition to wilderness than many Idahoans, and he had achieved a measure of trust working with Herb Blewett, a local utility executive and Grangeville Chamber of Commerce leader, on other environmental issues. Jack Olsen of the Wickes mill wanted a solution to the log supply crisis and looked to Church as a fair broker.[8]

The first meeting, termed an exploratory session, took place in Grangeville on April 28, 1977, with Scott, Baird, Brigham, and Lechefsky representing the preservation interests, and Olsen, Blewett, and three other Grangeville businessmen representing the development side. The Grangeville interests came to the table with a proposal for a 105,000-acre wilderness study area, whereas the environmentalists insisted on "instant" wilderness for the core area. Nevertheless, Mort Brigham reported to Governor John Evans that it had been "a hopeful beginning" and that his side had offered to release about eighty thousand acres for logging around the periphery of the area.[9]

Thus far the negotiations had been closely guarded from the public, but a representative of Idaho's mining industry got word of the sessions and demanded a seat at the table. Much of the area had "proven mineral potential," he said, but the Grangeville contingent realized that they could never reach an agreement if intransigent antiwilderness groups were involved. Other environmental leaders presumably learned of the negotiations, too, but they knew and trusted Baird and Brigham, who had deserved reputations as tireless advocates. The group conducted an additional daylong meeting and pursued ideas informally with each other over a period of two months. It was an intense time for all of the participants; Baird nearly canceled a honeymoon trip with his wife-to-be, Lynn. As they got off the plane upon their return, there was Doug Scott, waiting to resume work. Intense negotiations ensued, this time leading to agreement on a 220,000-acre wilderness and release of 78,000 acres of timberlands for development.[10]

Frank Church and his colleague James McClure presented the compromise proposal to Congress in August 1977 as the "Gospel-Hump Roadless Area Land Allocation Act." McClure was not as committed to the negotiations and introduced a separate bill that called for a wilderness study for Gospel-Hump.[11] Steve Symms gave indications he would not support either proposal. While both parties to the negotiations had their reservations about the agreement, they decided it was in their interest to proceed. Donald MacKenzie of the Wickes firm defended Church's bill but said it should not "set a pattern for future settlements. Too many user groups such as the miners, off road vehicle people and recreational users other than preservationists were not included."[12] At a hearing Church led that summer in Grangeville, Baird called the compromise proposal "in many ways wilderness on the rocks," but he endorsed it as a means of

protecting valuable roadless land within the political limitations of a rural timber county. "You don't get very far producing wilderness areas when you have
people losing their jobs at the same time. We have to have some kind of compromise in between," he said. Doug Scott added the national Sierra Club's impri-
matur to the deal, and even Mort Brigham, the dig-in-his-heels veteran of the
Clearwater and Selway battles, agreed.[13]

Opposition to the compromise was fierce. Off-road vehicle interests were
becoming more organized in the state and small-time miners and antigovernment zealots were a strong presence in northern Idaho. Speaking for these
interests, gubernatorial candidate C. L. "Butch" Otter submitted a statement
opposing "the Federal Government controlling the lives of Idaho people." It was
"abhorrent," he stated, that "entire communities have to bow to the wishes of a
few preservationists because the preservationists have influenced the Congress
and have the laws on their side."[14] It was a curious statement, calculated to appeal
to those who saw little value in a public estate managed by a representative body.

Mort Brigham decried the vociferous attacks made on Senator Church during the August 24 Senate field hearing on the bill, telling him that never in the
past fifty years had he seen a public official shown less respect.[15] To accommodate those interests, Church trimmed the proposed wilderness to 206,000 acres,
and later that year he attached his bill as an amendment to S. 1180, his Endangered American Wilderness Act. The combined bill passed Congress and was
signed into law on February 24, 1978. During the negotiations the Forest Service went ahead with its own planning efforts for the area, urged on by James
McClure, but these largely became moot under the new legislation.

The agreement on Gospel-Hump was possible because of an unusual align-
ment of events: the successful Sierra Club appeals that stalled timber sales over
a large area, Frank Church agreeing to take on another contentious land-alloca-
tion battle, and the willingness of the Grangeville timber and business interests
to discuss a compromise. Had more interest groups taken part in the negotiations, or if the participants had not built a basic level of trust, nothing would
have resulted. Dennis Baird took part in further talks with wilderness opponents in the early 1980s in an attempt to reach agreement on a general Idaho wilderness bill, but by that time the hard-core opponents of wilderness were better
organized and shut down the process.[16]

More radical wilderness advocates, too, lambasted the Gospel-Hump com-
promise for releasing significant roadless lands, particularly a portion of the
"Dixie Tail" area north of the Salmon River. The area, named Jersey Jack in
RARE and later called Cove-Mallard, was located between the Gospel-Hump

area and the Salmon River Breaks Primitive Area.[17] Most Idaho activists, however, saw the compromise as the only way to overcome the increasingly organized opposition to wilderness among the state's timber industry and off-road vehicle users. Baird recalls that "we were losing a wilderness—and Mort and I did the best we could." There was no existing primitive area to anchor a larger wilderness, as in the River of No Return, and the remote, hard-to-reach area was (and remains) a lightly visited destination for serious hikers, anglers, and hunters. Baird insisted that environmentalists abide by the agreement, noting that the timber industry also did—which helped keep open the lines of communication as controversy flared in other parts of the Nez Perce National Forest. The Gospel-Hump agreement was a harbinger of the approach other mainstream wilderness groups such as the Idaho Conservation League and Montana Wilderness Association would take in the future.

The success of the talks in Grangeville naturally led to speculation that Frank Church would employ the same approach with the River of No Return proposal, but this was a far larger area and involved many more constituent groups than Gospel-Hump, making an accommodation unlikely. Ted Trueblood met with Church during the summer recess of 1977 and was taken aback when the senator asked him twice if his group would accept a smaller wilderness or some trade-off involving a different area. Trueblood refused, subsequently calling it "unthinkable" that they would sit down with the timber interests in a brokered negotiation. "Only in Congressional hearings—which you have promised—can the people express their wishes," he told Church. He was somewhat reassured when late that year, Church told him that it was never his intention to deal with the River of No Return through closed-door negotiations, but soon afterward Trueblood lamented that "Frank Church told us in August that 1.8 [the 1.8-million-acre proposal advanced by Gov. Cecil Andrus] is maximum and there is no way we can enlarge it."[18]

The Andrus proposal offered a convenient middle ground, and the senator was known for favoring the artful compromise. This left Trueblood and his friends with only one option—to build as much support as they could for the larger proposal. Doug Scott offered his help in Washington, where he directed legislative affairs for the Sierra Club along with John McComb and the Wilderness Society's Tim Mahoney and John Hooper. All four men were experienced lobbyists, but Scott told the Idaho activists that it was up to them to beat the drums for their 2.3-million-acre proposal. The campaign for the central Idaho wilderness would come down to the Idahoans' ability to craft a compelling story for protecting the largest wilderness in the Lower 48.

21

Mountains and Rivers without End
The Salmon River Wilderness, 1977–1980

Outfitter Norm Guth owned a rustic hunting lodge alongside the rushing waters of the Salmon River, deep within an unroaded canyon that for centuries had enticed as well as repulsed explorers. He employed a shallow-draft jet boat to gain passage down and back up the River of No Return, maneuvering through rapids with names like Gunbarrel and Devils Teeth. His passengers could watch the fir-clad hillsides pass in review and imagine themselves homesteading a river bar like Sylvan Hart, the colorful, tough-talking "Buckskin Bill" who still lived along the river. Guth sometimes called the Salmon the "river of no financial return," although its growing popularity allowed him to sustain his remote camp. In August 1978 Norm and his brother Bill hosted Jimmy and Rosalynn Carter and their family on a three-day whitewater raft trip down the Middle Fork. Secretary of Interior Cecil Andrus had invited the president to accompany him down the Salmon's wildest tributary in order to discuss the various wilderness proposals soon to come before Congress.[1] The trip gave unprecedented coverage to the River of No Return controversy and was almost certainly a factor in increasing the size of the administration's wilderness recommendation.

Although preservationists were delighted to have Carter on board, what mattered most was support within Idaho itself—especially among Guth's colleagues. As president of the state outfitters and guides association, Norm was in a position of some influence over wilderness legislation. Unlike in Montana, where guides and outfitters often originated wilderness proposals, the Idaho association's support was by no means certain. Along with Richard Smith, a fellow outfitter from Salmon who was vice chairman of the Sierra Club's Northern Rockies Chapter, Guth acted as liaison with environmental groups and helped bring the outfitters into the preservation camp. In April 1977 they hosted a meeting of the Sierra Club's regional leaders, including Doug Scott, at Guth's outfitting camp. The club reaffirmed that jet boats, aircraft landings, and outfitter camps would be permitted in the wilderness at existing levels of use. The River of No Return Wilderness Council, which included many Idaho sportsmen, agreed. Some of them may have swallowed hard at accommodating the noisy airplanes and river craft, but no wilderness bill was going to pass without strong support from Idaho's hunting and boating enthusiasts.

Following the 1976 presidential election Ted Trueblood, Ernie Day, and Bruce Bowler had lunch with Frank Church and learned that he was "optimistic" about a central Idaho wilderness bill. Doug Scott drafted a bill for a 2.3-million-acre wilderness, including in it specific language allowing commercial services such as jet boats. He told Fred Hutchison, Church's legislative aide, that by having these provisions "right in the bill itself, in plain black-and-white," wilderness proponents could "easily and decisively" refute arguments that it would put outfitters out of business.[2] Norm Guth testified at a subsequent Senate hearing that his industry brought $23 million annually in direct income to the state, and "if provided with ample amounts of wilderness, the outfitting and guiding industry along with other forms of dispersed recreation will continue to grow and be an ever more valuable asset to the state of Idaho."[3]

There was some urgency to the legislation, for the Forest Service was preparing unit management plans for the roadless country surrounding the two central Idaho primitive areas, and the first examples were not encouraging. A recently released plan for the rugged slopes east of the Salmon River Breaks Primitive Area recommended turning the Horse Creek and Reynolds Creek drainages into a "motorized backcountry area," open to trail bikes and snow machines. The plan acknowledged that roads built for timber harvest operations would "dissect substantial areas of importance to wildlife" and would reduce water quality in streams flowing into the main Salmon River. Timber removal from the river breaks area— the most sensitive in the planning unit—would be accomplished at a net loss to the federal treasury, the plan noted.[4] Other unit plans around the periphery of the Idaho Primitive Area showed a similar orientation, comprising what the preservationists called "chainsaw legislation"—attempts by the Forest Service to limit the potential expansion of the two primitive areas by building roads up to their edges.

Despite Frank Church's long record of support for wilderness, it was not clear that he would go to the mat for the wilderness council's proposal. Timber availability was becoming a key issue in central and northern Idaho; sawmills had excess headrig capacity after the buildup of the late 1960s, and their owners were looking toward the wild interior of the state for new log supplies. In 1974 Church advised Forest Service chief John McGuire that "a shutdown of these sawmills— oftentimes the major employer of an Idaho town—could cause economic chaos." He urged McGuire to complete the unit plans, release roadless areas not selected for wilderness study, and free up more money to build access roads.[5]

As the nationwide recession continued, sawmills faced high prices for raw logs and poor demand for finished lumber. This led one mill in the town of Horseshoe Bend to close temporarily in early 1975. Its 325 workers accepted pay cuts in order to continue working, but its president, Theodore Hoff Jr., urged Church to place a moratorium on new wilderness designations until a "careful appraisal of the effects of classification upon the long-term economy of Idaho" had been made.[6] In August 1976 Boise Cascade announced that it would close its sawmill in McCall and transfer or lay off 156 workers, citing reduced log supplies from the nearby Payette and Boise National Forests. Intermountain regional forester Vern Hamre offered to put an additional ten million board feet of timber per year up for bidding, but the company deemed this insufficient.[7] Frank Church scheduled a hearing on the timber supply issue the following June in McCall, at which more than three dozen witnesses expressed anger and frustration over the lack of adequate timber supplies. Harry Adams, manager of Boise Cascade's operations in central Idaho, warned that administrative appeals of timber sales in roadless areas on the Payette National Forest "make planning almost impossible and certainly heighten the probability of additional mill closures." But Forest Service spokesmen said the harvest reductions had less to do with roadless areas than with new environmental standards that restricted logging on other forestlands.[8]

Idaho's timber industry had benefited from a drastic and probably unsustainable increase in logging on the national forests, the result of a Forest Service program designed to convert millions of acres of mature and "overmature" timber into younger, faster-growing stands. The statistics were telling: from 1966 to 1975 the Boise and Payette National Forests offered an average of 230 million board feet of timber for sale annually, whereas by 1976, with new environmental safeguards in place, this was reduced to 176 million board feet. Future harvests were expected to remain at that level unless substantial amounts of timber from central Idaho's roadless areas were made available.[9] Dan Lechefsky, whom Clif

Merritt had hired as the Wilderness Society's new field organizer in Idaho, tried to contain the political damage caused by the mill closures. He cited opinion polls showing strong statewide support for protecting roadless areas, but timber supply would play a major role in future wilderness debates in the Gem State. At the McCall hearing Church told a representative of the industry-oriented group Outdoors Unlimited that "where you have large acreages of commercial timber, you don't have an area that ought to be wilderness. . . . That is how we have to draw the line."[10]

Church emphasized that "it was a question of balance—drawing the line in such a way to give us the unique attraction of wilderness while keeping a healthy wood products industry."[11] He predicted that the Idaho and Salmon River Breaks Primitive Areas would be reclassified in their entirety, along with enough adjacent lands to bring the total to 1.5 million acres. Outside this area, only those roadless lands that did not jeopardize area sawmills would be included in the wilderness. This drew the line, in effect, between timberlands and the high country, much as the Forest Service insisted be done. Such statements unnerved Idaho's preservation advocates, who took scant comfort when President Carter announced in December 1978 that he would be sending a revised wilderness recommendation of 1.9 million acres to Congress early in 1979. It included Chamberlain Basin, which now appeared safe from the timber industry. Frank Church included the administration proposal as one of three "by-request" bills he introduced the following January. Numbered S. 95, S. 96, and S. 97, they represented the full spectrum of proposals, ranging from the Idaho Forest Industry Council's 1.3 million acres to the River of No Return Wilderness Council's 2.3 million. The latter would also designate 237 miles of the Salmon River under the Wild and Scenic Rivers Act, with provisions for continued jet boat use. In discussions with Morris Udall, the chairman of the House Interior Committee, Church predicted that the final result would be an "amalgam" of all three proposals.

These statements gave the strong impression that the skids were greased for something like the Andrus or Carter proposals. Preservation interests probably could have settled fairly easily for the administration proposal, which after all exceeded their original goal of a unified wilderness of about 1.5 million acres. Protecting the existing primitive areas and some small additions around their periphery would have matched many Idahoans' idea of wilderness and would not have led to appreciable losses of available timber. By substantially increasing the size of its proposal, the council risked losing support among "soft" wilderness supporters—especially among the sporting fraternity. This was where the vocal advocacy of respected outdoorsmen such as Ernie Day, Ted Trueblood,

and Norm Guth proved so valuable. With solid support among outdoors enthusiasts of many persuasions, the preservationists were able to withstand, with two
notable exceptions, concerted attacks from the timber and mining industries as
the Church bills came before hearings in Idaho in the spring of 1979.

Senators Church and McClure opened the sessions in Lewiston on April 2.
The timber industry focused on the availability of forested lands north of the
Salmon River, which they believed were needed to support sawmills in Elk City,
Kooskia, and Grangeville. These and other nearby firms had a maximum processing capacity of 186 million board feet of timber per year, whereas the Nez
Perce National Forest was offering only 112 million feet. According to a spokesman for the Wickes mill in Grangeville, this shortfall forced them to harvest
timber from private lands before it was fully mature. The RARE II areas between
the Gospel-Hump Wilderness and the Salmon River Breaks Primitive Area were
needed, he said, to ensure these mills' future.[12]

Maintaining the undisturbed watersheds of the Salmon and Selway River
basins formed much of the pro-wilderness testimony, with the 1964–65 disaster
in the South Fork of the Salmon held up as an example of what could happen
elsewhere in these drainages. Fred Rabe, an aquatic biologist at the University of Idaho, spoke of how the streams in this region had evolved for the past
seven thousand years into "more than just inanimate water courses containing
particles of sand and silt, dissolved gases and minerals headed downstream."
They were "living communities" that were easily disturbed by human activities.[13] Several outfitters in the Elk City area called for more active management
to promote big game habitat, while others, including Moscow outfitter David
Petersen, pointed out that increased road access would drive animals out of
areas where he led trips. Dennis Baird responded that while environmentalists
could not support "elk ranching" as a form of forest management, it was time to
reexamine the agency's fire control policy and begin controlled burns to restore
natural conditions in the wilderness.[14] James McClure questioned him closely
on this point, but Baird felt that such manipulation was needed to undo the
effect of decades of fire suppression.

Nelle Tobias, a 40-year resident of McCall, Idaho, treasured Idaho's expansive forests as an endowment from an older era. "Without the land which grows
the trees, which measures out the clean water, which renews the salmon industry, which refreshes the air we breathe, we and our country are bankrupt," she
said at the Lewiston hearing. Keeping this wilderness intact would mean that
the timber industry "would lose nothing but a covetous dream."[15] To advocates
such as Tobias, wilderness designation was both an ideal of American society

and a political tool by which they might corral an overzealous federal agency.

By appealing to sporting interests as well as urban environmentalists, the River of No Return Wilderness Council was able to obtain two-to-one majorities in Lewiston and Salmon and a narrow plurality in Boise. Of the 591 people who testified, 381 supported the maximum wilderness proposal, according to the council.[16] Despite this showing, they faced challenges on virtually the whole circumference of their proposal. They had filed administrative appeals of several planning units on the Payette and Boise National Forests, alleging losses to wildlife and roadless lands. RARE areas north of the main Salmon River in the "Dixie Tail" also remained under dispute. Dennis Baird pleaded with Frank Church to retain the Running Creek and Upper Bargamin areas in the wilderness and to refrain from releasing Meadow Creek, a tributary to the Selway River. These areas had come under concerted attack from Elk City residents who wanted an assured timber supply for their local mill, but to Baird they comprised "a quarter million acres where rock turns to sand, where trees grow thin and slow, where erosion from the presence of even trails causes massive slumps."[17] Church indicated he was willing to support a large wilderness in the core of the Salmon River Mountains, but outlying areas with significant timber conflicts would be a hard sell.

As the River of No Return bills headed into final negotiations in Congress, Church was faced with another thorny issue: minerals. The Blackbird cobalt deposit, located on the eastern side of the area in the Clear Creek and Panther Creek drainages, had been mined during the height of the Cold War, but with the United States now importing most of its supply of this strategic mineral from Africa, James McClure sought an amendment that would exclude this and another mining district on the western side of the Idaho Primitive Area from the wilderness.[18] Church favored language that would retain the Blackbird area in wilderness classification under "relaxed" rules that would permit underground mine development. Although the acreage involved was relatively small, environmentalists worried that large-scale mine development would endanger salmon runs and a sizable resident herd of bighorn sheep.[19] Church nonetheless pressed for the exception over James McClure's objections—another example of his seeking compromise avenues to protect wilderness.

In December 1979 the Senate Energy and Natural Resources Committee adopted a new bill, written by Church and his staff, as a substitute for the three bills he had introduced by request. It called for 2.2 million acres of wilderness in the Salmon River drainage and added 105,000 acres in the Magruder

Corridor, including Running Creek and Upper Bargamin, to the Selway-Bitter-root Wilderness. The bill was approved by the full Senate on November 20 on a 69 to 18 vote and was referred to the House. The Jersey Jack–Mallard Creek RARE II areas were left out of the bill in deference to Elk City residents who wanted the area opened to logging.[20] With these concessions, the final Central Idaho Wilderness Act passed the House on June 1, 1980, and, following a con-ference committee to iron out differences between the bills, the 2,239,000-acre wilderness was signed into law on July 23. The cobalt issue remained a sticking point until the end, with the conference committee endorsing a "special min-ing management zone" within the wilderness that established mineral extraction as a dominant use. Aircraft landings and jet boat use were permitted at 1978 lev-els, as determined by the Forest Service. The bill established a 97-mile-long wild river along the main Salmon downstream from the Corn Creek landing, with a 46-mile recreational river above that point. (The Middle Fork was already classi-fied as wild under the Wild and Scenic Rivers Act.)

The decades-long campaign to protect the largest national forest wilder-ness in the Lower 48 ended as an astonishing success. Beginning in the sum-mer of 1964 when Doris and Kelsey Milner had heard a bulldozer start up in the dark woods of the upper Selway, preservation advocates had tried at every turn to prevent the further dismemberment of the roadless expanse that had once thrilled Bob Marshall. This work originated at the grass roots and contin-ued to be a campaign of local advocates, many of whom were sportsmen and women. By tying the fate of the Salmon River and upper Selway wilderness to its great herds of elk and mountain sheep and its streams full of wild trout, these advocates gained significant support among conservative Idahoans. They had to accept many compromises that whittled the area's boundaries, but far less than they initially feared. The national environmental groups provided skilled lobby-ing, organizational guidance, and access to nationwide mailing lists, but with-out these dedicated individuals and their friends, the Salmon-Selway wilderness would almost certainly be a fractured series of smaller, unconnected areas, its wild creatures subject to far more pressure from humans.

Perhaps the most extraordinary aspect of the Idaho wilderness story was how Frank Church, in parallel with Lee Metcalf, emerged from his longtime sup-port of timber and reclamation interests to become one of the preservationists' strongest allies. He ultimately backed the River of No Return council's pro-posal because he thought it had significant support among Idaho citizens—and because he thought it was the right thing to do. His initial statements favored limiting wilderness designation to the contours of the existing Idaho and

Salmon River Breaks Primitive Areas, but in the end he agreed to protect some seven hundred thousand additional acres of de facto wilderness. As he remarked in 1976 at the introduction of the Endangered American Wilderness Act, "Congress, having launched a wilderness preservation policy, must maintain its oversight responsibilities to see to it that this important policy is fulfilled, not only in the initial program mandated by the Wilderness Act, but for those areas of 'de facto wilderness' which we find merit full protection." In a 1977 interview he suggested that the nation's wilderness system ought to take in about twice as much land as its initial framers anticipated, including some twenty to thirty million acres of de facto wilderness outside Alaska.[21] This was a substantial revision of his earlier stands and spoke to his political courage as well as to the dedication of Idaho's wilderness proponents.

Morris Udall and John Seiberling in the House of Representatives were also indispensable to the bill's passage—especially by erecting a wall against legislative "hard release" provisions, which would continue to be debated as other statewide wilderness bills came up for consideration. Nonetheless, Church's advocacy came at a price. Four months after the bill was signed into law, Idaho voters elected Steve Symms, an avowed opponent of wilderness preservation, as their new senator. Four years later Congress voted to add Frank Church's name to the wilderness he had skillfully helped create. Stricken with pancreatic cancer, he died at his home in Maryland that April. Doug Scott recalled visiting him shortly before he passed away and reported that the senator was "thrilled" to be so recognized.[22] Church's work would not have been possible, however, without the extraordinarily patient work of Idaho citizens who knew the lands in question. Refusing to back away from a vision of a grand wilderness, they gave a dozen years of effort to a campaign that established the largest protected landscape in the national forests of the contiguous United States.

22

Watershed Moments
The Big Hole and the Rattlesnake, 1976–1987

The need to protect the free-flowing rivers and streams of the Northern Rockies helped coalesce an effective preservation movement in the 1940s and 1950s, but concern for the "blue-ribbon" waters of Idaho and Montana remained long after the threat of major dams had passed. Flowing water tied together many interests, from anglers and boaters to those who simply appreciated the glint of sunlight on a clear mountain pool. Two very different streams—the famed fishing waters of southwestern Montana's Big Hole River and the municipal watershed of Rattlesnake Creek near Missoula—drew attention from citizens who feared damage from logging and unrestricted vehicle use. Their efforts to safeguard these drainages illustrate the innovative approaches that preservationists were forced to adopt during the difficult years of the Sagebrush Rebellion.

In the early summer of 1976 one of Norm Guth's guests on the Salmon River was a lanky, sideburned young man whose home for the past few years had been the high Big Hole Valley east of the Continental Divide. Kenneth Bohlig had taught school with his wife, Clara, in the village of Wisdom, Montana, for only a few years when the local school board decided not to rehire them. The unstated reason was his outspoken views and unusual teaching methods. A native of upstate New York, Ken wanted these ranchers' sons and daughters to know something of the world beyond, so at the end of each school year he invited several of his best students to cram into his four-seat Toyota Land Cruiser and drive east for a visit to the nation's capital. He made certain to include Gary, Indiana, on their route so that these youngsters who breathed the purest air in the world would see what industrial growth could bring.

Bohlig stirred anger among conservative Big Hole residents when he filed an administrative appeal of a timber sale in Little Lake Creek, a lodgepole-lined drainage that flowed down from the Continental Divide. The sale threatened to open up thousands of acres in an inventoried RARE area called the West Big Hole, which the Forest Service had not selected for wilderness study. Although the area formed part of the Big Hole River's watershed, it did not appear on any wilderness group's must-protect list. With his coappellant, rancher Jon Roush, Bohlig won reconsideration of the sale, and he set about trying to gain other converts for his backyard wilderness. His activism caught the attention of Holway Jones, the chair of the Sierra Club's national wilderness committee, who offered him a job as a field organizer, comparable to Bill Cunningham's position with the Wilderness Society. Briefing sessions in Washington followed, after which Bohlig moved to Atlanta to help with the "Conservationists for Carter" campaign early in the election year. That June he got a choice field assignment: to meet with Idaho outfitters and guides to shore up their support for the River of No Return Wilderness Council's 2.3-million-acre proposal, which included wild river status for seventy-nine miles of the main Salmon. He headed out to a familiar part of the West to meet Norm Guth, Richard Smith, and other outfitters and guides who were friendly to the wilderness cause. An affable, outgoing fellow, Bohlig relished the task. Wild places drew him like a lodestone; the chance to do some good for the wilderness beckoned.

Early one evening on a trip down the main Salmon River with the Guth outfit, Bohlig left camp in search of a vantage point on the steep slopes that lined the canyon. His friends had observed his fearless approach to the heights, but rocks can crumble and grassy inclines can be especially treacherous, and high above the Salmon River Bohlig began to slide. He made desperate attempts to halt his tumbling fall, leaving boot prints in the soil to be found later by his stunned companions. News of his death shocked his fellow activists, but no one more than Dale Burk, Bohlig's close friend and fishing companion. That spring, while on the Big Hole River, they had talked of floating Burk's home waters across the mountains in the Bitterroot Valley. Bohlig's parting words to his friend were "I'll see you soon—on the other side of the Great Divide."[1]

Several of Ken Bohlig's friends vowed to continue his fight to preserve the West Big Hole and West Pioneer roadless areas, which flanked this expansive high mountain basin, or "hole." A gift from Montana's past, uncluttered with ranchettes, ski areas, or mining scars, the Big Hole supplied its namesake river with clear, constant waters that earned it blue-ribbon designation from the Montana Fish and Game Department. Framing this setting were the peaks lining the Continental Divide, a vista as spectacular as that of Idaho's Sawtooth Range from Stanley Basin, according to a teacher and former state senator from Butte named Al Luebeck. An avid outdoorsman, he had spent part of his boyhood in the remote country around Arrastra Creek northwest of Lincoln, Montana, where his father operated a small sawmill. Beginning in the mid-1950s he took numerous backpack trips into the Lincoln Back Country, sometimes running into Tom Edwards, who kept a permanent camp in the North Fork of the Blackfoot River. Like Edwards, Luebeck grew concerned about the logging roads that were beginning to encircle the area, and in 1960 he walked into Cecil Garland's store and learned of the effort to protect the Back Country. He went on to participate in this campaign and became active in the Montana Wilderness Association.

The Northern Region planned to develop the lands surrounding the Big Hole as well, and in 1975 Luebeck and his friend Tony Schoonen of the Anaconda Sportsmen's Club organized an ad hoc group called Beaverhead Forest Concerned Citizens to oppose the extensive logging and road building slated for the area. Luebeck was a friend of Pat Williams, a fellow teacher and Democratic Party activist from Butte who was running for Montana's western district congressional seat in 1978. During the campaign Luebeck invited Williams to his home to meet some of his fellow sportsmen and discuss the West Big Hole area. He handed Williams a photo of the two of them enjoying a fishing trip in the area some years earlier and asked him to sponsor a wilderness bill for the area.

Williams was running for Congress primarily to work on education and labor issues, but once he was elected, the importance of natural resource issues to his district led him to seek appointment to the House Interior Committee. Ron Marlenee already sat on this committee, but Williams prevailed on the House leadership to allot him a position as well. In September 1979, hoping to point the way toward an equitable resolution of the roadless area question, Williams announced that he would introduce a bill to establish a West Big Hole wilderness of not more than eighty-six thousand acres on the east slope of the Continental Divide. (Lands west of the divide on the Salmon National Forest were not included and were generally too steep to log.) Its boundaries were to be established through meetings between preservation groups, local ranchers, and the timber industry, with a separate recreation area to be designated on the lower slopes adjoining the Big Hole Valley. No consensus could be reached among the disparate groups Williams invited to the table, so he introduced a wilderness bill with boundaries drawn by Luebeck's group.[2]

House Interior Committee chairman Morris Udall agreed to hold a field hearing on the bill the following March. Luebeck and his supporters urged Williams to hold the hearing in Butte, but the representative instead chose Dillon, the county seat of Beaverhead County and home to a stud mill owned by the F. H. Stoltze Company of Columbia Falls. Stoltze had acquired the mill in 1972 with assurances from local Forest Service officers of a continued supply of timber from the surrounding Beaverhead National Forest. Nearby mills in Philipsburg and Deer Lodge, Montana, and in Salmon, Idaho, also expanded their capacities, however, and by 1973 the Beaverhead's annual harvest of 28.3 million board feet was fully subscribed. Five years later, roadless area studies under RARE II reduced the cut to 24.3 million board feet, with further reductions likely if areas such as the West Pioneers and West Big Hole remained off limits.[3]

Managed for decades as a low-use east-side forest providing cattle forage, posts and poles for ranchers, and a small supply of sawlogs, the Beaverhead escaped much attention from conservationists during the 1960s. When the forest proposed five new wilderness study areas in 1973 as part of the first RARE program, the conservative populace of Beaverhead County voiced its strong displeasure. Two of the larger study areas encompassed the craggy, sparsely timbered East Pioneer Mountains, but even these 11,000-foot peaks contained likely mineralization. Ruth Koch, an MWA leader from Butte, recalled a stormy public meeting in 1972 at which mining industry representatives from Spokane, Portland, and Salt Lake City joined local leaders in condemning any wilderness designations in the Pioneer Range. There was, she told Clif Merritt, "a real and very vitriolic back-lash against the Sierra Club as 'outsiders' . . . I heard this kind of thing in the hotel lobby, in the grocery store and on the street."[4]

Eight years later the West Big Hole proposal met with an even more hostile reaction. Placards, a banner-draped log truck, and overt anger greeted Morris Udall and Pat Williams when they opened the hearing before an audience of seven hundred at Western Montana College in Dillon. Luebeck's group and its friends in the MWA and Sierra Club argued that the high-elevation forest surrounding the Big Hole was a poor prospect for intensive timber management, but ranchers living there were wary of any designation that might restrict their grazing rights and bring outsiders to their remote valley. Many Dillon residents spoke of the important economic contribution the Stoltze mill made to their community.

Following the hearing, Udall told Williams that it had been one of the most contentious sessions he had ever attended, comparable to those he had held in Alaska on pending parks and wilderness legislation. Williams recalled that "the place had the look of the lynch mob," and Bill Cunningham believed it was only Udall's extraordinary patience and humor that prevented a riot.[5] By this time the Sagebrush Rebellion had popularized the idea that traditional western interests—livestock grazing, timber cutting, mining, and vehicle use—were under siege from radical environmentalists. This was not a new thesis in rural Montana, whose residents had enjoyed a comfortable relationship with development-minded federal agencies for decades, but the movement's emphasis on public protest and theatrics (which it borrowed from the Left and from the more flamboyant environmentalists) encouraged citizens in such communities to take media-worthy action.

At the request of the Beaverhead County Chamber of Commerce, Pat Williams postponed action on his West Big Hole bill to permit the chamber to study the economic effects of potential wilderness designations. Its report, delivered a year later, contained little new information, but with his mail running overwhelmingly against designating any wilderness in Beaverhead County, Williams announced that he would likely abandon his West Big Hole measure. Instead he would seek some kind of administrative plan that offered protection for the entire headwaters of the Big Hole River.[6]

Montana's preservation leaders should not have been shocked by the bitter opposition they encountered in Dillon, a complete turnabout from the 1968 Great Falls hearing on the Scapegoat wilderness. The RARE studies, coming on the heels of major reforms in federal timber practices, served to further depress sawlog availability from the national forests, but the problem ran deeper than that. Environmental regulations and restrictions on motorized use of the backcountry threatened the open relationship that people living in the rural West enjoyed with federal lands, which amounted to a sense of ownership and control. It was the mirror image of the anger that many Idaho and Montana sportsmen felt about dams and logging in the 1950s and 1960s, in which an uncomprehending federal bureaucracy interfered with their use of undisturbed forests, rivers, and mountains. That so many rural residents now felt that the tables had turned reflected on the success of the preservation movement, which had substantially broadened its aims beyond protecting a handful of signature mountain areas such as the upper Flathead, Selway, and Blackfoot. Every part of western Montana and central and northern Idaho was a contested landscape, with no room left to search for timber or minerals in some adjacent, overlooked drainage.

Concern over wilderness designations was not limited to outlying corners of these states. Shortly before the March 1980 hearing in Dillon, Pat Williams commissioned an opinion poll of voters in his district in which 42 percent of the respondents "strongly disagreed" with designating more federal land in Montana as wilderness. Bill Cunningham obtained the report and was disturbed to note that opposition to wilderness had increased sharply from a similar poll the representative had conducted before the 1978 election. The poll had "extremely serious implications to the cause of wilderness that cannot be ignored," Cunningham reported to MWA leaders. Wilderness activists could no longer assume that the public was automatically with them, he said, and he called for a "concerted and carefully thought out program" of public education on the values of wilderness.[7] But the MWA lacked the resources to conduct an extensive media campaign, and its members were dealing with dozens of new Forest Service multiple-use plans as well as the ongoing reviews of the S. 393 wilderness study areas. Successful wilderness campaigns required local grassroots groups to build support among community leaders, drawing on the reservoir of interest in wild country that still existed in Montana and Idaho. These campaigns succeeded only where they could demonstrate that federal classification of wilderness could work in locals' interest.

Residents of the college town of Missoula produced the one notable success of the post-RARE years: a backyard wilderness in the Rattlesnake Creek drainage north of town. This stream issued from a mountain reservoir operated by the Montana Power Company, which owned intermingled sections of land in the area. Used for years as a source of municipal water and for local recreation, the drainage was showing signs of overuse by the early 1970s. A road following the creek was popular with motorcyclists, leading to conflicts with other users. Side trails and trash were proliferating, according to Cass Chinske, a nearby resident who helped found a citizen group called Friends of the Rattlesnake.[8]

At first the group favored a backcountry-type designation for the 85,000-acre area, but Stewart Brandborg and local advocates encouraged the group to seek full wilderness status. The group then proposed that the upper half of the drainage be designated wilderness and the lower portion reserved for nonmotorized recreation. In June 1979 Pat Williams held a hearing in Missoula at which strong support for protecting the area was evident, leading him to introduce legislation that September. A land trade with Montana Power took time to arrange, however, and a motorcyclist group, hoping to retain access to lakes in the upper drainage, led a protest against the measure during Morris Udall's visit to Montana the following March.[9] John Melcher took their side and introduced his version of the bill in August 1980, which included a five-mile-long corridor along the creek that would remain open to motorbikes. With this agreement, and dropping a provision to create a federally funded nature education center in the lower drainage, Congress enacted the 33,000-acre Rattlesnake Wilderness that October. (The Forest Service later closed the canyon road to motorcycles, citing user conflicts and resource damage.) The bill included an adjoining 28,000-acre national recreation area and provided for exchange of Montana Power's lands for coal leases in eastern Montana, where the company maintained a large generating station.[10] It was a sole bright spot in a difficult year for Montana preservation advocates, showing once again how a locally based citizen group, through persistence and judicious compromise, could protect a landscape treasured by thousands of city dwellers.

In April 1981 Pat Williams surprised many observers by introducing a statewide RARE II release bill that was similar to nationwide bills introduced by Republican senators Samuel Hayakawa and Jesse Helms. The bills would exempt the Forest Service's programmatic environmental impact statement on RARE II from further judicial review and open the way for development of all nonselected roadless areas. Williams's version was limited to Montana RARE areas, and like the others it did not pass, but the issue came to dominate post–RARE II discussions nationwide during the early to mid-1980s.[11] The release bills, as they were known, were spurred by a state of California lawsuit that successfully challenged the Forest Service's RARE II environmental impact statement. Industry officials and the Forest Service worried that similar lawsuits would be filed in other states, tying up resource development in hundreds of roadless areas. Williams released a statement calling his bill an attempt to "get off dead center on this wilderness study issue" and indicated that he would support some new wilderness proposals as well. The move was widely seen as an attempt to shore up his support among rural Montanans in the wake of the Beaverhead controversy and serve notice to the preservation community that litigation over RARE II would be counterproductive.

The MWA was, in fact, contemplating a RARE II lawsuit for Montana's national forest areas, despite Bill Cunningham's warning that such an attempt would result in Congress rubber stamping the agency's decision for the 3.5 million acres of nonselected RARE II areas in Montana. In a lengthy memo to the MWA governing council the previous November, he had insisted that "key Congressional staff and public lands lobbyists"—including Doug Scott and Wilderness Society conservation director Chuck Clusen—agreed "to a person."[12]

Even though the MWA did not pursue legal avenues to RARE II, the Williams bill seemed to confirm Cunningham's analysis. With Lee Metcalf gone and John Melcher no great friend of Montana wilderness, Cunningham saw a cloudy future ahead. "Public support for wilderness in Montana has dropped substantially due to a well-funded industry propaganda campaign combined with difficult economic times," he warned. "Congress won't act to protect Montana wilderness without the support or at least consent of the Montana Congressional Delegation." But with Williams nursing his wounds from Dillon and Max Baucus reluctant to take on the contentious issue, preservation activists were left to seek other avenues.

One approach was through administrative channels under the new forest plans mandated under the National Forest Management Act of 1976. One of the first to be issued was for the Beaverhead National Forest, which had already embarked on an experiment in forest-wide land use planning using computer models to forecast various "resource outputs" under different management scenarios. The analyses were based on the Forest Service's "FORPLAN" computer model and were impenetrable to most readers, but the Beaverhead Forest Concerned Citizens group invited a young economist from Oregon named Randal O'Toole to analyze the plan. He found that the Beaverhead's planners had failed to include all the costs of timber management in their analyses, leading them to ascribe positive financial returns to higher cutting levels. O'Toole noted that their model runs used prices bid for stumpage during the high-demand period of 1976–81, before the nationwide recession. "Incredibly, and without explanation," he wrote, "these already inflated prices were tripled when fed into the computer. This major error led planners to conclude that 90% of the Beaverhead Forest could make money when managed for timber." O'Toole's reanalysis using prices from 1981 and after showed that timber sales on nearly 80 percent of the forest would lose money.[13]

The Beaverhead Forest Concerned Citizens group went on to file an administrative appeal of the forest plan, which proceeded for some years without resolution. The question of below-cost timber sales grew into a national issue, led by analysts with the Natural Resources Defense Council and the Wilderness Society,[14] but the question was largely irrelevant to the political situation in Beaverhead County and other east-side forests. Forest Service planners had assumed since the early 1960s that virtually all the timber on their forests would be made available for harvest, regardless of economic return, and had promised steadily increasing cutting levels for local mills. As was the case throughout the West, any withdrawal of potential commercial forest (and most of the RARE II areas

were designated as such) meant reductions in allowable cuts. Economic dislocations in rural communities such as Dillon were therefore inevitable, guarantee-
ing a strong political reaction to wilderness proposals.

Towns such as Butte and Anaconda, on the other hand, bridged the urban-
rural divide to some extent. Hunting and fishing occupied many residents'
weekends, and for local anglers the Big Hole River stood out as an outstanding
destination. This stream had a history of conflict over water withdrawals for irrigation and even a proposed dam near the town of Divide, to which were added
concerns over the Forest Service's timber sale program in the river's headwaters.
Roscoe Nickerson of the Anaconda Sportsmen's Club took up the case in his
outdoors column in the *Montana Standard,* contrasting the clarity of this stream
with the often murky waters of the Madison, Ruby, and Beaverhead Rivers,
which he said experienced siltation from logging and overgrazing. With fifty or
more timber sales planned in the Big Hole's headwaters over the next decade, he
predicted that the hundreds of anglers who descended on the river each spring
would find it less productive and seek other destinations. "The economic loss to
the community would be inestimable," he wrote.[15]

These allegations were difficult to prove, but Al Luebeck and Tony Schoonen
were able to persuade several Big Hole ranchers that the Forest Service's road-
building program posed a threat to their operations. Their entrée to this isolated
and conservative community came from a newcomer to the Big Hole, a rancher
named Jim Welch, who had purchased the Arrow Ranch on the north side of the
valley in 1981. Having made his wealth in California's housing boom, Welch was
seeking a location far from congestion and pollution. A year after moving to the
Big Hole, he was appalled to find the Forest Service building a new timber haul
road along the lower slopes of the forest behind his ranch, with numerous clear-
cuts to follow. He invited Luebeck and Bill Cunningham, who was now working
for the MWA, to see the road and discuss his options. A 400-acre timber sale
was planned for the Howell Creek drainage, close by the Anaconda-Pintler
Wilderness, which Welch said would sell at a net loss of more than a thousand
dollars an acre. He also feared disruption of a major elk calving ground and
possible siltation in this tributary of the Big Hole River. Moose, black bear, and
deer used the area, and a broad meadow was noted for an unusual population of
freshwater clams.[16] The two advocates were impressed with the wildlife they saw
in the area and agreed to help.

That evening, Welch invited fellow rancher Jack Hirschy and his family to
join them for dinner, and while Hirschy was cool to wilderness designation,
he had a problem of his own. The next morning he invited Luebeck and

Cunningham to visit his ranch, where they could see bulldozers at work in the nearby West Pioneer Mountains. "Jack was really upset," Luebeck recalled. "That's when it finally broke." It was not just the new road and clear-cuts that bothered Hirschy, but the subsidization of the sale: the agency invested $800,000 in the road and gained only $50,000 from the timber sale, according to Luebeck. The cost of such roads could be justified only as part of a major timber sale program that would transform the mountains surrounding the Big Hole.

Around this time Luebeck obtained a forest planning map showing anticipated timber sales over the next ten years. The logging road network reached into virtually every side drainage of the Big Hole, linked by a collector road system circling the valley that would bring many more visitors to what had been something of a private preserve for locals. He showed the map to the Big Hole ranchers, who could see their solitude and their unpolluted streams vanishing. Based on their distaste for this high-impact timber program, Welch, Hirschy, and several fellow ranchers made common cause with the two wilderness advocates.

Jim Welch, unwilling to let the administrative appeal process grind to its conclusion, placed fliers in the Dillon, Butte, Anaconda, and Helena newspapers asking citizens to help stop the Howell Creek sale. A postage-paid response form addressed to Montana's congressional delegation called for including the sale area as a 12,000-acre addition to the nearby Anaconda-Pintler Wilderness. The responses ran in the thousands, many from people who normally did not write on such issues. Timber and cattle associations criticized Welch as a newcomer, and John Melcher accused him of simply wanting to increase the value of his property, but eight local ranchers backed Welch and submitted a petition opposing the road and timber sale to the Montana congressional delegation. They and their neighbors did not necessarily care for environmentalists, but faced with intensive logging in their backyards, some were willing to consider wilderness classification.[17]

Welch's activism fit the pattern established by Phil Yeckel, Pete Combs, and Jeanette and John McIntire in other parts of the state. Each had purchased a ranch beneath a scenic mountainscape but was upset to see the Forest Service push roads and clear-cuts into the area. Their wealth and community standing gave them access to public officials, but equally important was their outreach to their neighbors. Hirschy, Clayton Huntley, and other Big Hole ranchers formed "Montanans for the Protection of the Big Hole," which brought a lawsuit against the Forest Service to halt a planned timber sale in the Steel Creek drainage east of the town of Wisdom. By 1987 the group included about twenty-five ranchers and had gained statewide attention for their unlikely alliance with the Butte-Anaconda sportsmen. They still did not favor wilderness, but they remained opposed to the agency's plans to radically transform the forests surrounding their homes.

Although Pat Williams's bill to designate the West Big Hole wilderness did not pass, the combined pressure brought to bear on the Forest Service had an effect. Timbering was drastically reduced around the periphery of the Big Hole and the planned road system was scaled back. "Below cost" sales became a national issue, eventually forcing the Northern Region to abandon its 30-year dream of placing these marginal, high-elevation forests under intensive management. Subsequent forest plans set aside the upper reaches of the West Big Hole as a recommended wilderness, and the West Pioneers remained under S. 393's interim protection provision, although expanding motor vehicle use presented conflicts in both areas.

Pat Williams later recalled that the March 1980 hearing in Dillon was "historic in the life of environmentalism in Montana." He may have been trying to put a good face on an exceptionally difficult situation, but he noted that for years afterward he heard from many county residents who had moderated their opposition to wilderness—if only a little.[18] Williams called it a "long learning process" for himself and his constituents. He recalled in 1997 that he had not come to Congress as a conservationist, but left it as one. Williams, like many present-day political leaders, hoped to find a consensual basis for action on public lands issues. For the Butte-Anaconda sportsmen and the Big Hole ranchers, the common ground lay in the largely undeveloped watershed of one of Montana's finest trout streams. Montana anglers knew from sad experience that a river lives only by the grace of its headwaters. As Winton Weydemeyer noted in 1948, it had been human folly to overgraze, impound, denude, or pollute too many of the Treasure State's streams, but in this far-off valley a small group of sportsmen reached out to the ranching community in an attempt to create a better blueprint for a river's future. The work that had begun with a lone activist from Wisdom had swelled to embrace two divergent cultures.

23

The Last Wilderness
Jack Creek and the Madison Range, 1970–1983

The 36,000-acre drainage of Jack Creek boasted none of the lofty peaks that studded the rest of the Madison Range, yet this timbered valley was the pivot point for a much larger wilderness that stretched from the Spanish Peaks south to Yellowstone. Montana preservation advocates faced a dilatory federal bureaucracy and a major corporation that had other plans for this drainage. The contest pitted conservation-minded citizens, some of whom were extraordinarily well connected, with a railroad that since 1864 had benefited from extraordinary federal largesse. With wilderness enthusiasts still uncertain of how much was within their reach, this unbroken sweep of mountain wildland stood in the balance.

Since the 1960s, landowners in the Madison Valley had been trying to protect Jack Creek as part of an expanded Spanish Peaks wilderness. The Northern Pacific Railway, however, wanted to complete land exchanges that would give it access to the "checkerboard" lands it owned in Jack Creek. The Forest Service largely acceded to these plans when it released a promised study of Jack Creek's wilderness potential in December 1969. Bill Worf, the Northern Region's chief of recreation and lands, presented the findings at a meeting of conservationists in Bozeman. Madison Valley ranchers Ed Beardsley and Pete Combs joined Clif Merritt, Florence and Ken Baldwin, and eight others as Worf outlined the difficulties in setting aside such a highly conflicted area. The agency admitted that most of the drainage qualified for protection under the terms of the Wilderness

Act, but the railroad still considered it part of a timber unit—as it had since 1957, when Ed Barry, Worf's predecessor, had opened negotiations on the subject. Several smaller trades were in the works, but Worf noted that the railroad might be willing to relinquish its Jack Creek holdings if it were offered more productive timberlands in the Swan Valley. The group was not enthusiastic about losing valuable wildlife habitat in the Swan, but the same problem existed almost anywhere they might look.[1] Northern Pacific representatives declined to attend the meeting, leaving the conservationists with little to go on.

Within months of the meeting, two major corporate events placed further pressure on the Madison Range wildlands. In March 1970 the Northern Pacific merged with the Great Northern and two other rail lines to form Burlington Northern, Inc. (BNI). The new company continued to pursue development of its checkerboard land holdings. Also that year, construction began on Chet Huntley's Big Sky Resort in the upper West Fork of the Gallatin.[2] These developments gave a sense of urgency to the conservationists' campaign to designate wilderness in major parts of the range.

Not all Madison Valley residents supported wilderness designation for Jack Creek; some Ennis business owners welcomed a road through the drainage that would connect their town with Big Sky and the Gallatin Valley. Lee Metcalf's and Arnold Olsen's bills to reclassify the Spanish Peaks Primitive Area included enough of Jack Creek to block the proposed transmountain road, in contrast to the Department of Agriculture's recommended wilderness of about half that size. Cecil Garland, the newly elected president of the MWA, noted that the administration's proposal would protect mostly "goat rocks" that were "esthetically beautiful and highly desirable" yet would not form an ecological unit. "Any wilderness, in order to support a community of wildlife must have the lower lands to supply habitat for the species that are going to survive," he said.[3]

With real estate development associated with Big Sky occupying much of the historic winter range along the West Fork of the Gallatin, protecting Jack Creek was all the more critical. Chet Huntley insisted that his resort would be planned with environmental values in mind and that removing cattle from the West Fork would open up the range for big game. His vision was subsumed into larger corporate aims after Chrysler Realty went bankrupt in the recession of 1974 and Big Sky was picked up by Boyne Resorts, a Michigan ski area developer. Expansion resumed and by the 1980s Big Sky had emerged as Gallatin County's top recreational attraction and income generator. Lone Mountain, which had once presided over Ken and Florence Baldwin's elk hunts in the West Fork, now served as a backdrop for elegant resort living.

Lee Metcalf's death in January 1978 delayed action on reclassifying the Spanish Peaks Primitive Area as the Montana delegation dealt with his holdover bills for the Absaroka-Beartooth and Great Bear Wilderness areas. The Forest Service also needed to complete its study of the adjacent Taylor-Hilgard area under Metcalf's S. 393.[4] Both Taylor-Hilgard and a companion study area in the Gallatin Range known as Hyalite–Porcupine–Buffalo Horn were subject to conflicting claims from snow machine users, ski resort builders, and BNI's timber division. On December 12, 1974, BNI's logging contractor, Yellowstone Pine Company of Belgrade, Montana, requested permission from the Forest Service to survey a logging road into some of its holdings between the Taylor Fork and Buck Creek, another side drainage to the north. The area to be logged lay within the proposed Taylor-Hilgard study area, but the agency granted the request four days later. Howard and Bonnie Kelsey of the Nine Quarter Circle guest ranch on the Taylor Fork were alarmed at the new incursion, as were a number of their clients, including Senator Bill Brock of Tennessee, who spent a week at the ranch during the first part of August 1975. Yellowstone Pine was "cutting timber on slopes that look much steeper than 45 degrees," Brock said in a letter to Agriculture Secretary Earl Butz. It was leaving "the most unsightly slash I've ever seen, building roads that are soon to wash out with heavy rain and snow, and doing no replanting whatsoever," he wrote.[5]

Brock was in touch with two Stanford Business School professors who had also been guests of the Kelseys. Robert Jaedicke and John Seidl took up the issue at some length with Agriculture Department officials, arguing that the Forest Service had a responsibility to prevent damage to the overall landscape in the Taylor Fork. Deputy assistant director Paul Vander Myde dismissed their claims, replying that "there is no legislation giving the Forest Service authority to regulate logging practices in private lands [and thus] it would be wrong to regulate the activities indirectly by conditioning access."

The professors continued to ask for stronger oversight, charging that Lewis Hawkes, the forest supervisor, was far too accommodating to BNI and its contractor. Hawkes admitted that a road failure had spilled debris onto adjacent Forest Service land, yet he fined the contractor a grand total of ninety-five dollars. This occurred not long after Yellowstone Pine filed a $2,500,000 suit for damages against the Forest Service, claiming it was denied access to railroad lands in Porcupine Creek on the other side of the Gallatin River. The suit was dismissed, but the company experienced no further problems with gaining access.[6] The Montana Wilderness Association filed an administrative appeal of the Buck Creek road project, but in September 1978 regional forester Robert

Torheim issued an adverse ruling. The MWA engaged the Bozeman law firm of Goetz and Madden on a pro bono basis to contest the decision in court, but no relief was forthcoming.

For years environmentalists had claimed that the western timber industry enjoyed undue influence with the Forest Service, but in the Madison Range it appeared that Burlington Northern and Yellowstone Pine were virtually dictating policy. Richard Behan, who had observed many public lands controversies in Montana and the West, blamed BNI for some of the worst corporate plundering of the public domain. "No law, no agency, no dedicated public land manager, no professional standards, no tradition, no policy, and no precedent could or would stand in the way of the corporate acquisition of public wealth," he wrote in 2001.[7] Yet it was not just a matter of corporate influence over public land policy; the near congruence of management goals among Forest Service and BNI timber planners from the 1950s through the 1970s made such practices almost inevitable. The 1958 agreement that led to the Hilgard Hold Area omitted timberlands in the lower Buck Creek drainage along with the private lands in Taylor Fork. Little had changed since then. The timber resources of the Madison Range needed to be developed, according to agency officials, and they hoped to pursue their goals in concert with the railroad.

In April 1977, faced with continued opposition to its timbering, Burlington Northern offered to trade the 177,000 acres it owned in the Gallatin and Beaverhead National Forests for an equal value of national forest timberland, preferably in the Flathead or Kootenai Forests. Those lands comprised valuable wildlife habitat and recreational areas as well, and little progress resulted. The issue became moot in October 1978 when Senator John Melcher attached an amendment to a national parks omnibus bill that required Congress to approve any national forest land exchange of more than 6,400 acres.[8] The need for the amendment was unclear, and the other members of the Montana congressional delegation expressed surprise and irritation at the sudden move. Rick Applegate, another Bozeman attorney who was working closely with the MWA on the Buck Creek issue, characterized the amendment as "hit and run legislation" designed to subvert the land trade.[9] The Forest Service put its environmental analysis of the land swap on hold and issued a permit to Yellowstone Pine to build a road into Buck Creek. Clear-cuts soon appeared in a neat checkerboard pattern on the ridges north of Taylor Fork, cutting into part of the land under study in S. 393.

Adding to the urgency for MWA leaders was a proposed ski area that would impinge on the slopes of Monument Mountain in the southern part of the

Taylor-Hilgard study area. "Ski Yellowstone" was to be a combined downhill ski area and second-home development patterned after Big Sky, effectively sandwiching the study area between two major resorts and increasing the demand for snowmobiling and trail biking between them. Rick Applegate went so far as to propose an alternative resort, which the MWA would develop on public lands north of Mount Hebgen. Envisioned as a low-impact, cross-country ski area without associated real estate sales, it would include twenty-nine miles of trails and an overnight hut as part of what Applegate called a "viable, reasonable alternative to this high density recreation and second home development." He offered to withdraw the plan if the state fish and game department found it to be detrimental to grizzly bears—in which case supervisor Hawkes would be "morally and legally obligated" to disapprove Ski Yellowstone as well.[10]

Ski Yellowstone's developers had difficulty lining up investors and the resort was never built, but the Madison Range remained "the most threatened de facto wilderness in Montana," according to Bill Cunningham, who worked for the MWA in Helena.[11] He encouraged Bozeman-area conservationists to form an ad hoc group to meet the various challenges in the region north of Yellowstone, which led in early 1979 to the formation of the Madison-Gallatin Alliance (MGA) under the leadership of an avid hiker and skier named Joan Montagne. The daughter-in-law of John Montagne, a founder of the MWA, Joan helped the new group set an ambitious agenda. She recruited a Bozeman physician named Richard Tenney and a young activist named Rick Meis, who together tried to push other organizations, including the MWA, toward larger wilderness proposals. Protecting Yellowstone's grizzlies was a key concern for the MGA, which wanted to see stricter controls on development of public and private lands north of the park.

In August 1979 Burlington Northern announced that it would build a logging road into a section of its land in the headwaters of Jack Creek, just west of Big Sky. Both the MGA and MWA hoped that Pat Williams, Montana's newly elected western district representative, would help stop the incursion, and in October he held a fact-finding hearing in Bozeman at which thirty pro-wilderness supporters spoke. Shortly thereafter, Williams joined Senators Baucus and Melcher in requesting regional forester Tom Coston to expedite studies of Jack Creek, which had been placed in a "further planning" category in RARE II. Bill Cunningham worried that this presaged an attempt to introduce "release" legislation that would throw Jack Creek back into nonwilderness status.[12]

Senator Melcher, perhaps realizing that a release bill would meet significant opposition, instead submitted an amendment to the Alaska National Interest

Lands Conservation Act, which specified that the secretary of agriculture must provide access to all private land inholdings and that no other law or departmental regulation could interfere with "the reasonable use and enjoyment thereof." The amendment appeared to be a direct attempt to grant BNI access to its holdings in the Madison Range. Melcher explained that his amendment did not prevent the Forest Service from attaching "terms and conditions" for landowner access, but that "reasonable access" must be allowed private landowners.[13]

This was public land politics in its rawest form. The way was now clear for BNI to begin road construction and logging in both Buck Creek and Jack Creek regardless of their effect on public land or extant wilderness proposals. The Goetz and Madden law firm filed suit in federal district court on behalf of the MWA, Wilderness Society, and Nine Quarter Circle Ranch to seek an injunction against the road project but was unsuccessful; soon large clear-cuts appeared in upper Jack Creek as well.[14] The dream of a single Madison Range wilderness area reaching from Cowboys Heaven to Yellowstone National Park had entranced outfitters, ranchers, sportsmen, and hikers for a quarter century, but long ago Congress had planted the seeds of its destruction in the 1864 Northern Pacific land grant. No officer of the Department of Agriculture or any member of the Montana congressional delegation was willing to take on one of America's corporate giants or challenge the land-disposal policy of a previous century.

With few avenues left to protect the Madison Range in its entirety, preservation groups turned to the Forest Service's study of the Taylor-Hilgard area mandated under S. 393. Gallatin Forest supervisor John Drake presented the agency's findings to a packed meeting in Bozeman in early November 1980. Within the 289,000-acre study area, the agency believed that 157,000 acres should be designated wilderness, with the remainder allocated to timber harvesting, off-road vehicle use, and other uses requiring mechanized equipment or vegetative manipulation. To the wilderness advocates' dismay, the entire Monument Mountain section west of Yellowstone National Park was missing from the proposal, as was the lower part of Buck Creek.[15] Jack Creek was not included in the study area.

John Craighead was "amazed and disappointed" at the lack of protection given Monument Mountain, which the Fish and Wildlife Service had designated as critical grizzly bear habitat following a 12-year study. "I have personally covered much of this area on foot, have radiotracked bears there and have evaluated the habitat," Craighead wrote. Its omission "would result in adverse modification of habitat and would surely lead to a high man-caused death rate among the grizzly bears of the area."[16] The chief obstacle to classifying the area as wilderness was the Big Sky Snowmobile Trail, a Forest Service–approved route that ran along Little Wapiti Creek south of Taylor Fork, past Sage Peak (the highest point in the Monument Mountain area) to Cabin Creek on the Hebgen Lake side of the mountains. Some six to eight thousand enthusiasts traveled the route each winter, with a typical weekend seeing two hundred machines, according to a 1970 Sierra Club report. Clif Merritt said that conservationists had "good reason to feel they were betrayed" by the Forest Service in establishing the snowmobile route and omitting the eastern part of the Taylor-Hilgard area from the original RARE recommendation.[17]

The MGA, which styled itself as "more aggressive, more political and more effective" than "the usual milk-toast group," decided to press ahead with its own comprehensive proposal for both the Madison and Gallatin Ranges. In June 1980 the group unveiled a 534,000-acre wilderness to be named for the late Lee Metcalf. It took in the Spanish Peaks and Cowboys Heaven, the contested lands in Jack Creek, and the Taylor-Hilgard wilderness study area, including Buck Creek and the Monument Mountain area, effectively shutting off the Big Sky snowmobile trail. Its boundaries were no less sweeping within the Gallatin Range, reaching from Palisade Mountain near Hyalite Lake south to the Porcupine and Buffalo Horn drainages and beyond to Yellowstone National Park. Some indication of the difficulty facing the proposal lay in the more than one hundred thousand acres of Burlington Northern land spread throughout much of the proposed wilderness.[18] The alliance hoped that a trade or purchase of these lands could be arranged to speed their designation as wilderness, and in January 1980 Joan Montagne, Howard Kelsey, Vic Benson, and Bill Cunningham met with Senator Max Baucus to ask for his support. Baucus agreed to try to reinstate the administrative process leading to a comprehensive land exchange, but John Melcher would not agree, leaving Burlington Northern to pursue its timber management goals within the two ranges.[19]

The notion that Yellowstone's magnificent wildlife populations depended on a larger ecosystem was gaining credence in the late 1970s, thanks to the pioneering research of Frank and John Craighead. By documenting the wide range of the Yellowstone grizzly bear, they concluded that its survival depended on unprotected habitats that were at least as extensive as the park itself. John Craighead recalled that as early as 1959 he and his brother were discussing the concept of a larger ecosystem incorporating the park, and during the late 1970s they introduced the term "greater Yellowstone ecosystem." Conservationists Rick Reese of Bozeman and Ralph Maughan of Pocatello began applying the concept to landscape conservation efforts in the early 1980s, and Reese's 1985 book *Greater Yellowstone* placed the term in popular usage.[20] Reese was active in the MGA and along with its leaders helped organize the Greater Yellowstone Coalition in 1983, which worked to firm up protection for the lands surrounding Yellowstone and Grand Teton National Parks.

The uses made of private lands within this region were critical to migratory wildlife such as elk, bison, grizzly bear, and pronghorn. But with a large-scale land trade in the Madison and Gallatin Ranges unlikely, any wilderness designations in that area would necessarily be small and fragmented.[21] Joan Montagne and her colleagues resigned themselves to working with Senators Melcher and Baucus to secure as much protected land as possible. They warned their members that the delegation's bill would "probably be barely a skeleton of our original proposal. . . . Each agency and representative group has been allowed to take its respective chomp out of the original Lee Metcalf Wilderness Proposal." This "piecemeal approach to planning," she wrote, led to "haphazard boundary adjustments, diminishing wildlife habitat areas, [and] lack of ecological unity."[22] It no doubt came as a difficult realization that the days of entrusting Lee Metcalf or Mike Mansfield to carry a strong wilderness bill past the opposition were over in Montana. Their early successes under the Wilderness Act would be replaced by difficult maneuvers on many fronts—administrative as well as congressional—to achieve conservation objectives.

Montagne's fears were realized in February 1982 when John Melcher introduced the "Lee Metcalf Wilderness and Management Act," which proposed 202,000 acres of wilderness in three disconnected parts: the Spanish Peaks Primitive Area, the Taylor-Hilgard peaks, and the rugged Beartrap Canyon of the Madison River, which was a Bureau of Land Management property located west of the primitive area. It called for a separate wildlife management designation for the Monument Mountain area, which would remain open to winter snow machine use. The measure was freighted with several "release" provisions, which specified nonwilderness status for Jack Creek, Mount Henry in northwestern Montana, and the Tongue River Breaks in eastern Montana, where coal strip mining was a possibility.[23]

Melcher introduced his bill without the support of Max Baucus, who expressed disappointment that he was not consulted. Melcher responded that Baucus's and the environmentalists' displeasure "tickles me like horsefeathers," since he had been working with them for four years to reach a consensus on the measure. He accused the wilderness groups of "pursuing their dedicated course to put as much land as possible into permanent wilderness" without regard for the "thousands of Montanans" who recreated in the area with vehicles.[24] He was running for reelection, however, and with environmentalists expressing strong displeasure with the bill, he agreed to add a 30,660-acre wilderness in the Monument Mountain area. Joan Montagne, who had stepped down as MGA president to take the same post with the MWA, welcomed the amendments but said they fell far short of what was needed to honor Lee Metcalf. Metcalf's widow, Donna, said the bill was "diminishing to the environment."[25]

Melcher did not try to advance his bill until the Ninety-Eighth Congress convened in 1983, when he reintroduced it as S. 96. It still consisted of four separate parcels separated by Burlington Northern's checkerboard holdings—an arrangement Montagne derided as "a proposal accommodating to all and satisfactory to none." Still, she advised her supporters to accept the bill as the best they could get, given the real possibility that with an unsympathetic administration in power, further incursions into the area could occur.[26] Pat Williams and Max Baucus were receptive to enlarging the bill's overall wilderness boundaries, which reached 259,000 acres by the time it passed Congress on October 31, 1983. The final bill included the rugged Beartrap Canyon area of the lower Madison River, the first BLM wilderness designation in the country. The bill also directed the secretary of agriculture to exchange 11,810 acres of national forest land in the Jack Creek drainage for 24,723 acres of BNI land located within the wilderness area.[27] Joan Montagne observed that "Senator Melcher has whittled the area down and politically maneuvered us into accepting his knife job on such a special area. It is certain that we won't get any more out of a delegation such as ours right now."[28]

Enactment of the Lee Metcalf Wilderness brought to a close negotiations that had been going on since 1958 between reluctant Forest Service officers and local conservationists. The intervening quarter century had brought a major ski area and real estate development to the upper Gallatin, along with a road across Jack Creek and the transfer of much of the land within it to Burlington Northern. The company would eventually sell large parcels to the developer of another high-end ski and second-home resort known as Moonlight Basin. The participants in the 1958 meeting at the Nine Quarter Circle Ranch had foreseen these developments in outline if not in detail, but even the growing strength of the MWA and MGA was not sufficient to forestall major losses to the range's wilderness character. The ironically named Lee Metcalf Wilderness, sectioned into four pieces like a peeled orange, did offer protection to the high country of the Spanish Peaks and Hilgard Basin, which remained splendid places for a summertime adventure. Gone, however, was the sense of freedom that outfitter Vic Benson reported when he traveled with Olaus Murie and others across mile upon mile of lake-spangled subalpine basins. The area's grizzly bears, elk, and mountain sheep would have to adjust to the new reality as well, their habitat increasingly fragmented by roads and riven with the sound of machines.

Such conflicts over public land designation arose in part from the legacy of old railroad land grants, but new pressures made them especially acute. America's growing population, coupled with its increasingly intense use of natural resources, laid claim to every available acre of the national forest system. There was no longer any slack in the gears that drove resource production. Unlike in the Scapegoat and Selway battles, timbering could not be shunted to some other uncut locality. Future wilderness designations would be paid in precious capital: one roadless tract traded against another in increasingly difficult negotiations. The Lee Metcalf Wilderness was the final seal on the bargain that Charles Tebbe and Ed Barry had offered the Gallatin Canyon outfitters in 1958: the timber country for the high country, with the unforeseen complication of long-distance snow machine routes tossed in. The result was a wilderness that looked very much like what the Forest Service had intended to allow all along.

24

Deadlock
Post–RARE II Legislation in Idaho and Montana, 1983–1988

The designation of the River of No Return Wilderness in 1980 marked high tide for the preservation movement in the Northern Rockies. The addition of Frank Church's name to the 2.2-million-acre area in 1984 was a fitting tribute to one of the Senate's great wilderness advocates, whereas the quartered and shrunken Lee Metcalf Wilderness, enacted the year before, fell well short of a memorial to the man who shepherded three of Montana's largest wilderness areas and a major wild river into law. Though reluctant to oppose the timber industry and the Forest Service early in their careers, Senators Church and Metcalf ultimately left a tremendous legacy of protected landscapes. The citizen movement that pushed for this legislation was to some extent the victim of its own success, however. Each new designated area, from the Scapegoat Wilderness in 1972 to the Great Bear, Absaroka-Beartooth, and River of No Return in the intervening years, represented forestland taken out of production. With ongoing wilderness studies placing more timber off limits, many rural residents in the Northern Rockies felt it was time to let the curtain fall on further protective designations. To them a way of life was at stake—one that depended on extracting useful commodities from the land and using vehicles for their recreation. Just as outfitters and horse users had used preservation-of-lifestyle arguments against the would-be developers of the upper Flathead, the Lincoln Back Country, and Chamberlain Basin, these citizens began to apply persistent and effective pressure on their congressional representatives. Any new wilderness designations in the 1980s and beyond would require significant trade-offs in the form of released forest acreage—a price that some preservation leaders were not willing to pay.

One of the most active groups opposing new wilderness designations was the Western Environmental Trade Association (WETA), which was formed in Oregon in 1971 as a coalition of labor unions, trade groups, and businesses opposed to new environmental regulations. WETA established a Montana branch in 1976, which drew considerable support among industrial workers who had formerly been allied with progressive and environmental causes. Outdoors Unlimited, based since 1967 in Coeur d'Alene, Idaho, helped coordinate lobbying efforts in similar fashion for off-road vehicle users. Enthusiasts of jeeps, trail bikes, and snow machines represented one of the fastest-growing segments of outdoor recreation, especially during the 1980s when new, user-friendly all-terrain vehicles became generally available. They found considerable sympathy among Steve Symms, John Melcher, and especially Ron Marlenee, who told a Great Falls wilderness activist that he wanted "as many Montanans as possible [to] be able to experience our open spaces and mountains. Fulfilling outdoor experiences should not be limited to hikers of great skill." John Melcher urged those "who want a place to park their camper, or the handicapped, or those who want to be close to the fishing and hunting" to speak out.[1] This was the same program that Ed Barry, the Northern Region's recreation director, had advanced during the 1950s and 1960s, and wilderness supporters suspected that now, as then, an interest in resource development lay just beneath the surface.

Most of the RARE II areas came with these built-in conflicts. The wilderness areas established by Congress in 1964 had been off limits to resource extraction and motor vehicle use since the 1930s, which allowed Frank Church and Lee Metcalf to legitimately claim that their designation would have little effect on log supplies or developed recreation. But outside these core areas lay roadless areas containing significant timber stands as well as primitive roads and trails favored by jeep and motorbike users. Preservation groups recommended further additions to the wilderness system from these lands amounting to 4.5 million acres in Idaho and 2.2 million acres in Montana—far more than the activists of the 1950s and 1960s had dared to suggest.[2] To wilderness opponents these were staggering numbers, suggesting that preservationists wanted to drastically curtail their activities on public lands. Unlike most previous wilderness legislation, which dealt with one area at a time, the RARE studies and subsequent statewide wilderness legislation created a climate of fear that made further progress all but impossible.

The continuing impasse over RARE II lands led to an unexpected announcement from Assistant Secretary of Agriculture John Crowell in February 1983 that
the Reagan administration would revisit the roadless area reviews through the
national forest management plans then under preparation. Quickly dubbed RARE
III, Crowell's program alarmed the timber industry with the promise of yet more
delays. Preservation groups suspected that was his intention; the Sierra Club's
Mike McCloskey called RARE III an "artificial crisis" that would panic Congress
into adopting nationwide release legislation.[3] He and his colleagues favored a
state-by-state approach, which would give grassroots activists more say in the process. Industry needed access to roadless areas, so the preservationists' quid pro
quo was substantial wilderness designations. Working through their champions
in Congress—the environmentalists with Ohio representative John Seiberling,
chair of the House Public Lands Subcommittee, and industry with Idaho's James
McClure, who chaired the Senate Energy and Natural Resources Committee—
the two sides hammered out a 1984 compromise that became the template for a
series of wilderness bills passed during President Reagan's second term. It provided that roadless areas that were not covered in a RARE II wilderness or further
planning recommendation, or that were undergoing a congressionally mandated
wilderness study, would be made available to development for the duration of one
forest planning cycle, typically ten to fifteen years. After that, the agency could
again evaluate their wilderness potential.[4] This "soft release" language was agreed
to in bills for many western states, including Oregon, Washington, and Wyoming.
With Doug Scott and Tim Mahoney at the helm for the environmentalists, a flo-
tilla of wilderness bills from other states made their way through Congress in 1984.
In a rare show of bipartisanship, Congress passed and President Reagan signed
twenty-one of these bills in his last year of office.

Efforts to reach a comprehensive post–RARE II agreement in Montana and
Idaho proved far more difficult, however. John Melcher convened field hearings in three Montana cities in July 1983, announcing that he and his colleagues
were seeking a consensus on which areas to designate as wilderness and which
to release from RARE's clutches. James McClure held hearings in Idaho that
summer with the same intention. As the chief interest groups staked out dia-
metric positions, it became clear that no simple accommodation was possible.
Many familiar faces appeared before the two delegations: Bob Helding from
the Montana Wood Products Association told Melcher's subcommittee that the
Montana timber industry must have stability if it was to recover from the "dev-
astating" recession. Larry Blasing of the Inland Forest Resource Council made
the quite reasonable observation that RARE I and RARE II had been designed

to allocate roadless lands so that industry would know where it could count on available resources. He told McClure's committee in Boise that "after 12 years, here we are requesting that Congress act to resolve that same issue." John McBride of St. Regis Paper said there was "no question" that his industry would go along with small wilderness designations along the margins of the Cabinet Wilderness and in Scotchman Peak, if other roadless areas were released for timber harvest. Doris Milner, whose 16-year campaign to protect the upper Selway had ended in success just three years earlier, remarked that "we are all weary of the interminable struggle" over roadless wildlands, but that areas such as the Sapphire Mountains still deserved to be protected.[5]

The effects of timber development on wildlife, which had dominated discussions of roadless lands in the Northern Rockies for more than three decades, remained a key concern. Hadley Roberts, a retired Forest Service wildlife biologist from Salmon, described how his agency's aggressive road-building program in Idaho's Lemhi Range had left hundreds of miles of roads open to hunters and encouraged four-wheel drive and motorbike users to branch out even farther. The loss of hiding cover forced deer and elk to migrate upslope, where still more timber sales were planned. He said local ranchers "have seen enough cutting and roading" in the range and were considering filing an appeal.[6] But Idaho state senator David Little of Emmett spoke for many of his constituents who wanted to hunt, fish, or gather firewood on their ATV or other vehicle. "Why shouldn't [these areas] be available to the senior citizen and the fellow who works and has to leave on a Friday night and be back on a Monday morning?"[7]

The two sides were miles apart and growing no closer. In Idaho the preservationists' wilderness alternative comprised slightly more than half of the state's remaining RARE II lands, whereas the timber industry's proposal comprised about 6 percent. In Montana the contrast was only slightly less stark, with the MWA and its allies proposing that 39 percent of the RARE II inventory be designated as wilderness and the timber industry generally endorsing less than 5 percent of the total.[8] MWA leaders participated in discussions with timber industry and Forest Service officials during the summer of 1983 as a means of showing good faith. As Bill Cunningham told John Melcher, it was an "opportunity to maintain timber programs and to maintain jobs and at the same time protect what is truly unique about Montana." They toured planned timber sales and held extensive map sessions to delineate acceptable boundaries but were able to reach agreement on only one area—a high-elevation ridge on the Helena National Forest called, predictably, Mount Baldy.[9] Lacking timber, it was emblematic of the gulf separating the groups.

In June 1984 the four members of the Montana delegation (John Melcher, Max Baucus, Pat Williams, and Ron Marlenee) introduced companion bills in the Senate and House that would designate 749,000 acres of wilderness in twenty-one areas, many of which had been proposed for such status in RARE II. Williams recalled in a 1997 interview how the four men met over a period of months, spreading maps on the floor of each other's offices, "with ties pulled down and coats off . . . on our hands and knees and literally on the floor" going over mining claims, snowmobile and jeep trails, and wildlife migration corridors in an effort to devise a proposal each of them could support.[10] Areas such as the Tobacco Root Mountains, West Big Hole, northern Sapphire Mountains, and Crazy Mountains were whittled down in a process that allowed any one of the four members to veto a wilderness proposal. In the case of the Rocky Mountain Front, a collection of RARE II areas along the windswept eastern edge of the Bob Marshall Wilderness, the delegation could agree on only a single 20,700-acre wilderness, whereas the MWA and its affiliates had recommended 320,000 acres in a substantial eastward expansion of this wildlife-rich area. Marlenee wanted to keep most of the Front open to those he termed "average recreationists," saying in a news interview that "we're not going to shut out the elderly or the people with campers who want to go out for the weekend."[11]

MWA president Ed Madej termed the twin bills a "wilderness axe" that would break faith with the long tradition of protecting Montana's wildland resources. James Curtis of Missoula, representing a new group called the Bob Marshall Alliance, informed Pat Williams that he was "flabbergasted and bewildered" by the delegation's proposal. He termed Marlenee's recreation argument a proxy for oil and gas interests that wanted access to the Overthrust Belt, a geologically complex feature along the eastern edge of the Rockies that was undergoing a major boom in natural gas development. There was even a short-lived proposal to conduct seismic exploration within the Bob Marshall Wilderness, which had spurred the alliance's formation and a vocal "Don't Bomb the Bob" campaign. Curtis cited U.S. Geological Survey figures showing potential natural gas production from the Front's roadless areas as sufficient to meet U.S. consumption for less than a month. Referring to Williams, Baucus, and Melcher, he said he "did not vote for my Democratic Congressman and Senators with the expectation that they would participate in a process that allows a notoriously reactionary Republican supporter of James Watt to dictate allocation decisions for federal lands."[12]

Curtis and other wilderness advocates had participated in a two-hour meeting with Pat Williams that summer, which Bill Cunningham characterized as "intense, open and blunt." The MWA staffer told the representative that he had misinterpreted the "mood of Montanans toward their wildland heritage." While wilderness advocates wanted to be done with RARE II, they would not support the wholesale abandonment of popular wilderness proposals, he said.[13] But the delegation had agreed, at Melcher's insistence, to allow no amendments to the consensus package. By midsummer both bills were dead in the water, victims of an unrelenting barrage of criticism from both sides of the wilderness divide.

Pat Williams expressed surprise at the vehement reaction against the 1984 bill, which seemed only to polarize the opposing sides. Ed Madej recalled that it took several failed attempts at passing a Montana wilderness bill for Williams to realize that he would encounter "the same degree of opposition over a hundred thousand acres or a million acres of wilderness." Montana's three Democrats in Congress were often not on speaking terms, Madej said, and could not agree on a wilderness package even when environmentalists tried to collaborate with the timber industry.[14] Subsequent efforts to enact comprehensive statewide wilderness legislation for Montana—and there would be many, spanning the next several decades—would be pursued individually, with Williams gradually taking stronger pro-wilderness positions.

Activists expressed similar concerns about bills that Idaho's Senator James McClure and Representative Larry Craig introduced in 1984 that would have added nine wilderness areas comprising 526,000 acres to the state's 3.6-million-acre tally.[15] These included a portion of the popular White Cloud Peaks east of the Sawtooth Range, where a proposed molybdenum mine had been at issue since the 1970s, as well as Borah Peak, the state's highest. Less well known was a 30,500-acre tract adjacent to the Mallard-Larkins Pioneer Area and a 124,500-acre portion of the proposed Great Burn wilderness. As originally introduced, the bill called for "hard release" of all other RARE II areas, meaning there would be no further consideration of their wilderness values in forest plans. Even some of these designations came under fire from the timber industry. The Idaho side of the Great Burn, according to Joseph Hinson of the Idaho Forest Industry Council, should be limited to no more than 21,500 acres in order to maintain timber supplies for a sawmill located across the state line in Superior, Montana.

Ernie Day called the McClure measure a "wilderness extinction bill" at a hearing held in Washington in April 1984. "We are being directed by this bill to trade our best for a bit of rocks and ice, and not much rocks and ice either. There is no quid pro quo here; hard release and destruction for a pittance."[16] But McClure's Energy and Natural Resources Committee issued a favorable report that May and sent the bill to the Senate floor. Larry Craig's companion bill ran into trouble in John Seiberling's House Public Lands Subcommittee, with Idaho governor John Evans among those expressing his reservations. Two weeks later, Representatives Peter Kostmayer of Pennsylvania and Jim Moody of Wisconsin introduced a bill to designate 3.4 million acres of Idaho wilderness, somewhat less than the preservation groups' 4.5-million-acre proposal. Neither bill made it out of Seiberling's committee. Steve Symms believed the Idaho delegation could have agreed on a 700,000–800,000-acre bill had Evans and Seiberling not been involved.[17] That fall Evans challenged Symms for his Senate seat, going down to a narrow defeat. The 1986 election saw the emergence of organized support for Symms from off-road vehicle users, including the BlueRibbon Coalition, which quickly grew to represent many off-road vehicle users in the region.[18]

Rick Johnson, a volunteer with the Idaho Conservation League (ICL) at the time, later recalled that the two sides were close to reaching an agreement on the McClure-Craig bill, and that its demise led to "political toxicity" that took "years to overcome." He believed that the resistance to the 1984 bill prevented Idaho conservationists from "moving into the post-Church era," referring to the sponsor of every wilderness bill that had been passed in their state.[19] Johnson, a Sun Valley resident and former Sierra Club lobbyist, headed the ICL beginning in 1995 and steered it toward a more collaborative approach with resource user groups. In a 2006 white paper he cowrote with Lindsay Slater, an aide to Idaho representative Mike Simpson, he said that it was simply too difficult to craft a single legislative solution for 9.3 million acres of roadless lands spread across the length and breadth of the state. "There were just too many 'special places' with too many interests," he believed.[20]

It was into this increasingly hostile atmosphere that Peter Kostmayer reintroduced his Idaho Wilderness Act in two successive congresses, increasing its size to 3.9 million acres, yet with no real chance of passage. James McClure stayed out of the fray until 1988, when he and Cecil Andrus (who was reelected to the governorship in 1986) offered a 1.4-million-acre compromise bill. Even this attempt failed to bridge the widening gap between development and preservation interests. By this time the Idaho Wildlands Defense Coalition, a consortium of preservation groups including the Wilderness Society, Sierra Club, and Idaho Conservation League, had enlarged their proposal to 5.7 million acres.[21]

Unlike in the Gospel-Hump compromise of 1977–78, failure was almost guaranteed for "consensus" legislation, since the mining and energy industries as well as the increasingly vocal off-road vehicle lobby insisted they be cut in on any deal. Rare indeed was a roadless area in either state that did not contain merchantable timber, promising minerals, or jeep roads and trails favored by wheeled adventurers. To the preservationists, the consensus approach was equivalent to taking the least common denominator of the RARE II areas—a return to the Forest Service's "rocks and ice" approach. Tom Hurlock, a Kalispell activist, said the industry-favored process would leave only barren ridges as wilderness in northwestern Montana—what he called "scraps, nothing but scraps." He urged a more deliberate approach. "There is a final nervous rush to develop the land as though it were needed," he stated at John Melcher's 1983 hearings. "I think we need to cool it, to be relaxed, to do our damn best to do a good job."[22] Some participants in these ongoing battles agreed and used the wreckage of the 1984 bills as a starting point for serious negotiation with the affected user groups. These ranged from professionally mediated efforts in Idaho to purely ad hoc attempts in Montana.

The latter characterized Al Luebeck's and Bill Cunningham's continuing dialogue with ranchers in the Big Hole Valley. Their shared concern over watershed protection, taxpayer-funded logging roads, and wildlife habitat did not always extend to wilderness classification, which remained anathema in Beaverhead County. Yet stopping the Forest Service's extensive road-building program in the foothills surrounding their valley was a matter of conservatism, according to Jack Hirschy, who asked, "In a time of trillion dollar federal deficits, why doesn't Congress begin its budget cuts here?" He was particularly concerned about the spread of spotted knapweed, which infested "virtually every clear-cut in the valley" and which vehicles spread even farther. The weed secreted soil toxins that displaced useful browse plants and was a serious threat to the nonirrigated margins of the Big Hole.[23]

Because of their overriding concern about roads, Hirschy and his fellow ranchers agreed in early 1988 to support a small wilderness area in the upper reaches of the West Big Hole, along with a national recreation area for the remainder of the RARE area. Clayton Huntley, speaking for the ranchers' association, requested the Senate Public Lands Subcommittee to adopt "very specific language excluding all commercial timber sales and logging roads in the recreation area." Remarkably, the group also endorsed wilderness legislation for the East Pioneer Mountains. "This is a complete turn around for the ranchers," Huntley acknowledged, and was achieved "after many years of evaluation and discussion about what really lies in our best interest."[24]

Hirschy's and Huntley's statements were in response to a new set of wilderness bills that Max Baucus and Pat Williams introduced in 1987. Both carried the cumbrous title "Montana Natural Resources Protection and Utilization Act," reflecting the antipathy that the mere mention of wilderness tended to evoke. Williams's 1.4-million-acre wilderness bill kept the West Big Hole in "further planning" status and established a national recreation area in the West Pioneer Mountains. He announced that April that he was "through making deals" with Ron Marlenee and would push the bill over his objections. At a markup session in September 1987, the House Public Lands Subcommittee rejected a substitute bill Marlenee offered that would have removed or weakened wilderness protections from nearly five million acres of RARE II lands. The eastern district representative said he was "incensed" by the subcommittee's action, and that Williams's bill was "a rape of the rights of Montanans to recreate" in places such as the Rocky Mountain Front.[25]

The House of Representatives passed Williams's bill in October 1987, but differences remained with Max Baucus's 1.3-million-acre Senate version. John Melcher combined features of both bills in a third measure calling for 1.4 million acres of wilderness, but it contained numerous special provisions, and few Montanans were enthusiastic about it. Nonetheless Melcher, who was running for reelection against Conrad Burns, a Billings broadcaster and county commissioner, obtained its passage. In a move thought to be aimed at helping Burns, President Reagan pocket vetoed the measure. Burns defeated Melcher, resetting the wilderness debate to the starting point.

Ron Marlenee sometimes spoke of his desire to represent "Joe Montana," the average recreationist who could not take time for a lengthy backpack or horse ride in the wilderness. Joe was ordinarily "a pretty tolerant guy," Marlenee observed, but lately he was feeling pushed around by wilderness advocates. "I've been in enough bars and coffee shops that I've learned where the fighting point begins—and friend, we're at it," he told members of the Senate Energy Committee in March 1988 during hearings on the Williams-Baucus bills. He said that snowmobiling—a favorite Joe Montana activity—had the greatest potential for tourism promotion in areas where wintertime unemployment was high. Tourists were not going to pay for a room just to look at the wilderness, he said, nor would "Joe the Hunter" benefit from closing off game management options.[26]

Marlenee's emblematic recreationist demanded a seat at the negotiating table, but wilderness advocates preferred to work with those whose interests could, in some cases, be satisfied with less sensitive forestlands. In 1990 the Flathead chapter of the MWA, working with the Libby-based Cabinet Resource Group, was able to reach an agreement with unionized sawmill workers in northwestern Montana over the disposition of roadless areas on the Kootenai

National Forest. The MWA held concurrent negotiations with millworkers and sportsmen over roadless areas in the western half of the Lolo National Forest, reaching agreements for both forests that would preserve 670,000 acres as wilderness and release 532,000 acres for logging and other uses. Max Baucus sponsored legislation to enact what was known as the Kootenai-Lolo accords, but opposition from snowmobile groups and the Western Environmental Trade Association, along with a lukewarm-to-hostile reception from some wilderness supporters, prevented its passage.

Although the agreements in the Big Hole and in northwestern Montana produced no immediate results, they fostered a degree of trust between former antagonists. This was a rare commodity during the timber wars of the 1980s, when accelerated logging of private and public forests in the northwestern states collided with newly organized activists wielding the Endangered Species Act of 1973 and the National Forest Management Act of 1976. These laws created enforceable legal requirements to protect the habitats of spotted owls, grizzly bears, lynx, bull trout, and other wildlife, leading timber industry executives to claim that environmentalists could halt federal timber sales with little more than the postage needed to file an administrative appeal. The Northern Region's timber sale program declined steadily from 1,125 million board feet in 1983 to 188 million in 1995, while employment in Montana's forest industries fell from a high of approximately 13,500 in 1978 to 9,500 in 1982, a recession year.[27] Industry ascribed job layoffs in timber-dependent communities such as Libby, Bonners Ferry and Potlatch to decreased federal timber supplies, but environmentalists blamed heavy cutting of private lands, including Champion International's rapid liquidation of its old-growth timber to pay off its bond issues.[28] Regardless of the cause, the layoffs led to steadily worsening polarization and occasional violence. "Cabins burned mysteriously in the dark," one reporter recalled of that era. "Cars were vandalized. People were attacked, literally beaten for beliefs."[29] Reaching any agreement with environmental and wilderness interests under such conditions represented a remarkable achievement.

In Idaho, interest groups pursued a formal negotiation process with ground rules established at the outset and commitments to abide by the results. In 1990 the Idaho legislature appropriated $150,000 to hire a mediation firm to work with the Idaho Wildlands Defense Coalition and antiwilderness groups in separate meetings covering northern and southern Idaho. Participants in a public meeting in Lewiston focused on the Clearwater National Forest, turning matters over to a small group of negotiators. The environmentalists selected Dennis Baird and his University of Idaho colleague Don Crawford, while Kevin Boling, a forest manager for the Potlatch firm, took the lead among several timber industry representatives. They reached agreement on numerous RARE II areas but were not able to obtain support from other interest groups. Negotiations over RARE areas in central and southern Idaho began in May 1991 between the Sierra Club, Idaho Conservation League, livestock industry, BlueRibbon Coalition, and the lumber mill in Salmon. These negotiations began hopefully but dissolved in acrimony and recrimination. Democratic representative Larry LaRocco, a former aide to Senator Frank Church, introduced a 1.3-million-acre wilderness bill in 1993, incorporating much of the agreement reached in the northern Idaho negotiations. He was unable to bring along the rest of Idaho's Republican congressional delegation, leaving the state no closer to resolution of the RARE II issue.[30]

Dennis Baird observed that negotiations require an immense commitment of time from volunteers who also have jobs and families.[31] In the case of the Gospel-Hump, each side had a strong reason for wanting to settle, and they dealt with only one area. Even then, other interest groups almost scuttled the agreement. In the 1990 negotiations, ranchers and off-road vehicle users were better organized, and there was added pressure from property-rights and antigovernment forces. Environmental interests were likewise split, with a growing segment of the wilderness fraternity opposed to any release of RARE II areas. They supported the Kostmayer bill and a subsequent, even more ambitious wilderness proposal that took in vast swaths of roadless and partially developed forestland in both states. Polarization had separated preservationists from resource users for decades; now it was about to divide wilderness interests as well.

25

Visions of the Wild Rockies
A Fractured Preservation Movement, 1990–2010

The wilderness debate in the Northern Rockies grew increasingly divisive during the 1990s, not only between traditional opponents but also among preservation groups that could not agree on strategy and goals. The Montana impasse resumed in April 1990 when Senator Max Baucus introduced a statewide bill to designate 900,000 acres of wilderness, while his colleague, Conrad Burns, attempted to lower the bar with a 620,000-acre bill. Burns termed his effort a "simple, non-contentious partial solution," which would release 2.8 million acres of Montana RARE II lands and leave 2.6 million acres unresolved. MWA president Emily Sieger said the bill meant more "abusive roadbuilding, logging, and mineral development" and cited recent congressional testimony from regional forester John Mumma that his agency was being pressured to cut more than was sustainable. She said that Burns's bill would permit "the kind of corporate looting the Forest Service was created to guard against 100 years ago."[1] In this highly polarized debate, the issues that had figured prominently in the state's wilderness politics for the past forty years—the protection of wildlife habitat and stream quality—tended to be overlooked. This reflected the enormous stakes involved in statewide legislation affecting thousands of workers, tens of thousands of recreationists, and millions of acres of potential timberland. Yet many advocates, including a new and much more radical organization, persisted in their efforts to place wildlife at the center of the debate.

Neither the Baucus nor Burns measures made it out of committee. That fall the two senators reached an agreement on a 1.2-million-acre bill that they introduced in September 1991. Action proceeded swiftly, with the Senate Energy Committee reporting the bill in November and the full Senate passing the bill the following March. Numerous areas of long-standing concern to preservation groups were slated for release under the bill, including the Sapphire and Middle Fork Judith S. 393 areas, the Crazy Mountains, Cowboys Heaven at the northern end of the Madison Range, and Trout Creek on the Kootenai National Forest, which the MWA described as an "elk factory" and excellent grizzly bear habitat. John Gatchell, the group's conservation director, believed they had no choice but to work with the two senators and their staffs to obtain what improvements they could in the bill. The group enlisted Pat Williams and other supporters in the House to add 270,000 acres to the measure, substantially increase the wilderness study acreage, and adopt the "soft release" language of the 1984 bills.

The MWA no longer held unquestioned leadership on wilderness issues in the state, however. In 1989 a former seasonal park ranger named Mike Bader decided it was time to approach the wilderness issue not from the timber industry's need for releasing RARE areas, but from the habitat needs of endangered and threatened wildlife. Not content to craft locally negotiated compromises with timber and off-road vehicle interests, he proposed a "Wild Rockies National Lands Act," which would set aside major wildland ecosystems in the contiguous Northern Rockies. Consisting of national forest, national park, and Wild and Scenic River designations, its goal was to ensure genetic interchange between these ecosystems and maintain overall biodiversity. "We've paid for all the roads and clearcuts and we can never get the money back. But we can get the land back, and it's time we did," Bader said.[2]

By emulating the nationwide lobbying techniques the Sierra Club and Wilderness Society used to pass the Alaska National Interest Lands Conservation Act, Bader's new organization, the Alliance for the Wild Rockies, hoped to overcome the entrenched resistance of the Idaho and Montana congressional delegations. It found a willing sponsor in Peter Kostmayer, who had already introduced a large Idaho wilderness bill. In September 1992, as the Burns-Baucus bill was nearing its denouement, Kostmayer introduced the Northern Rockies Ecosystem Protection Act (NREPA), a staggeringly comprehensive bill that would (among other actions) designate sixteen million acres of wilderness in Idaho, Montana, Wyoming, and parts of eastern Oregon and Washington; establish protected corridors between many of the wilderness areas; and set up a "National Wildland Restoration and Recovery System" to undo the damaging effects of past logging and road-building practices. Instead of releasing nonselected RARE II areas for development, it called for further area-by-area reviews. "Wilderness as a resource has been degraded enough," Bader wrote. "It is time we take what is politically viable and replace it with what is ecologically correct."[3]

The alliance gained considerable publicity for its campaign when singer-songwriters Carole King (who owned a ranch on the Salmon River) and John Oates appeared in Washington to lobby for the bill. More significant was its endorsement by a crew of wildlife biologists, including the Craighead brothers, the noted mountain lion researcher Maurice Hornocker, and grizzly bear researcher Charles Jonkel. In a 1991 statement in support of the bill, they noted that the Northern Rockies contained the "last large intact mammal and predatory bird fauna in the lower 48 states," but that "unique wildlife treasures" such as the grizzly bear and gray wolf were in danger of extirpation. Piecemeal wilderness designations as provided in the Burns-Baucus legislation were insufficient to protect these habitats, they maintained.[4]

Concern for the habitat of elk, native trout, and salmon had motivated wilderness activists in the Northern Rockies since the 1940s, but NREPA focused on rare and nongame species, including predators such as wolves that sportsmen often regarded as competitors for their elk. Research in the emerging field of conservation biology was emphasizing the importance of wolves and grizzly bears as "keystone" or "umbrella" species, which regulated populations of many other species and prevented overbrowsing of ranges by ungulates such as elk.[5] The biologists also proposed establishing migration corridors linking protected park lands and wilderness areas, a concern Clif Merritt had raised in the 1950s when trying to halt timber roads and hydropower reservoirs in the upper Flathead drainage. Following his dismissal from the Wilderness Society in 1977, Merritt went on to cofound the Denver-based American Wilderness Alliance, which increasingly focused on biodiversity issues. Merritt remarked to Dallas Eklund, his fishing buddy from his Flathead days, that he had been urging the MWA to expand its Alternative W to "protect more of the lower elevation roadless areas so important in their wild state as critical habitat for our world-class wildlife."[6] In truth, the MWA had been working on this goal for decades, and in 1992 it adopted biodiversity as the theme for its annual meeting. The new, more strident preservationists personified by Mike Bader were extending a principle, not inventing one. Their disagreement with the MWA was a matter of political strategy more than one of science or policy. It was nonetheless a substantial difference, which brought considerable rancor to formerly amicable strategy discussions.

Along with NREPA, 1992 saw the appearance of political tactics developed in the woods wars of Oregon and California. Groups affiliated with Earth First! and the Alliance for the Wild Rockies held rallies to denounce the Burns-Baucus legislation and support the Kostmayer proposal. Four activists locked themselves to a pillar inside Max Baucus's Missoula field office in protest of his bill.[7] Pat Williams's office was the scene of a lunchtime rally involving more than a hundred peaceful protesters, including Bill Cunningham, who told the crowd that important roadless lands such as those in northwestern Montana's Yaak Valley were missing from the bill. Williams refused to try to kill the Burns-Baucus bill, telling a *Missoulian* reporter that he wanted to "get this issue past us and allow Montana to get on with protecting what needs protecting and producing where we can produce."[8] Yet the new players in the movement were unwilling to settle for the compromises of the past. That spring, Earth First! spearheaded a lengthy road-blockading action to delay timber sales in the Mallard Creek drainage, an upland forest area located in the "Dixie Tail" between the Gospel-Hump and River of No Return Wilderness areas. A decade earlier Dennis Baird had been unable to secure its inclusion in the Central Idaho Wilderness Act, and the area, formerly known as Jersey Jack, now lay open to timber harvesting. The Idaho legislature hastily passed a law to make such protests illegal, and an injunction arising from a 1995 Sierra Club–led lawsuit was quickly dissolved. Yet the delays and the ensuing controversy eventually resulted in cancellation of further sales.[9]

Congress came close to passing the Baucus-Burns bill in the waning hours of the 102nd Congress, but an unrelated filibuster ran out the clock. The pattern continued in subsequent Congresses: initial conferences were held among each state's Senate and House delegations, followed by introduction of one or more bills containing fewer than two million acres of wilderness. Interest groups demanded changes, leading to the bills' demise near the end of each session. The preservationists' hopes rose in November 1992, when Pat Williams defeated Ron Marlenee for what was now Montana's sole seat in the House. In the following session of Congress he was able to shepherd a 1.7-million-acre bill—his largest to date—through that body. Max Baucus was not able to proceed as far with the latest version of his 1.2-million-acre Montana National Forest Management Act, nor was Conrad Burns able to advance his ominously titled Montana Jobs Security and Land Protection Act. Burns's bill provided, among other things, for most national forest land in the state to be designated as "multiple-use resource recovery lands," in which the Forest Service would have to meet output targets for timber, minerals, and forage. Its inclusion of 778,000 acres of wilderness areas and additional special management areas was not calculated to draw support from the wilderness groups. Larry LaRocco introduced a 1.26-million-acre bill for his congressional district, covering lands in northern and western Idaho, but ran into opposition from Senator Larry Craig, who continued to favor a statewide approach.[10]

With Peter Kostmayer losing his bid for reelection, it fell to New York representative Carolyn Maloney (along with sixty-three cosponsors) to reintroduce NREPA—at 16.3 million acres still the far outlier in the field.[11] It called for an Interior Department study of a proposed Flathead National Park and Preserve in the Whitefish Range and the closure of various backcountry roads, including those in the Magruder Corridor and the South Fork of the Flathead River. This was in line with the wilderness restoration or "rewilding" concept being advocated by some conservation biologists and the former Earth First! leader Dave Foreman. The bill received a hearing in Washington in May 1994 at which John Craighead reviewed the long history of legislation to protect America's wild places. The veteran biologist observed that laws such as the Wilderness Act and the Wild and Scenic River Act "emerged spontaneously and piecemeal at the grassroots level of our society" and helped secure portions of our natural resource heritage, although "most, if not all, were initially opposed by the governing status quo." These public land laws "might have led to a comprehensive holistic policy of sustainable resource preservation and management," he said, but had failed in doing so partly because of divisions between the responsible federal agencies, which had fractured the management of public lands despite their wide-ranging biota. Holistic resource management, Craighead said, could take the form of an "ongoing experiment that can result in sustainable management of extractive resources while preserving the biodiversity of our wildlands ecosystems."[12]

MWA leaders expressed support for NREPA in concept but called for changes to correct what they termed "serious inaccuracies" and the inclusion of certain heavily impacted areas, such as a developed ski run, open roads, and recent logging areas. Biological corridors encompassed significant private land and were politically unworkable, the group believed.[13] The two organizations' differences were symptomatic of a growing split in the wilderness preservation movement. From its inception the MWA chose to work closely with Montana's political leaders, whether friendly and relatively united (as in the halcyon Mansfield-Metcalf years) or strongly divided, as they had been since 1978. This approach yielded spectacular results when it could count on strong champions in the Senate, but with conservative administrations in power and Congress split along partisan lines, only modest wilderness proposals stood any chance of passage. The wilderness movement faced a fundamental choice: either moderate its demands to fit the new political reality, or press forward with proposals for full biotic preservation and hope that enough Americans would join them. Bader's Alliance for the Wild Rockies was willing to take that risk, but the MWA, with far more experience in legislative campaigns, chose to work with the Montana delegation and gain what protections it could.

With Congress proving to be a formidable barrier, wilderness advocates sought to protect endangered wildlands through administrative channels, an avenue they had downplayed ever since the Wilderness Act was passed. In 1997 activists working to protect the Rocky Mountain Front from oil and gas leasing scored a notable success when Lewis and Clark National Forest supervisor Gloria Flora withdrew an entire ranger district from further mineral leasing. Existing leases were not affected, but the decision won time for advocates of what MWA executive director Bob Decker called "a place where every superlative is justified."[14] A far more sweeping administrative action came in 2001 when President Clinton announced that the Department of Agriculture would prohibit road construction in any national forest roadless area of one thousand acres or more. Environmentalists campaigned for the so-called roadless area rule partly as a way to deal with the high maintenance costs and environmental impacts of a four-decade legacy of timber roads in the backcountry. Subsequent efforts under the two Bush administrations to limit or dismantle the rule met with some success, notably in Idaho, but it stands as the largest advancement for wilderness protection since the spate of congressional bills in 1984. Some observers argue that the rule usurps Congress's authority, but with that body virtually deadlocked on public lands issues, many environmental groups appear quite satisfied with their end run around antiwilderness legislators from the western states.[15]

Other preservation groups in the Northern Rockies have drawn on collaborative efforts begun in the 1980s. In 2009 Senator Jon Tester introduced the Montana Forest Jobs and Recreation Act, the latest in a series of complex, multipurpose bills lacking the word "wilderness" in their title. In its latest version it would establish eighteen new national forest wilderness areas or wilderness area additions, five Bureau of Land Management areas, and seven recreation-area classifications; release other roadless areas on the Beaverhead-Deerlodge and Kootenai National Forests; and provide for forest restoration work and mandate forest "treatments" for specified acreages on both national forests. Significantly, it would establish wilderness areas in parts of the long-contested East and West Pioneers, West Big Hole, and Sapphire roadless areas; establish an adjoining West Big Hole national recreation area; and release other lands in these areas, including the bulk of the West Pioneer S. 393 study area.[16]

This attempt to break the wilderness deadlock encountered vocal opposition from those who felt they were excluded from the drafting of the bill and who objected to the mandated timber harvest levels. Bill Worf, a 33-year Forest Service veteran, said that Tester's bill would permit a return to the overcutting he had witnessed in the national forests in the 1960s. Stewart Brandborg, who had retired to the Bitterroot Valley but remained active in public lands issues, said it would override a century's worth of federal resource protection laws and would open a "Pandora's box of special loopholes and subsidies for a handful of corporations." Matthew Koehler of the WildWest Institute stated that the bill would set a poor precedent for all future wilderness legislation. He and Brandborg both preferred the status quo of the roadless area rule.[17]

There remains strong support for Tester's bill, which he reintroduced in 2011 and 2013, among those who advocate a more collaborative process to resolve long-standing public land disputes. Robyn King of the Yaak Valley Forest Council said that the conflict over logging and wilderness in northwestern Montana was "tearing our communities apart . . . everyone lost, and no one gained."[18] Tester's bill and similar legislation appears motivated as much by a desire to heal some of these wounds as to enact new wilderness designations. It represents a new era in public lands legislation and stands a far better chance of passage than NREPA-style bills. But in doing so, it has contributed to the severe rift within the conservation community—one that shows little sign of abatement.

In 2009 Idaho senator Mike Crapo succeeded in gaining the state's first wilderness designation since 1980 with his bill to set aside 517,000 acres in the BLM-managed Owyhee River canyon lands of southeastern Idaho. The bill, which also released 200,000 acres of roadless lands, was a product of a collaborative process involving conservationists, ranchers, vehicle users, and the Shoshone-Paiute Tribes. Building on this effort, Crapo and his House colleague Mike Simpson returned to a long-simmering controversy over the Boulder–White Cloud Peaks east of Stanley—the final unprotected element of the great Salmon River Wilderness. Their measure called for 319,000 acres of wilderness and the release of 132,000 acres, but it met with significant opposition from off-road vehicle and mountain bike users, indicating that so-called place-based land use initiatives must thread a narrow course through an array of incompatible land uses.

In 2008 Crapo convened the Clearwater Basin Collaborative, an advisory group consisting of twenty-one organizations including off-road vehicle users, the Rocky Mountain Elk Foundation, the Wilderness Society, and the Nez Perce Tribe. First suggested by Dale Harris of the Great Burn Study Group and Alex Irby, an Idaho Fish and Game commissioner from Orofino, the project receives funding from the Department of Agriculture and is pursuing various forest restoration and wildfire reduction initiatives. John McCarthy, a longtime activist with the Idaho Conservation League who now works with the Wilderness Society, believes there is a "growing recognition" of the need to work with other interest groups to deal with increasingly complex land use issues. "It's bringing people together in a very interesting way," he stated in a recent interview. "Folks who maybe will fight over some things and some places—like ATV guys and wilderness guys—are looking at how do we work on projects that improve conditions overall." But Gary Macfarlane of the advocacy group Friends of the Clearwater believes that collaborative groups unfairly bypass normal review procedures established under laws such as the National Environmental Policy Act. "The integrity of NEPA is compromised when the agency reaches a deal or understanding with the collaborative forest planning group before the NEPA process even begins," he states.[19]

It remains unclear whether collaborative groups can reach agreement on contentious land allocation issues without a strong legal impetus such as in the Gospel-Hump negotiations. Many citizens in communities close to national forests are growing weary of the endless disputations over public lands, but some wilderness advocates are unwilling to relinquish the congressional procedures that netted a sizable wilderness system in the first place, and that guaranteed citizens everywhere at least a nominal say in the process. Few wilderness bills would have passed Congress without the support of "outsiders" who consider the national forests their domain as surely as the residents of rural Idaho and Montana.

Wilderness preservation in the United States has always depended on the close alliance of concerned individuals at the grass roots and the politically sophisticated lobbying apparatus of the nation's major conservation groups. Neither could function without the other, nor has this formula changed in any substantive way since the days when Olaus Murie and Stewart Brandborg traveled the western states, speaking to any group that would listen. Today's grass-roots advocates make better use of scientific and economic research, opinion polls, and mass media than ever before, but they remain the spiritual successors to Ken and Florence Baldwin, Mort Brigham, Doris Milner, Jerry Jayne, Cecil Garland, and Joan Montagne. They may no longer type letters at their kitchen table, but they still engage in the person-to-person outreach that has been the hallmark of the American wilderness movement. Consider the Friends of Scotchman Peaks Wilderness, whose members sponsor hikes, conduct research on native wildlife, set up information booths at county fairs, organize comments on forest plans, and one day may gain permanent protection for the 88,000-acre wilderness that Mike and Linda Comola's little band of Clark Fork Valley residents identified in 1976.

There is inspiration, too, in the continuing work of the Great Burn Study Group, still led by a seemingly tireless Dale Harris, who claims to have lost only eighty acres from the proposed wilderness in four decades. Harris and his cohorts have met with motorcycle and ATV riders to seek agreement on trail use, yet they also pay for aircraft overflights to monitor wintertime snow machine trespass into their study area. There is the aforementioned Yaak Valley Forest Council, which seeks to protect the few remaining roadless lands on the Kootenai National Forest through advocacy and dialogue, as well as taking part in on-the-ground forest and stream restoration work in this heavily impacted region. In Idaho, the Friends of the Clearwater evolved out of the confrontations of Cove-Mallard to take on the longer-term work of monitoring and commenting on forest plans, filing appeals, and instigating the occasional lawsuit. The decades-long effort to protect more of the Swan Crest east of Kalispell occupies the members of the Swan View Coalition, which eschews the collaborative approach in favor of traditional administrative and legal channels.

There are many others, too, ranging from purely collaborative efforts to more aggressive citizen committees and no-holds-barred legal institutes. Their work is more sophisticated, and the issues more complex than those that grassroots groups faced a half century ago, but together they have amassed an amazing record of citizen action that has transformed resource politics in the Northern Rockies. Empowering citizens to influence federal land policy is as much a legacy of the postwar wilderness movement as the actual designations it achieved. The Forest Service may have originated the first wildland protection measures in this region, but it has largely ceded the field to citizens, who have decisively repudiated the Progressive-era paradigm of management by government experts.

The question now before the citizens of Idaho, Montana, and the rest of the country is whether wilderness and its native wildlife will continue to play a strong role in their lives or be dismissed as the private domain of a handful of elite recreationists. Just as in the 1940s, 1950s, and 1960s, preservation advocates must once again present a compelling story about the meaning of wilderness lands to human lives. They would do well to remember that the sportsmen and outfitters who built the preservation movement in the Northern Rockies were trying to accomplish something more significant than just fencing off forests and mountains as recreational preserves. Whether they were hunters and anglers, or simply connoisseurs of the wild, those activists understood wilderness to be a living and dynamic landscape. They also knew that humans needed such places for sanity, spiritual growth, and wonder. The science of biodiversity conservation, though it has enriched our understanding of the natural world and led to exciting new initiatives, cannot by itself capture this essential and too-easily-severed connection between humans, wild creatures, and the landscapes in which they might live and move freely. People need to derive both pleasure *and* meaning from the lands around them, and the challenge for today's preservationists, as in Leopold's and Murie's day, is to show that the most lasting enjoyment and the most significant meanings are obtained using primitive and elemental tools—on foot and on horseback, alert to one's surroundings and in close touch with wild creatures.

The meaning of wildlife and wild country to modern humans was a question that obsessed Olaus Murie, and one to which we must return again and again. As he asked in 1958 at the dawn of the space age, "Have we not had the experience, when we have been in the midst of a beautiful wilderness, of feeling a deep satisfaction, a fundamental reverence for a mountain, a forest, or a river scene?" He spoke of Americans seeking a higher view of their destiny, a quest that he hoped would take us not out of Earth's orbit in a spaceship, but closer to our origins. "Above all things in this world," he said, "man needs inspiration."[20] Such inspiration is to be found in the landscapes that these men and women worked to protect—and it can also be found in their immense dedication to this unending task. These visionaries believed in the reality of the wild, and in the role that such places must continue to play in American life.

Afterword
The Scapegoat Wilderness, 1988–2012

In late June 1988, while the Montana and Idaho congressional delegations were debating the latest round of post–RARE II wilderness bills, outfitter Smoke Elser and his friend Bill Cunningham—two of Montana's most active wilderness proponents—were enjoying an afternoon in camp in the western part of the Scapegoat Wilderness. A lightning strike from a passing thunderstorm ignited an old log a short distance from their camp, so the two men cleared brush from around it to safeguard their half-dozen guests. There was no cause for alarm; winds were light and the Forest Service generally did not respond to such strikes deep within a designated wilderness. The fire wandered for several weeks within a limited area, scorching some trees while bypassing others. Little or no rain fell that summer, however, and by late August the Canyon Creek fire had covered some thirty-four thousand acres. A Forest Service crew was working to control its spread southward out of the wilderness, but most of the agency's resources were occupied with the gigantic blazes in and around Yellowstone National Park. Then, in early September, jet stream winds drove the fire in a single raging charge across the Continental Divide and down to the prairies east of the mountains. By the time rain and snow arrived on September 11, the fire had covered 247,000 acres and charred most of the wilderness.

The Forest Service suspended and later revised its wilderness fire policy to better account for dry fuel conditions and weather patterns, and today about half of the naturally caused wildfires in the Bob Marshall region are still allowed to burn. Grasses, forbs, and shrubs cover much of the burned area of the Scapegoat Wilderness and provide renewed forage for big game. Outfitters who witnessed the loss of their hunting grounds now report lush conditions and improved sight lines. The fire, however, was a harbinger of drastic changes. Beginning in 2000 the Northern Rockies experienced repeated severe fire seasons affecting millions of acres of both wilderness and nonwilderness lands. The fires sparked intense debate over the ecological role and social acceptability of wildfire.

Probably none of the participants in the wilderness battles of the 1950s, 1960s, and 1970s anticipated the degree to which large wildfires would return to the region's forests. Preservation advocates argued for retaining areas where ecological processes could run their course unfettered by humans, often without acknowledging the primary role of wildfire in shaping the Northern Region's forests. Insects, too, are leaving their unmistakable imprint on these forests, causing many citizens to wonder whether we can afford to give such forces free rein. Science points to the regenerative effects of these processes and the resulting diversity of forest landscapes they create, but the American wilderness has always existed in a social context, and if the populace at large cannot see the virtue in leaving large landscapes alone, intervention is sure to follow.

The advocates of an earlier generation bequeathed a tremendous legacy of designated wilderness areas to the citizens of Idaho and Montana. They accomplished this by focusing public attention on particular places such as the upper Selway, Clearwater, Flathead, and Blackfoot Rivers, which otherwise would have been homogenized into managed forest or inundated under reservoirs. They minimized the cost of such land withdrawals to regional timber harvests and eventually the bills came due, for reasons only partly of their making. Opponents of wilderness, ever mindful of those costs, have hardened their stance. In an environment of growing resource scarcity, new wilderness legislation will be achieved only through painful trade-offs of roadless land.

Proponents of sweeping ecological restoration measures such as NREPA call for taking a global perspective, examining whole bioregions in order to select lands needed for the security and free movement of wildlife. An additional perspective—one that accounts for human needs—might also be beneficial. A truly visionary approach to land preservation would show how human societies might coexist with large wilderness areas. Could a wood products economy based on demonstrably sustainable timbering practices make a comeback in the Northern Rockies, sensitively utilizing nonwilderness lands in perpetuity? Is there room for cattle ranching and elk hunting in areas frequented by the grizzly bear and wolf? Can recreation areas be partitioned so that places for motorized adventure and for silent contemplation will both exist in abundance? These questions require us to address the uses of both public and private lands, not just the national forest system, and they require that every special interest own up to its ultimate goals.

To put it in the simplest terms, how do we want the mountains of Idaho and Montana to appear a century from now? Teddy Roe, Lee Metcalf's legislative aide, explained this in stark terms to an angry constituent in 1977. Roe predicted that unless we acted soon, we would "find the timber gone, the mills closed, small trout streams barren and silt-laden, tourists repelled by visually disturbing clearcuts, and erosion and flooding heightened by damage to the watershed." His warning can be rephrased in hopeful terms as well. A century hence, the Northern Rockies could be a place where generations of loggers still work in the woods, passing along their knowledge of good practices; where families can drive to and camp by peaceful lakes and clear, undammed streams; where agricultural lands fill verdant valleys. And where, within sight of those farms and towns and campgrounds and logging shows, one can see the edge of wilderness, extending for miles back into the mountains.

It is not easy to imagine how we might arrive at such a future, but without a vision of a landscape in harmony with its human population, we are committed to overuse, incessant conflict, and the decay of our dreams. To hope for such a future may seem absurd in a world that is drilling every known deposit for its hydrocarbons and challenging the very atmosphere with its exhausts. But it is possible to find hope. Whatever humans have done to these mountains, we, like Olaus and Mardy Murie and thousands of others, still seek inspiration in them. One need only set out on the trail to a place such as Heart Lake in the burned-over Scapegoat Wilderness. Walking alone and quietly, one hears woodpeckers at work on the snags left from a 2003 wildfire. Fireweed blooms among the dense, knee-high lodgepole pines. The voices of wolves carry from a nearby hillside. The land is charged with mystery as it renews itself before our eyes. We reach Heart Lake and sit by its silent shore. Beyond Red Mountain, beyond even Scapegoat's rampart, lies unseen country. It is a gift of the rarest kind.

Acknowledgments

I am indebted to the staffs of numerous university and public archives for access to manuscript and photograph collections. Of these, special thanks to Anna Barker, Dennis Baird, Claudia Jensen, Donna McCrea, and the entire crew at the Montana Historical Society Research Center. My thanks to Forest Service archivists and historians Cindy Schacher, Carlie Magill, Shandy Lemperlé, Richa Wilson, and Mary Williams for assistance in locating materials and photographs.

It was my pleasure to interview or correspond with many individuals who were involved in the events described herein. My thanks go to Dennis Baird, Stewart Brandborg, Dale Burk, Bill Cunningham, Tom Davis, Arnold Elser, Cecil Garland, John Gatchell, Dale Harris, Jerry Jayne, Ray Karr, Matthew Koehler, Al Luebeck, Gary Macfarlane, Joan Montagne, Jim Murry, Duncan Patten, Fred Quivik, and Teddy Roe. Pen Edwards provided insights into the activities of his father, "Hobnail" Tom Edwards, as well as access to his family's papers. Any errors of fact or interpretation are, of course, my own.

My research was assisted greatly by the Montana Historical Society's James H. Bradley Fellowship. John Alley of the University of Utah Press was instrumental in keeping both author and project on track and in focus, while Laurel Anderton provided a skilled copyedit. Finally, a word of thanks to my Montana and Idaho hosts and hostesses, who give me much reason to return, and to Bessann, for the same.

Notes

Abbreviations for manuscript collections are listed in the Bibliography.
Series, box, and folder number (where applicable) are separated by slashes
(e.g. TWS 4/40/12).

Introduction

1. While Fox notes that amateur conservationists in the early twentieth century were often men of independent means, the movement broadened considerably in the second half of the century (*American Conservation Movement*, 341–45). Although most of the local activists portrayed in these pages are male, few were independently wealthy and several lived close to the economic margins.
2. The Forest Service's RARE program and its RARE II successor are discussed in chapters 15 and 19.
3. Sutter, *Driven Wild*, 14. Sutter notes that "road building continued to threaten wilderness after World War II, and roadlessness remained the defining characteristic of wilderness" (255–56). While this is true, I argue that the need to maintain both huntable and watchable populations of wildlife took on increasing importance in the Northern Rockies.
4. Groups such as the MWA played "pivotal roles in wilderness politics," according to Turner (*Promise of Wilderness*, 8).
5. Kevin Marsh's *Drawing Lines in the Forest* discusses important wilderness battles in Oregon and Washington from 1950 to 1984, which is roughly the time period covered in this book. Howard Zahniser also took a personal interest in many of these

battles. Harvey, *Wilderness Forever*, 160–65.

6. See especially Neil, *To the White Clouds*; Norton, *Snake Wilderness*; and Robert D. Baker et al., *National Forests of the Northern Region.*

7. William Baker, "Indians and Fire in the Rocky Mountains."

8. Marsh, *"This Is Just the First Round,"* 229.

Prologue. The Headwaters of the Gallatin River, September 1958

1. Murie served as a half-time employee of the Wilderness Society with the additional title of director, while his colleague Howard Zahniser, the society's executive secretary, handled political affairs in the nation's capital. Theirs was an effective collaboration that established the Wilderness Society's dual role of organizing citizens in the field and lobbying on Capitol Hill.

2. The conversations at the 1958 meeting at the Nine Quarter Circle Ranch are recorded in a typewritten set of minutes (OMP-DPL 3/2). No author is listed. Howard Kelsey also elaborated on the meeting in a letter to Howard Zahniser, October 22, 1956, TWS 4/43/5.

3. Michael Childers's *Colorado Powder Keg* provides a useful history of the development of Forest Service recreation policy in the early twentieth century. He notes that while recreational visits to the national forests increased exponentially in the 1920s, "many in the agency deemed recreation a minor use" when compared to grazing and timber (11). This attitude persisted into the 1950s.

4. Marsh observes that in contrast to the ideal of preserving areas of completely unsullied nature, wilderness designation in actual practice "was mainly a form of land use in which—in contrast to most areas in the national forests—road building, logging, and other forms of industrial development were not allowed." *Drawing Lines in the Forest*, 6.

5. See Newfont, *Blue Ridge Commons* for analysis of the commons idea as applied to forest management policy.

6. These included the Gila Primitive Area in New Mexico (created out of the former Gila Wilderness Reserve), the Three Sisters Primitive Area in Oregon, and the Glacier Peak Limited Area in Washington. All were formed under Forest Service regulations dating to the 1920s (see chapter 2).

7. For an overview of the emergence of conservation biology in the United States, see Meine, "Conservation Biology—Past and Present." Clifton Merritt, whose work figures strongly in these pages, spent much of his later career trying to identify and protect corridors for migrating wildlife in the West through the group American Wildlands. This was a direct outgrowth of his early work in Montana, only part of which is chronicled here.

Chapter 1. The Blueprint for Our Folly

1. The standard work on Progressive-era conservation is Samuel P. Hays's *Conservation and the Gospel of Efficiency*. For other interpretations, see Adam Rome, "Conservation, Preservation, and Environmental Activism: A Survey of the Historical Literature," National Park Service History series, http://www.nps.gov/history/history/hisnps/NPSThinking/nps-oah.htm.

2. U.S. Army Corps of Engineers, *Columbia River and Tributaries*, 159, table 4-13.

3. Mansfield recalled in 1999 that he personally appealed to President Roosevelt to halt the Flathead Lake plan. He evidently saw little drawback to flooding the South Fork of the Flathead, a valley of no great importance, according to his biographer. Oberdorfer, *Senator Mansfield*, 59–60.

4. For comparison with rural residents opposing forest industrialization in a different part of the country, see Newfont, *Blue Ridge Commons*, 19.

5. National Park Service statement on Glacier View Dam, April 10, 1947, OMP-DPL 2/13.

6. Ibid., May 4, 1948.

7. The Bureau of Reclamation announced plans to build two dams in Dinosaur National Monument in 1943, when it filed a *Federal Register* notice of power withdrawals at Echo Park and Split Mountain, but open battle with conservationists did not begin until 1950, when Interior Secretary Oscar Chapman came out in support of the dams (Cosco, *Echo Park*, 17; Harvey, "Battle for Dinosaur"). Testimony in opposition to Glacier View is cited in Buchholz, *Man in Glacier*, chap. 6; and Murie, "Intangible Resources of Wild Country," 499.

8. Murie recounted meeting Winton Weydemeyer in a speech to the Montana Wildlife Federation in Kalispell, January 11, 1958, OMP-MC, drawer FX-4, fd. 1.

9. Weydemeyer testimony, May 25, 1948, OMP-DPL, 2/14.

10. Drury to "Conservationists" (mimeo), ibid., April 27, 1949.

11. Mansfield to Krug, ibid., February 25, 1949.

12. Secretary of the Interior (Krug) to Mansfield, ibid., April 6, 1949.

13. "Mansfield in Favor of Glacier View Dam," *Kalispell (MT) Daily Inter Lake*, September 25, 1955.

14. Metcalf to Gus Norwood, February 17, 1954, LMP 253/2. Norwood was head of the Northwest Public Power Association, a lobbying group for consumer electric cooperatives and public utility districts.

15. Zahniser to editor, *Daily Inter Lake*, November 28, 1956.

16. Metcalf to Ruder, October 11, 1955, LMP 121/9.

17. "Objects to H. H. News Column," *Columbia Falls (MT) Hungry Horse News*, March 20, 1959.

18. Eklund to editor, *Daily Inter Lake*, October 24, 1955; Eklund to Jack Rose, Montana Wildlife Federation, October 6, 1955, CMP 3/12.

Chapter 2. Selway Wilderness

1. Parsell, *Major Fenn's Country*, 20–21. The Forest Service's backcountry lookouts and guard stations communicated over single-strand, nine-gauge telephone wire. The Selway National Forest was dissolved in 1934 and parceled out to the Lolo, Clearwater, and Nez Perce National Forests.

2. Marshall's note on his Lolo Pass jaunt is cited in Lynn Baird and Dennis Baird, *In Nez Perce Country*, 223. The Lolo Pass truck trail reached the Powell Ranger Station in 1928, where it turned northward to follow the route of the old Lolo Trail. See also Bud Moore, *The Lochsa Story*, 175–76. Marshall's years at Missoula are described in Glover, *A Wilderness Original*, 67–97, and in Sutter, *Driven Wild*, 206–7.

3. Marshall, "Impressions from the Wilderness."

4. Construction on the Lolo Motorway began in the summer of 1930 and was completed in the fall of 1934. It was opened to public travel the following summer. The route generally followed ridges to the north of the Lochsa. Steve F. Russell, "Lolo Motorway 1934," http://www.public.iastate.edu/~sfr/trails/motorway.html.

5. Koch, "Passing of the Lolo Trail." According to Lynn Baird and Dennis Baird, the noted District 1 photographer K. D. Swan joined Koch in his opposition to the truck trail projects (*In Nez Perce Country*, 250).

6. Leopold, "Last Stand of the Wilderness."

7. Gilligan, "Development of Policy and Administration," vol. 1, 85.

8. Ibid., 85–86.

9. Gilligan also discussed the Kneipp inventory in an important report he prepared for the Outdoor Recreation Resources Review Commission in 1962 (Wildland Research Center, *Wilderness and Recreation*, 18–19). The report was widely cited by those working to pass the Wilderness Act.

10. Greeley to district foresters, December 30, 1926, quoted in Gilligan, "Development of Policy and Administration," vol. 1, 102, 104.

11. Marshall compiled his 1927 inventory on a handwritten card, according to wilderness activist and author Dave Foreman, who discovered it among Marshall's personal papers at the University of California's Bancroft Library. It is reprinted in Foreman and Wolke, *Big Outside*, appendix 5.

12. Leon F. Kneipp, "Land Planning and Acquisition, U.S. Forest Service," oral history interview by Amelia R. Fry, Edith Mezirow, and Fern Ingersoll, 1964–1965, Bancroft Library, University of California–Berkeley, Regional Oral History Office, 115.

13. Gilligan, "Development of Policy and Administration," vol. 1, 116, fig. 6.

14. Morrell to Reed, March 22, 1926, NAS, Northern Region History files, reprinted in AnneMarie Moore and Baird, *Wild Places Preserved*, 42–43.

15. Morrell to Reed, March 24, 1926, NAS, Northern Region History files, reprinted in AnneMarie Moore and Baird, *Wild Places Preserved*, 44–46.

16. Gilligan, "Development of Policy and Administration," vol. 2, 1. The word "inspiration" was dropped in 1930. Regulation L-20 also set up natural areas and experimental forests, which were reserved primarily for research.

17. Stuart to district foresters, March 11, 1929, reprinted in AnneMarie Moore and Baird, *Wild Places Preserved*, 50–51.

18. The Beartooth and Cabinet park proposals are described in Dilsaver and Wyckoff, "Failed National Parks in the Last Best Place." See also Rothman, "Shaping the Nature of a Controversy." In the case of the Selway-Bitterroot there was no serious park proposal, and there was genuine interest in its preservation among a handful of well-placed individuals within the agency, notably Elers Koch and Bitterroot National Forest supervisor G. M. Brandborg.

19. See Dennis Baird and Lynn Baird, "Campfire Vision," 50–58. Stuart's letter to Rutledge, dated February 2, 1931, is reprinted in U.S. Senate, Committee on Energy and Natural Resources, *River of No Return Wilderness Proposals*, pt. 1, 23–24.

20. Marshall to Silcox, September 6, 1935, reprinted in AnneMarie Moore and Baird, *Wild Places Preserved*, 94–95.

21. Marshall to Kelley, April 5, 1935, reprinted in AnneMarie Moore and Baird, *Wild Places Preserved*, 88–91; Marshall, "Three Great Western Wildernesses," 10.

22. Kelley to chief forester, August 1, 1935, quoted in Cunningham, "Magruder Corridor Controversy," 25–27.

23. The order establishing the Selway-Bitterroot Primitive Area is reprinted in AnneMarie Moore and Baird, *Wild Places Preserved*, 107–8. The land south of the Magruder Road was retained as the Salmon River Breaks Primitive Area when the secretary of agriculture established the Selway-Bitterroot Wilderness in 1963.

24. Evan Kelley, "Recreation on the National Forests," speech given at Recreational Conference of the Idaho State Planning Board, Hailey, ID, August 30, 1936. U. S. Forest Service, Northern Regional historical files, series 1680-1, fd. "Evan W. Kelley—Speeches and Writings."

25. I discuss the Lost Horse Canyon road project in *The Bitterroot and Mr. Brandborg*, 46–48.

26. Marshall and Dobbins, "Largest Roadless Areas in United States," reprinted in Foreman and Wolke, *Big Outside*, appendix C.

27. Merriam, "Irony of the Bob Marshall Wilderness," 80–87.

28. Wolff's remarks are in an undated memo to a regional office staffer and are quoted in Roholt, "Montana Wilderness Study Bill," 59.

29. The spelling was changed to "Anaconda-Pintler" in the 1970s.

30. Koch, in "The Passing of the Lolo Trail," argued that "the whole United States Army, if it were on the ground, could do nothing but keep out of the way" of such wildfires. His superiors disagreed, and the policy of total fire control remained in place in the Selway until the 1970s. See especially Earl Loveridge's retort, "Is Back Country Fire Protection a 'Practical Impossibility'?" Selway-Bitterroot Wilderness History Project, http://sbw.lib.uidaho.edu/Pages/33.pdf.

31. News release, August 26, 1937, cited in Slusher, "Notes from Study of Files," in AnneMarie Moore and Baird, *Wild Places Preserved*, 185. Ed Slusher, the chief of the Northern Region's wilderness management branch in the 1960s, compiled and summarized much of the correspondence between the regional office and the individual forest supervisors in charge of the Selway. Dennis Baird believes the originals of this correspondence were lost.

32. Slusher, "Notes from Study of Files," in AnneMarie Moore and Baird, *Wild Places Preserved*, 185–86.

33. Kelley to chief, Forest Service, June 27, 1940, cited in Slusher, ibid.

34. The U regulations were established on September 19, 1939, under 36 CFR 251. The "U" refers to "undeveloped" lands; U-4 provided for research and natural areas.

35. In his book *National Parks: The American Experience*, Alfred Runte developed the thesis that Congress would consider designating only economically worthless lands as national parks. The same philosophy crops up in early discussions of national forest wildlands. In 1946, for example, Meyer Wolff (a wilderness supporter on the Region 1 recreation staff) appeared to favor excluding lands with a "high present or future commodity value" from a reclassified Selway-Bitterroot wilderness area. M. H. Wolff, "Notes on the Reconsideration of the Selway-Bitterroot Primitive Area," memo to file, June 18, 1946, cited in Cunningham, "Magruder Corridor Controversy," 38.

Chapter 3. The "Bob" Besieged

1. Wolff, "Bob Marshall Wilderness Area."

2. Harold E. Aldrich, "Review—Sun River Basin," LMP 263/5; Cooney to editor, *Living Wilderness*, February 13, 1947, TWS 4/40/23.

3. Cooney to Murie, October 31, 1947, TWS 4/40/43; Zahniser to Murie, November 14, 1947, and Murie to Cooney, December 19, 1947, OMP-DPL 1/18. The order establishing the Bob Marshall, which was signed by Agriculture Secretary Henry Wallace on August 16, 1940, said that "the boundary of the wilderness area will be automatically adjusted to exclude such portion of this withdrawal as becomes unsuited to the wilderness classification by reason of improvement or uses by the

Reclamation Service." Lucile V. Batts, acting chief, Division of Recreation and Lands, to Zahniser, July 28, 1947, TWS 4/40/23.

4. Zahniser to Reid, July 17, 1947, reply July 24, 1947, TWS 4/40/23.

5. Cottam to Zahniser, August 11, 1947; Zahniser to White, July 17, 1947, TWS 4/40/23.

6. News item, *Living Wilderness* 13 (Summer 1948): 22.

7. DeVoto mentioned the Glacier View project in a July 22, 1950, article in the *Saturday Evening Post* entitled "Shall We Let Them Ruin Our National Parks?" He made several fact-finding visits to Montana around this time for his articles on the so-called stockmen's bills; see, for example, "Sacred Cows and Public Lands," *Harper's Magazine*, July 1948, reprinted in DeVoto, *Easy Chair*, 257–81.

8. Cooney to Murie, October 31, 1947; Murie to Cooney, November 6, 1947, TWS 4/40/23.

9. Keller, *Making of a Masterpiece*, 32–35.

10. U.S. Fish and Wildlife Service, *Teton Slope Unit*, 19–24.

11. Ibid., 21–24. The infamous "Gardiner firing line" of 1919, in which massed hunters waited at the northern boundary of Yellowstone National Park for elk to leave their sanctuary following a heavy snowfall, left Montana's wildlife managers with an evil taste in their mouths for decades. They frequently raised this specter as an example of what could happen when elk herds were denied their customary wilderness travel routes. See Zirngibl, "Elk in the Greater Yellowstone Ecosystem," 55–56.

12. "Annual Spring Ride, Sun River Game Conservation Committee," June 9, 1951, OMP-DPL 1/18. The Allan ranch, a 40-acre private inholding at the edge of today's Bob Marshall Wilderness, is now run by the Klick family as the K Bar L Guest Ranch.

13. Howard Zahniser notes, TWS 4/40/23. Hanson wanted his opposition to the dam kept quiet, since he was cooperating with conservationists in an attempt to forestall congressional legislation that would have given cattlemen special rights to graze on national forest lands.

14. Cooney to Murie, October 21, 1952; Joel D. Wolfson, acting secretary, to Penfold, August 29, 1952, OMP-DPL 1/18.

15. "Rain Disrupts Highway, Railroad Travel," *Great Falls (MT) Tribune*, June 4, 1953. Vernon was quoted in the *Helena (MT) Independent Record*, June 25, 1953.

16. Cooney to Callison, June 26, 1953, OMP-DPL 1/18; C. Allan Friedrich, "Factors Contributing to the 1953 Floods in the Vicinity of Great Falls, Montana," LMP 127/7.

17. Cavallo, *Fiction of the Past*, 64. Cavallo examines the cult of expertise in reference to the intelligentsia of the 1950s, which enjoyed profound respect among middle-class Americans.

18. Zahniser to McKay, July 20, 1953, OMP-DPL 1/18. Zahniser's use of runoff data to dispute the Bureau of Reclamation's analysis of the 1953 Sun River flooding anticipated David Brower's challenge to the bureau's evaporation predictions for the Echo Park Dam, which the Sierra Club leader presented at a hearing in January 1954. Cosco, *Echo Park*, 75.

19. Peters, "Forever Wild," 59.

Chapter 4. The Battle of Bunker Creek

1. U.S. Forest Service, Northern Region, "Trends in Volume and Value of Timber Harvests," unnumbered table in "Regional Fact Sheet," 1957, NAS 95-60A70, box 3. Depression-era figures for volume cut (not sold) are from Calkin, *Historic Resource Production*, table 5.

2. Holsten, et al., *Spruce Beetle*; Bolle, "Bitterroot Revisited," 164; University of Montana School of Forestry, "Study of Policies, Guidelines, and Enforcement Procedures," 62.

3. Flathead National Forest, "Timber Harvesting," *Trails of the Past: Historical Overview of the Flathead National Forest, Montana, 1800–1960*, http://www.foresthistory.org/ASPNET/Publications/region/1/flathead/chap10.htm.

4. P. D. Hanson, memo to supervisors of west-side forests, July 14, 1953, NAS 95-63A209, box 7. The Northern Region's beetle control policy was explained in an internal memo dated April 15, 1954, TWS 4/40/53.

5. Edward P. Cliff, "Timber Access Road Problems on the National Forests," speech to Pacific Logging Congress, November 4, 1953, Edward Cliff papers, Merrill-Cazier Library, Utah State University, Logan, UT.

6. "Timber Volumes Cut and Sold—Flathead National Forest," table in University of Montana School of Forestry, "Study of Policies, Guidelines, and Enforcement Procedures," 52. Timber sale volume on national forests affected by the bark beetle often exceeded the allowable cut, since salvage sales did not count toward the "programmed" harvest.

7. Rollie Saylor, interview by Chris Roholt, Spotted Bear Ranger Station, May 1971, cited in Roholt, "Montana Wilderness Study Bill," 76.

8. Neitzling to regional forester, February 11, 1954; Dallas Eklund, interview by Chris Roholt, 1971, both cited in Roholt, "Montana Wilderness Study Bill," 76–77.

9. Merriam, "Bob Marshall Wilderness Area of Montana—Some Socio-Economic Considerations," 791.

10. Petition of Flathead Lake Wildlife Association, February 27, 1954, TWS 4/40/23. These figures may have been overstated for the lightly used upper Flathead, but the forty outfitters working in the Bob Marshall generated some $258,000 in direct income per year, according to a 1960 study. Merriam, "Bob Marshall Wilderness

Area of Montana—A Study in Land Use," 103–4.

11. The sportsmen's resolutions are in TWS 4/40/23. Tolke's comments are from Robert L. Baker, "Dude Wrangler Gives Capital O.K.," *Washington Post and Times-Herald*, 1954, clipping in TWS 4/41/2.

12. Resolution of Montana Fish and Game Commission, May 1954, TWS 4/40/23. Cooney used similar words in a letter to Howard Zahniser, June 24, 1954 (same file).

13. Neitzling to Zahniser, March 12, 1954, TWS 4/40/23.

14. Merritt to Murie, May 9, 1954, TWS 4/40/23. Merritt was drawing from a Forest Service research report titled *Forest Resources of Montana*, authored by S. Blair Hutchison and Paul Kemp of the agency's Northern Rocky Mountain Experiment Station in Missoula, Montana.

15. Clifton R. Merritt, "Beyond the Roads," CMP 110/10.

16. Weller to Murray, October 13, 1954, CMP 4/4.

17. John Castles, memo to record, November 23, 1954, cited in Roholt, "Montana Wilderness Study Bill," 79; "Timber Volumes Cut and Sold," fiscal years 1954 and 1955; Hanson to Zahniser, January 3, 1955, TWS 4/40/24.

18. For Merritt's account of the establishment of the Jewel Basin Hiking Area, see "The Land of Snow-Painted Peaks and Jewel-Like Lakes," *Swan View's News*, www.swanview.org/newsletters/Holidays_2008_e.pdf.

19. Merritt to Hudoba, January 5, 1955, cited in Robert N. Baker, "Clif Merritt and Wilderness Wildlife," 103.

Chapter 5. Idaho's Lifeblood

1. McCollister and McCollister, "Clearwater River Log Drives."

2. River and Harbor Act of 1945, Pub. L. No. 79-14, March 2, 1945; U.S. Army Corps of Engineers, *Columbia River and Tributaries*.

3. See Ewert, "Evolution of an Environmentalist."

4. Murphy and Metsker, *Inventory of Idaho Streams*, 7, table 1.

5. "Clearwater Dam Support Is Voiced," *Spokane (WA) Spokesman-Review*, November 21, 1953; "27 Speakers Express Approval of Plan for Two Clearwater Dams," *Lewiston (ID) Morning Tribune*, November 21, 1953.

6. "Game Dept. Fears Dams on Clearwater," *Lewiston Morning Tribune*, November 13, 1948.

7. "Idaho Dam Threat," news item, *Living Wilderness* 47 (Winter 1953–54): 38–40.

8. Stewart Brandborg, interview by author, Hamilton, MT, October 9, 2010.

9. Hanson to O'Connor, March 5, 1954; Hanson to Zahniser, March 3, 1954, TWS 4/29/10.

10. Harmon to chief, Forest Service, January 19, 1954; Sieker to Region 1, February

2, 1954; Harmon to Zahniser, March 26, 1954, all cited in AnneMarie Moore and Baird, *Wild Places Preserved*, 188–89.

11. Brigham to Murie, April 17, 1954, OMP-DPL 4/4.

12. Brandborg is quoted in "Idaho Dam Threat," *Living Wilderness* 47 (Winter 1953–54), 38–40. The Corps of Engineers rebuttal is from A. B. Curtis's statement to the Board of Engineers for Rivers and Harbors, Washington, D.C., February 26, 1954, 7, in the Dworshak Dam collection, Special Collections and Archives, University of Idaho Library.

13. John Corlett, "Idaho Wildlife Federation Like 'Spoiled Child,'" *Lewiston Morning Tribune*, January 15, 1954.

14. "Lewiston Writer Takes Issue with Columnist on Dams Issue," *Lewiston Morning Tribune*, January 18, 1954.

15. The Corps of Engineers ultimately decided in favor of a hatchery rather than providing fish passage facilities at the 700-foot-high structure. Operated by the U.S. Fish and Wildlife Service, the facility has been plagued with disease problems and has often failed to meet its production goals. Miller, "Review of Dworshak National Fish Hatchery Mitigation Record."

16. Stewart Brandborg, interview by author, Hamilton, MT, May 7, 2011.

17. Stewart Brandborg, transcript of interview by Joanna Tenny, Missoula, MT, July 12, 2002, Wilderness Institute, University of Montana, tape 1, side B.

18. Brandborg to Dondero, May 20, 1954, TWS 4/27/27.

19. Mort Brigham observed in a 1957 letter to Frank Church that floods in the Clearwater Basin during the sixty-two years since 1894 had produced estimated total damages of $4.5 million, whereas the Corps of Engineers pegged the combined annual flood control benefits from the Penny Cliffs and Bruces Eddy Dams at $62 million for the period. Brigham discounted as insignificant the potential flood control benefits occurring farther downstream, owing to the Clearwater's relatively small contribution to the Columbia system. Brigham to Church, January 2, 1957, LMP 120/5. Church quotation is from Ewert, "Evolution of an Environmentalist," 39.

20. "Report of the District Engineer," in U.S. Senate, *Middle Snake River*, 86, 115; Brigham to Neuberger, May 3, 1957, LMP 120/5; Sewell, "Nez Perce Dam."

21. Brigham to Nadel, June 12, 1956, TWS 3/1/3.

Chapter 6. Partitioning Eden

1. Kelley to chief, Forest Service, February 23, 1937, reprinted in AnneMarie Moore and Baird, *Wild Places Preserved*, 125–26.

2. Bud Moore, *Lochsa Story*, 316–18.

3. Ibid., 322.

4. Ibid., 323.

5. John McCarthy, "Reflecting on the Life of Conservation Champion Bud Moore," December 2, 2010, The Wilderness Society, http://wilderness.org/content/reflecting-life-conservation-champion-bud-moore.

6. R. J. Henderson and A. E. Allen, "Mechanization of Trail Maintenance and Travel Interim Report," Equipment Development Report TEB #326, Missoula, MT, January 17, 1955, NAS Series 95-60A70, box 7A, fd. "Roads & Trails–Bitterroot–C. Y. 1955."

7. Marshall to Murie and Zahniser, July 22, 1953, OMP-DPL 1/18.

8. Hanson to Zahniser, February 1, 1954, Slusher, "Notes from Study of Files," in AnneMarie Moore and Baird, *Wild Places Preserved*, 188.

9. Broome, *Faces of the Wilderness*, 88.

10. Wilderness Society council minutes, August 24, 1955, TWS 4/29/10.

11. Leopold, "Last Stand of the Wilderness."

12. Scott, *Enduring Wilderness*, 39; Yard to Kenneth Reid (Izaak Walton League), February 17, 1939, TWS 1/3/27.

13. Scott, *Enduring Wilderness*, 42; Harvey, *Wilderness Forever*, 82.

14. Harvey, *Wilderness Forever*, 190.

15. Ibid., 187–88, 212.

16. Memos dated March 18 and April 30, 1958, Slusher, "Notes from Study of Files," in AnneMarie Moore and Baird, *Wild Places Preserved*, 193–95.

17. Ed Slusher's 1958 summary lists these various issues in regional office memos from August 23, 1956; November 7, 1956; January 6, 1958; and January 22, 1958 (ibid.).

18. Worster, "The Nature We Have Lost," in *Wealth of Nature*, 9–10.

19. Stewart Brandborg, telephone conversation with author, December 4, 2012; "Wilderness Bill Is Protection, Brandborg Says," *Lewiston Morning Tribune*, October 28, 1961; Zahniser to Stewart Brandborg, January 17, 1961, TWS 2/6/21.

20. Stewart Brandborg, interview by Roger Kaye, Darby, MT, March 3, 2003, http://digitalmedia.fws.gov/utils/getfile/collection/document/id/924/filename/925.pdf.

21. Inland Empire Multiple Use Committee, "Proposal for the Selway Bitterroot Wilderness Area," February 1961, Mansfield Library, University of Montana–Missoula.

22. "North Idaho Wilderness Proposal Brings Conflicted Testimony," *Boise Statesman*, March 10, 1961.

23. Caldwell and Visser, "Tourist Packer Services in Primitive Areas."

24. Remarks of Stewart Brandborg in "Selway-Bitterroot Hearings," *Living Wilderness* 77 (Summer–Fall 1961): 43; statement of G. M. Brandborg, March 7, 1961, LMP 41/3.

25. "Statement by Morton R. Brigham on Reclassification of Selway-Bitterroot Wilderness," OMP-DPL 2/33.

26. Remarks of Frank Cullen in "Selway-Bitterroot Hearings"; "North Idaho Wilderness Proposal Brings Conflicted Testimony," *Boise Statesman*, March 10, 1961.

27. "Selway-Bitterroot Hearings," 44.

Chapter 7. A Book and Its Cover

1. Tebbe to Baldwin, October 17, 1958, CMP 45/2.

2. Mrs. Ernest Miller to Ed Barry, September 19, 1960, OMP-DPL 4/37.

3. Baldwin to Murie, September 11, 1958, OMP-DPL 3/2.

4. Ken and Florence Baldwin, oral history interview by Scott Bischke, June 13, 2002, Montana Historical Society OH 2079, tape 1, side 1.

5. Ibid.

6. Cooney to Murie, October 31, 1947, TWS 4/40/23.

7. Baldwin to "Friends of Wilderness," March 19, 1958; "Outline of Montana Wilderness Society," both in Montana Wilderness Association records, Helena, MT. I am indebted to Joan Montagne for collecting these and other documents related to the MWA's beginnings.

8. Summary of first meeting of Montana Wilderness Association, March 28, 1958, MWA records.

9. The MWA's creation is described in notes compiled by Ken Baldwin in Joan Montagne, "Montana Wilderness Association History 1958–1983" (MWA records) and in Clif Merritt's papers (CMP 4/2).

10. Yeckel to Craighead, January 23, 1962, TWS 4/43/5. The Gravelly Range lies to the west of the Madison Valley.

11. Kenneth Baldwin, John Montagne, and Russell Berg, "Statement of the Montana Wilderness Association for Spanish Peaks Wilderness Hearing," September 9, 1966, copy in Montana State University Library; Merritt to Brandborg, July 6, 1966, TWS 4/43/6.

12. Yeckel to Metcalf, March 31, 1966, TWS 4/43/6.

13. Yeckel to Metcalf, June 10, 1966, LMP 42/1.

14. Koessler statement, October 5, 1966, LMP 42/1.

15. Baldwin, Montagne, and Berg, "Statement of the Montana Wilderness Association for Spanish Peaks Wilderness Hearing."

16. Montagne to regional forester, September 11, 1966, LMP 42/1.

17. Combs to Metcalf, August 30, 1966; Orr to Neal Rahm, September 17, 1966, LMP 42/1.

18. Metcalf-Yeckel correspondence, December 1966, LMP 42/1; Metcalf to L. A. Chamberlain, January 12, 1967, LMP 41/7. Chamberlain was director of the Ennis Commercial Club.

19. Witter to Metcalf, April 12, 1967, LMP 41/7.

20. Cliff to Metcalf, July 14, 1967, LMP 41/7.

21. Yeckel to Metcalf, April 17, 1967, LMP 41/7; Menk to Yeckel, August 8, 1967, LMP 41/6; Greeley to Metcalf, August 8, 1967, LMP 41/6.

22. Correspondence between Edward Beardsley, Humphrey's assistant William Connell, and Lee Metcalf, dated November 28 to December 20, 1967, LMP 41/7; Jackson to Freeman, April 5, 1968, LMP 41/6.

23. Freeman to Jackson, April 16, 2012, LMP 41/6. The administration proposal was transmitted on March 29, 1968. The Olsen bill was H.R. 16547.

24. After hearing that regional forester Neal Rahm was reluctant to proceed with the Jack Creek study, Lee Metcalf dispatched a letter to Secretary Freeman reminding him of his commitment. "Please implement the agreement promptly," Metcalf concluded. Metcalf to Freeman, June 20, 1968, LMP 41/6.

Chapter 8. Wild River

1. This account is based on John Craighead's typewritten journal from his second Middle Fork trip, July 15–20, 1957, CMP 4/4.

2. Merritt recalled in his memoirs how he and John Craighead were "shooting the rapids of the wild Upper Middle Fork . . . on that morning in July, 1956 when he first mentioned the concept, which he said he had just thought of." "Beyond the Roads," Spruce Park chapter, CMP 100/10. Craighead's letter to Baldwin was reprinted as an article titled "Wild River" in the Montana Wildlife Federation *News*, June 1957, 15–20.

3. Frank Craighead to Udall, February 22, 1961, SBP 65/5.

4. Udall to Merritt, November 27, 1963, CMP 110/10.

5. Cliff to Metcalf, April 16, 1962, CMP 1/9.

6. Leo L. Laythe to H. T. Nelson, February 5, 1957, CMP 1/9. Laythe worked in the Fish and Wildlife Service office in Portland, Oregon. Nelson was a regional director of the Bureau of Reclamation in Boise, Idaho.

7. Kenneth Holum to Metcalf, October 4, 1965, LMP 98/9. Holum was assistant secretary of the interior for water and power development.

8. William L. Spence, "Torrents of Rain, Miles of Misery," *Kalispell (MT) Daily Inter Lake*, May 8, 2011; Holum to Metcalf, October 4 1965, LMP 98/9; Metcalf to Allen J. Ellender, June 16, 1965, LMP 98/9. Ellender chaired the House Public Works Subcommittee.

9. Dominy to Metcalf, July 15, 1964; Sykes to Metcalf, July 29, 1964, both in LMP 98/9.

10. Metcalf to Dominy, May 17, 1965, LMP 100/2; Metcalf to John M. Dalimata, March 5, 1965, LMP 98/8.

11. John Montagne, "Summary of Technical Factors Concerning Flood Control along the Sun River Drainage, Montana," LMP 110/1. The reports on which his paper was based were prepared by Theodore T. Williams, P.E. (letter to Montagne dated July 3, 1965), and Joseph Caprio ("Climate Review in the Sun River Basin," dated July 3, 1965), both in LMP 110/1.

12. Theodore Fosse to Metcalf, September 17, 1965, LMP 110/1; Englund, note to "Lee," September 1965, LMP 110/1. Fosse was a Cascade County extension agent.

13. John F. Kraft, Inc., "Study of Voter Attitudes in Montana," September 1966, LMP 8/625. Kraft's opinion survey was conducted in the fall of 1965 for use in Metcalf's reelection campaign.

14. Metcalf to Francis Van Rinsum, March 12, 1965, LMP 98/9. Frank Church's S. 1446, which he introduced on March 8, 1965, designated portions of six rivers as the initial components of a national wild rivers system, including the undeveloped reaches of Idaho's Salmon and Clearwater Rivers.

15. U.S. Forest Service, *Waters of the Flathead*. The agency proposed to classify 219 miles of the North, Middle, and South Forks under the Wild and Scenic Rivers Act's three classifications.

16. Merritt memoirs, "Spruce Park," CMP 100/10.

17. Merriam, "The Bob Marshall Wilderness Area of Montana—A Study in Land Use," 118.

18. Merritt to John Craighead, May 27, 1964, CMP 52/5.

Chapter 9. Full Use and Development

1. Timber harvest data are from Northern Region fact sheets, NAS series 95-60A70, box 4.

2. Tebbe to Hon. James E. Murray and others, December 31, 1958, in U.S. Forest Service, *Full Use and Development*, xiv.

3. Ibid., 28–29.

4. Ibid., 30. For further discussion of the *Full Use and Development* report, see Swanson, *Bitterroot and Mr. Brandborg*, 119–22.

5. Robert D. Baker, *National Forests of the Northern Region*, table 12.3.

6. "Statement of Congressman Lee Metcalf on Behalf of the Montana Congressional Delegation, Before the Subcommittee of Public Works of the United States Senate Public Works Committee, in Missoula, Montana, December 14, 1957," LMP 664/5.

7. James Murray, Lee Metcalf, Mike Mansfield, and LeRoy Anderson to Ezra Taft Benson, May 27, 1958, LMP 2/35; Metcalf statement on forest roads and trails budget for 1959, LMP 35/7.

8. Edwards to Metcalf, February 7, 1959, courtesy of Edwards family.

9. Metcalf to Edwards, February 16, 1959, ibid.; Hirt, *Conspiracy of Optimism*, 152–57.

10. Tom Edwards, handwritten notes for lecture, 1959, courtesy of Edwards family.

11. Merriam, "Bob Marshall Wilderness Area of Montana—A Study in Land Use," 100-101.

12. Hirt, *Conspiracy of Optimism*, 140–41.

13. Ibid., 192–98.

14. Sierra Club news release, July 28, 1960, HJP 1/9; Brower to Murie, June 30, 1960, OMP-DPL 4/10 (emphasis in original). The 1926 Kneipp survey identified 55 million acres of wildland tracts of 230,000 acres of more; the losses Brower identified were presumably based on James Gilligan's studies for the Outdoor Recreation Resources Review Commission, which were released in 1962. Gilligan was considering only those roadless areas of 100,000 acres or more; many smaller wildland tracts were being developed as well.

15. Church to Brower, October 13, 1960, HJP 1/9 (emphasis in original).

16. Church's presentation is in Senate Report 109, 88th Cong., 1st sess., April 3, 1963, cited in Keane, "Wilderness Act as Congress Intended."

17. U.S. Senate, *Federal Timber Sale Policies*, 179–81.

18. Statement of Howard Zahniser, in American Forest Products Industries, *Proceedings, Forest Land Use Conference*, 38.

19. David R. Brower, notes for Sierra Club board meeting, December 5–6, 1960, HJP 13/23.

Chapter 10. The Storekeeper and the Kleinschmidt Hoss

1. Arnold Elser, interview by author, Missoula, MT, May 5, 2011; Thelma Elser, "Fifty Years in the Bob Marshall," Back Country Horsemen of Montana *News*, February 2008.

2. Merriam, "Irony of the Bob Marshall Wilderness," 85. Biographical details are from the Edwards family.

3. Statement of Donald A. Roos, in U.S. Senate, *Lincoln Back Country Wilderness Area*, 53–54.

4. Statement of Frank Dunkle, ibid., 4; Edwards to Metcalf, December 29, 1954, LMP 36/5; Edwards to Hanson, January 30, 1955, cited in Merriam, "Irony of the Bob Marshall Wilderness," 84.

5. Tom Edwards, handwritten notes for lecture, 1959, courtesy of Edwards family. Author Michael Korn traces the phrase "the hush of the land" to outfitter Eli Laird, who operated a dude ranch at Lindbergh Lake in the 1920s (Korn, "Hobnail Tom"). Edwards would likely have known Laird, who died in 1943.

6. Tom Edwards, handwritten notes for lecture, 1959, courtesy of Edwards family.

7. Behan, "Lincoln Back Country Controversy," 14.

8. U.S. Forest Service, Northern Region, "Timber Management Plan, Lincoln Working Circle, Helena National Forest, Montana, 1959," in Mansfield Library, University of Montana–Missoula.

9. Garland, telephone conversation with author, December 12, 2011; Garland to Hamre [1962], CGP 1/1.

10. Metcalf to Garland, January 25, 1962; Rasmussen to Garland, June 25, 1962, both in CGP 1/1.

11. Garland delivered these remarks to the MWA's second annual convention, which was held in Lincoln in 1964. They are part of a 1969 recollection by various MWA presidents. Montana Wilderness Association history files, Helena, MT.

12. U.S. Forest Service, *Long Range Plan*.

13. Garland to Zahniser, May 21, 1963; Garland to Brower, April 8, 1963, both in TWS 4/42/4.

14. Behan, "Lincoln Back Country Controversy," 23.

15. Stanley M. Arkwright to Garland, April 22, 1963, CGP 1/1.

16. Cecil Garland, recollections of the MWA's second annual convention, 1969, in MWA files, Helena; also Garland, telephone interview by author, January 8, 2008.

17. Quoted in Roth, *Wilderness Movement*, 30.

18. Cecil Garland, recollections of the MWA's second annual convention.

19. John Craighead to Rasmussen, April 30, 1963, TWS 4/42/4; Schoonover to Hamre, June 17, 1963, CMP 1/10.

20. Garland to Hamre, May 17, 1963, CGP 1/1.

21. "Modified Plan Announced for Lincoln North Area," *Helena (MT) Independent Record*, June 16, 1963.

22. Merritt to Schoonover, July 11, 1963, CMP 1/10.

23. Weisel and Aldrich to Cliff, August 13, 1963, CMP 28/12.

24. Brandborg to John Craighead, May 31, 1963, TWS 4/42/4.

25. Statement of Cecil Garland, in U.S. Senate, *Lincoln Back Country Wilderness Area*, 9–10.

26. Edwards to Weisel, April 11, 1963, LBCPA 1/3.

27. Battin to Brandborg, August 20, 1963, TWS 4/42/4; Roe to Mansfield, July 3, 1963, MMP 8/60/1.

28. Metcalf to Garland, June 7, 1963, CGP 1/1; staff memo to Mansfield, June 24, 1963, MMP 8/60/1; Greeley to Mansfield, June 28, 1963, MMP 8/60/1.

29. Boyd Rasmussen, "Statement on Long Range Plans for the Lincoln District," October 1963, CMP 28/12.

30. Mansfield to Allen J. Ellender, November 20, 1963, MMP 8/60/1.

31. Weisel to Garland, February 5 and February 14, 1964, CMP 28/12.

32. Merritt to Kreck, February 9, 1964, CMP 28/12.

33. Merritt to Brandborg, March 6, 1964, CMP 28/12.

34. Zahiniser to Merritt, March 16, 1964; Merritt to Brandborg, March 18, 1964, both in CMP 28/12. The wilderness proposal is described in notes of the spring meeting of District 1 of the Montana Wildlife Federation, Missoula, MT, April 4, 1964, CMP 1/10.

Chapter 11. Rumblings along the Magruder Road

1. Cunningham, "Magruder Corridor Controversy," 66, table 3.

2. The Anaconda-Pintlar Wilderness was designated as a 159,000-acre wilderness area in December 1962 under regulation U-1. Its name was changed in 1978 to Anaconda-Pintler to reflect local usage. The Cabinet Mountains became a 94,272-acre "wild area" in May 1963 under regulation U-2. Both areas became "instant" wilderness areas under the 1964 Wilderness Act.

3. Andersen to regional forester, January 29, 1963, Bitterroot National Forest archives, Hamilton, MT.

4. Brandborg to Olsen, February 22, 1963, BEP 12/6; Montana Wilderness Association, "Memorandum for Interested Members and Cooperators," January 16, 1963, OMP-DPL 4/4.

5. Metcalf to Freeman, March 2, 1962, LMP 40/1.

6. Freeman to Metcalf, April 1963, ibid.

7. Cliff to Metcalf, September 9, 1963, SBP 31/6.

8. Clifton Merritt oral history interview, CMP 113/10.

9. Doris Milner to Leland Schoonover (and others), December 3, 1964; "Save the Wilderness of the Upper Selway" (brochure), both in SBP 41/1.

10. Rahm to chief forester, June 8, 1965, cited in Cunningham, "Magruder Corridor Controversy," 77; Andersen to Morton R. Brigham, January 5, 1965, SBP 41/1.

11. Cliff to Olsen, August 6, 1965, SBP 41/1.

12. Kelsey C. Milner to Mansfield, January 12, 1965, ibid.

13. Andersen to Brigham, January 5, 1965, ibid.

14. Church to Bowler, April 14, 1965, ibid.

15. Montagne to Merritt, October 4, 1965, TWS 4/43/3.

16. Zahniser to Merritt, March 16, 1964, CMP 4/2.

17. Brandborg to Doris Milner, June 22, 1965, TWS 4/43/3.

18. Doris Milner oral history interview OH 413-03, July 18, 1975, Special Collections and Archives, University of Montana–Missoula.

19. Milner to Cliff (draft), March 1, 1965, TWS 4/30/7.

20. Cliff to Metcalf, July 2, 1965; Brigham to Doris Milner, June 22, 1965; both in DMP-UI 2/3.

21. Donald Aldrich, "Inspection Trip Made into Selway River Headwaters," Montana Wildlife Federation *News*, January 1966; Doris Milner to Metcalf, August 6, 1965, BEP 12/35.

22. Reynolds to Church, n.d., Western Montana Fish and Game Association records, Special Collections and Archives, University of Montana–Missoula, 11/8.

23. Brandborg to Montagne, October 11, 1965, TWS 4/43/3.

24. Doris Milner and Brigham to Sens. Mansfield, Metcalf, and Church and Reps. Olsen and Battin, December 13, 1965, BEP 12/32.

25. Brigham to G. M. Brandborg, May 17, 1966, TWS 4/30/7. A copy of Brigham's tracing is in CMP, box 12, fd. "Proposed Forest Service Logging Area."

26. Brigham to Pegues, April 13, 1966, BEP 12/34.

27. Shackelford to forest supervisor, February 10, 1967, Bitterroot National Forest Archives, file 2410, "Plans—Magruder Block."

28. Don Aldrich, "Missoula Meeting with the Upper Selway Study Committee," Montana Wildlife Federation *News*, January 1967.

29. Stewart Brandborg, notes on Selway issue, SBP 54/5; Freeman to Metcalf, June 9, 1966, TWS 4/30/10.

30. For the composition and activities of the Selke committee see Swanson, *Bitterroot and Mr. Brandborg*, 135.

31. Cunningham, "Magruder Corridor Controversy," 112; Stewart Brandborg memo to conservation leaders, January 4, 1967, BEP 12/32.

32. "Statement by Secretary Freeman on the Report of the Review Committee for the Magruder Corridor," April 20, 1967, Bitterroot National Forest archives, Magruder Corridor file. Merrill Englund, Metcalf's administrative assistant, reported Freeman's reaction to the report in a letter to Don Aldrich, July 17, 1967, LMP 40/12.

Chapter 12. The Green of Our Forests

1. Mort Brigham described some of his early experiences in the St. Joe–Clearwater forests in a letter to Jim Calvert of the Idaho Environmental Council, February 6, 1969, TWS 4/28/29.

2. "Ed Myers: From Flunky to Fire Lookout," http://www.fs.usda.gov/Internet/FSE_DOCUMENTS/fsm9_018536.pdf. 13. Moreland, known as the "Ridgerunner," is described in a write-up on the Mallard-Larkins Pioneer Area, http://www.summitpost.org/mallard-larkins-pioneer-area/288752.

3. Billie Jean Plaster, "Timber Town," *Sandpoint Magazine*, Winter 1996.

4. Calkin, *Historic Resource Production*, tables 4 and 7.

5. Janet Brigham Rands kindly provided these insights about her father in a conversation with the author in Salt Lake City, UT, November 23, 2011.

6. Brigham to McArdle, February 28, 1957, CMP 1/3.

7. John A. Morrison, "Big Game Management Problems in Idaho Primitive Areas," Idaho Fish and Game Department, TWS 4/28/17.

8. Brigham to Hilding, June 20, 1961, TWS 4/27/27.

9. Brandborg to Brigham, June 26, 1961, ibid.

10. "Bruces Eddy Plan Ready—Church," *Lewiston (ID) Morning Tribune*, May 30, 1961; "House Votes to Authorize Bruces Eddy," ibid., October 13, 1962.

11. Bruces Eddy (later renamed Dworshak) Dam was authorized under the Flood Control Act of 1962.

12. "Bruces Eddy: The Future Now Is Here," *Lewiston Morning Tribune*, October 13, 1962.

13. "Bruces Eddy Dam Will Jeopardize Operations at Lewiston—Cancell," *Lewiston Morning Tribune*, August 17, 1963; Morton R. Brigham, news release, October 21, 1963, CMP 2/1.

14. Brigham to Nancy Mae Larson, October 29, 1968, TWS 4/27/28.

15. Mary Ann Reese, "Forestry Board Shuns Fire Bill Vote," *Idaho Daily Statesman* (Boise), November 18, 1966. Thompson was addressing the Idaho State Cooperative Board of Forestry, a joint government-industry group.

16. Brigham, "Proposed St. Joe Wilderness."

17. U.S. Forest Service, Northern Region, "Mallard-Larkins Pioneer Area Established in North Idaho's St. Joe, Clearwater National Forests," news release, May 1969, TWS 4/28/11.

18. "Notice—Act Now," flier, Outdoors Unlimited [1969], TWS 4/28/11.

19. Brigham to Calvert, February 6, 1969, TWS 4/28/29.

20. Brigham to Calvert, March 5, 1969, ibid.

21. Brigham to Calvert, January 23 and February 15, 1969, ibid.

22. Brock Evans, speech given October 16, 1970, ibid.

23. Brigham to "cooperators," August 13, 1971, ibid.

Chapter 13. The Hush of the Land

1. Roth, *Wilderness Movement and the National Forests*, 2.

2. Stewart Brandborg, interview by author, Hamilton, MT, May 7, 2011. Brandborg called the requirement for affirmative congressional action "a great liberating force" since it required active grassroots organizing, which became a chief source of strength for the movement. Scott, *Enduring Wilderness*, 63.

3. Mansfield to Allen J. Ellender, November 20, 1963; Metcalf to Calvert, December 23, 1963, both in MMP 8/60/1.

4. Cecil Garland, telephone conversation with author, December 12, 2011. As any wilderness traveler can attest, civilized comforts at the end of a trip can cast a favorable

glow over the whole outing.

5. Clif Merritt, "Campaign Started to Save Back Country," news release, May 15, 1964, CMP 1/13.

6. Merritt to Leland Schoonover, July 8, 1964, CGP 1/2.

7. Merritt described the encounter in his "Beyond the Roads" memoir, CMP 110/12.

8. Merritt to Thomas Kimball, July 26, 1964, CGP 1/2. Kimball was head of the National Wildlife Federation.

9. Merritt to Garland, January 20, 1965, CGP 1/3. Merritt thanked Mansfield and Metcalf for introducing the bill, which he said would be "warmly received and strongly supported," and did not immediately press for its expansion. Merritt to Mansfield, January 14, 1965, MMP 8/60/1.

10. Metcalf made this statement in a news release issued during his 1972 Senate campaign (LMP 651/6).

11. Garland to Smith, March 12, 1965, ERSP 19/15.

12. Excerpt from Tom and Helen Edwards's "White Tail Tattler" of January 1954, courtesy Edwards family. This was an annual or semiannual newsletter the couple sent to their guests, which recounted the previous seasons' adventures and was illustrated with many of Hobnail Tom's humorous and evocative cartoons.

13. Statement of Tom Edwards, in U.S. Senate, *Lincoln Back Country Wilderness Area*, 37.

14. R. H. "Buff" Hultman to county commissioners, Missoula County, 1967, TWS 4/42/6. The commissioners had voted to oppose the wilderness designation, but after the outfitters protested, they reversed their stance—an indication of the outfitters' clout.

15. Delaney to Metcalf, April 7, 1965, CMP 28/13.

16. Clyde Reichelt, "Lincoln Concerned about Back Country Future," *Great Falls (MT) Tribune*, January 19, 1964.

17. Morgan to Merritt, June 1, 1965, TWS 4/42/4; Garland to Metcalf, June 24, 1965, LMP 100/2.

18. Garland to Battin, March 27, 1965, CMP 28/13; Garland, telephone conversation with author, December 12, 2011. The Battin bill was H.R. 7266. Clif Merritt's account of the genesis of the Battin bill is substantially different; he recalled persuading a reluctant Garland to support the larger proposal and helping him draw the boundaries (Merritt interview by Scott Bischke, December 19, 2002, MHS OH 2075). However, Merritt's letter of January 20, 1965 (note 9) suggests that Garland was already pushing for such a bill.

19. Edwards to Garland, April 15, 1965, CGP 1/3.

20. Correspondence to Mike Mansfield on the Scapegoat issue for 1965 is in MMP 8/60/2.

21. U.S. Forest Service, *Patterns for Management*, 7–8, 11–13.

22. Statement of Cecil Garland, in U.S. Senate, *Lincoln Back Country Wilderness Area*, 12–13.

23. Tom Edwards to guests, May 15, 1968, courtesy of Edwards family.

24. Ralph Pomnichowski, "Wilderness Backers Prevail," *Great Falls Tribune*, September 24, 1968. Battin's companion bill was H.R. 7148.

25. Statement of Tom Edwards, in U.S. Senate, *Lincoln Back Country Wilderness Area*, 36–38.

26. U.S. Senate, *Lincoln Back Country Wilderness Area*, statements of Frank Dunkle, 5; John Craighead, 117; and George Weisel, 111.

27. Ibid., statement of Cecil Garland, 10.

28. Ibid., statements of Dr. Horace H. Koessler, 93; Robert N. Helding, 56; Allen R. White, 178–79.

29. Ibid., statement of Lee Metcalf, 46.

Chapter 14. One Powerful Senator

1. Stewart M. Brandborg, "The Wilderness Act: The First Three Years," in Maxine McCloskey and Gilligan, *Wilderness and the Quality of Life*, 31–32.

2. Brandborg to Hultman, December 6, 1968, TWS 4/40/1.

3. Roth, *Wilderness Movement and the National Forests*, 32. In his memoir of the Lincoln-Scapegoat battle, Clif Merritt named Morgan the unsung hero of the Lincoln-Scapegoat, working behind the scenes to create some grudging acceptance for the citizens' wilderness proposal within the Forest Service. Merritt, "Beyond the Roads," CMP 110/12.

4. Robert Morgan, notes of meeting, March 13, 1969, quoted in Roth, *Wilderness Movement and the National Forests*, 35.

5. Bud Moore recalled this key meeting in an interview with the author, Condon, MT, September 29, 2007.

6. Neal Rahm statement, in U.S. Senate, *Lincoln Back Country Wilderness Area*, 15.

7. Uttley to Mansfield, March 28, 1969, MMP 8/60/4.

8. F. M. Gannon, report to Helena Wilderness Riders, CGP 2/1.

9. Brandborg to Merritt, April 18, 1969, TWS 4/42/7. Section 4(d)(2) of the Wilderness Act required that the Geological Survey and the Bureau of Mines examine the mineral resources of *designated* national forest wilderness areas on a "planned, recurring basis"; the policy of requiring a mineral survey of *candidate* areas appears to have originated in the House conference committee report on the act. House Report 1829, 88th Cong., 2nd sess.

10. Cecil Garland recollections, author's possession, courtesy of Montana Wilderness

Association. The "something" that Aspinall wanted turned out to be a water project in Colorado, according to some reports.

11. Mansfield to Aspinall, October 28, 1969, CGP 2/1.

12. Jackson to William T. Pecora, February 19, 1970, MMP 8/60/3. Pecora was director of the U.S. Geological Survey.

13. Albert Quie, telephone conversation with author, May 13, 2013; Quie to Garland, September 16, 1970, CGP 2/2.

14. Cecil Garland recollections, author's possession.

15. Tom Edwards to "Friends of the Scapegoat Lincoln Back Country," December 31, 1971, courtesy of Edwards family.

16. The Mansfield-Metcalf bill, S. 484, became P.L. 92-395 (92nd Cong., 2nd sess.). Consisting of three brief paragraphs, the bill referenced a long legislative history and designated 240,000 acres as the Scapegoat Wilderness contiguous to the southern border of the Bob Marshall Wilderness. The Agriculture Department letter to Wayne Aspinall, dated October 20, 1971, stated it had "no objection to enactment of legislation to designate a Scapegoat Wilderness involving a major portion of the Lincoln Back Country area." This, and Tom Edwards's letter of August 21, 1972, are in TWS 4/42/8.

17. Burk, *Great Bear, Wild River*, 29–30.

18. Dale A. Burk, "Concern Grows for 'Wild' Middle Fork River Area," *Missoulian* (Missoula, MT), n.d., filed in LMP 117/9; Dale A. Burk, "Montana Wilderness," *Sierra Club Bulletin*, November–December 1970, 12–15. Christopher Ransick discussed Burk's activist journalism in "The Bitterroot Controversy."

19. Flathead National Forest, Spotted Bear Ranger District, "Multiple Use Survey Report (Stage II), Spotted Bear River Road #568.1 and Dean Ridge Loop Road #564.1," LMP 38/1.

20. Mel Ruder, "Spotted Bear Roading May Threaten Elk Herd," *Missoulian, November 22, 1969* (from *Hungry Horse News*); Dunkle to Metcalf, February 9, 1970, LMP 38/1.

21. See Swanson, *Bitterroot and Mr. Brandborg*, chap. 16.

22. Mansfield, Metcalf, and Olsen to Cliff, May 21, 1970, LMP 38/1.

23. Hanson to Metcalf, June 4, 1970, LMP 37/8.

24. Cliff to Metcalf, June 5, 1970, LMP 38/1.

25. The cooperative studies are summarized in Lyon et al., *Coordinating Elk and Timber Management*.

26. Merritt to Kreck, June 30, 1970, CMP 20/4.

27. Hultman to Brandborg, n.d., ibid. Chadwick's report was relayed to Stewart Brandborg in a December 19, 1972, letter from Robert R. Ream, Chadwick's faculty adviser at the University of Montana (TWS 4/40/2). Chadwick described his

seasons in Bunker Creek in his book *A Beast the Color of Winter.*

28. Paul D. Dalke, Idaho Cooperative Wildlife Research Unit, to Stewart Brandborg, October 10, 1967, TWS 4/27/28; Brigham to Bill Cunningham, February 27, 1969, TWS 4/30/1. Cunningham, a graduate student at the University of Montana, was writing a thesis on the Magruder Corridor controversy.

29. Brigham to Church, January 19, 1969, FCP 152/17.

30. U.S. Forest Service, Bitterroot National Forest, "Magruder Corridor Resource Inventory," 1–2.

31. Loren Knudson, brief submitted to Magruder Corridor Advisory Committee, TWS 4/30/1.

32. Knudson, ibid., citing Parker v. United States, 309 F. Supp. 593, 1 ERC 1163 (D. Colo. 1970). The Parker case, which Clif Merritt helped prepare, set an important precedent for environmentalists concerned about the primitive area reviews. Dennis Roth's Forest Service history provides a good discussion (*Wilderness Movement and the National Forests*, 20–22).

33. Stewart Brandborg, telephone interview by author, October 9, 2011.

34. S. 4575, 91st Cong., 2nd sess., December 9, 1970.

35. U.S. Forest Service, Bitterroot National Forest, "Management Proposal for the Magruder Corridor."

36. Doris Milner, letter to Save the Upper Selway Committee members, September 16, 1971, in author's possession; "Industry Groups Criticize Five Year Moratorium on Magruder Corridor," *Western Timber Industry*, November 1971.

37. Remarks of Frank Church, *Congressional Record*, 92nd Cong., 1st sess., v. 117, no. 123, August 2, 1971; also FCP, series 7.9, 13/5. The bill was S. 2390.

Chapter 15. Wilderness Made Rational

1. Lucas and Stankey, "Social Carrying Capacity," 16, 20; Lucas, "Backcountry Concept."

2. Worf, "National Forest Wilderness, a Policy Review," cited in Roth, *Wilderness Movement and the National Forests*, 5.

3. Ibid.

4. Costley, "An Enduring Resource," 11; Roth, *Wilderness Movement and the National Forests*, 7.

5. The purity issue became a central focus in the debate over wilderness designations in the eastern national forests from 1973 to 1975. In this campaign, and in the debate on the Endangered American Wilderness Act in 1977–78, Doug Scott (who was then working for the Sierra Club) argued that Congress did not intend to set an impossibly high standard for either the classification or

management of wilderness areas. "Our Nationwide Wilderness Preservation System," 49–50.

6. Section 2(c) of the Wilderness Act requires that an area so classified be "without permanent improvements or human habitation" and that it "generally appears to have been affected primarily by the forces of nature, with the imprint of man's work substantially unnoticeable."

7. The May 1969 directive stated that "Regional Foresters will identify and submit a brief report on unclassified areas which seem to warrant further and more intensive study." See Dave Foreman, "A Little National Forest Roadless Area History," *The Rewilding Institute* 21, April 14, 2008, http://rewilding.org/rewildit/images/21-Forest-Service-Roadless-Areas.pdf.

8. Roth, *Wilderness Movement and the National Forests*, 36.

9. John Hendee, George Stankey, and Robert Lucas give a good overview of the first RARE study in their book *Wilderness Management*, 99–104.

10. Roholt, "Montana Wilderness Study Bill," 116.

11. Additional staff included M. Rupert Cutler, a journalist and Michigan native who became Brandborg's assistant executive director in 1965, and Doug Scott, a Michigan activist who had been recruited by Cutler and who replaced him in 1969. James Turner details some of these organizational changes in *The Promise of Wilderness*, 47–49.

12. Robert A. Rowen to Scott, December 1, 1971, TWS 3/10/1.

13. U.S. Forest Service, *Roadless and Undeveloped Areas*, table 2.

14. Thomas Rickart provides a thorough overview of the RARE program in "Wilderness Land Preservation," 886–97.

15. Evans to Yurich, August 13, 1971, TWS 4/40/2.

16. Alex Sakariassen, "Guarding the Burn," *Missoula (MT) Independent,* July 18, 2011.

17. These and other features are described in Clyde M. Eriksen and Mary Ann Eriksen, "A Proposal for the Study of Wilderness Designation, Pioneer Mountains, Beaverhead County, Montana," December 31, 1970, ERSP 32/3.

18. The lawsuit, Sierra Club, et. al. v. Butz, civil no. 72-1255, 349 F. Supp. 935, (N.D. Calif. 1972), was dismissed and the injunction dissolved on December 11, 1972. Rickart, "Wilderness Land Preservation," 890.

19. The draft RARE recommendations are summarized in U.S. Forest Service, *Proposed New Wilderness Study Areas.*

20. Evans to Sierra Club staff, January 24, 1973, TWS 3/10/3.

21. Saylor's H.R. 19784 (91st Cong., 2nd sess.) included the Lincoln Back Country, Jewel Basin, and Magruder Corridor, among other areas.

22. U.S. Forest Service, *New Wilderness Study Areas.*

23. Aldrich to McGuire, April 5, 1973, TWS 4/40/3.

24. Merritt sent the final list of study areas to Lee Metcalf in a letter dated August 19, 1974 (CMP 5/6). Teddy Roe recalled Lee's reaction in a telephone conversation with the author, June 18, 2012. The development of the Montana Wilderness Study Act is discussed in some detail in Roholt, "Montana Wilderness Study Bill." S. 4066 was reintroduced in the 94th Congress as S. 393.

25. Metcalf also introduced S. 3729, his Great Bear wilderness bill, in the second session of the 93rd Congress. It was reintroduced as S. 392 in the following session.

26. McGuire to Henry M. Jackson, October 4, 1974; McGuire reply, November 13, 1974, both in CMP 5/6.

Chapter 16. The Organization of Spirited People

1. Jim Calvert, memo dated September 9, 1969, GJP 3/19.

2. Jim Calvert, record of meeting held on November 1 and 2, 1969, GJP 3/19.

3. Rahm, "Salmon: River of No Return."

4. Cited in J. M. Herbert to Floyd Iverson, August 15, 1968, Selway-Bitterroot Wilderness History Project, http://sbw.lib.uidaho.edu/pages.html.

5. John A. Morrison, "Big Game Management Problems in Idaho Primitive Areas," Idaho Fish and Game Department, TWS 4/28/17.

6. Wilson to chief, U.S. Forest Service, June 3, 1947, OMP-DPL 4/4.

7. Swift to Zahniser, March 3, 1949, TWS 4/28/16.

8. Sierra Club, "Idaho Primitive Area: Report of Exploration and Reconnaissance May 1964," University of Idaho Library; Morrison, *River of No Return Wilderness*, 8–9.

9. Charles R. Joy, memo to record, April 2, 1968, Selway-Bitterroot Wilderness History Project, http://sbw.lib.uidaho.edu/pages.html.

10. Herbert to Iverson, August 15, 1968, ibid.

11. Iverson to Brandborg, March 17, 1970, TWS 4/28/18.

12. Morrison, "River of No Return Wilderness," ii.

13. Jerry Jayne, notes on formation of River of No Return Wilderness proposal, provided to author via e-mail, July 13, 2012.

14. Jim Deane, interview with Ernie Day, *Living Wilderness* 43 (September 1979): 19–22.

15. Don Aldrich, meeting notes of February 24–25, 1973, TWS 4/28/20.

16. "Forest Service Salmon, Primitive Proposals Criticized as Inadequate," *Idaho State Journal* (Pocatello), February 28, 1973.

17. "Proposed Wilderness Areas near Salmon Add 53,000 Acres to Forest Service Study," *Idaho Falls (ID) Post Register*, January 23, 1973. The new study areas were first identified in the RARE review. They included Clear Creek–Garden Creek (43,264

acres) and Big Deer Creek (9,540 acres), bringing the total study acreage to about 1.6 million acres.

18. "Time for Facts," advertisement in *Idaho State Journal*, November 28, 1973.

19. "Backers of Idaho Wilderness Outnumber Foes by 4-1 Ratio," *Lewiston (ID) Tribune*, December 6, 1973; Merritt to Brigham, December 13, 1973, TWS 4/28/22.

20. Statement of Carl J. Hocevar at Pocatello meeting, November 30, 1973, FHP 2/3.

21. "Idaho Wilderness Heritage at Stake in Three Hearings," *Aberdeen (ID) Times*, November 15, 1973. Tom Davis provided useful background on the River of No Return Wilderness Council in a July 3, 2012, e-mail to the author.

22. Platts and Megahan, "Time Trends," 229–30.

23. Merritt to Crandell, February 15, 1973, TWS 4/28/20. Merritt had been discussing the same issue with Doug Scott as well.

24. Quoted in Bob Johnson, "Salmon Wilderness Classification Draws Support of Few," *Salt Lake Tribune* (Salt Lake City, UT), December 10, 1973.

25. Trueblood, "Forest Service versus the Wilderness Act."

26. Church's statements were presented in his May 1973 constituent newsletter under the heading "How Much Wilderness? A Common Sense Answer" (FCP 152/19).

27. Greg Stahl, "Ernie Day Was Giant of Idaho Conservation," *Idaho Mountain Express* (Sun Valley), February 29, 2008. The first quotation is from Andrus's second inaugural address, cited in "Biographical Sketch of Cecil D. Andrus," Andrus papers, Albertson Library, Boise State University, available at http://library.boisestate.edu/special/andrus/index.shtm.

28. Morache to Church, January 27, 1977, FHP 2/14.

29. Dean Lokken, "Plans Arouse Debate," *Spokane (WA) Daily Chronicle*, November 26, 1973; editorial, *Idaho State Journal*, December 8, 1974; "Andrus Seeks States' Help," *Spokane Daily Chronicle*, November 6, 1975.

30. Scott to Church, August 14, 1973, with follow-up memo to Idaho wilderness cooperators and national leaders, August 29, 1973, both in TWS 4/28/21.

31. Symms's mimeographed statement is in TWS 4/28/22.

32. Church to David Arcano, December 17, 1974, FCP 152/20.

33. Merritt to Crandell, February 24, 1975; Merritt to Brigham, March 2, 1975, both in TWS 4/28/22.

34. Frank Church, letter to constituents, November 4, 1976, FCP 153/2.

Chapter 17. Lee Metcalf and the Politics of Preservation

1. Cecil Garland recollections, Montana Wilderness Association records, Helena, MT.

2. Dale A. Burk, "Concern Grows for 'Wild' Middle Fork River Area," *Missoulian* (Missoula, MT), undated newspaper clipping in LMP 117/9; Middle Fork

Preservation Committee, "Great Bear Wilderness Area," 3–4, University of Idaho Library, Moscow, ID.

3. Jean Warren, testimony on S. 392, TWS 4/41/23.

4. See U.S. Forest Service, *Waters of the Flathead.*

5. Colorado senator Floyd Haskell requested the wilderness study provision. George Alderson (of the Wilderness Society) to Merritt, December 23, 1975, TWS 4/41/22.

6. "Statement of Senator Lee Metcalf on S. 393," May 9, 1975, LMP 662/45.

7. Statement of Royce Satterlee, in U.S. Senate, *Montana Wilderness,* 103, 108–9.

8. Ibid., 118.

9. "Statement of Senator Lee Metcalf on S. 393."

10. Merritt to Doris Milner, May 29, 1975, CMP 5/6.

11. Statement of Hap Kramlich, in U.S. Senate, *Montana Wilderness,* 199.

12. J. D. Holmes, "Wood Products Industry Asks Judge to Oppose Metcalf Bill," *Missoulian,* May 17, 1975.

13. Scott to Judge, May 20, 1975, LMP 557/1.

14. Metcalf to Wambach, June 12, 1975, LMP 557/1.

15. Robert F. Wambach, "Summary of Conclusions for Governor Thomas L. Judge: The Potential Impact of the Montana Wilderness Study Act of 1975, S. 393," LMP 557/1.

16. Merritt to Baucus, November 13, 1975, TWS 4/40/7.

17. Bud Moore, "Sapphire Roadless Area," July 15, 1974, DMP-UMT, box 2, fd. "Sapphire Wilderness."

18. Moore's hopeful statement was premature; in 2000 great swaths of the Sapphires burned in the Bitterroots' worst fire season in human memory.

19. "Statement of John Firebaugh" (on Moose Creek timber sale, 1975); John Firebaugh, report for Montana Fish, Wildlife and Parks Division, n.d., both in DMP-UMT, box 2, fd. "Sapphire Wilderness."

20. Burns to Milner, February 28, 1978, ibid.

21. Stu Burns, comments to Ravalli County Fish and Wildlife Association, March 26, 1973, DMP-UMT, box 11. Burns was the club's president at the time.

22. Burns to Milner, February 28, 1978.

23. Crandell to Melcher, July 22, 1976, TWS 4/40/10. Melcher requested that S. 393 be "vitiated," or recalled, after Mansfield secured its passage (Metcalf was not on the Senate floor that day).

24. Marlenee to Wilbur Anderson (president, Dillon Chamber of Commerce), September 15, 1977, RMCP 1/92.

25. President Carter signed P.L. 95-150, the Montana Wilderness Study Act, into law on November 1, 1977. It provided for nine wilderness study areas: West Pioneer

(151,000 acres), Taylor-Hilgard (289,000), Blue Joint (61,000), Sapphire (94,000), Ten Lakes (34,000), Middle Fork Judith (81,000), Big Snowies (91,000), Hyalite–Porcupine–Buffalo Horn (151,000), and Mount Henry (21,000).

Chapter 18. Timber and the Mountain Fortress

1. Statement of Robert N. Helding, March 1, 1977, in U.S. House of Representatives, *Endangered American Wilderness Act*, 491, table 1; also statement of Forrest Dobson, ibid., 474.

2. Statement of John McBride, ibid., 477.

3. Statement of Don Nettleton, ibid., 473, 511.

4. Doug Scott, memo to "Key Conservation Leaders," March 18, 1974, TWS 4/41/29. NEPA is the National Environmental Policy Act, the law requiring environmental review of major federal decisions affecting the environment.

5. Statements of John McIntire and Jeanette Nolan McIntire, in U.S. Senate, *Montana Wilderness*, 77, 79. The House version of S. 393 did not include Mount Henry.

6. Kelley's statement is from Richard Aarstad, "The J. Neils Lumber Company" (typescript, n.d.), Montana Historical Society files. The combined plan, known as a cooperative sustained-yield unit, operated under a 1944 law that was applied in only a few localities in the West. See Swanson, *Bitterroot and Mr. Brandborg*, 93–94.

7. Statement of Douglas Chadwick, U.S. House of Representatives, *Endangered American Wilderness Act*, 543, 545.

8. Bill Cunningham, notes for speech to Montana Wilderness Association, 2008, provided to author.

9. In a six-month period beginning in June 1971, more than three hundred observations of seven radio-collared elk were made along the Sapphire Mountain divide. Only three of these were made in clear-cut areas or along logging roads; two of those were on roads blocked by snowdrifts. U.S. Forest Service, et al., "Montana Cooperative Elk-Logging Study," 58.

10. Metcalf granted Frank Church his proxy in the conference on the Endangered American Wilderness Act with the proviso that Church would join Oregon senators Mark Hatfield and Bob Packwood in opposing the controversial North Kalmiopsis area in that state (Metcalf to Church, November 29, 1977, LMP 306/3). Such "log-rolling" was commonplace in the final negotiations on such legislation.

11. This was the "Natural Diversity Act," which Metcalf introduced and which gained sixteen cosponsors. The Senate took no action on it. Congress did pass the strip mining bill and the Alaska National Interest Lands Conservation Act, both of which were top priorities for the Sierra Club and Wilderness Society.

12. Statement of Lee Metcalf before Senate Parks and Recreation Subcommittee,

September 20, 1977, LMP 662/4.

13. Mike Comola to Jack Bingham, December 6, 1976, TWS-NRRO, box 1. Bingham was a project coordinator in ASARCO's Wallace, Idaho, office. Linda Comola to Russell Smith, November 16, 1976, ibid.

14. The Comolas related these events at the annual meeting of the Montana Wilderness Association in Kalispell, December 1976, and in conversations with the author.

15. D. Thatcher Hubbard Sr. to C. C. McCall, June 16, 1976, LMP 20/3.

16. Koch to Neal Rahm, October 28, 1968, CMP 3/4; Sierra Club Wilderness Classification Study Committee, "Report to Sierra Club Foundation," January 1972, 52, TWS 3/9/8.

17. Merritt to John Hall, October 31, 1968, TWS 4/40/12. Hall was the assistant executive director of the Wilderness Society.

18. Brandborg to Rahm, October 30, 1968, TWS 4/40/12.

19. Bob Anderson, "Absaroka and Beartooth Primitive Area Study Information Summary," July 1971, 65–66, 102, ERSP 1/11.

20. Notes in Elizabeth Reitell Smith papers, 1/3 and 1/6.

21. Ed Carrell Jr., "Mayor's View," *Livingston (MT) Enterprise*, January 27, 1972; Domasco to Metcalf, January 27, 1975, LMP 4/23; Rate to Steve Yurich, March 30, 1974, ERSP 4/1.

22. News release, Gallatin National Forest, July 21, 1976, ERSP 12/1.

23. S. 1671, June 10, 1977, 95th Cong., 1st sess.

24. Marlenee to Rate, October 18, 1977; R. A. Barker to Metcalf, October 13, 1977, both in ERSP 1/1.

25. Bill Cunningham to Bob Anderson and others, October 9, 1977, ERSP 1/1.

26. "Lee Metcalf, Consumer, Education Advocate, Dies," *Washington Post*, January 13, 1978.

27. Brower, "Lee Metcalf, 1911–1978."

28. Marlenee to Russell J. Warchola, March 31, 1978, RMCP 16/7.

Chapter 19. RARE Redone

1. H.R. 8745, 95th Cong., 1st sess.

2. Marlenee's statement is from a form letter sent in response to pro-wilderness letters from constituents (RMCP 16/7).

3. The Sagebrush Rebellion dates to 1979, when the Nevada state legislature passed a resolution calling for the transfer of BLM lands to the states (Cawley, *Federal Land, Western Anger*, ix, 14). It had much older antecedents, including the so-called stockmen's bills of the 1940s and 1950s.

4. Scott to Marita, July 25, 1974; Scott to Sierra Club and Wilderness Society staff,

September 10, 1974, both in TWS 3/10/12.

5. Karr, "Forests for the People," 121–22.

6. Statement of Rupert Cutler, in U.S. House of Representatives, *Endangered American Wilderness Act*, 96–98. Cutler recalled later that he came up with the idea for RARE II while testifying before Roncalio's committee. During the hearing "it became embarrassingly clear that the Forest Service had insufficient data on its roadless areas. . . . After checking over my shoulder with Chief John McGuire as to whether his agency could do such a review and getting an affirmative answer, I told the House subcommittee the Forest Service would review the whole National Forest system for its wilderness potential within two years." "Father of RARE II Shares History," Friends of Allegheny Wilderness newsletter, June 2011, http://www.pawild.org/fawn/faw_v11n02.pdf.

7. Dale Burk, "Timber Industry Wanted Roadless Area Review," *Missoulian* (Missoula, MT), July 21, 1977.

8. Karr, "Forests for the People," 132.

9. Ibid.

10. U.S. Forest Service, *RARE II: Draft Environmental Statement*, 4. Region 1 figures are from a computer printout entitled "Percent of Total National Forest System Area in Recommended Final Inventory," TWS-NRRO, box 10. Acreage totals vary depending on whether the count includes "gross acres" (9,368,445) or "net acres" (which exclude private inholdings) (8,989,232).

11. The inventoried RARE areas comprised 105 of the 242 ecosystems delineated in Robert G. Bailey's *Ecoregions of the United States* (cited in U.S. Forest Service, *RARE II: Draft Environmental Statement*, 13, 14). State-by-state employment losses are displayed in a table on p. 103 of the RARE II Draft EIS.

12. Don Schwennesen, "Conservationists Unveil RARE 'Alternative W,'" *Missoulian*, August 30, 1978.

13. Industry recommendations are from Inland Forest Resource Council, "1979 Unaudited RARE II Wilderness Recommendations" (table), March 15, 1983, courtesy of Bill Cunningham.

14. Karr, "Forests for the People," 62.

15. U.S. Forest Service, *RARE II: Final Environmental Statement*, i, appendix J.

16. Ibid., appendix G.

17. News release, Montana Wilderness Association, April 1979, TWS-NRRO, box 10.

18. Inland Forest Resource Council, "A Forest Products Industry Alternative," January 29, 1979, courtesy of Bill Cunningham.

19. News release from Wilderness Society, Friends of the Earth, and Sierra Club, April 1979, TWS-NRRO, box 10.

20. "Administration Changes to RARE II Final EIS," April 16, 1979, TWS 3/10/3. Doug Scott's telegram to Cutler is the author's recollection.

21. "RARE II—The Results," memo from Citizens for America's Endangered Wilderness, January 1979, TWS-NRRO, box 10.

22. Roth, *Wilderness Movement and the National Forests*, 59. The case was California v. Bergland, 483 F. Supp. 465. In 1982 the appeals court for the Ninth Circuit generally upheld the decision in California v. Block, 690 F.2d 753.

23. "Background Information—Federal Court Ruling in California concerning Forest Service RARE II decision," 1979, TWS-NRRO, box 10.

24. Nationwide about 2.8 million acres of RARE II roadless lands have been developed through timber harvest, road building, or other uses since 1979. Nie, "Administrative Rulemaking," 699.

25. Keegan, Fiedler, and Dillon, *Montana Challenge*, 9, fig. 7.

26. Dave Foreman, memo to Celia Hunter and others, June 11, 1977, CMP 9/3.

27. Cunningham and Comola to conservation leaders, December 1, 1978, TWS-NRRO, box 10, fd. "RARE II."

Chapter 20. Negotiating a Wilderness

1. Brigham to Church, November 19, 1976, FHP 5/44.

2. Sam McNeill to Brigham, January 14, 1976; Greenley to Church, March 4, 1976, both in FHP 5/4. McNeill was a regional game manager for the Idaho Fish and Game Department.

3. Whitfield to "Forest Supervisors and Staff Directors," June 23, 1976, SCNRC 2/2.

4. Brigham to Biddison, April 25, 1975, SCNRC 2/14; Scott to Greenley, July 2, 1976, FHP 6/1.

5. Fred Hutchison, "Land Use Planning within the Gospel-Hump Area," background statement for Senator Frank Church, FHP 5/44.

6. MacKenzie to Church, March 21, 1977, FHP 6/1.

7. Scott to Baird, Brigham, and Lechefsky, March 27, 1977, SCNRC box 10, fd. "Gospel Hump."

8. Dennis Baird, interview by author, Moscow, ID, September 13, 2012; Larry LaRocco, memo to Fred Hutchison, March 28, 1977, FHP 6/2.

9. Baird to Church, March 23, 1977; Lechefsky, telegram to Church, May 11, 1977, both in FHP 6/1; Blewett to Church, April 13, 1977; Brigham to Evans, May 2, 1977, both in FHP 6/1.

10. "Mine Leader Attacks Closed Door," *Northern Idaho Press* (Wallace, ID), May 18, 1977; Baird interview, September 13, 2012.

11. Church's bill was offered as an amendment to S. 1180, 95th Cong., 1st sess. (see U.S.

Senate Committee on Energy and Natural Resources, *Gospel-Hump Wilderness Area*, 6–11). McClure's S. 2035 called for a wilderness study of a 220,000-acre core area.

12. MacKenzie to Symms, August 11, 1977, FCP 153/10.

13. Statements of Dennis Baird, Douglas Scott, and Mort Brigham, in U.S. Senate Committee on Energy and Natural Resources, *Gospel-Hump Wilderness Area*, 49, 55, 63; MacKenzie to Symms, August 11, 1977, FCP 153/10. Historian Sara Dant called the Gospel-Hump agreement an example of Frank Church's pragmatism in dealing with wilderness issues in his home state. She describes Church meeting with Dennis Baird, Mort Brigham, Dan Lechefsky, and Doug Scott in a Lewiston motel room "down on his hands and knees . . . poring over maps of central Idaho" to hammer out the compromise. Baird noted that at a negotiation session in Grangeville, "half the sheriff's department" stood outside to discourage violence from armed "militia types." Dant, "Making Wilderness Work," 237, 261.

14. Statement of C. L. "Butch" Otter, in U.S. Senate Committee on Energy and Natural Resources, *Gospel-Hump Wilderness Area*, 163–64.

15. Brigham to Church, August 30, 1977, FCP 153/11.

16. See Baird, Maughan, and Nilson, "Mediating the Idaho Wilderness Controversy."

17. Roselle, *Tree Spiker*, 163. During the August 24 hearing, Doug Scott specified that the compromise did not apply to the "Dixie Tail" area where the later Cove-Mallard timber sales were located. It remained an issue, however, in the ongoing negotiations over the central Idaho wilderness bills.

18. Trueblood recounted his August 18, 1977, conversation in an October 12, 1977, letter to Church, TTC 1/11. Trueblood's fears about Church were expressed in a January 7, 1978, note intended for Doug Scott, which he did not mail (RNRWC 1/14). The note nonetheless displayed his worries about whether the wilderness council could achieve its 2.3-million-acre proposal.

Chapter 21. Mountains and Rivers without End

1. "River Rafts, Equipment Readied for Carter's Salmon River Run," *Spokane (WA) Spokesman-Review*, August 28, 1978.

2. Scott to Fred Hutchison, December 21, 1976, in Ted Trueblood, memo to directors of River of No Return Wilderness Council, January 6, 1977, TTC 1/4.

3. Statement of Norm Guth, in U.S. Senate Committee on Energy and Natural Resources, *River of No Return Wilderness Proposals*, 919–20.

4. U.S. Forest Service, *Draft Environmental Statement for the Beartrap-Dutchler Planning Unit*, 3, 6, 16, 117–18.

5. Church to McGuire, May 14, 1974, FHP 2/3.

6. Theodore Hoff Jr., "Statement on Salmon River Wilderness and Salmon Wild and

Scenic River" [1975], FCP 152/20.

7. "Sawmill to Close," *Spokesman-Review*, August 11, 1976; "Mill Shutdown Blame Leveled," *Spokane Daily Chronicle*, August 23, 1976; "Timber Offer Unlikely to Stop Mill Closure," *Kennewick (WA) Tri-City Herald*, October 6, 1976.

8. Statement of Harry Adams in U.S. Senate Committee on Energy and Natural Resources, *Roadless Areas in Central Idaho*, 53.

9. Statement of Jim Hardin, Wickes Forest Industries, ibid, 69–72.

10. Statement of Dan Lechefsky, ibid. Church's comment was in response to the statement of Jean Nelson of Kooskia, Idaho, who headed a local chapter of Outdoors Unlimited (ibid., 15).

11. Dana Howard, "Church Hopes for Fast Wilderness Action," *Idaho Falls (ID) Post Register*, December 18, 1978.

12. U.S. Senate Committee on Energy and Natural Resources, *River of No Return Wilderness Proposals*, pt. 1, 32–33.

13. Ibid., 95–96.

14. Ibid., 50–53, 76.

15. Ibid., 84.

16. Mimeo to "Friends of the River of No Return Wilderness," RNRWC 2/8; Trueblood statement, U.S. Senate Committee on Energy and Natural Resources, *River of No Return Wilderness Proposals*, pt. 3, 926.

17. Baird to Church, October 12, 1979, FCP 154/14.

18. J. Allen Overton Jr. (of the American Mining Congress) to Church, April 24, 1980, HCP 7/10.

19. Church to Philip Lindstrom (of the Hecla Mining Co.), December 1, 1979, FCP 154/16; William O. Hickey to John Seiberling, April 15, 1980, HCP 7/10.

20. Frank Church constituent letter, December 1979, FCP 154/14. The relevant Senate Committee on Energy and Natural Resources report is *River of No Return Wilderness: Report to Accompany S. 2009.*

21. Frank Church, remarks upon introduction of Endangered American Wilderness Act, *Congressional Record* 122, June 29, 1976; Books, "Interview with Senator Frank Church."

22. James Hagengruber, "N. Idaho Wilderness Proposal Gets Push," *Spokesman-Review*, October 28, 2006.

Chapter 22. Watershed Moments

1. Dale Burk recalled Ken Bohlig in a eulogy he gave at the Montana Wilderness Association's convention in Kalispell in December 1976. Richard Smith recalled the search efforts in a conversation with the author while on the Salmon River in April 1977. Other recollections are the author's from conversations with Bohlig in 1974 and 1975.

2. Williams to Joan Montagne, December 21, 1979, Montagne files. The bill was H.R. 5344, 96th Cong., 1st sess.

3. Heffner, Duckett, and Kirkpatrick, *Decision by Default*, 13; Michael J. Lyngholm, "A Report on the Local Lumber Industry and How It Can Survive," ibid., B-19.

4. Koch to Merritt and Francis Walcott, April 10, 1972, CMP 34/10.

5. Pat Williams, oral history interview by Bill Cunningham, Special Collections and Archives, University of Montana, OH 362-1, side 1; Bill Cunningham, interview by author, June 11, 2011.

6. Montana Department of Fish, Wildlife and Parks, *Montana Wilderness Synopsis*, 6–7.

7. Cunningham to MWA governing council, April 12, 1980, TWS 4/43/22.

8. Larry Wills, "Wilderness on the Edge," *Spokane (WA) Spokesman-Review*, May 28, 1984.

9. Albert Borgmann to Brandborg, July 10, 1974, TWS 4/40/4; Sherry Hodges, "Wilderness Opponents Give Udall an Earful," *Missoulian* (Missoula, MT), March 22, 1980.

10. Rattlesnake National Recreation Area and Wilderness Act, P.L. 96-476, October 19, 1980.

11. The Hayakawa-Helms bill was S. 842, while Williams's was H.R. 2392, 97th Cong., 1st sess.

12. Cunningham to MWA council, May 31, 1980, TWS 4/40/26.

13. CHEC (Cascade Holistic Economic Consultants), "Review of the Beaverhead Forest Plan," May 1986, personal files of Bill Cunningham. O'Toole discussed the Beaverhead case in his book *Reforming the Forest Service*, 3–5.

14. Barlow et al., *Giving Away the National Forests*.

15. D. Roscoe Nickerson, "Timber Sales Could Wreck the Big Hole," *Montana Standard* (Butte), July 15, 1984.

16. Jim Welch, news release, July 10, 1984, Cunningham files.

17. "Sportsmen, Melcher Fight over Road," *Great Falls (MT) Tribune*, September 24, 1984; petition from North Big Hole ranchers, Cunningham files; Ralph Nichols, quoted in "Big Hole Mailslide," *Helena (MT) Independent Record*, August 8, 1984; Melcher to Ellen Knight, September 7, 1984, Cunningham files.

18. Williams interview, OH-362-1, side 2. The Forest Service released its West Pioneer study in August 1980. U.S. Forest Service, *Proposal and Report*.

Chapter 23. The Last Wilderness

1. "Summary, Forest Service Statement on Jack Creek, Bozeman, Montana, December 11, 1969," LMP 41/5.

2. The development of the Big Sky Resort is covered in Lyle Johnston's biography of newscaster Chet Huntley (*"Good Night, Chet,"* 129–46), and in Rick Graetz, "Big

Sky Resort," *Helena (MT) Independent Record*, February 24, 2000.

3. Cecil Garland, statement on S. 1849 (Spanish Peaks), CGP 3/5.

4. Peggy McLaughlin to Rolf Y. H. Olson, January 30, 1978, LMP 306/2.

5. Brock to Butz, September 22, 1975, LMP 557/1.

6. Jaedicke and Seidl to Vander Myde and John R. McGuire, July 16, 1976, LMP 20/3.

7. Behan, *Plundered Promise*, 35. The Northern Pacific land grant had multiple reper-
cussions in the Northern Rockies, including BNI's eventual spinoff of its timber
holdings to Champion International (later Plum Creek Lumber), which cut them
heavily in the 1980s.

8. C. R. Binger to James R. Wolf, April 21, 1977, TWS-NRRO, box 2. Binger was president of BNI's resources division, while Wolf was a concerned stockholder from
Rockville, Maryland.

9. Thomas Kotynski, "Melcher's Land-Swap Measure Seen as 'Hit and Run' Legislation," *Great Falls (MT) Tribune*, October 14, 1978.

10. Montana Wilderness Association, "Preliminary Proposal for a Special Nonmech-
anized Winter Recreation Area on and Adjacent to Mt. Hebgen," June 1975, LMP
23/2.

11. Bill Cunningham, activity report for October 1976, CMP 5/4.

12. Melcher, Baucus, and Williams to Coston, November 26, 1979; Cunningham to
Joan Montagne (and ten others), both courtesy of Joan Montagne.

13. Melcher's amendment was adopted as sec. 1323 of P.L. 96-487.

14. In Montana Wilderness Association v. United States (U.S. Court of Appeals, Ninth
Circuit, 655 F.2d 951), the appeals court decided that Congress intended Melcher's
amendment to apply to the entire national forest system.

15. U.S. Forest Service, *Proposal and Report*, map depicting Alternative D.

16. "Statement of Dr. John Craighead on the Proposed Taylor-Hilgard Wilderness
Area, Dillon, Montana, November 5, 1980," ERSP 23/2.

17. Sierra Club Wilderness Classification Study Committee, report on Taylor-Hilgard
area, 61, TWS 3/9/8; Merritt to Grace Miller, n.d., TWS 4/43/18.

18. The Madison-Gallatin Alliance presented its wilderness proposal in a tabloid publication titled "The Lee Metcalf Wilderness Proposal," dated June 1980, courtesy of
Joan Montagne.

19. Cunningham to Baucus, January 12, 1980, ERSP 23/2.

20. Rocky Barker, "Sheridan, Craigheads Invent Greater Yellowstone," http://www.
rockybarker.com/yelhist.html. See also Clark and Zaunbrecher, "Greater Yellowstone Ecosystem," 8–9.

21. John Melcher supported a much smaller land trade with BNI that would consoli-
date private lands in Jack Creek in exchange for railroad lands farther south in the

Taylor Peaks area, but not in Buck Creek. Preservation interests said this would
swap timbered public lands for high-elevation private lands that were unlikely to be
developed in any event. Cunningham to Benson, November 16, 1979, courtesy of
Joan Montagne.

22. Madison-Gallatin Alliance newsletter, July/August 1981, ERSP 23/2.

23. S. 2210, 97th Cong., 2nd sess., February 11, 1982. On the same day, Melcher introduced bills to create special "management areas" in the Elkhorn Mountains (S. 2111)
and the West Pioneers (S. 2112) as looser substitutes for wilderness designation.

24. "Baucus's Disappointment Horsefeathers—Melcher," *Billings (MT) Gazette*, February 14, 1982.

25. "Metcalf Wilderness Bill Ready for a Vote," *Missoulian* (Missoula, MT), September 23, 1982; "Metcalf's Widow Criticizes Proposed Bill," *Great Falls (MT) Tribune*,
November 1, 1982.

26. Madison-Gallatin Alliance newsletter, January/February 1983, courtesy of Joan
Montagne.

27. The law was P.L. 98-140.

28. Madison-Gallatin Alliance newsletter, January/February 1983.

Chapter 24. Deadlock

1. Marlenee to Lance A. Olsen, May 9, 1980, and to John and Jeanette McIntire, October 15, 1981, RMCP 16/7; Dennis Swibold, "Melcher Speaks Out," *Bozeman (MT)
Daily Chronicle*, September 25, 1984.

2. Wilderness acreages in Idaho and Montana: Gorte, *Wilderness: Overview and Statistics*, tables 4 and 5; Idaho citizen recommendations: Dennis Baird, Maughan, and
Nilson, "Mediating the Idaho Wilderness Controversy," 232.

3. Michael McCloskey and Desautels, "Primer on Wilderness Law and Policy." Udall
was chair of the House Interior Committee. John Crowell's announcement was in
response to the Ninth Circuit Court's decision in *California v. Block*, which required
further analysis of nonselected roadless areas in that state.

4. "Agreement Reached in Wilds Dispute," *Salt Lake City (UT) Deseret News*, May 3,
1984. James Turner calls the release-for-wilderness trade-off "a major shift in how
wilderness legislation was negotiated." *Promise of Wilderness*, 199.

5. Testimony from U.S. Senate Committee on Energy and Natural Resources, *Montana Wilderness*.

6. Statement of Hadley B. Roberts, in U.S. Senate Committee on Energy and Natural
Resources, *Idaho Wilderness*, 681–82.

7. Statement of David Little, ibid., 25.

8. The Idaho figures did not include the RARE II lands that were made part of the

River of No Return Wilderness.

9. Statement of Bill Cunningham, U.S. Senate Committee on Energy and Natural Resources, *Montana Wilderness*, 56; Ed Madej, interview by author, Helena, MT, September 29, 2011.

10. Pat Williams, oral history interview by Bill Cunningham, May 12, 1997, Special Collections and Archives, University of Montana, OH 362-1, side 2.

11. Steve Shirley, "Wilderness Supporters Castigated," *Helena (MT) Independent Record*, July 14, 1984. The bills were S. 2850 and H.R. 6001, 98th Cong., 2nd sess.

12. "Wildlands Bill Blasted Again," *Spokane (WA) Spokesman-Review*, July 12, 1984; Curtis to Williams, July 10, 1984, personal collection of Bill Cunningham.

13. Cunningham to Williams, July 19, 1984, personal collection of Bill Cunningham; "Wilderness Bill Changes Warned Against," *Independent Record*, July 15, 1984; Steve Shirley, "Young Wilderness Bill Sparks 'Real Dilemma,'" *Independent Record*, July 15, 1984.

14. Ed Madej, interview by author, Helena, MT, September 29, 2011.

15. McClure's bill was S. 2457, the Idaho Forest Management Act of 1984. Craig's companion measure was H.R. 5425, 98th Cong., 1st sess.

16. U.S. Senate Committee on Energy and Natural Resources, *Idaho Forest Management Act of 1984*, 117, 270.

17. Sherry Devlin, "Wilderness Issue Draws Symms' Fire," *Spokane (WA) Chronicle*, August 24, 1984.

18. Clark Collins, "A Chronology of the BlueRibbon Coalition," BlueRibbon Coalition, Inc., http://www.sharetrails.org/magazine/article/chronology-blueribbon-coalition.

19. Rick Johnson, "Jim McClure," *Idaho Conservation League* (blog), February 28, 2011, http://www.idahoconservation.org/blog/2011-blog-archive/jim-mcclure.

20. Johnson and Slater, "Central Idaho Economic Development."

21. Dennis Baird, Maughan, and Nilson, "Mediating the Idaho Wilderness Controversy," 232.

22. Statement of Tom Hurlock, U.S. Senate Committee on Energy and Natural Resources, *Montana Wilderness*, 33.

23. Statement of Jack Hirschy, March 22, 1988, personal collection of Bill Cunningham.

24. Statement of Clayton Huntley, March 22, 1988, ibid.

25. "Wilderness Consensus 'Fails,'" *Billings (MT) Gazette*, April 16, 1987. Marlenee's remarks are from his notes for the markup session on September 9, 1987, RMCP 195/5.

26. Ron Marlenee, statement before Senate Energy and Natural Resources Committee, March 22, 1988, RMCP 195/6.

27. Calkin, *Historic Resource Production*, table 5; Keegan et al., *Montana's Forest Products*

Industry. Montana timber industry employment rebounded to 12,000 by 1984 as the recession eased and the industry diversified into other fields such as log homes.

28. Richard Manning's *Last Stand* discusses Champion International and the timber wars in western Montana.

29. Michael Jamison, "Tester Wilderness Bill Product of Years of Local Effort," *Missoulian* (Missoula, MT), August 1, 2009.

30. Dennis Baird, Maughan, and Nilson, "Mediating the Idaho Wilderness Controversy," 232–39.

31. Ibid.

Chapter 25. Visions of the Wild Rockies

1. Conrad Burns, news release, April 7, 1990, RMCP 194/10; MWA news release, November 19, 1991, and Sieger to Sen. Dale Bumpers, November 19, 1991, RMCP 195/1. Baucus's bill was S. 2403, the Montana Interim Roadless Lands Release and Conservation Act of 1990; Burns's was S. 2235, the Montana Federal Lands Management Act of 1990. John Mumma resigned in the face of pressure from Washington to increase allowable cuts. Wilkinson, *Crossing the Next Meridian*, 152.

2. Bader, "Wild Rockies Ecosystem Protection Act."

3. Ibid.

4. John J. Craighead (and eleven others) to Sen. Dale Bumpers, October 11, 1991, personal collection of Bill Cunningham.

5. Noss et al., "Conservation Biology."

6. Clif Merritt, note to Dallas and Fae Eklund, December 15, 1992, CMP 3/7.

7. Karen Coates and Randi Erickson, "Four Protesters Arrested at Baucus' Missoula Office," *Montana Kaimin* (Missoula), February 11, 1992.

8. Sherry Devlin, "Williams Unmoved by Rally's Demands," *Missoulian* (Missoula, MT), January 29, 1992.

9. Natalie Shapiro, "Looking Back on Cove-Mallard," *Clearwater Defender* (Friends of the Clearwater newsletter), Fall 2012.

10. Bills introduced in the 103rd Congress by the Montana and Idaho delegations were S. 2125 (Burns), S. 2137 (Baucus), H.R. 2473 (Williams), and H.R. 1570 (LaRocco).

11. Maloney's NREPA bill was H.R. 2638.

12. Statement of John Craighead, in U.S. Senate, *Northern Rockies Ecosystem Protection Act*, 34–35. Craighead's concept of holistic resource management is not to be confused with Allan Savory's range management method, which bears the same name.

13. Montana Wilderness Association, *Legislating the Wild* (brochure), CMP 4/3.

14. Julie Cart, "Critics Fear Energy Plan Will Tame a Wild Land," *Los Angeles Times*, November 9, 2003.

15. Martin Nie examines the roadless area rule from a policy-making standpoint in "Administrative Rulemaking and Public Lands Conflict." He argues that "Congress ought to intervene and resolve what are essentially value- and interest-based political conflicts over public land management." James Turner looks at the political development of the rule in *The Promise of Wilderness*, 351–61.

16. S. 37 (formerly S. 268 and S. 1470), 113th Cong., 1st sess. In December 2013 the Senate Energy and Natural Resources Committee favorably reported the bill with certain amendments. At the time of writing (July 2014) it had not passed the full Senate.

17. Bill Worf, "Gutting the Forest Service Is Not the Solution," *New West*, http://www.newwest.net/main/article/usfs_retiree_on_tester_bill_gutting_the_usfs_is_not_the_solution/; Stewart Brandborg, "Tester Bill Threatens Wild Northern Rockies," *Missoulian*, March 8, 2010; Matthew Koehler, interview by author, Missoula, MT, June 16, 2011.

18. Michael Jamison, "Tester Wilderness Bill Product of Years of Local Effort," *Missoulian*, August 1, 2009.

19. John McCarthy, interview by Bruce Reichert, summer 2011, "The People's Land," Idaho Public Television, http://www.idahoptv.org/outdoors/shows/thepeoplesland/johnMcCarthy.cfm; Gary Macfarlane, "U.S. Forest Service Must Follow the Law," *Moscow-Pullman (ID) Daily News*, March 18, 2013, http://dnews.com/opinion/article_1207ba0f-0a26-5e2d-a44f-ac89653a0672.html (subscription required).

20. Olaus J. Murie, "Inspiration in Wilderness," talk given to Northwest Wilderness Conference, Seattle, WA, March 1958, OMP-MC.

Bibliography

Manuscript Collections

BEP   Brock Evans Papers, University of Washington Library, Seattle, Washington

CGP   Cecil Garland Papers, Archives and Special Collections, Maureen and Mike Mansfield Library, University of Montana, Missoula, Montana

CMP   Clifton R. Merritt Papers, Archives and Special Collections, Maureen and Mike Mansfield Library, University of Montana, Missoula, Montana

DMP-UI   Doris Milner Papers, Special Collections and Archives, University of Idaho Library, Moscow, Idaho

DMP-UMT   Doris Milner Papers, Archives and Special Collections, Maureen and Mike Mansfield Library, University of Montana, Missoula, Montana

ERSP   Elizabeth Reitell Smith Papers, Archives and Special Collections, Maureen and Mike Mansfield Library, University of Montana, Missoula, Montana

FCP   Frank Church Papers, Special Collections and Archives, Albertsons Library, Boise State University, Boise, Idaho

FHP   Fred H. Hutchison Papers, Special Collections and Archives, Albertsons Library, Boise State University, Boise, Idaho

GJP   Gerald A. Jayne Papers, Special Collections and Archives, University of Idaho Library, Moscow, Idaho

HCP   Harry Crandell Papers, Denver Public Library, Denver, Colorado

HJP   Holway R. Jones Papers, Special Collections and University Archives, University of Oregon Libraries, Eugene, Oregon

LBCPA   Lincoln Back Country Protective Association Records, Archives and Special Collections, Maureen and Mike Mansfield Library, University of Montana, Missoula, Montana

LMP   Lee Metcalf Papers, Montana Historical Society, Helena, Montana

MHS   Montana Historical Society Research Center, Helena, Montana

MMP   Mike Mansfield Papers, Archives and Special Collections, Maureen and Mike Mansfield Library, University of Montana, Missoula, Montana

NAS   National Archives, Pacific Alaska Region, Seattle, Washington

OMP-DPL   Olaus J. Murie Papers, Denver Public Library Conservation Collection, Denver, Colorado

OMP-MC   Olaus J. Murie Papers, Murie Center Archives, Moose, Wyoming

RMCP   Ron Marlenee Congressional Papers, Montana State University Library, Bozeman, Montana

RNRWC   River of No Return Wilderness Council Records, Special Collections and Archives, University of Idaho Library, Moscow, Idaho

SBP   Stewart Brandborg Papers, Archives and Special Collections, Maureen and Mike Mansfield Library, University of Montana, Missoula, Montana

SCNRC   Sierra Club Northern Rockies Chapter Records, Special Collections and Archives, University of Idaho Library, Moscow, Idaho

TTC   Ted Trueblood Collection, Special Collections and Archives, Albertsons Library, Boise State University, Boise, Idaho

TWS   The Wilderness Society Records, Denver Public Library, Denver, Colorado

TWS-NRRO   The Wilderness Society–Northern Rockies Regional Office Records, Montana Historical Society, Helena, Montana

American Forest Products Industries. *Proceedings, Forest Land Use Conference*, Washington, D.C., September 21–22, 1961. Washington, D.C.: American Forest Products Industries, 1961.

Bader, Mike. "The Wild Rockies Ecosystem Protection Act: A New Approach to Ecosystems Protection." *Words on Wilderness* (Wilderness Institute, University of Montana, 1991): 10–11.

Bailey, Robert G. *Ecoregions of the United States*. Washington, D.C.: USDA Forest Service, 1976.

Baird, Dennis, and Lynn Baird. "A Campfire Vision: Establishing the Idaho Primitive Area." *Journal of the West* 26 (July 1987): 50–58.

Baird, Dennis, Ralph Maughan, and Douglas Nilson. "Mediating the Idaho Wilderness Controversy." In *Mediating Environmental Conflicts: Theory and Practice*, edited by

J. Walton Blackburn and Willa M. Bruce, 229–45. Westport, CT: Quorum Books, 1995.

Baird, Lynn, and Dennis Baird, eds. *In Nez Perce Country: Accounts of the Bitterroots and the Clearwater after Lewis and Clark.* Moscow: University of Idaho Library, 2003.

Baker, Robert D., Larry Burt, Robert S. Maxwell, Victor H. Treat, and Henry C. Dethloff. *The National Forests of the Northern Region: Living Legacy.* College Station, TX: Intaglio, 1993.

Baker, Robert N. "Clif Merritt and Wilderness Wildlife: Learning How to Live in Paradise." Master's thesis, University of Montana, 2005.

Baker, William R. "Indians and Fire in the Rocky Mountains: The Wilderness Hypothesis Revisited." In *Fire, Native Peoples, and the Natural Landscape,* edited by Thomas R. Vale, 41–76. Washington, D.C.: Island Press, 2002.

Barlow, Thomas, Gloria Helfand, Trent Orr, and Thomas Stoel Jr. *Giving Away the National Forests—An Analysis of U.S. Forest Service Timber Sales below Cost.* Natural Resources Defense Council, 1980.

Behan, Richard W. "The Lincoln Back Country Controversy: A Case Study in Natural Resource Policy Formation and Administration." Missoula: School of Forestry, University of Montana, 1969.

———. *Plundered Promise: Capitalism, Politics, and the Fate of the National Forests.* Washington, D.C.: Island Press, 2001.

Bolle, Arnold W. "The Bitterroot Revisited: A University [Re]View of the Forest Service." In *American Forests: Nature, Culture, and Politics,* edited by Char Miller, 163–76. Lawrence: University Press of Kansas, 1997.

Books, Dave. "An Interview with Senator Frank Church." *Western Wildlands* 4 (Fall 1977): 2–5.

Brigham, Morton R. "Proposed St. Joe Wilderness." *Living Wilderness* 33 (Summer 1969): 15–18.

Broome, Harvey. *Faces of the Wilderness.* Missoula, MT: Mountain Press, 1972.

Brower, David R. "Lee Metcalf, 1911–1978." *Not Man Apart,* March 1978.

Buchholz, C. W. *Man in Glacier.* West Glacier, MT: Glacier Natural History Association, 1976.

Burk, Dale A. *Great Bear, Wild River.* Eureka, MT: Stoneydale Press, 1977.

Caldwell, Harry H., and Cornelius Visser. "Tourist Packer Services in Primitive Areas." *Land Economics* 29, no. 4 (November 1953): 351–56.

Calkin, David. *Historic Resource Production from USDA Forest Service Northern and Intermountain Region Lands.* Research Note PNW-RN-540. Portland, OR: USDA Forest Service, Pacific Northwest Research Station, 1999.

Cavallo, Dominick. *A Fiction of the Past: The Sixties in American History.* New York: St.

Martin's Press, 1999.

Cawley, R. *Federal Land, Western Anger: The Sagebrush Rebellion and Environmental Politics.* Lawrence: University Press of Kansas, 1993.

Chadwick, Douglas. *A Beast the Color of Winter: The Mountain Goat Observed.* San Francisco: Sierra Club Books, 1983.

CHEC (Cascade Holistic Economic Consultants). "Review of the Beaverhead Forest Plan and Final Environmental Statement: A CHEC Forest Plan Review." Eugene, OR: CHEC, 1986.

Childers, Michael W. *Colorado Powder Keg: Ski Resorts and the Environmental Movement.* Lawrence: University Press of Kansas, 2012.

Clark, Tim W., and Dusty Zaunbrecher. "The Greater Yellowstone Ecosystem: The Ecosystem Concept in Natural Resource Policy and Management." *Renewable Resources Journal* 5, no. 3 (Summer 1987): 8–16.

Cosco, Jon M. *Echo Park: Struggle for Preservation.* Boulder, CO: Johnson Books, 1995.

Costley, Richard J. "An Enduring Resource." *American Forests* 75, no. 6 (June 1972): 8–11.

Cunningham, William P. "The Magruder Corridor Controversy: A Case History." Master's thesis, University of Montana, 1968.

Dant, Sara. "Making Wilderness Work: Frank Church and the American Wilderness Movement." *Pacific Historical Review* 77 (2008): 237–72.

DeVoto, Bernard. *The Easy Chair.* Boston: Houghton Mifflin, 1955.

Dilsaver, Larry M., and William Wyckoff. "Failed National Parks in the Last Best Place." *Montana: The Magazine of Western History* 59, no. 3 (Autumn 2009): 3–24.

Ewert, Sara E. Dant. "Evolution of an Environmentalist: Senator Frank Church and the Hells Canyon Controversy." *Montana: The Magazine of Western History* 51 (Spring 2001): 36–51.

Foreman, Dave, and Howie Wolke. *The Big Outside: A Descriptive Inventory of the Big Wilderness Areas of the U.S.* Tucson, AZ: Ned Ludd Books, 1989.

Fox, Stephen. *The American Conservation Movement: John Muir and His Legacy.* Madison: University of Wisconsin, 1981.

Friedrich, C. Allan. *Factors Contributing to the 1953 Floods in the Vicinity of Great Falls, Montana.* Research Note No. 122. Missoula, MT: USDA Forest Service, Northern Rocky Mountain Forest and Range Experiment Station, 1953.

Gilligan, James P. "The Development of Policy and Administration of Forest Service Primitive and Wilderness Areas in the Western United States." 2 vols. PhD diss., University of Michigan, 1953.

Glover, James M. *A Wilderness Original: The Life of Bob Marshall.* Seattle: Mountaineers, 1986.

Gorte, Ross W. *Wilderness: Overview and Statistics*. Congressional Research Service Report No. 94-976 ENR. Washington, D.C.: The Service, 1994.

Harvey, Mark W. T. "Battle for Dinosaur: Echo Park Dam and the Birth of the Wilderness Movement." *Montana: The Magazine of Western History* 45 (Spring 1995): 32–45.

———. *Wilderness Forever: Howard Zahniser and the Path to the Wilderness Act*. Seattle: University of Washington Press, 2007.

Hays, Samuel P. *Conservation and the Gospel of Efficiency: The Progressive Conservation Movement, 1890–1920*. Pittsburgh: University of Pittsburgh Press, 1999. First published 1959 by Harvard University Press.

Heffner, Robert A., Sharon Duckett, and Gary Kirkpatrick. *Decision by Default: The Southwest Montana Mill Crisis*. Helena: Montana Dept. of Commerce, 1989.

Hendee, John C., George H. Stankey, and Robert C. Lucas. *Wilderness Management*. Miscellaneous Publication No. 1365. Washington, D.C.: USDA Forest Service, 1978.

Hirt, Paul W. *A Conspiracy of Optimism: Management of the National Forests since World War Two*. Lincoln: University of Nebraska Press, 1994.

Holsten, E. H., R. W. Thier, A. S. Munson, and K. E. Gibson. *The Spruce Beetle*. Forest Insect and Disease Leaflet 127. Washington, D.C.: USDA Forest Service, 1999.

Hutchison, S. Blair, and Paul D. Kemp. *Forest Resources of Montana*. Forest Resources Report No. 5. Missoula, MT: USDA Forest Service, Northern Rocky Mountain Experiment Station, 1952.

Johnson, Rick, and Lindsay Slater. "Central Idaho Economic Development and Recreation Act of 2005." In *Collaborative Conservation Strategies: Legislative Case Studies from Across the West; A Western Governors' Association White Paper*. Denver, CO: Western Governors' Association, 2006.

Johnston, Lyle. *"Good Night, Chet": A Biography of Chet Huntley*. Jefferson, NC: McFarland, 2003.

Karr, Raymond W. "Forests for the People: A Case Study of the RARE II Decision." PhD diss., University of Montana, 1983.

Keane, John T. "The Wilderness Act as Congress Intended." *American Forests*, February 1971, 40–43, 61.

Keegan, Charles E., Carl E. Fiedler, and Thale Dillon. *Montana Challenge: Forest Management and the Forest Products Industry*. Missoula: Bureau of Business and Economic Research, University of Montana, 2007.

Keegan, Charles E. III, Krista M. Gebert, Alfred L. Chase, Todd A. Morgan, Steven E. Bodmer, and Dwane D. Van Hooser, *Montana's Forest Products Industry: A Descriptive Analysis, 1969–2000*. Missoula: Bureau of Business and Economic Research,

University of Montana, 2001.

Keller, David. *The Making of a Masterpiece: The Stewardship History of the Rocky Mountain Front and the Bob Marshall Wilderness Complex*. Missoula, MT: Boone and Crockett Club, 2001.

Koch, Elers. "The Passing of the Lolo Trail." *Journal of Forestry* 33 (February 1935): 98–104.

Korn, Michael. "Hobnail Tom." *Montana Outdoors*, July–August 1988, 37–41.

Leopold, Aldo. "The Last Stand of the Wilderness." *American Forests and Forest Life* 31 (October 1925): 599–605.

———. *A Sand County Almanac: And Sketches Here and There*. New York: Oxford University Press, 1949.

Lucas, Robert. "The 'Backcountry Concept': A Positive Viewpoint." *Montana Outdoors* 11, no. 6 (November/December 1980): 24–25.

Lucas, Robert, and George H. Stankey. "Social Carrying Capacity for Backcountry Recreation." In *Outdoor Recreation Research: Applying the Results*. Symposium, June 19–21, 1973. General Technical Report NC-9. Marquette, MI: USDA Forest Service, North Central Experiment Station, 1974.

Lyon, L. J., T. N. Lonner, J. P. Weigand, C. L. Marcum, W. D. Edge, J. D. Jones, D. W. McCleerey, and L. L. Hicks. *Coordinating Elk and Timber Management: Final Report of the Montana Cooperative Elk-Logging Study 1970–1985*. Helena: Montana Department of Fish, Wildlife and Parks, 1985.

Manning, Richard. *Last Stand: Logging, Journalism, and the Case for Humility*. Salt Lake City: Peregrine Smith Books, 1991.

Marsh, Kevin R. *Drawing Lines in the Forest: Creating Wilderness Areas in the Pacific Northwest*. Seattle: University of Washington Press, 2007.

———. "This Is Just the First Round." *Oregon Historical Quarterly* 103 (Summer 2002): 210–33.

Marshall, Robert. "Impressions from the Wilderness." *Nature Magazine* 44 (1951): 481.

———. "Three Great Western Wildernesses." *Living Wilderness* 1 (September 1935): 10.

Marshall, Robert, and Althea Dobbins. "Largest Roadless Areas in United States." *Living Wilderness* (November 1936): 11–13.

McCloskey, Maxine E., and James P. Gilligan, eds. *Wilderness and the Quality of Life*. San Francisco: Sierra Club, 1969.

McCloskey, Michael, and Jeffrey Desautels. "A Primer on Wilderness Law and Policy." *Environmental Law Reporter* 13 (1983). http://elr.radcampaign.com/sites/default/files/articles/13.10278.htm.

McCollister, Charles, and Sandra McCollister. "The Clearwater River Log Drives: A Photo Essay." *Forest History Today*, Fall 2000, 20–26.

Meine, Curt. "Conservation Biology—Past and Present." In *Conservation Biology for All*, edited by Navjot S. Sodhi and Paul R. Ehrlich. London: Oxford University Press, 2010.

Merriam, Lawrence C. "The Bob Marshall Wilderness Area of Montana—Some Socio-Economic Considerations." *Journal of Forestry* 62 (November 1964): 789–95.

———. "The Bob Marshall Wilderness Area of Montana—A Study in Land Use." PhD diss., Oregon State University, 1963.

———. "The Irony of the Bob Marshall Wilderness." *Journal of Forest History* 33, no. 2 (April 1989): 80–87.

Miller, William H. "A Review of Dworshak National Fish Hatchery Mitigation Record." U.S. Fish and Wildlife Service, Dworshak Fisheries Assistance Office, Report FR-1/FAO-88-2, 1987.

Montana Department of Fish, Wildlife and Parks. *Montana Wilderness Synopsis*. Helena: Montana Department of Fish, Wildlife and Parks, 1981.

Moore, AnneMarie, and Dennis Baird. *Wild Places Preserved: The Story of Bob Marshall in Idaho*. Moscow: University of Idaho Library, 2009.

Moore, Bud. *The Lochsa Story: Land Ethics in the Bitterroot Mountains*. Missoula, MT: Mountain Press, 1996.

Morrison, Peter, ed. *River of No Return Wilderness: A Report of Sierra Club Wilderness Studies of the Idaho and Salmon River Breaks Primitive Areas and Adjacent Lands*. San Francisco: Sierra Club, 1972.

Murie, Olaus J. "The Intangible Resources of Wild Country." In *Renewable Natural Resources: Proceedings of the Inter-American Conference on Conservation of Renewable Natural Resources*, Denver, CO, September 7–20, 1948, sec. 4, 496–500. Washington, D.C.: U.S. Department of State, 1949.

Murphy, Leon W., and Howard E. Metsker. *Inventory of Idaho Streams Containing Anadromous Fish: Pt. II, Clearwater River Drainage*. Boise: Idaho Department of Fish and Game, 1962.

Neil, J. M. *To the White Clouds: Idaho's Conservation Saga, 1900–1970*. Pullman: Washington State University Press, 2005.

Newfont, Kathryn. *Blue Ridge Commons: Environmental Activism and Forest History in Western North Carolina*. Athens: University of Georgia Press, 2012.

Nie, Martin. "Administrative Rulemaking and Public Lands Conflict: The Forest Service's Roadless Rule." *Natural Resources Journal* 44 (Summer 2004): 687–742.

Norton, Boyd. *Snake Wilderness*. San Francisco: Sierra Club Books, 1972.

Noss, Reed, Howard B. Quigley, Maurice G. Hornocker, Troy Merrill, and Paul C. Paquet. "Conservation Biology and Carnivore Conservation in the Rocky Mountains." *Conservation Biology* 10 (August 1996): 949–63.

Oberdorfer, Don. *Senator Mansfield: The Extraordinary Life of a Great American States-man and Diplomat.* Washington, D.C.: Smithsonian Books, 2003.

O'Toole, Randal. *Reforming the Forest Service.* Washington, D.C.: Island Press, 1988.

Parsell, Neal. *Major Fenn's Country: A History of the Lower Lochsa, the Upper Middlefork of the Clearwater, and Surrounding Lands.* Grangeville, ID: USDA Forest Service, Nez Perce National Forest, 1986.

Peters, Gregory Merrill Deschaine. "Forever Wild: Journeys through the North Fork." Master's thesis, University of Montana, 2009.

Platts, William S., and Walter F. Megahan. "Time Trends in Riverbed Sediment Composition in Salmon and Steelhead Spawning Areas: South Fork Salmon River, Idaho." Ogden, UT: USDA Forest Service, Intermountain Forest and Range Experiment Station, 1975.

Rahm, Neal M. "Salmon: River of No Return." *National Parks Magazine* 40 (May 1966): 8–12.

Ransick, Christopher T. "The Bitterroot Controversy: Dale Burk's Dual Role as Journalist and Activist." Master's thesis, University of Montana, 1988.

Reese, Rick. *Greater Yellowstone: The National Park and Adjacent Wildlands.* Helena: Montana Geographic Series, 1985.

Rickart, Thomas M. "Wilderness Land Preservation: The Uneasy Reconciliation of Multiple and Single Use Land Management Policies." *Boston College Environmental Affairs Law Review* 8, no. 4 (August 1980): 873–917.

Roholt, Christopher M. "The Montana Wilderness Study Bill: A Case History." Master's thesis, University of Montana, 1977.

Roselle, Mike. *Tree Spiker: From Earth First! to Lowbagging; My Struggles in Radical Environmental Action.* New York: St. Martin's Press, 2009.

Roth, Dennis M. *The Wilderness Movement and the National Forests: 1964–1980.* Forest Service History Series FS 391. Washington, D.C.: USDA Forest Service, 1984.

Rothman, Hal. "Shaping the Nature of a Controversy: The Park Service, the Forest Service, and the Cedar Breaks Proposal." *Utah Historical Quarterly* 55 (Summer 1987): 213–35.

Runte, Alfred. *National Parks: The American Experience.* Lincoln: University of Nebraska Press, 1979.

Scott, Douglas W. *The Enduring Wilderness: Protecting Our Natural Heritage through the Wilderness Act.* Golden, CO: Fulcrum Publishing, 2004.

———. "Our Nationwide Wilderness Preservation System." In *People, Places, and Parks: Proceedings of the 2005 George Wright Society Conference on Parks, Protected Areas, and Cultural Sites,* edited by David Harmon. Hancock, MI: George Wright Society, 2006.

Sewell, W. R. D. "The Nez Perce Dam and the Value of a Fishery." *Land Economics* 37 (August 1961): 257–60.

Sutter, Paul. *Driven Wild: How the Fight against Automobiles Launched the Modern Wilderness Movement.* Seattle: University of Washington Press, 2004.

Swanson, Frederick H. *The Bitterroot and Mr. Brandborg: Clearcutting and the Struggle for Sustainable Forestry in the Northern Rockies.* Salt Lake City: University of Utah Press, 2011.

Trueblood, Ted. "The Forest Service versus the Wilderness Act." *Field & Stream,* September 1975, 16, 18, 40.

Turner, James Morton. *The Promise of Wilderness: American Environmental Politics since 1964.* Seattle: University of Washington Press, 2012.

University of Montana School of Forestry. "A Study of Policies, Guidelines, and Enforcement Procedures Affecting Prevention, Control, and Abatement of Air and Water Pollution Resulting from Forestry Practices on the Flathead National Forest, Montana." Prepared for U.S. Environmental Protection Agency, 1974.

U.S. Army Corps of Engineers. *Columbia River and Tributaries.* H.R. Doc. No. 531, 81st Cong., 2nd sess., 1950.

U.S. Fish and Wildlife Service. *Teton Slope Unit: A Preliminary Report on Fish and Wildlife Resources.* Billings, MT: The Service, 1952.

U.S. Forest Service. *Draft Environmental Statement for the Beartrap-Dutchler Planning Unit, 1976.* Ogden, UT: USDA Forest Service, 1976.

———. *Full Use and Development of Montana's Timber Resources.* S. Doc. No. 9, 86th Cong., 1st sess. Washington, D.C.: Government Printing Office, 1959.

———. *Long Range Plan, Northern Half Lincoln Ranger District.* Missoula, MT: USDA Forest Service, Northern Region, 1953.

———. *New Wilderness Study Areas: Roadless Area Review and Evaluation.* Current Information Report No. 11. Washington, D.C.: Government Printing Office, 1973.

———. *Patterns for Management, Blackfoot–Sun River Divide Area, Lolo–Helena–Lewis and Clark National Forests.* Missoula, MT: USDA Forest Service, Northern Region, 1968.

———. *A Proposal and Report: Mount Henry, Taylor-Hilgard, and West Pioneer: Montana Wilderness Study Act Areas; Beaverhead, Gallatin, and Kootenai National Forests, Montana.* Washington, D.C.: Government Printing Office, 1980.

———. *Proposed New Wilderness Study Areas: Roadless Area Review and Evaluation.* Current Information Report No. 9. Washington, D.C.: Government Printing Office, 1973.

———. *RARE II: Draft Environmental Statement: Roadless Area Review and Evaluation.* Washington, D.C.: Government Printing Office, 1978.

————. *RARE II: Final Environmental Statement: Roadless Area Review and Evaluation.* Washington, D.C.: Government Printing Office, 1979.

————. *Roadless and Undeveloped Areas (Final Environmental Statement): Selection of Final New Study Areas from Roadless and Undeveloped Areas on the National Forests.* Washington, D.C.: Government Printing Office, 1973.

————. *Waters of the Flathead: A Proposal.* Missoula, MT: USDA Forest Service, Northern Region, 1973.

U.S. Forest Service, Bitterroot National Forest. "Magruder Corridor Resource Inventory." 1970.

————. "Management Proposal for the Magruder Corridor." June 1, 1971.

U.S. Forest Service, Montana Fish and Game Department, Bureau of Land Management, and University of Montana. "Montana Cooperative Elk-Logging Study, Progress Report for the Period January 1–December 31, 1971." Region 1, U.S. Forest Service, Intermountain Forest and Range Experiment Station, Montana Fish and Game Department, Bureau of Land Management, and School of Forestry, University of Montana, 1972.

U.S. House of Representatives. *Endangered American Wilderness Act: Hearings on H.R. 3454 Before the Subcommittee on Indian Affairs and Public Lands of the Committee on Interior and Insular Affairs,* 95th Cong., 1st sess. Parts 1 and 3 (1977).

U.S. Senate. *Federal Timber Sale Policies: Joint Hearings Before a Special Subcommittee on the Legislative Oversight Function of the Committee on Interior and Insular Affairs, United States Senate, and the Subcommittee on Public Works and Resources of the Government Operations Committee, House of Representatives,* 84th Cong., 1st and 2nd sess., Redding, CA. (1955).

————. *Lincoln Back Country Wilderness Area, Montana: Hearing on S. 1121 Before the Subcommittee on Public Lands of the Committee on Interior and Insular Affairs, United States Senate,* 90th Cong., 2nd sess. (Great Falls, MT, September 23, 1968).

————. *Middle Snake River, Snake River and Tributaries, Wyoming, Idaho, Oregon, and Washington.* Letter from the Secretary of the Army, April 25, 1955. S. Doc. No. 51, 84th Cong., 1st sess., June 14, 1955.

————. *Montana Wilderness: Hearing on S. 393 Before the Subcommittee on Environment and Land Resources of the Committee on Interior and Insular Affairs, United States Senate,* 94th Cong., 1st sess. (1975).

————. *Northern Rockies Ecosystem Protection Act of 1993: Joint Hearing on H.R. 2638 Before the Subcommittee on Specialty Crops and Natural Resources of the Committee on Agriculture and the Subcommittee on Environment and Natural Resources of the Committee on Merchant Marine and Fisheries,* 103rd Cong., 2nd sess. (1994).

U.S. Senate Committee on Energy and Natural Resources. *Gospel-Hump Wilderness*

Area: Hearing on S. 1180 (amendment no. 826) Before the Subcommittee on Parks and Recreation of the Committee on Energy and Natural Resources, United States Senate, 95th Cong., 1st sess., Grangeville, ID (1977).

———. *Idaho Forest Management Act of 1984: Hearings on S. 2457 Before the Subcommittee on Public Lands and Reserved Water* (1984).

———. *Idaho Wilderness: Hearings Before the Subcommittee on Public Lands and Reserved Water . . . to Review the Idaho Wilderness Recommendations.* Part 1 (1983).

———. *Montana Wilderness: Hearings Before the Subcommittee on Public Lands and Reserved Water . . . to Review the Montana Wilderness Recommendations* (1984).

———. *River of No Return Wilderness Proposals: Hearing on S. 95, S. 96, and S. 97 Before the Subcommittee on Parks, Recreation and Renewable Resources of the Committee on Energy and Natural Resources,* 96th Cong., 1st sess. Part 1: Lewiston, ID (1977); Part 3: Washington, D.C., (1979).

———. *River of No Return Wilderness: Report to Accompany S. 2009, Nov. 14, 1979.* S. Rep. No. 96-414, 96th Cong., 1st sess.

———. *Roadless Areas in Central Idaho: Hearing on National Forest Roadless Areas,* 95th Cong., 1st sess., McCall, ID (1977).

U.S. Senate Committee on Interior and Insular Affairs, Subcommittee on Public Lands. *Lincoln Back Country Wilderness Area, Montana: Hearing on S. 412, 91st Cong., 1st sess. (Washington, D.C., March 7, 1969).*

Wildland Research Center. *Wilderness and Recreation—A Report on Resources, Values, and Problems.* Outdoor Recreation Resources Review Commission Report No. 3. Washington, D.C.: Government Printing Office, 1962.

Wilkinson, Charles F. *Crossing the Next Meridian: Land, Water, and the Future of the West.* Washington, D.C.: Island Press, 1992.

Wolff, Meyer H. "The Bob Marshall Wilderness Area." *Living Wilderness* 6 (July 1941): 5–7.

Worf, William A. *National Forest Wilderness: A Policy Review.* Washington, D.C.: USDA Forest Service, 1972.

Worster, Donald. *The Wealth of Nature: Environmental History and the Ecological Imagination.* New York: Oxford University Press, 1993.

Zirngibl, Wendy Marie. "Elk in the Greater Yellowstone Ecosystem: Conflicts over Management and Regulation Prior to Natural Regulation." Master's thesis, Montana State University, 2006.

Index

Numbers in *italics* refer to photographs.